The Business Cycle Today

NATIONAL BUREAU OF ECONOMIC RESEARCH
General Series 96

Economic Research: Retrospect and Prospect

THE BUSINESS CYCLE TODAY

Fiftieth Anniversary Colloquium I

Edited by

VICTOR ZARNOWITZ

*University of Chicago
and National Bureau of Economic Research*

NATIONAL BUREAU OF ECONOMIC RESEARCH
NEW YORK 1972

Distributed by COLUMBIA UNIVERSITY PRESS
NEW YORK AND LONDON

Relation of National Bureau Directors to Publications
Reporting Proceedings of the Fiftieth Anniversary Colloquia

Since the present volume is a record of colloquium proceedings, it has
been exempted from the rules governing submission of manuscripts to,
and critical review by, the Board of Directors of the National Bureau.
(Resolution adopted July 6, 1948, as revised
November 21, 1949, and April 20, 1968)

Prefatory Note

This volume of the Fiftieth Anniversary Series contains the proceedings of The Business Cycle Today, a colloquium held in New York City on September 24, 1970. We are indebted to the members of the Bureau's Board of Directors who helped to plan and coordinate the session: R. A. Gordon, Crawford H. Greenewalt, Gottfried Haberler, Geoffrey H. Moore, Henry Theil, Willard L. Thorp and W. Allen Wallis. We are also grateful to Gnomi Gouldin, Virginia Meltzer, Ester Moskowitz, and Ruth Ridler who prepared the manuscript for publication.

VICTOR ZARNOWITZ

Fiftieth Anniversary Colloquium and Publication Series

To commemorate its fiftieth anniversary the National Bureau of Economic Research sponsored a series of colloquia to explore the effects of pending and anticipated policy issues on future research priorities for areas of long-standing Bureau concern. As a basis for the panel and audience discussions, economists specializing in the subject area prepared papers in which they reviewed relevant research advances through time and presented their opinions for the direction of future effort. These papers, and in some instances edited transcripts of panelists' comments, appear as part of the National Bureau's Fiftieth Anniversary publications series. Papers developed for the colloquia and publications series and participants in the program included:

THE BUSINESS CYCLE TODAY
September 24, 1970—New York City

Moderators:
    Morning session: Paul A. Samuelson
    Afternoon session: F. Thomas Juster

Presentations:
    "Dating American Growth Cycles"   *Ilse Mintz*
    "The 'Recession' of 1969–1970"   *Solomon Fabricant*
    "The Cyclical Behavior of Prices"   *Geoffrey H. Moore*
    "Forecasting Economic Conditions: The Record and the Prospect"
                                           Victor Zarnowitz
    "Econometric Model Simulations and the Cyclical Characteristics
        of the U.S. Economy"   *Victor Zarnowitz*
    "A Study of Discretionary and Nondiscretionary Monetary and
        Fiscal Policies in the Context of Stochastic Macroeconometric
        Models"   *Yoel Haitovsky and Neil Wallace*

Panelists:
Morning session: Otto Eckstein, Henry C. Wallich
Afternoon session: Bert G. Hickman, Arthur M. Okun

FINANCE AND CAPITAL MARKETS
October 22, 1970—New York City

Moderator: Robert V. Roosa

Presentation:
"Finance and Capital Markets"   *John Lintner*

Panelists: William J. Baumol, Sidney Homer, James J. O'Leary

A ROUNDTABLE ON POLICY ISSUES AND RESEARCH OPPORTUNITIES IN INDUSTRIAL ORGANIZATION
November 5, 1970—Chicago, Illinois

Moderator: Victor R. Fuchs

Presentations:
"Industrial Organization: Boxing the Compass"
James W. McKie
"Antitrust Enforcement and the Modern Corporation"
Oliver E. Williamson
"Issues in the Study of Industrial Organization in a Regime of Rapid Technical Change"   *Richard R. Nelson*
"Industrial Organization: A Proposal for Research"
Ronald H. Coase

PUBLIC EXPENDITURES AND TAXATION
December 2, 1970—Washington, D.C.

Moderator: Walter W. Heller

Presentation:
"Quantitative Research in Taxation and Government Expenditure"
Carl S. Shoup
Panelists: James M. Buchanan, Richard R. Musgrave

ECONOMIC GROWTH
December 10, 1970—San Francisco, California

Moderator: R. Aaron Gordon

Presentation:
"Is Growth Obsolete?"
William D. Nordhaus and James Tobin

Panelists: Moses Abramovitz, Robin C. O. Matthews

HUMAN RESOURCES
May 13, 1970—Atlanta, Georgia

Moderator: Gary S. Becker

Presentation:
"Human Capital: Policy Issues and Research Opportunities"
Theodore W. Schultz

Panelists: Alice M. Rivlin, Gerald S. Somers

THE FUTURE OF ECONOMIC RESEARCH
April 23, 1971—South Brookline, Massachusetts

Presentation:
"Quantitative Economic Research: Trends and Problems"
Simon Kuznets

Contents

THE BUSINESS CYCLE TODAY: AN INTRODUCTION
Victor Zarnowitz   1

DATING AMERICAN GROWTH CYCLES   Ilse Mintz   39

THE "RECESSION" OF 1969–1970   Solomon Fabricant   89

THE CYCLICAL BEHAVIOR OF PRICES
Geoffrey H. Moore   137

DISCUSSION—MORNING SESSION   167

FORECASTING ECONOMIC CONDITIONS: THE
RECORD AND THE PROSPECT   Victor Zarnowitz   183

ECONOMETRIC MODEL SIMULATIONS AND THE
CYCLICAL CHARACTERISTICS OF THE U.S.
ECONOMY   Victor Zarnowitz   241

A STUDY OF DISCRETIONARY AND NONDISCRETION-
ARY MONETARY AND FISCAL POLICIES IN THE
CONTEXT OF STOCHASTIC MACROECONOMETRIC
MODELS   Yoel Haitovsky and Neil Wallace   261

DISCUSSION—AFTERNOON SESSION   311

INDEX   323

The Business Cycle Today: An Introduction

Victor Zarnowitz
University of Chicago and National Bureau of Economic Research

I

The National Bureau of Economic Research has been engaged in studying business cycles almost from its beginning fifty years ago. The intensive concern with the major problem of economic instability reflected the need of the times as well as the central scientific interests of several of the main contributors to the Bureau's work. Foremost among these was Wesley Mitchell, the director of research of the National Bureau in the first quarter-century of its history. Mitchell's close associates and principal coworkers, Arthur F. Burns, Solomon Fabricant, and Geoffrey H. Moore, successively guided the Bureau's progress in the two decades after his death in 1948. Basic research on the nature, causes, and indicators of pervasive fluctuations in economic activity continued to mark this phase of the Bureau's growth.

This long-standing involvement in studies relating to business cycles made the subject a fitting choice for the first in a series of six colloquia that the Bureau organized to celebrate its fiftieth anniversary. This colloquium, entitled "The Business Cycle Today," was held at the Hotel Pierre in New York City on September 24, 1970. Its program included papers by members of the Bureau's research staff: Ilse Mintz, Geoffrey H. Moore and Solomon Fabricant in the morning session; and Victor Zarnowitz and Yoel Haitovsky and Neil Wallace in the afternoon session. There were opening remarks by

John Meyer, president of the National Bureau, and invited comments on the presentations by Otto Eckstein, Harvard University; Bert G. Hickman, Stanford University; Arthur M. Okun, The Brookings Institution; and Henry C. Wallich, Yale University. Paul A. Samuelson, of the Massachusetts Institute of Technology, was chairman of the conference in the morning; and F. Thomas Juster of the National Bureau, in the afternoon; the discussion they led included audience participation. Herbert Stein, member of the President's Council of Economic Advisers, gave a luncheon address. The present volume is based on the proceedings of the two working sessions of the meeting.

II

A widely accepted conception of business cycles of historical experience includes recurrent (but nonperiodic) cumulative expansions and contractions, which are diffused over a multitude of economic processes and involve such major aggregates as national income and product. This is consonant with the well-known working definition by Burns and Mitchell.[1] In the period after World War II, fluctuations have clearly become much milder than they were during most of the recorded business history of the nineteenth and first four decades of the twentieth century. In the industrial countries of western Europe and Japan, they took predominantly the form of accelerations and decelerations in the rates of economic growth; sustained declines in aggregate economic activity occurred but sporadically. In the United States and Canada, the moderation of the cycle when compared with the prewar patterns is also apparent, although four recessions are generally recognized to have interrupted economic growth between 1948 and 1961; so, the survival of business cycles conforming to the older, "classical" concept was still not seriously questioned. As the long expansion of the U.S. economy in the 1960's persisted beyond most economists' expectations, such questioning did begin to spread, however. Indeed, the basic question "Is the Business Cycle Obsolete?" was explicitly raised by an international conference held in April 1967.[2] The answer was, in general, negative but importantly qualified by the acknowledgment that absolute declines in aggregate economic activity have become smaller and shorter; that in fact, in many countries, the cycle came to be largely limited to fluctuations in positive growth rates; and that some of

[1] A.F. Burns and W.C. Mitchell, *Measuring Business Cycles,* New York, National Bureau of Economic Research, 1946, p. 3.

[2] Martin Bronfenbrenner, ed., *Is the Business Cycle Obsolete?,* New York, Wiley-Interscience, 1969.

the fluctuations may be due mainly to lags and excesses of alternating economic policies aimed at combating inflation and unemployment.

Looking ahead, Burns in 1968 noted the possibility that a "recession" may come to mean "merely a reduced rate of growth of aggregate activity instead of an actual and sustained decline" but added that "there is as yet insufficient ground for believing that economic developments will generally conform to this model in the near future."[3] He called for continuation of basic research on business cycles and of efforts to improve forecasting and policies for economic stabilization. The contributions to this colloquium agree with the spirit of these recommendations.

As suggested by its title, the colloquium focused on the analysis of the economic fluctuations of recent times rather than on the long historical record of cyclical movements as compiled and examined in NBER studies. But the reports and discussion proceeded on the basis of that record: Understanding the new developments and their implications presupposes a tested knowledge of facts and relationships that must rely on data of the past. Furthermore, our title presumes that a "business cycle" is still going on at the present time, the thesis here being that the central process and many of its attendant phenomena are not "obsolete" but that they did and do undergo important changes. The evolution of the economic system and of its institutions and of economic policies requires that observations of a new type be made and new analytical tools developed and applied in business cycle research. This is the particular theme of Mintz and Fabricant, who believe that the time has come to attempt a revision of the National Bureau definition of business cycles; both consider alternative concepts, though they differ in some important respects on methods and terminology. Moore warns in the discussion against premature adoption of new and untested methods but does not contest the need for their thorough consideration; in fact, he too uses a new (and still different) approach in his report on the cyclical behavior of prices.

That the concepts and tools of research in business cycles must be reappraised and if need be revised by "economists of each generation" was early recognized by Mitchell.[4] Cumulative changes in the organization of the economy affect the nature of the economy's motion over time. The very

---

[3] Arthur F. Burns, "Business Cycles," in *International Encyclopedia of the Social Sciences,* 1968, Vo. 2, p. 244, reprinted as "The Nature and Causes of Business Cycles," in Burns, *The Business Cycle in a Changing World,* New York, NBER, 1969, pp. 50–51.

[4] See Wesley C. Mitchell, *Business Cycles.* Berkeley, University of California Press, 1913, pp. 582–583, reprinted in *Business Cycles and Their Causes,* Berkeley, University of California Press, 1941, p. 168.

attempts to reduce economic instability in the large (of which business cycles, broadly defined, are a primary manifestation) may alter the structure of the economy and thereby change the character of its cyclical fluctuations; and such effects are not necessarily limited to successful attempts only. Much has been written about the progress toward economic stability made here and abroad since the depression of the 1930's, and there is indeed abundant evidence of some real gains on this front. In the morning session of the colloquium, Paul Samuelson contrasted the business cycles of the pre-World War II era with those of the last quarter-century by comparing them with a dinosaur and a lizard, respectively. But some others doubted that the battle against cyclical instability had been so decisively won; even if the old beast is indeed extinct (a major depression is widely regarded as unlikely), the new one is still in many ways recognizable as its offspring and is, though much tamer, by no means innocent. The developments of 1969—70 can be read as a lesson that broad declines in the nation's productive activities with associated increases in unemployment are not yet a thing of the past and that our knowledge of how to achieve and maintain prosperity without inflation is far from adequate. Dealing with this latest episode in the United States experience, Fabricant concludes that the different course of today's business cycles "does not of itself compel us to stop thinking of them as members of the same species" [as the cycles 'of earlier days']. "The causes of business cycles have not vanished. . . . A tiger caged is not the same as a tiger loose in the streets, but neither is it a paper tiger. There are good reasons for not forgetting that important fact."[5]

In brief, it is the old but ever-changing problem of economic instability, conceived in evolutionary and comprehensive terms, that in one form or another engages the attention of all reports and comments in this colloquium. Forecasting economic conditions is a response to the uncertainty generated by this instability and a requirement of government and business policies. In my paper I deal with predictions of recent economic developments, their main sources, characteristics, and accuracy; I try to evaluate the performance of those who regularly forecast the course of the economy and of some econometric forecasting models. Haitovsky and Wallace report on their experiments with stochastic simulations of the effects of selected monetary and fiscal policies as carried out with three quarterly econometric models of the U.S. economy in the periods after World War II or the Korean War. Thus perhaps the main general purpose of the colloquium can be described as an

[5] Solomon Fabricant, "The 'Recession' of 1969–1970," p. 135, below. As it happens, the world of animals provided the colloquium participants with subjects for a few rather different metaphors.

attempt to approach current problems in cyclical analysis, forecasting, and policy in ways that vary and are partly new, so as to stimulate discussion and learn in the process.

III

Developments following the depression of the 1930's and World War II are now widely believed to have altered the nature of business cycles and reduced the importance of economic instability relative to other major economic and social problems of the nation. Some reflections upon this process and its sources are prompted by the present occasion.

National Bureau studies identify four recessions in the U.S. economy between 1948 and 1961, with durations varying from nine to thirteen months and averaging ten. Over the preceding period of nearly one hundred years (since 1854), twenty-two recessions are counted, which lasted twenty months on the average and more than ten months in all but three cases. There is no precedent in the past for a sequence of contractions so brief and mild as those observed in the last quarter-century (including the 1969–70 episode as it appears at the present time, in January 1971).

Moreover, business cycle expansions seem to have become longer in recent times. Their length varied from 25 to 45 months in 1949–61, averaging 36 months. If the last expansion is counted as lasting 105 months (!), from February 1961 to November 1969 (Fabricant's tentative peak date), the average increases to 49 months. The twenty-two expansions between 1854 and 1945 varied from 10 to 80 months and averaged 29 months.

Conceivably, differences of this kind could be due to differences in the intensity of external disturbances to which the economy is exposed, but it is not at all clear that such "shocks" were weaker (or stronger) in the post-World War II period than in the preceding century (allowing for the growing size of the economy). Probably the strongest shocks are caused by major wars; wartime expansions, for example, are particularly long.[6] U.S. history before 1945 includes, of course, three large-scale armed conflicts——the Civil War and World Wars I and II——but the later times were plagued by the wars in Korea and Vietnam as well as by the often high tensions of the Cold War and the associated growth and fluctuations in

[6] The 1938–45 expansion lasted 80 months; the 1861–65, 1914–18, and 1949–53 expansions, 44–46 months each. (These episodes correspond to the Civil War, World Wars I and II, and the Korean War. The very long expansion of the 1960's includes the period of the protracted conflict in Vietnam.)

defense expenditures. When the wartime cycles are excluded, recent contractions still appear shorter and more moderate, and recent expansions longer if not always more vigorous, than their historical counterparts.[7]

Nevertheless, one cannot so simply refute the hypothesis that shocks of different kinds and lesser intensities account to some extent for the observed moderation of cyclical fluctuations. The distinction between what constitutes external disturbances and their effects and what is properly attributable to the pattern in which the economy reacts to and propagates such impulses is in practice rather vague and arbitrary. Erik Lundberg illustrates this with references to the role of balance of payments changes in some countries of Western Europe and notes that the problem is "especially pertinent with regard to government policy reaction."[8]

If weaker disturbances in the years since World War II were the whole answer, one could speak of a period of greater stability but not of progress toward greater stability. The latter implies improvements in the operational characteristics of the economy or in economic institutions or policies, as a result of which the system became less vulnerable to the variety of shocks experienced in the past.

Most of the explanations of the relative shortness and mildness of recent recessions stress the stabilizing impact of structural, institutional, and policy changes. The principal factors in this development include the great increase in public revenue from personal and corporate income taxes and the introduction of the pay-as-you-go system of income tax collection; the expansion of unemployment insurance and other social security programs and transfer payments; and the rising importance of private pension plans and corporate policies of stable dividend distribution. The effect of each of these "built-in-stabilizers" is to loosen the once close link between the fluctuations in aggregate output and those in total personal income and consumer spending. The upward trend in the proportion of the labor force accounted for by the cyclically more stable sectors, notably the service industries and the "white-collar" (overhead labor) types of occupation, has similar stabilizing

[7]The average duration of "peacetime" contractions, for example, was over 21 months in the period before World War II and a little less than 10 months in the period 1948–61 (these measures exclude the contractions immediately following the Civil War, the two world wars, and the Korean War). The corresponding figures for the peacetime expansions are 25 and 32 months, respectively.

[8]See Erik Lundberg, *Instability and Economic Growth,* New Haven and London, Yale University Press, 1968, p. 95. Lundberg continues: "The actual postwar instability patterns in the various countries may be heavily influenced by policy changes, taken as exogenous factors or regarded as responses to actual or expected deviations from certain targets or norms."

implications. The insurance of mortgages, savings and loan accounts, and (most important) bank deposits are postdepression reforms that have undoubtedly strengthened confidence in the financial system and continue to prevent crises.[9]

Stabilization of the economy at high levels of activity (promotion of "maximum employment, production, and purchasing power") was declared, in the Employment Act of 1946, to be a continuing policy goal of the federal government. The postwar period saw a growing acceptance of the view that the government has both the responsibility and the ability to prevent prolonged large-scale unemployment. This position repeatedly received support from the events, beginning with the fact that, contrary to many forecasts, no major depression materialized during and after the demobilization. There was then even less surprise at the brevity and moderation of the successive business contractions. Expectations of a high and rising level of economic activity became predominant during the 1950's and 1960's, and this itself is believed to have had stabilizing effects in the sense of favoring strong consumer and business demand for goods and services.[10]

By the same token, however, it often appeared that government policies were oriented more toward checking any developing recession than toward checking any developing inflation, an observation which tended to impart an inflationary bias to the public's expectations. To the extent that such expectations induce pressures which contribute to actual inflation and impede anti-inflationary policies, they can clearly be destabilizing, and this has indeed become a recurring problem in the postwar era.

Apart from their effects *via* expectations, have the discretionary economic policies been stabilizing, that is, have they made a significant net contribution to the moderation of business cycles? Not surprisingly, the question does not have a simple, generally accepted answer. Probably many, perhaps most

[9]The foregoing summary draws upon A.F. Burns, "Progress Towards Economic Stability," *American Economic Review,* March 1960, reprinted in *The Business Cycle in a Changing World,* Chap. 3.

[10]Growth of confidence in future economic stability has been tentatively interpreted as a major cause of the shift to a rising trend in the velocity of circulation of money in the postwar period; see Milton Friedman and Anna Jacobson Schwartz, *A Monetary History of the United States, 1867–1960,* Princeton University Press for NBER, 1963, Chap. 12. Alternative explanations of this trend (seen as a decline in the demand for money relative to income) stress mainly the prevalence of upward movements in interest rates (Henry A. Latané, "Income Velocity and Interest Rates: A Pragmatic Approach," *Review of Economics and Statistics,* November 1960, pp. 445–449) and the growth of nonbank financial intermediaries whose liabilities are viewed as close substitutes for money (J.G. Gurley and E.S. Shaw, *Money in a Theory of Finance,* Washington, D.C., The Brookings Institution, 1960).

economists would affirm that monetary policy has on the whole been more successful in the postwar than in the interwar period and that several fiscal policy measures (mainly tax reductions in times of sluggish demand) have also made positive contributions. But all serious attempts to appraise the effectiveness of stabilization policies suggest a mixed record and demonstrate that it is exceedingly difficult to reach conclusive results in this area. I shall return to this subject in the next section of this essay.

IV

An important but difficult question that may now be raised concerns the contribution of economic theory and research to the observed moderation of the business cycle. The answer is bound to depend on the analysis of the causes of that moderation. For example, to the extent that weaker external disturbances are to be credited, advances in economic knowledge and its applications would seem rather immaterial. The institutional and structural changes whose importance can hardly be questioned are prima facie attributable largely to such broad historical developments as the growth of the governmental sector (which was particularly fostered by wars and defense-related programs). It appears difficult to link many of these changes directly and importantly to the progress in economics and other social sciences. Thus, records going back to the 1870's "show that even before World War I federal revenues tended to move in loose harmony with the business cycle, while expenditures ordinarily rose during contractions as well as expansions. In other words, 'built-in' fiscal stabilizers are not an invention of recent years, although their importance has gained immensely with the growth of the federal budget."[11]

To be sure, some of the changes that proved beneficial started as conscious innovations prompted by the pressure of events. Federal insurance of bank deposits and the pay-as-you-go basis for income taxation may serve as examples. Certainly these and some other institutional improvements have been informed by economic logic. But they cannot be credited to the great advances in economics that have been made since the depression experiences and the appearance of Keynes' *General Theory* in the 1930's. Among the main concerns of that time, of course, was widespread unemployment, its causes, and effective ways to combat it. The problem is to a large extent a cyclical one, associated with business contractions or slowdowns, as shown

[11] A. F. Burns, *Business Cycle Research and the Needs of Our Times,* Thirty-third Annual Report of the NBER, May 1953, reprinted in A. F. Burns, *The Frontiers of Economic Knowledge,* Princeton for NBER, 1954, p. 182. The evidence referred to comes from John M. Firestone, *Federal Receipts and Expenditures During Business Cycles, 1879–1958,* Princeton for NBER, 1960.

recurrently by the course of the Unites States economy after World War II. One would therefore expect the latter period, which witnessed an enormous increase in economists' output and presumably a substantial increase in tested economic knowledge, to result in the development and application of effective stabilization policies, particularly the discretionary monetary and fiscal policies now chiefly in use.

As already noted, however, the record of such policies is mixed. Almost any observer's scorecard would contain a sufficiently large proportion of failures to make it appear doubtful that governmental measures to stabilize the economy are about to eliminate fluctuations in aggregate business activity and bring within our reach the ideal of sustained prosperity without inflation.

In this context, some of the most serious deficiencies in our knowledge relate to the magnitude, timing, and interaction of the effects of different policies. Economic theory and research made considerable progress in identifying the signs of important policy parameters, so that in many cases the direction in which a single specific policy change would work can be fairly well predicted. But much more than a model that can provide such qualitative information is required for a successful choice and application of economic policies. It is widely recognized that discretionary policies operate with distributed lags that may be complex and variable, but dependable measurements of such lags are not yet available. There is much controversy among American economists about the relative effectiveness of monetary vs. fiscal policy, but these policies interact and are carried out simultaneously in various combinations which makes it very difficult to estimate their separate consequences. A further complication is that a policy's immediate impact may differ greatly from its longer-term effects, even qualitatively. Still another problem is presented by what appears to be at least a partial and short-term conflict between the full-employment and the stable-price-level objectives of policy. And, last but not least, considerations of domestic politics or foreign policy may sometimes inhibit governmental action required for economic stabilization or indeed motivate destabilizing action.

The outlook for our ability to maintain a satisfactory rate of growth while keeping economic fluctuations small can be evaluated more realistically and reliably when account is taken of all the problems just listed. One is then inclined to take a longer and broader view of the entire subject: just as the cumulation of economic knowledge is a gradual and laborious process, not without some setbacks and probably inevitable limitations, so are the advances in the application of that knowledge to such practical tasks as the reduction of economic fluctuations. The progress toward economic stability is itself likely to prove slower and less "linear" than we might wish it to be. Yet to expect less of the stabilization policies in the near future need not mean to be less hopeful in the long run; and furthermore this attitude should generate more rather than less appreciation for the progress already made.

In this connection, it is important to note the discussion of postwar "policy cycles" in Western Europe. Government intervention is believed to have succeeded in limiting fluctuations in output and employment to a narrower range at higher levels, but also to have induced setbacks (interruptions of the generally strong growth trends) through the introduction of restrictive, anti-inflationary measures.[12] In the United States, some critics complained about the instability of federal spending, particularly on defense, while others stressed that the monetary policy moves were at times destabilizing, by being too late and too strong, even if in the right direction.[13] (However, even these economists would tend to agree that the postwar policies were an improvement upon the interwar policies.)

V

I think that most students of the subject would accept, though agreeing it is difficult to prove, that the development of modern macroeconomics contributed importantly to the potential of economic policy by teaching the profession about the probable directional effects of different policy measures. Such lessons are usually applied with lengthy lags, but men of affairs and the interested sections of the public showed rather more receptiveness to them than many would have expected. Beyond that, great advances in economic statistics and econometrics gave increasingly powerful analytical tools to those concerned with quantitative economic research and its applications to questions of policy. Both the quantity and quality of economic data have increased immensely in what has been termed "the statistical revolution" that in most countries started during the Second World War.[14]

[12] See Angus Maddison, "The Postwar Business Cycle in Western Europe and the Role of Government Policy," *Banca Nazionale del Lavoro Quarterly Review,* June 1960, especially pp. 114–125; and Milton Gilbert, "The Postwar Business Cycle in Western Europe," *American Economic Review, Papers and Proceedings,* May 1962, pp. 93–109. For an appraisal of these views, see Lundberg, *Instability* [fn. 8], pp. 135–140; and Lundberg, "Postwar Stabilization Policies," in Bronfenbrenner, ed., *Is the Business Cycle Obsolete?* [fn. 2], Chap. 15.

[13] See Bert G. Hickman, *Growth and Stability of the Postwar Economy,* Washington, D.C., The Brookings Institution, 1960, p. 215; and R.A. Gordon, "The Stability of the U.S. Economy," in Bronfenbrenner, ed., *Is the Business Cycle Obsolete?* p. 23. For the most comprehensive critique of discretionary monetary policies, see Friedman and Schwartz, *A Monetary History* [fn. 10]; also, Milton Friedman, "The Role of Monetary Policy," *American Economic Review,* March 1968, pp. 1–17.

[14] Lundberg, *Instability* [fn. 8], pp. 16–18.

No attempt can be made here to trace all these lines of progress, of course, but this is an appropriate occasion for recalling at least some of the more important contributions of the National Bureau. These are by no means limited to the research classified specifically (and somewhat narrowly) as "studies in business cycles." At the Bureau, and elsewhere, inquiries in various fields have resulted in new materials and knowledge that proved helpful in dealing with the problem of economic instability.

That this is so can be seen most readily in the case of the massive studies that have led to the development of systematic national income accounting and its worldwide diffusion. Thanks in a large measure to these time series data, "there now exists in all Western counties a relatively well-organized statistical universe to which our notions of development and stability refer. . . . Economic reality is a product of systematic statistical observations in a more serious sense today than it was during earlier decades."[15] The pioneering National Bureau work in this area goes back to the earliest NBER publication, by Mitchell, W. I. King, F. R. Macaulay, and O. W. Knauth,[16] but the main contributions here are those by Simon Kuznets and his associates, which appeared in the years 1937–46.[17] The great influence this research had on the development of economics since the 1930's is today generally recognized.[18]

Other basic measures developed in National Bureau studies concern business and household capital formation, consumption, and financing (Kuznets, Fabricant, Goldsmith, Lipsey, Becker, Juster and Shay); output, employment, labor force, productivity, prices, and wages (Fabricant, Kendrick, Wolman, Long, Easterlin, Mincer, Mills, Stigler, Rees, Kravis and Lipsey); money flows, interest rates, and the stock of money (Copeland, Macaulay, Durand, Braddock Hickman, Conard, Guttentag, Cagan, Friedman and Schwartz); government, business, and consumer financing (Seltzer,

[15]*Ibid.*, p. 16.

[16]Wesley C. Mitchell et al., *Income in the United States: Its Amount and Distribution, 1909–1919, I, Summary,* New York, NBER, 1921; and Mitchell, ed., *II, Detailed Report,* 1922.

[17]Simon Kuznets, *National Income and Capital Formation, 1919–1935,* New York, NBER, 1937; *National Product in Wartime,* 1945; S. Kuznets assisted by L. Epstein and E. Jenks, *National Income and Its Composition, 1919–1938,* 1941; *National Product Since 1896,* 1946.

[18]For example, Harry G. Johnson observes that Keynes' "original concept of the propensity to consume was very strongly influenced by national income accounting (in fact, the development of the Keynesian theory can be related fairly closely to the development of national income accounting)." See H.G. Johnson, *Essays in Monetary Economics,* Cambridge, Mass., Harvard University Press, 1967, p. 86.

Holland, Kahn, Saulnier, Haberler, Moore); etc.[19] Without the groundwork laid by these investigations, much of the recent economic research, particularly of a quantitative nature, would have been seriously impaired if not frustrated. This includes studies dealing with business cycle problems, some of them undertaken by the authors who developed the materials just listed (e.g., Friedman and Schwartz and Cagan[20]).

Of course, in large part the Bureau's efforts in data collection and measurement originated directly in the program of research on business cycles initiated by Wesley Mitchell. Gradually, a uniquely rich library of well over two thousand time series on almost every aspect of economic activity was built up, with full annotations, seasonal adjustments, measures of cyclical timing, amplitude, conformity, etc. These data were assembled and used in the course of many studies, including, in addition to those mentioned above, the massive investigations by Mitchell and Burns of how to define, measure, and analyze business cycles; research on cyclical movements in transportation by Hultgren, in inventories by Abramovitz and Stanback, in personal income by Creamer, in consumption by Mack, in exports by Mintz; and studies of business cycle indicators by Moore, Shiskin, Hultgren, Bry, and Zarnowitz.[21] I believe it is fair to say that the materials assembled and analyzed in all these reports add up to a large proportion of our factual knowledge of how the various economic activities and aggregates behaved during the historically observed sequence of business expansion, downturn, contraction, and upturn——that is, in each phase of the uneven but pervasive fluctuations that

[19]This recital is very incomplete, yet it is already so long that references would take up too much space here. Each of the annual reports of the National Bureau includes a full list of the NBER publications.

[20]Phillip Cagan, *Determinants and Effects of Changes in the Stock of Money, 1875–1960,* New York, NBER, 1965; Cagan, *Changes in the Cyclical Behavior of Interest Rates,* New York, NBER, 1966; Friedman and Schwartz [fn. 10].

[21]Let me add to this sentence an abbreviated list of references (all are volumes in the NBER series of Studies in Business Cycles; a more complete list of the Bureau's business cycle publications is given at the end of this book): W. C. Mitchell, *Business Cycles: The Problem and Its Setting,* 1927; A. F. Burns and W. C. Mitchell, *Measuring Business Cycles,* 1946; W. C. Mitchell, *What Happens During Business Cycles,* 1951; Thor Hultgren, *American Transportation in Prosperity and Depression,* 1948; Moses Abramovitz, *Inventories and Business Cycles,* 1950; Thomas M. Stanback, Jr., *Postwar Cycles in Manufacturers' Inventories,* 1962; Daniel Creamer assisted by Martin Bernstein, *Personal Income During Business Cycles,* 1956; Ruth P. Mack, *Consumption and Business Fluctuations,* 1956; Geoffrey H. Moore, ed., *Business Cycle Indicators,* 1961; Ilse Mintz, *Cyclical Fluctuations in the Exports of the United States Since 1879,* 1967.

marked the process of the economy's growth. To be valid, the theoretical explanations of economic growth and fluctuations must conform to the major facts disclosed by these largely empirical studies; to be useful, they will also have to incorporate the more important and durable of the findings of this research.

Those engaged in the study of economic fluctuations at the National Bureau placed their hope in the cumulation of economic knowledge: that their "quest of the lessons of experience will aid other students, as well as laymen who must wrestle practically with business cycles."[22] Their work has been primarily in the nature of basic research——on how business cycles come about, vary, and interact with structural and operational changes in the economy——because this strategy promised to contribute most in the long run to the improvement of the analysis of current business conditions, economic forecasting, and policies. There is evidence in support of this strategy in the wide use made of various tools and results of this research, e.g., the reference chronology of business cycle peaks and troughs, the identification of mild and severe contractions, systematic amplitude differences among individual economic processes, the classification of the latter by characteristic cyclical timing, etc. Serious criticism also appeared, but it centered on the methodology of the Bureau's cyclical analysis rather than on the substantive findings of this analysis.[23]

Recent literature on the behavior, determinants, and influence of such key economic variables as consumption, types of investment, prices, and money

[22] A. F. Burns, *Economic Research and the Keynesian Thinking of Our Times,* Twenty-sixth Annual Report of the NBER, June 1946, reprinted in Burns, *Frontiers* [fn. 11], p. 24. Having illustrated some problems in business cycle research that are of great importance to men concerned with economic policy ("Whether a cyclical downturn can be recognized promptly enough to permit immediate governmental intervention, whether cost-price relations are of slight consequence in the termination of a boom, whether inflationary tendencies become important only as 'full employment' is approached..."), Burns continues: "True, the most painstaking studies of experience will not always lead to conclusive answers; but they should at least narrow the margins of uncertainty, and thus furnish a better basis than now exists for dealing with grave issues of business cycle theory and policy."

[23] Tjalling C. Koopmans, "Measurement without Theory," *Review of Economic Statistics.* August 1947; Rutledge Vining, "Koopmans on the Choice of Variables to be Studied and of Methods of Measurements," *ibid.,* May 1949; T. C. Koopmans, "A Reply," *ibid.*; R. Vining, "A Rejoinder," *ibid.* This debate, with an "Additional Comment" by Koopmans (1957), is reprinted in R. A. Gordon and L. R. Klein, eds., *Readings in Business Cycles,* Homewood, Ill., Irwin, for the American Economic Association 1965, pp. 196–231.

shows continuing concern with a number of economic relationships explored
in the National Bureau reports. For example, fixed-investment functions in
most of the major aggregate econometric models employ profit variables that
have long been stressed in these reports.[24] The accelerator variables appear to
be working with rather long distributed lags in these functions, which is
consistent with the view that they explain long-run tendencies much better
than short-run behavior.[25] In the determination of inventory investment, the
accelerator has a role to play and an important nexus exists involving new and
unfilled orders, shipments, production, and price changes; this theme has
received much attention in the work of Abramovitz, Stanback, Mack, and
Zarnowitz and increasing recognition in more recent econometric studies.[26]

In the theory of consumption, formulations that are consistent with
observation of both the short-term instability and the long-term stability and
higher values of the proportion of income consumed have in effect
superseded Keynes' simpler concept of a stable relationship between
consumer expenditures and current income. The failure of early postwar

[24] Cyclical changes in actual and prospective profits have a strategic part in Mitchell's
Business Cycles (1913). Mitchell viewed the encroachment of unit costs on prices as one
of the main factors limiting the boom and, correspondingly, the improvement in the
price-cost ratios and profit margins as one of the main factors limiting the contraction
and stimulating the revival. Reports by Hultgren on cyclical changes in labor costs and
the diffusion of profits and by Kendrick on productivity changes provide evidence that is
generally favorable to this hypothesis; Edwin Kuh, "Profit, Profit Markups, and
Productivity," *Employment, Growth, and Price Levels,* Study Paper 15, Joint Economic
Committee, 86th Cong. 1st sess., 1960, is similarly informative. For further references
and a concise account of the cyclical role of profits, see G. H. Moore, *Tested Knowledge
of Business Cycles,* Forty-second Annual Report of the NBER, June 1962; reprinted in
Gordon and Klein, eds., *Readings,* pp. 496−502.

[25] This view is well represented in the literature on the determinants of investment in
capital goods. See A.F. Burns, "Hicks and the Real Cycle," *Journal of Political
Economy,* February 1952, pp. 1−24 (reprinted in Burns, *Frontiers,* pp. 236−267),
where tests by Kuznets, Tinbergen, and Hultgren are cited in support of this position.
(These tests, however, refer to the simple old version of the "accelerator principle,"
which is now in disuse; recent and current studies employ instead the "flexible" or
distributed lag forms of the accelerator.) The econometric models of Tinbergen, Klein
and associates, and Suits use primarily profits in their investment equations; some newer
efforts such as the massive SSRC-Brookings model rely more on the modern stock
adjustment (accelerator) formulations. For references, see two survey articles: Marc
Nerlove, "A Tabular Survey of Macro-Econometric Models," *International Economic
Review,* May 1966, pp. 127−175, and Bert G. Hickman, "Dynamic Properties of
Macroeconometric Models: An International Comparison," in Bronfenbrenner, ed., *Is
the Business Cycle Obsolete?* [fn. 2], Chap. 13.

[26] The Bureau reports include, in addition to the studies by Abramovitz, Stanback,
and Mack listed in footnote 21 above, Victor Zarnowitz, "The Timing of Manufacturers'
Orders During Business Cycles," in Moore, ed., *Business Cycle Indicators,* Chap. 14;
Zarnowitz, *Unfilled Orders, Price Changes, and Business Fluctuations,* 1962 and Ruth
Mack, *Information, Expectations, and Inventory Fluctuations,* 1967. The other studies

forecasts and Kuznets' data showing a rough constancy of the share of capital formation in U.S. output[27] led to doubts about the validity of Keynes' concept, at least as an explanation of the long-run savings-income relation, and to the emergence of the "relative income," "permanent income," and "lifetime income" hypotheses of Duesenberry, Friedman, and Modigliani and Brumberg and Ando.[28] In empirical work, lagged consumption or income terms and measures of assets or wealth are now commonly included in the consumption equations. The National Bureau was actively involved in these developments.[29]

In their massive work on money, Milton Friedman and Anna Schwartz have forcefully argued that changes in the supply of money act as a major causal factor in business cycles. This position, which has important implications for economic policy, is in the center of one of the most intensive controversies in the history of economic thought. Both these studies and the debate they touched off promise to advance economic knowledge substantially.[30]

---

include the contributions of Paul G. Darling, Michael C. Lovell, and Gary Fromm to *Inventory Fluctuations and Economic Stabilization,* Joint Economic Committee, 87th Cong. 1961–62; and M.C. Lovell, "Determinants of Inventory Investment," in *Models of Income Determination,* Studies in Income and Wealth, Vol. 28, Princeton for NBER, 1964 (see *ibid.* for further references). Also, Otto Eckstein and Gary Fromm, "The Price Equation," *American Economic Review,* December 1968, pp. 1159–1183; T.J. Courchene, "Inventory Behavior and the Stock-Order Distinction," *Canadian Journal of Economics and Political Science,* August 1967, pp. 325–357; and Courchene, "An Analysis of the Price-Inventory Nexus with Empirical Application to the Canadian Manufacturing Sector," *International Economic Review,* October 1969, pp. 315–336.

[27]S. Kuznets, *National Income: A Summary of Findings,* New York, NBER, 1946, pp. 52–54.

[28] J.S. Duesenberry, *Income, Saving, and the Theory of Consumer Behavior,* Cambridge, Mass., Harvard University Press, 1949; F. Modigliani and R.E. Brumberg, "Utility Analysis and the Consumption Function: An Interpretation of Cross-section Data," in K.K. Kurihara, ed., *Post-Keynesian Economics,* New Brunswick, N.J., Rutgers University Press, 1954; M. Friedman, *A Theory of the Consumption Function,* Princeton for NBER, 1957; A. Ando and F. Modigliani, "The 'Life Cycle' Hypothesis of Saving: Aggregate Implications and Tests," *American Economic Review,* March 1963, pp. 55–84.

[29]In addition to Friedman's *A Theory of the Consumption Function* [fn. 28], the NBER publications in this area include: Dorothy S. Brady and Rose D. Friedman, "Savings and the Income Distribution," in *Studies in Income and Wealth,* Vol. 10, 1947; Franco Modigliani, "Fluctuations in the Saving–Income Ratio: A Problem in Economic Forecasting," in *Studies in Income and Wealth,* Vol. 11, 1949; and Robert Ferber, *A Study of Aggregate Consumption Functions,* 1953. For a critical review of the pre-1952 contributions, see A.F. Burns, *The Instability of Consumer Spending,* Thirty-second Annual Report of the NBER, May 1952, reprinted in *Frontiers* [fn. 11], pp. 152–169.

[30]This is not the place to argue these issues, but some attention will be given later to related points. For references, see footnotes 10 and 20 above.

Studies of business cycle indicators, diffusion indexes, anticipations data, and short-term economic forecasting all grew out of the Bureau's basic program of cyclical research, but their results are much more directly applicable to the practical problems of decision makers in government and business. The selection of the indicators was based on studies of hundreds of economic time series and successive reviews of the results, most recently in 1965 by Moore and Shiskin;[31] since 1961, up-to-date charts, tabulations, and various analytical measures for these data are published in a monthly report by the Bureau of the Census.[32] The literature and the data on economic forecasts collected from a variety of sources indicate clearly that the materials and techniques developed in these studies have become important and widely used tools in the analysis and prediction of business conditions.[33] Here the story of the Bureau's efforts has a linkage with the broader subject of the development and present state of economic forecasting which has recently become something of a "growth industry," reflecting the growth of both the economy and the concern with economic instability.

As noted before, it is proper to take a broad view in trying to evaluate any advance in economics, for we are dealing essentially with gradual processes of increased understanding, not without occasional setbacks, rather than with a definite progress measurable directly in terms of the resulting improvements in dealing with current economic problems (e.g., of inadequate growth, instability, inequity, etc.). Thus viewed in this brief and very incomplete survey, the work of the National Bureau is believed to have resulted in many important and potentially useful contributions.

[31] G. H. Moore and J. Shiskin, *Indicators of Business Expansions and Contractions,* New York, NBER, 1967. For references to earlier lists of indicators in NBER publications by Mitchell and Burns, Moore, and Shiskin, see *ibid.,* p. 1.

[32] *Business Conditions Digest* (formerly *Business Cycle Developments*). This publication brings together a large number of economic time series found useful by business analysts and forecasters, classifying them by topic, as national income and product, cyclical indicators, anticipations and intentions, etc. It is prepared under the guidance of a committee established by the Bureau of the Budget and headed by Julius Shiskin.

[33] Thus, most forecasts of the economy's course in the near future use the framework of the national income accounts, but business cycle indicators are consulted by a large majority of the forecasters in the samples we have reviewed and are ranked along with the "GNP models" as the principal approaches actually employed. See Victor Zarnowitz, "New Plans and Results of Research in Economic Forecasting," paper presented at the annual meeting of the American Economic Association and the American Statistical Association, December 30, 1970; published in *Fifty-first Annual Report* of the NBER, 1971.

VI

Theories of business cycles deal with the effects and interaction of two sets of factors, the exogenous disturbances (e.g., variation in weather, inventions, wars, political and perhaps economic policy changes) and the endogenous components of the economic system (quantities demanded and supplied, prices, etc., usually collected in large aggregates by major categories of markets or spending). There are some hypotheses that rely primarily on the first set, attributing the cyclical movements of the economy to cycles in the external disturbances (such as weather-induced harvest cycles). More common are theories that stress the second set, trying to identify endogenous causes of instability in the economic system:

> [But virtually] all serious explanations are neither purely exogenous nor purely endogenous. . . . Even if one assumes a weather cycle, the peculiar response of the business system, which converts harvest variations into a general alternation of prosperity and depression, has still to be explained. On the other hand, a purely endogenous theory is hardly satisfactory. It is not likely that, without outside shocks, a cyclical movement would go on forever: and, even if it did go on, its course would certainly be profoundly influenced by outside shocks——that is, by changes in the data (however these may be defined and delimited by economically explained variables).[34]

Most business cycle theories, old and new, are dynamic in the sense of being designed to "explain how one situation grows out of the foregoing."[35] Dynamic models incorporate lags in response, that is, relationships among variables whose magnitudes pertain to different points of time.[36] Such models with lags can generate growth and cycles endogenously, that is, even without changes in the parameters, in the exogenous variables or in the disturbances. More generally, however, changes in these outside "data,"

[34] Gottfried Haberler, *Prosperity and Depression,* 1937; new ed., Cambridge, Mass., Harvard University Press, 1957, p. 9. It may be added, however, that Haberler suggests that methodologically "For various reasons, it seems desirable, in the explanation of the business cycle, to attach as little importance as possible to the influence of external disturbances" (*ibid.,* p. 10).

[35] Ragnar Frisch, "Propagation Problems and Impulse Problems in Dynamic Economics," *Economic Essays in Honor of Gustav Cassel,* London, 1933, reprinted in Gordon and Klein, eds., *Readings* [fn. 23], pp. 155–156.

[36] Other dynamic devices closely related to lags include uses of differences or derivatives, expressing rates of change over time, and of cumulated variables (see Carl F. Christ, "Aggregate Econometric Models," *American Economic Review,* June 1956, reprinted in Gordon and Klein, eds., *Readings* [fn. 23], p. 309).

which may be either random or systematic-autonomous, are included in the analysis, and the models are then used to show how the cyclical response system in the economy converts such changes into recurrent, pervasive fluctuations. In this view, external impulses as well as the internal propagation mechanism are required for the cyclical movements in economic activity to persist; nevertheless, some writers who accept this type of theory still interpret business cycles as "self-generating," that is, having their essential traits determined primarily by the economy's organization and *modus operandi*, not by the nature of any disturbing causes "outside" the economic system.

It is probably this broad conception of self-generating cyclical fluctuations that best describes the core of the theory accepted by Wesley Mitchell, although his comprehensive "analytic description" of business cycles includes some very different elements as well, in subsidiary roles.[37] Exogenous forces and accidental events can accelerate or retard an expansion, alleviate or aggravate a contraction. These movements, which are basically endogenous, may also sometimes run into barriers, e.g., an expansion may be halted by the upper limit on the supply of money under the gold standard. But there is no evidence that the business cycle peaks (troughs) are caused typically by a concentration of unfavorable (favorable) external disturbances. Also, the expansionary and contractionary processes, while "cumulative," are usually self-limiting due to the stresses and imbalances that they themselves create; they are rarely terminated by any identifiable barriers. Thus, the economy is definitely not viewed as fundamentally unstable in the sense of generating potentially "explosive" fluctuations which are constrained by some limiting factors.[38]

The National Bureau studies in business cycles show no commitment to any particular cyclical theory but rather deal with aspects of various theories and their empirical validity. This is probably to a large extent a reflection of the strong influence of Mitchell's work, in which business cycles are treated as a set of complex phenomena with a plurality of causes and which is itself in effect a synthesis of elements of several theories, old and new.[39] There are

[37]See Milton Friedman, "The Economic Theorist" in A.F. Burns, ed., *Wesley Clair Mitchell, The Economic Scientist,* New York, NBER, 1952, pp. 252–257.

[38]The best-known theory of such fluctuations, based on a "strong" accelerator-multiplier interaction, was advanced much later by John R. Hicks in *A Contribution to the Theory of the Trade Cycle,* London, Oxford University Press, 1950. For a critique of this theory, with particular reference to the related evidence from the business cycle studies of the National Bureau, see Burns, "Hicks and the Real Cycle" [fn. 25].

[39]See Haberler, *Prosperity* [fn. 34], p. 13.

distinctive concepts here, notably of the differential responses in the price system, the lag of selling prices behind buying prices or costs, and the effects of the consequent changes in profit margins (and the totals and diffusion of profits) on investment and business activity in general. But there are also other important components such as the lags of induced expenditures behind receipts and of investment outlays and deliveries behind investment decisions and orders, the responses of the monetary and banking system, the resulting changes in the cost and availability of credit, in expectations, etc.[40] Evidence collected and evaluated by the National Bureau indicates that these processes, despite their diversity and complexity, displayed a substantial degree of consistency over the successive cycles. This is shown by the diffusion indexes that reveal the pervasiveness and early timing of the fluctuations in the *scope* of expansions and contractions, which are hidden behind the movements of economic aggregates. It is seen, too, in the persistence of timing sequences of different activities: orders, production, shipments, inventory change; investment commitments, expenditures, and realizatons; labor market adjustments; interest rates, bond and stock prices; industrial prices, costs, and profit margins.[41]

It seems fair to say that research of this kind and scope serves directly the purpose of analyzing the complex system of processes that are involved in business cycles rather than the purpose of constructing the simplest acceptable theory that could account for the basic features of business cycles. It works toward the latter objective but indirectly, in ways resembling a "roundabout" method of production, which seeks to be more efficient at the cost of being very time-consuming. Substantial contributions to the "tested knowledge of business cycles" have thus been made, but they do not add up to an integrated theory with demonstrated capacity to explain the past and predict the future phenomena in question. To be sure, this ultimate scientific goal may seem rather elusive in the context of dealing with complex processes

[40] In his essay on Mitchell, Friedman [fn. 37] writes (p. 271): "The business-cycle theory I have constructed from Part III of Mitchell's 1913 volume contains practically every element that is significant in the business-cycle theories that are currently prominent. Here are the multiplier process, the acceleration principle, the Pigovian cycles of optimism and pessimism, the Marshallian and Hawtreyan drain of cash from the banking system and the resultant tightening of the money market, a decline in the expected yield from new investment at the peak that is the counterpart of the Keynesian 'collapse of the marginal efficiency of capital' except that it is a continuous decline rather than a discontinuous 'collapse', the Keynesian changes in liquidity preference. Here, too, is an attempt at a reasoned explanation and integration of these phenomena."

[41] See the paper by Moore [fn. 24] for a report on the pre-1962 work of the National Bureau on the diffusion indexes, timing sequences, and other aspects of business cycles. Some of the later studies in these areas are included among the references in footnotes 20, 21, 26, and 31.

of economic change which are themselves subject to subtle historical alterations as are, also, the structure and institutions of the economy and the targets and tools of economic policy.

VII

More direct attempts to formulate "the" theory of business cycles, mainly by means of speculative thinking, deductive logic, and more or less abstract models, account for a large part of the literature on the economics of cyclical change and growth. There are intellectually attractive problems in economic dynamics, and some ingenious cyclical models have been constructed. It is, however, primarily by being confronted with historical evidence that such models can contribute to our understanding of the "real" business cycles, and not all of the models are testable. When the work of testing and synthesizing is outdistanced by model construction, this tends to result in a proliferation of different (but typically overlapping) theoretical constructs, not in progress toward a unified, validated theory. The latter clearly requires that both empirical and theoretical studies be pursued so as to profit from the quasi-symbiotic interaction of selective fact and disciplined thought.[42]

The decade of the 1930's saw the beginning of three important developments: (1) the formulation and interpretation of explicit and complete mathematical models of business cycles in highly aggregative form (Frisch, Kalecki, Samuelson);[43] (2) the reformulation of macroeconomic theory (Keynes);[44] and (3) the construction of econometric models of business cycles (Tinbergen).[45] These were originally rather distinct approaches to the study of the economy and its movements, but their evolution soon came to be shaped by strong cross-influences, both between the theoretical and the econometric models and between either type of models and the post- or neo-Keynesian analysis.

[42] To quote a pertinent passage from Burns' "Nature and Causes" [fn. 3], pp. 12–13: "The investigations that economists have currently under way focus on speculative model building, econometric model building, statistical studies of fluctuations in individual processes or in the economy at large, experiments with forecasting techniques, and studies of business-cycle policy. This variety of approaches sometimes leads to methodological controversies. But no serious student of business cycles any longer questions that empirical research must be guided by an analytic framework or that speculative theorizing must be tested by an appeal to experience."

[43] M. Kalecki, "A Macroeconomic Theory of Business Cycles," *Econometrica,* 1935, pp. 327–344; Paul A. Samuelson, "Interactions Between the Multiplier Analysis and the Principle of Acceleration," *Review of Economic Statistics,* 1939, pp. 75–78, reprinted in G. Haberler, ed., *Readings in Business Cycle Theory,* Homewood, Ill., Irwin for the American Economic Association, 1944, pp. 261–269; Frisch, "Propagation Problems" [fn. 35].

The mathematical models include a dynamically stable system, in which a given disturbance sets off fluctuations of an ever smaller amplitude, that is, a *damped* movement toward a new equilibrium. Frisch's linear model is of this mixed exogenous-endogenous type; it is essentially stochastic, but the external shocks which keep alive the fluctuations of this system in spite of dampening need not be entirely or necessarily random. Frisch notes that the shocks may be autonomous and more continuous and sees one of their sources in the innovations whose role in the economic process of growth and cycles was stressed by Schumpeter.[46] Another source of such autonomous impulses, which may be of increasing importance, is the public sector of the economy whose rapid growth in recent times is a well-known matter of record.

Kalecki's 1935 theory illustrates an attempt to construct a linear endogenous model with constant amplitude of fluctuations; but this system is unrealistically constrained to the thin line between stability (dampening) and instability (antidampening or explosive behavior) and, moreover, it is stable only in the nonstochastic case: if subjected to random disturbances, its expected motion would be swings with amplitudes increasing over time.[47] Subsequent work by Kalecki[48] is "Keynesian" in stressing the combined effects of the multiplier and the investment demand function, but it introduces interesting dynamic elements, notably the lag between investment decisions and realizations; it treats economic activity as *tending* toward the level equating savings and investment. Similarly, the trade cycle theories by Harrod[49] and Kaldor[50] have a basically Keynesian orientation, but different dynamic features, Harrod stressing the acceleration principle, and Kaldor,

[44] John Maynard Keynes, *The General Theory of Employment, Interest and Money,* London, Macmillan, 1936.

[45] Jan Tinbergen, *Statistical Testing of Business-cycle Theories,* 2 vols., Geneva, League of Nations, 1939.

[46] See Frisch, "Propagation Problems" [fn. 35], section VI, "The Innovations as a Factor in Maintaining Oscillations." Also see Joseph A. Schumpeter, *The Theory of Economic Development,* Cambridge, Mass. Harvard University Press, 1934 (first published in German in 1911) and *Business Cycles: A Theoretical, Historical, and Statistical Analysis of the Capitalist Process,* 2 vols., New York, McGraw-Hill, 1939.

[47] Paul A. Samuelson, *Foundations of Economic Analysis,* Cambridge, Mass., Harvard University Press, 1947, pp. 336–337.

[48] M. Kalecki, "A Theory of the Business Cycle," *Review of Economic Studies,* February 1937, pp. 77 ff, reprinted in Kalecki, *Essays in the Theory of Economic Fluctuations,* London, G. Allen & Unwin, 1939.

[49] R.F. Harrod, *The Trade Cycle,* Oxford, Clarendon Press, 1936.

[50] N. Kaldor, "A Model of the Trade Cycle," *Economic Journal,* March 1940, pp. 78–92.

investment and saving as nonlinear functions of the levels of output and capital.

Samuelson (1939) has shown how combining the multiplier with the accelerator results in a model which can produce cycles that are either damped or constant or explosive, depending on the numerical values of the two interacting parameters. A later model by Hicks[51] specifies the values that would produce explosive fluctuations. In this system, the boom is limited by a "ceiling" due to a shortage of resources and the slump by a "floor" due to the nonnegativeness of gross induced investment. This endogenous model, furthermore, generates the cycles around an upward equilibrium trend in national output (which basically reflects the growth in autonomous investment geared, not to the demand for output, but to continuing technological changes). Another endogenous model based on a nonlinear version of the accelerator principle was presented at nearly the same time by Goodwin.[52] Earlier Metzler[53] developed an endogenous linear accelerator-multiplier theory of "minor" business cycles in which the driving force comes from investment in inventories rather than in "longer-lived" capital goods (equipment and structures).

These models, in showing how the interaction of simple relationships determining investment and consumption can generate sustained fluctuations in output without any dependence on "outside" factors, illustrate ingeniously some interesting problems in economic dynamics. They are, however, likely to be more useful for the (somewhat circular) purpose of studying certain types of cyclical theories than for the really important purpose of studying the essential elements and causes of the observed fluctuations of the economy. Their explanatory or predictive power has not been demonstrated. Indeed, they may well be hiding much more than they reveal, since they pay little or no attention to the monetary and financial factors, the formation and influence of expectations, the variation in innovations and "autonomous" investment, the cyclical changes in the cost-price-profit relations, and so on. The heavy emphasis on induced investment, with high values for the accelerator, makes these models highly unstable, a feature others found difficult to reconcile with the historical (particularly, recent) course of the economy.

[51] See *A Contribution* [fn. 38].

[52] R.M. Goodwin, "The Non-Linear Accelerator and the Persistence of Business Cycles," *Econometrica*, January 1951, pp. 1—17.

[53] Lloyd Metzler, "The Nature and Stability of Inventory Cycles," *Review of Economic Statistics*, August 1961, pp. 113—129; "Business Cycles and the Modern Theory of Employment," *American Economic Review*, June 1946, pp. 278—291.

Reactions against the limitations of the endogenous accelerator models can be found, in various explicit or implicit forms, in both theoretical and applied work. Hansen[54] argued that the major fluctuations in aggregate demand are due primarily to movements in autonomous investment generated by invention, population growth, and the exploitation of frontier areas; the multiplier-accelerator process amplifies the resulting cycles in income, but its role is secondary. In Duesenberry's comprehensive theory,[55] which employs a relatively complex and disaggregated model, business cycles are ascribed to a "combination of exogenous factors working on the system" which include variations in innovations and autonomous investment; the effects of speculative booms associated with rapidly growing industries, the stock market, or actual and expected wage-price spirals; monetary disturbances; and random changes reflecting the effects of political events or expectations, changes in exports and the foreign balance, or shifts in economic policies. In Duesenberry's view, the historically observed variety of business cycles and structural changes in the economy are such as to preclude any monistic explanation of economic growth and fluctuations. His model is stable; it explains growth by the interaction of a capital-adjustment process with autonomous investment, downturns by the operation of the exogenous factors, and the recovery by corrective forces inherent in the system.[56]

The emphasis on the plurality of causes and diversity of elements in the individual business cycles will remind the reader of Mitchell's analysis and the evidence presented in the National Bureau studies. The similarities extend to several important components of the theory, notably the role of construction costs and profits in the explanation of investment.[57] There is certainly much

[54] Alvin Hansen, *Business Cycles and National Income,* New York, W.W. Norton and Co., 1951.

[55] James S. Duesenberry, *Business Cycles and Economic Growth,* New York, McGraw-Hill, 1958.

[56] For example, Duesenberry argues that "every shock which produces a depression tends ultimately to produce conditions which are favorable to recovery. But whether a recovery actually occurs (without a long period of capital decumulation) depends on what happens during the downswing" (*ibid.*, pp. 252–253).

[57] See *ibid.*, Chap. 5 and 7. Important antecedent models featuring profits in the investment functions are found in the studies by Tinbergen, *Statistical Testing* [fn. 45]; Lawrence R. Klein, "Studies in Investment Behavior," in *Conference on Business Cycles,* New York, NBER, 1951; Lawrence R. Klein and A.S. Goldberger, *An Econometric Model of the United States, 1929–1952,* Amsterdam, North-Holland, 1955; and John R. Meyer and Edwin Kuh, *The Investment Decision,* Cambridge, Mass., Harvard University Press, 1957.

less affinity between the Bureau's approach and those endogenous models which depend principally and rather rigidly on the acceleration principle.[58]

The construction of aggregate econometric models was originally (as in the pioneering work by Tinbergen in the 1930's) strongly oriented toward business cycle research.[59] In the postwar period, work on such models intensified and broadened, and its results are now being widely used for various purposes including forecasting, tests of macroeconomic hypotheses, and simulation of the likely effects of alternative policies. The models for the U.S. economy progressed from annual to quarterly units; they vary greatly in size and complexity; but the evolution so far appears to be in the direction of ever larger systems. The models, for the United States as well as for the other countries, generally utilize the structure of national income accounts and are for the most part of Keynesian persuasion. Many have similar features. This similarity in part reflects the importance and influence in this area of the work by Lawrence R. Klein and his associates.[60]

Since the views about the nature and causes of business cycles are quite diverse, as illustrated by the preceding brief survey of the different theories and models, it is important to ask what light the econometric studies throw upon the relation of the exogenous and endogenous factors that may be involved. The question must be raised in the context of two recent developments: (1) the increasing emphasis on exogenous factors among which

[58]See Burns' critique of Hicks' trade-cycle theory [fn. 25]. It is true that self-generating cycles are the central concepts in the work of Mitchell and others at the National Bureau and that the role of exogenous factors, though by no means disregarded, is treated as secondary. But the argument seems persuasive that the main ideas in this approach (that the nature of the cycle is determined primarily by the structure and institutions of the economy and that both prediction and control of the cycle must be sought in the understanding of the "processes which run regularly within the world of business itself") would not be substantively changed even if the role of the "disturbing causes" were more explicitly involved. See Friedman, "The Economic Theorist" [fn. 37], pp. 253–254.

[59]See Tinbergen, *Statistical Testing* [fn. 45]. Also see Jan Tinbergen, "Econometric Business Cycle Research," *Review of Economic Studies,* 1940, pp. 73–90, reprinted in Haberler, ed., *Readings* [fn. 43],pp. 61–86.

[60]See L. R. Klein, *Economic Fluctuations in the United States, 1921–1941,* New York, J. Wiley and Sons, 1950; Klein and Goldberger, *An Econometric Model* [fn. 57]; L. R. Klein, "A Postwar Quarterly Model: Description and Applications," in *Models of Income Determination,* Studies in Income and Wealth, Vol. 28, Princeton for NBER, 1964; M. K. Evans and L. R. Klein, *The Wharton Econometric Forecasting Model,* Studies in Quantitative Economics No. 2, Economic Research Unit, University of Pennsylvania, Philadelphia, 1967. See the survey articles by Nerlove and B. G. Hickman [fn. 25] for references to other U.S. and foreign econometric models.

are included political and economic policy changes, and (2) the challenge to certain tenets and applications of Keynesian theory raised in writings of several monetary economists, particularly Milton Friedman. In what follows, some attention will be given to these topics.

VIII

In a study of the Klein-Goldberger econometric model of the U.S. economy, Irma Adelman and Frank Adelman concluded that nonstochastic simulations based on smooth extrapolations of the exogenous variables do not enable that model to generate cyclical movements resembling the historically observed fluctuations nor do "type I" stochastic simulations, with random shocks superimposed upon the extrapolated values of the exogenous variables. They found, however, that "type II" stochastic simulations, with random shocks introduced into each of the fitted equations, do result in cycles whose average duration, conformity, and timing characteristics agree broadly with the measures developed by the National Bureau.[61] They interpreted these results as consistent with the Frisch hypothesis that highly developed capitalistic economies react to random impulses so as to convert them into the pervasive and recurrent fluctuations described as the business cycle. Similarly, in his survey of sixteen U.S. and foreign aggregate econometric models, Bert Hickman reported that "the weight of their evidence suggests strongly that modern mixed enterprise systems are characterized by stable response mechanisms and small dynamic multipliers. If that be so, then the cycles of experience must be kept alive by exogenous stimuli."[62]

In a comprehensive investigation of econometric model simulations, a team of National Bureau researchers, aided by the active cooperation of the builders of several quarterly U.S. models, found that nonstochastic sample-period simulations produce strongly damped cyclical movements.[63] Only the first one or two recessions covered are, in some attenuated form, reproduced in such simulations; beyond that the declines in the over-all aggregates tend to disappear. In simulations extending for a hundred quarters

[61]Irma Adelman and Frank L. Adelman, "The Dynamic Properties of the Klein-Goldberger Model," *Econometrica*, October 1959, pp. 596–625, reprinted in Gordon and Klein, eds., *Readings* [fn. 23], pp. 278–306.

[62]Hickman, "Dynamic Properties" [fn. 25], p. 429.

[63]Victor Zarnowitz, Charlotte Boschan, and Geoffrey H. Moore, with the assistance of Josephine Su, "Business Cycle Analysis of Econometric Model Simulations," *Econometric Models of Cyclical Behavior,* Studies in Income and Wealth, Vol. 36, New York, NBER, forthcoming.

into the future, the projected series are in general smooth and trend-dominated, indicating that these models do not generate cyclical movement endogenously. When shocks are applied to these long *ex ante* simulations, many fluctuations do occur, but they are in large part too short to qualify as cyclical, according to comparisons with the NBER reference-cycle measurements. It is only when these stochastic simulations are expressed as deviations from the trendlike deterministic ("control") solutions for the corresponding variables and models that they reveal characteristics closer to those of the historically observed cycles. The simulations based on autocorrelated shocks are much smoother and often appear more plausible than those with serially uncorrelated shocks. A somewhat updated summary version of the Zarnowitz-Boschan-Moore study, prepared by one of the authors, is included in this volume.[64]

The models examined in these simulation studies are in general stable. If it could be assumed that they are correctly specified, these experiments would provide some support for the Wicksell-Slutsky—Frisch theory of a dynamically stable (damped) response mechanism, with fluctuations being renewed and "kept alive" by erratic shocks. The support would appear strong in the case of the Adelmans' study and some of the models examined by Hickman. It must be viewed as much more limited and qualified, however, as far as the more recent and comprehensive reports of the 1969 NBER conference at Harvard are concerned.[65] Here the evidence suggests that random disturbances alone produce only weak fluctuations, visible in deviations from trends rather than in the stochastically simulated series proper. Smoother and longer (but similarly weak) fluctuations appear when the shocks to the equations are serially correlated. The cyclical aspects of the simulations would probably be strengthened by application of autocorrelated shocks not only to the equations with endogenous equations but also to

[64]V. Zarnowitz, "Econometric Model Simulations and the Cyclical Characteristics of the U.S. Economy," paper presented at the Second World Congress of the Econometric Society, Cambridge, England, September 1970. This paper includes some simulations of the Brookings model in addition to those of the Wharton, OBE, and FRB-MIT-PENN models included in the full NBER report.

[65]These include, in addition to the NBER study cited in footnote 63: M. K. Evans, L. R. Klein, and M. Saito, "Short-Run Prediction and Long-Run Simulation of the Wharton Model"; G. R. Green, in association with M. Liebenberg and A. A. Hirsch, "Short- and Long-Term Simulations with the OBE Econometric Model," and E. P. Howrey, "Dynamic Properties of a Condensed Version of the Wharton Model," all in *Econometric Models* [fn. 63]. See also the Introduction by Bert G. Hickman in *ibid.*

exogenous variables.[66] There are reasons to expect that wars, policy actions, technological change (innovations), etc., would indeed frequently result in autocorrelated, "autonomous" shocks to the economy.

However, the econometric models in question may not be correctly specified. If so, then the autocorrelations observed in the sample residuals for many equations in these models may in the main reflect these misspecifications. Frequent caveats on this score are expressed in the work on econometric model simulations.[67]

It is not easy to document specification errors in the models; economic theory provides broad guidelines, but it does not prevent arguments among economists with different views about what the correct formulations ought to be. Large-scale, complex models, in particular, pose many detailed specification problems that theory and empirical research have not yet been able to resolve with the existing information. The best tests available here are indirect, based on the predictive value of the model.[68]

The *ex ante* forecasts with econometric models typically involve judgmental elements: predictions of the exogenous inputs, modifications of the constant terms, and revisions of the model. After allowing for the "fine tuning," i.e., with the same adjustments of the intercepts (same guesses about the joint impact of the disturbances and model and data errors in the particular forecast period), the *ex ante* forecasts are often found superior to the *ex post* forecasts, even though the former include and the latter exclude the errors in exogenous variables. When the *ex ante* forecasts are recalculated without any constant-term adjustments, they are still frequently more accurate than the corresponding *ex post* predictions. These results come from a comprehensive study of the Wharton-EFU and OBE models by M.K. Evans, Y. Haitovsky, and G. I. Treyz.[69] In "Forecasting Economic Conditions: The Record and the Prospect," the survey of the NBER studies of economic

[66] A few such simulations were run for the OBE model by Green et al., with the result that cycle declines were increased in amplitude and duration. But the effects of shocks or fluctuations in exogenous variables were not given adequate attention in the 1969 conference studies.

[67] See Adelman and Adelman, [fn. 61], p. 301; Hickman, "Dynamic Properties" [fn. 25], pp. 428–429; and remarks by deLeeuw, Hickman, and Zarnowitz et al., in *Econometric Models* [fn. 63].

[68] See Carl F. Christ, "Econometric Models, Aggregate," *International Encyclopedia of the Social Sciences,* 1968, Vol. 4, pp. 346–347.

[69] "An Analysis of the Forecasting Properties of U.S. Econometric Models," in *Econometric Models* [fn. 63].

forecasting which is included in this volume, I interpret these findings as indicative of offsetting errors. Indeed, in the cases where the *ex post* forecast errors exceed the *ex ante* ones without adjustments, the single most plausible explanation left is that the model contains misspecifications which are more than offset by errors in the exogenous variables.[70]

IX

According to many critics, a major source of specification errors in recent econometric models is the neglect or inadequate handling of the monetary and financial factors. This view is stressed particularly by those economists who take a "monetarist" approach (as opposed to the "Keynesian" approach) to macroeconomics; the writings by Milton Friedman and his associates were most influential in the recent development of this line of thought.[71] However, some economists basically sympathetic to the so-called neo-Keynesian concepts have also urged that greater attention be given to the monetary and financial sectors in econometric models, and efforts in this direction are apparent in the latest models.[72]

Evidence assembled by Friedman and Schwartz leads them to conclude that "there is an extremely strong case for the proposition that sizable changes in the rate of change in the money stock are a necessary and sufficient condition for sizable changes in the rate of change in the money income."[73] For the minor U.S. economic fluctuations, "the case for a monetary explanation is not nearly so strong. . . ," but "it is plausible to suppose that changes in the stock of money played an important independent role, though certainly the evidence for these minor movements does not rule out other interpretations." The mechanism whereby monetary changes are

[70] Zarnowitz, "New Plans and Results" [fn.33].

[71] These writings include, in addition to those cited in footnotes 10, 13, and 20, the following: M. Friedman, *The Demand for Money: Some Theoretical and Empirical Results,* New York, NBER, 1959 (reprinted from the *Journal of Political Economy,* August 1959, pp. 327–351); M. Friedman and D. Meiselman, "The Relative Stability of Monetary Velocity and the Investment Multiplier in the United States, 1897–1958," in *Stabilization Policies,* Englewood Cliffs, N.J., Prentice-Hall for the Commission on Money and Credit, 1964, pp. 165–268; M. Friedman and A. J. Schwartz, "Money and Business Cycles," *Review of Economics and Statistics; Supplement;* February 1963, pp. 32–64; M. Friedman, "A Theoretical Framework for Monetary Analysis," *Journal of Political Economy,* March-April 1970, pp. 193–238; M. Friedman and A. J. Schwartz, *Monetary Statistics of the United States: Estimates, Sources, Methods,* New York, NBER, 1970.

[72] For example, H. P. Minsky in his "Comment" on Friedman and Schwartz, "Money and Business Cycles" [fn. 71] writes: "The belief that money is important is not inconsistent with acceptance of the basic validity of the modern income-expenditure approach to business cycles. To one holding such a view, the nonexistent or primitive

transmitted in ways that can produce cyclical fluctuations in income is viewed as a series of reciprocal adjustments of stocks to flows, which involve variable but often lengthy lags. Absorption of newly injected money, for example, requires alteration of yields and prices of different assets, which creates discrepancies between the actual and desired portfolios and prompts the banks and the public to reshuffle their balance sheets in the effort to reduce such discrepancies. The first impact of an increase in the monetary growth that usually occurs early in contraction is on the financial markets (bonds, then equities), but eventually the stimulus spreads to the markets for goods and services, causing rises in investment and in payments for real resources at large. In the process, interest rates first decline and then rise, the reversal being due to the increase in spending, income, and prices. The process will tend to overshoot and involve cyclical, presumably damped, adjustments to each monetary "shock." Moreover, the shocks are likely "to take the form of an unusually high or low rate of growth of the stock of money for some time, with a reversion to a previous level . . . equivalent to two shocks . . . in opposite directions. Hence the shock itself gives rise to a cyclical movement in addition to the cyclical adjustment to each shock separately."

This hypothesis envisages a "partly self-generating cyclical mechanism," in which disturbances in the growth of money supply induce cyclical adjustments and recur frequently enough to prevent the fluctuations from dying out. The stock of money is subject to large changes that are autonomous, i.e., not directly attributable to contemporary changes in income and prices. It is recognized that changes in business activity do affect money, but this is considered a "reflex influence" or a secondary "feedback." Thus, the monetary changes are here treated as a mainly exogenous and "causal" factor in a narrow but important sense.[74]

monetary and financial system incorporated in income and expenditure models such as those of Duesenberry, Eckstein, and Fromm, of Klein, and of Suits is a defect that should be corrected" (*Review of Economics and Statistics; Supplement,* February 1963, pp. 65–66). The increased concern about the role of the monetary-financial factors and their interaction with the "real" factors can be seen in the reports on the structure and performance of the large-scale Brookings-SSRC model and especially of the more recent FRB-MIT-PENN model. See Frank deLeeuw, "A Model of Financial Behavior," in J. S. Duesenberry, G. Fromm, L. R. Klein, and E. Kuh, eds., *The Brookings Quarterly Econometric Model of the United States,* Chicago, Rand-McNally, 1965, pp. 464–530. Also see F. deLeeuw and E. Gramlich, "The Federal Reserve–M.I.T. Econometric Model," *Federal Reserve Bulletin,* January 1968, pp. 11–40, and A. Ando and F. Modigliani, "Econometric Analysis of Stabilization Policies," *American Economic Review,* May 1969, pp. 296–314.

[73]The quotations in this paragraph are from Friedman and Schwartz, "Money and Business Cycles" [fn. 71], pp. 63 and 55.

[74]*Ibid.,* pp. 48–56, 63–64 *passim.*

Formally, the model of the economy that is conveyed by these studies is dynamically stable, converting random or systematic disturbances into cyclical fluctuations in major economic variables. Substantively, it is the monetary factor——changes in the rate of growth of the money stock——that is the major source of these disturbances. In particular, this factor is regarded as basically responsible for the major economic fluctuations; the evidence for the minor ones, taken alone, would not be inconsistent with the alternative view "that the close relation between money and business reflected primarily the influence of business on money."[75] In most applications, however, especially by others who have adopted Friedman's basic position, the distinction between the major and minor fluctuations plays no operational role and monetary changes are treated generally as the main independent force determining the movements in money income that are associated (sometimes identified) with business cycles. Friedman and Schwartz have emphasized that their account is tentative and not preclusive;[76] but the other factors that "no doubt . . . play a role" attract very little of their attention and are presumed secondary. The main rival theory, namely, that "real" rather than monetary factors are critical, with investment being the main motive force in business cycles, is explicitly rejected, but the monetary hypothesis is also sharply distinguished from the earlier "credit" theories of the cycle. This conception of business cycles as essentially a monetary phenomenon (resembling the "dance of the dollar" view of Irving Fisher) is also clearly different from the much broader conception of Mitchell.[77]

X

The monetary disturbances to which a crucial role is assigned in the current "monetarist" theory of business fluctuations need not be all directly associated with changes in monetary policy. Thus changes in the division of money holdings between currency and bank deposits, which depend on the public's decisions, have often acted as an important determinant of changes in the quantity of money. This fact, established by Cagan, may signify, in keeping with the monetarist position, a feedback effect related to prior autonomous shifts in policy and subject to potential offsets by subsequent

[75] *Ibid.,* p. 55. Friedman and Schwartz identify six deep depressions or major cycles among the twenty-one reference cycles between 1867 and 1960.

[76] *Ibid.,* pp. 55 and 64.

[77] This statement is, of course, entirely consistent with the fact that Mitchell attached great importance to the role of money in the structure and cyclical movements of contemporary industrial economies in the Western world.

shifts; but it is as such a manifestation of the business-to-money chain of influence which is stressed in other interpretations.[78] Moreover, major disturbances in the economic system may and do arise from other, nonmonetary sources, and the potential of monetary policy to counterbalance such forces is limited.[79]

Nevertheless, there is a marked tendency in recent discussions of problems of inflation and recession to emphasize the power of economic policy to do both good and evil——to stabilize and disturb. According to one view, the economy is rather unstable, in need of being stimulated by fiscal policies at some times and of being restrained by fiscal and perhaps monetary policies at other times. According to the monetarist view, the economy is fundamentally stable, and major business cycle movements are primarily attributable to "inappropriate movements in the money stock"; economic instability can therefore be minimized by controlling the rate of monetary expansion.[80] These are opposite positions, yet they have one important point in common, namely, that economic policy is potent enough to be, if correct, a major force working to promote or restore economic stability; and also to be, if erroneous, a major cause of, or at least contributor to, economic instability. It all depends only on the choice of the right policies at the right time, provided that the choice is defined broadly to include self-imposed institutional rules and automatic stabilizers as well as discretionary policies.

As usual, such positions are often exaggerated and vulgarized in popular debate. Also, extreme views on the powers of stabilization policies are not new.[81] But the increasing emphasis on exogenous and particularly policy factors in the analysis of business fluctuations is so manifest in recent professional writing as to merit serious attention. Is this emphasis based on new evidence or a revival of some old beliefs? Has it increased too much or too little or just about right?

[78] See Phillip Cagan, *Determinants and Effects of Changes in the Stock of Money, 1875–1960,* New York, NBER, 1965; Allan H. Metzler, "Money Supply Revisited: A Review Article," *Journal of Political Economy,* April 1967, pp. 169–182; Richard G. Davis, "Discussion," *American Economic Review,* May 1969, pp. 316–317.

[79] See Friedman, "The Role of Monetary Policy" [fn. 13], p. 14.

[80] Leonall C. Andersen and Keith M. Carlson, "A Monetarist Model for Economic Stabilization," *Federal Reserve Bank of St. Louis Review,* April 1970, p. 8.

[81] Thus Friedman reminds us that in the 1920's "it came to be widely believed that a new era had arrived in which business cycles had been rendered obsolete by advances in monetary technology.... The Great Contraction destroyed this naive attitude. Opinion swung to the other extreme." He expresses the fear that "now as then, the pendulum may have swung too far, that, now as then, we are in danger of assigning to monetary policy a larger role than it can perform. ..." See his "The Role of Monetary Policy" [fn. 13], pp. 1 and 5.

The evidence from econometric models and related simulation studies tends to support the view that exogenous factors play a major role.[82] Policy changes are generally treated as exogenous in these models. In a recent monetarist model, changes in total spending depend entirely (except for the error term only) on current and past changes in two exogenous policy variables.[83] But it must again be recognized that all these models represent only different ways of combining fragments of uncertain knowledge and outright hunches; they certainly contain serious errors of commission and omission, are implemented with very imperfect data, and are valuable primarily as vehicles of a continuing search for more and firmer understanding of the economy in motion. The models differ not only with respect to the underlying theories or intuitions, i.e., in specification, but also in size and complexity, sample periods, and methods of estimation and application to forecasting. With so many sources of incomparability, which cannot be eliminated, neutralized, or fully allowed for (without removing the distinctive properties of the models), conclusive discrimination among the models is very difficult. However, predictive and dynamic simulation tests, which are probably more convincing than the others, suggest at least a few broad propositions, as follows: (1) Both monetary and fiscal policy variables have significant effects on aggregate spending; neither set should be treated as dominant at all times or as negligible, and improvements in dealing with both sets pay off in better performance of the model.[84] (2) The combined influence of both sets of policy variables is far from sufficient to account for

[82] As noted by Hickman, Introduction to *Econometric Models,* [fn. 63], ". . . some classes of shocks may generate cycles when acting upon the models studied in this conference. It should be emphasized, however, that broadening the class of shocks to include perturbations in exogenous variables and to allow for serial correlation in the disturbances to equations and exogenous variables, diminishes the role of model structure as a cycle maker."

[83] See Andersen and Carlson, "A Monetarist Model" [fn. 80], p. 11. Here quarterly changes in nominal GNP are related to dollar changes in money stock (demand deposits and currency outside banks) and in high-employment federal expenditures with lags of zero to four quarters.

[84] See *ibid.* and, also, L. C. Andersen and Jerry L. Jordan, "Monetary and Fiscal Actions: A Test of Their Relative Importance in Economic Stabilization," *Federal Reserve Bank of St. Louis Review.* November 1968, pp. 11–23; F. deLeeuw and J. Kalchbrenner, "Monetary and Fiscal Actions: A Test of Their Relative Importance in Economic Stabilization––Comment," *ibid.,* April 1969, pp. 6–11, and Andersen and Jordan "Reply," *ibid.,* pp. 12–16. The St. Louis model in its present version (April 1970) indicates that the fiscal effects, though weaker and more temporary than the monetary effects, are significant. See also the references to the analysis of the FRB-MIT model [fn. 72]; in this larger and more elaborate model, both monetary and fiscal policy variables have pronounced effects on GNP.

the systematic component of changes in total spending (let alone for other important elements in economic fluctuations).[85] (3) Business cycle analysis and forecasting can benefit from econometric studies of structural models of various degrees of complexity, but inadequate knowledge and data, and perhaps also problems of coordinating the work of a large group of experts, impose definite limits upon the size of potentially useful models at the present time.[86]

There are, of course, good and easily understandable reasons why changes in economic policies attract much greater and more general attention now than in times past (but not so long ago) when both the weight of the government and the extent of its intervention in the economy were much smaller. But precisely because this is so, the chances have also increased that the potency of governmental policies would often be overestimated. Policy changes soon tend to become a matter of public record, although not all receive prompt and wide publicity, whereas the changes wrought by forces within the economy are more diffuse and subtle, hence often difficult to discern. Moreover, policy changes interact with other "outside disturbances" and endogenous forces so that the task of isolating and evaluating the effects of these factors on the movement of national income and other aggregates is very arduous, even conceptually and a fortiori in empirical applications. The policy variables can be exogenous only in the sense that they do not respond to *current* movements in the endogenous variables. They certainly do respond to earlier developments in the economy as policy makers try to counteract undesirable trends due either to internal causes or external disturbances (including the influence of past policies). These corrective efforts must frequently concur with the more "autonomous" policy initiatives, and both

[85] For example, the St. Louis equation "explains" nearly two-thirds of the variance of changes in GNP with changes in money stock and high-employment federal expenditures alone. This is a rather high R^2 considering the first-difference form of the model, but contemporaneous values of the policy variables as well as short-lag values are included, and there can be little doubt that there is some bias in this single-equation approach: the influence is not entirely from money to GNP but also in the opposite direction. Other formulations designed to reduce this basic and much-debated problem have led to lower correlations (see the deLeeuw-Kalchbrenner comment [fn. 84].

[86] These limitions are stressed by several reviewers of the largest of the U.S. models, the Brookings-SSRC model, which contains several hundred equations (see E. Mosbaek in *Econometrica*, January 1968, pp. 194–196, and Z. Griliches in the *Review of Economics and Statistics*, May 1968, pp. 215–234). On the other hand, the single-equation or reduced-form models such as the St. Louis model may be used to study the influence of certain exogenous policy factors but they are much too "underdeveloped" and structurally undetermined to be helpful in business cycle research.

affect aggregate spending, income, etc., only with lags which may be substantial and variable. When these lagged effects are cumulated and attributed fully to policy changes, the influence of these changes may often be significantly overestimated.

This way of looking at economic policies has however, other implications as well, namely, that the governmental actions may at times tend to cancel each other or have net destabilizing effects.[87] One explanation of the latter centers on the difference between the immediate and the delayed consequences of a policy, as in Friedman's analysis of the monetary authority's attempts to peg either interest rates or the rate of unemployment.[88] Another explanation would have policies alternate between the immediate goals of fighting inflation and of fighting unemployment, with the efforts to contain the rise in prices leading to a business recession or slowdown and efforts to reduce unemployment leading to renewed inflationary pressures, as in some analyses based on the Phillips curve.[89] The two hypotheses are not logically inconsistent and could both be valid. There is evidence to support the view that reactions to discretionary policy shifts involve patterns of lengthy and varying lags, although measurements of the distributed lags in the effect of monetary policy vary considerably and are far from conclusive. There is also evidence to support the relationship between wage changes and unemployment as summarized by the Phillips curve, although it is plausible that in the long run no stable trade-off would exist between unemployment and *anticipated* inflation.[90]

It is clear that we know much less about the working of economic stabilization policies than we need for both an objective appraisal of the past and as a guide to such conduct of current affairs as would command wide professional agreement. It is certainly difficult, even with the benefit of hindsight, to decide such questions as whether any of the postwar U.S. recessions could have been avoided by better policies and, if so, how, and at what alternative costs. But underlying such questions is the central problem of business cycle theory to which frequent reference was made here: What are the relative roles of exogenous factors and endogenous processes in

[87]This brings us back to the "policy cycles" noted early in this paper, as an extreme case of destabilizing action.

[88]See Friedman, "The Role of Monetary Policy" [fn. 13], pp. 5–11.

[89]See M. Bronfenbrenner and F. D. Holzman, "Survey of Inflation Theory," *American Economic Review,* September 1963, particularly pp. 626–628.

[90]See Friedman, "The Role of Monetary Policy" [fn. 13]; also, E. S. Phelps, "Money-Wage Dynamics and Labor-Market Equilibrium," *Journal of Political Economy,* July-August 1968, Part II, pp. 678–711 (with extensive references to the numerous Phillips curve studies of the recent years).

determining the course of the economy? There is great need for well-designed research on this subject, the eventual results of which could contribute much to a better understanding of current policy issues.

One approach to the study of how stabilization policies work is through simulation experiments with different econometric models and "policy rules." The paper by Haitovsky and Wallace included in this volume examines stochastic and nonstochastic simulations with various combinations of discretionary and nondiscretionary monetary and fiscal policies. The policy rules incorporate different assumptions about the monetary and fiscal responses to developments in the economy. The novel feature of the study is the wide range of stochastic elements considered: Not only the additive disturbances but also the coefficients and the noninstrument exogenous variables are random. The nonstochastic simulations are found to give poor estimates of the distributions of outcomes of the corresponding stochastic simulations. (Investigators should, therefore, rely on the latter, not on the former, lest they overstate the stability of the models and misjudge the relative effects of different policies.) This is an exploratory, experimental study which attempts to move onto new ground, and its main contribution is therefore methodological. Some of its substantive results have been questioned in the discussion and may be viewed as tentative and as an invitation to further research.

XI

I have tried to survey a wide area of fact and thought rather briefly and selectively so as to provide a background for the reports that follow. The topics included the apparent moderation of business cycles in recent times—some facts on the progress toward economic stability and some reflections on its possible causes; the role of economic theory and research in this development, with particular reference to National Bureau studies and their interaction with other work; the conception of business cycles and its evolution in the literature as influenced by the historical changes in the cycle; recent growth-cycle models and the "monetarist" view of economic fluctuations in the context of that evolution; the functions and relation of exogenous and endogenous factors in theoretical and econometric models of cyclical behavior; and some relevant evidence from forecasting, simulation studies, analyses of how monetary and fiscal policies work, etc. In reviewing these matters, several references were made to the papers prepared for the present occasion.

Having thus traveled over a varied terrain, it is well to come back to the starting place for another look and an afterthought: What are the main lessons of the colloquium reports as seen against the background provided here?[91]

1. Economic fluctuations have definitely become milder in the post-World War II period, here and in other highly developed market economies; slowdowns in the rate of growth of total spending and income have largely replaced sustained declines in these measures of aggregate economic activity. However, many features of the "classical" business cycle reappear, though perhaps in modified forms, in the recent "growth cycles." Thus downturns in the leading indicators predict either a decline (recession) or a marked retardation in economic activity, and upturns in these sensitive series predict either a recovery or a pronounced general speedup (Mintz). Comprehensive price indexes have never conformed very well to business cycles, but cyclical fluctuations in their *rates of change* how a one-to-one correspondence with the U.S. cycles of the postwar period, when both recessions and slowdowns are recognized (Moore).[92] In the 1969–70 period, too, the timing sequence and diffusion of business cycle indicators resembled well the economic changes characteristic of past recessions (Fabricant).

2. Structural changes in the economy have been given a large share of credit for the observed progress toward economic stability, but claims could also be raised here on behalf of such potential factors as increased knowledge about how to avoid destabilizing policy changes and how to offset other disturbances. However, we have yet to learn what the relative contributions of these factors are. The whole problem of the interaction of exogenous and endogenous forces, including any major historical changes in their relationship, requires much further study. Much of the material for these investigations is likely to come from simulation and forecasting tests of various econometric models of cyclical behavior. Simulation studies suggest a high degree of dynamic stability in the systems intended to represent the U.S. economy in recent years; outside disturbances play an apparently important role, but the cyclical responses to them in these models are weak. The latter feature, however, may apply much more to the models in question than to the realities of the economy. The major role of judgmental inputs into, and

[91] In what follows, the reports are occasionally referred to by the author's name given in parentheses. It should be noted that these references, along with those made earlier, are only intended as a brief guide: more complete summaries are not needed, since they are provided in the text of each essay. In particular, problems of forecasting have received little attention in this introduction because my paper, "Forecasting Economic Conditions: The Record and the Prospect," is itself in part a survey of this area of study.

[92] It is interesting to recall similar findings by Friedman and Schwartz, who showed that rates of change in money stock conformed much better and more uniformly to business cycles than did the levels ("Money and Business Cycles" [fn. 71], pp. 34–36).

the structural shortcomings of, the models obscure the validity of the evidence from the available simulation and forecasting studies (Zarnowitz). But this is not at all to argue against the usefulness of such studies, but only for the need to widen and deepen them considerably. This research needs to be extended simultaneously in three directions, to study the effects of fluctuations and disturbances in exogenous factors, learn more about the specification errors in the models, and include a greater variety of models.[93] Also greatly needed are stochastic simulation studies of the effects of specific economic policies treated as partly endogenous in the sense of being a response to certain economic developments (Haitovsky and Wallace).

3. Whatever their causes, the moderation and modification of business cycles in recent times require that the methods of cyclical analysis be altered in some respects. New tools of research are needed, particularly a more complete reference chronology which, ideally, should integrate the "classical" cycles as dated and analyzed in the Bureau's studies and the speedup-slowdown concept discussed at the colloquium of which this book is a product. The work by Ilse Mintz makes a major contribution to this end, but much further study is necessary.[94] This would probably include cyclical analyses of many rate-of-change series, similar to Moore's study that concentrated on price indexes, and could eventually result in considerable improvement of both the data and their interpretation.[95]

4. The 1969–70 developments disclose not only important similarities but also important differences when compared with earlier recessions. In particular, inflation persisted amidst a decline in production and a rise in unemployment more strongly than was ever previously recorded. This clearly has major implications for stabilization policies and also for further research, for it prompts a reconsideration of the criteria of severity of recessions.

[93] The last of these desiderata implies that particular attention should be paid to the most recent and as yet not well explored models that represent efforts to develop certain sectors or aspects of the economy which were previously rather neglected. The FRP-MIT-PENN model and the St. Louis Federal Reserve model would fall in this category. Similarly important here would be further work on the incorporation into an econometric model of major results of the NBER cyclical studies——a major task initiated by Gregory C. Chow and G. H. Moore in "An Econometric Model of Business Cycles," in *Econometric Models* [fn. 63].

[94] In this connection, some earlier work on minor or short fluctuations might prove helpful, including Ruth Mack's emphasis on "subcycles," in particular in the analysis of inventory movements and their implications.

[95] If the promise of such improvements became apparent, further work with data along these lines might be undertaken and the results included in the *Business Conditions Digest* [fn. 32].

Considerable debate on these criteria developed at the colloquium, centering upon the relative significance of real vs. pecuniary measurements of aggregate economic activity (Fabricant, Mintz, Moore). Further study is needed to help resolve this issue.

Finally, let me express the belief that the reports here presented, as well as the discussion they stimulated, will have contributed to the development of a fruitful research strategy in dealing with the phenomena that are summed up in the phrase "the business cycle today." It seems clear once more that these phenomena are still really important, despite the changes in their complexion due to the welcome advance toward greater economic stability. The pressure of other "new" socioeconomic problems does not mean that the old problem of instability no longer requires much attention. Indeed, in one sense, that pressure adds to the seriousness of this problem because it reduces society's tolerance for even mild economic declines, especially in the face of persistent inflationary developments.

Dating American Growth Cycles

Ilse Mintz

1. THE PURPOSE OF THE STUDY

The Revision of the Business Cycle Concept

Business cycles are a thing of the past, comparable to dinosaurs, some believe. Others, on the contrary, call the 1969-70 swing in the U.S. economy a traumatic experience. Why these differences in views?

Economic fluctuations have, since World War II, become much milder than they used to be.[1] A recession in the sense of an absolute and sustained decline in aggregate economic activity is a rare exception nowadays. Alternations of periods of fast growth with periods of slow growth have replaced, in most instances, the alternations between the rise and fall of economic activity which constituted the classical business cycle. This holds for most countries, including the United States. Here recessions prevailed in less than 17 per cent of the months, 1948–68, and in the later part of this period expansion was unbroken for eight years whether or not the later part of 1969 is classified as recession.

Note: This paper is a report on research in progress. Except for the Conclusions and the Postscript its coverage of data extends only through March 1970. Also, some findings have been obtained by short-cut methods rather than by complete analysis. The contemplated extension and revision is not likely to change the main findings, but some adjustments of detail are to be expected.

[1] See Arthur F. Burns, *The Business Cycle in a Changing World*, New York, NBER, 1969, pp. 50, 102. Also C. A. Blyth, *American Business Cycles 1945–50*, New York, Praeger, 1968, pp. 19, 22.

But the mildness of the fluctuations does not prevent experts and laymen, both in the United States and abroad, from paying great attention to them and from regarding periods of slow growth much as periods of decline used to be viewed in former days. Here, as everywhere, expectations have risen with achievements, and rising aggregate economic activity today does not preclude concern about subnormal performance.[2]

A period of low growth is, of course, in many ways quite different from a period of absolute decline. But in other ways the two are similar. Alternations between periods of, say, 4 per cent rises and 2 per cent falls (which qualify as classical business cycles) and alternations between periods of, say, 8 per cent rises and 2 per cent rises may be expected to show considerable family resemblance,[3] and this resemblance in duration, pervasiveness, and other aspects, will be affirmed by the findings of this study.

The time has come, therefore, to adjust the tools of business cycle analysis to the moderation of the cycle and this, essentially, is the task of the study of which the present paper is a preliminary report. The study tries to develop a working concept which can do for the analysis of growth cycles, as I shall call them, what the Burns-Mitchell definition has done for the analysis of classical cycles. It seems reasonable to expect that dating the phases of growth cycles will give precision to the variety of notions and impressions now encountered and will help in measuring the behavior and the interrelationships of the various sectors and aspects of the economy.

The proposed chronology will, moreover, facilitate comparisons between U.S. fluctuations and those in foreign economies which have had almost no experience with classical cycles after World War II.

The new chronology is not intended, it should be stressed, to supplant the traditional one. The treasure we possess in our knowledge of business cycles, cast in the framework of classical cycles, will continue to be used and

[2] "The American people have of late been more conscious of the business cycle, more sensitive to every wrinkle of economic curves, more alert to the possible need for contracyclical action on the part of government, than ever before in our history" (Burns, *Business Cycle*, p. 101).

"Only in relatively few cases (the United States, Canada, Switzerland and Belgium) can we register significant absolute declines in one or more years. However, we must refer these instability experiences to the much greater postwar ambitions with regard to full employment, as well as to the new ambitions of rapid and stable growth, that have become accepted more or less explicitly by all countries after the war. From this point of view a retardation of growth from a normal rate of 5 per cent to 1 per cent is regarded as quite a serious affair . . ." Erik Lundberg, *Instability and Economic Growth*, New Haven, Yale University Press, 1968, p. 87).

[3] For references to others who stress the similarity of relative and absolute decline, see Ilse Mintz, *Dating Postwar Business Cycles, Methods and Their Application to Western Germany, 1950–67*, New York, NBER, Occasional Paper 107, 1970, pp. 3,4.

elaborated further. The idea is to supplement it gradually by a similar body of information about growth cycles.

The existence of two cycle concepts and two chronologies creates however, a certain confusion, which is already evident in discussions of the subject today. To guard against this, it is most important to distinguish carefully between the two types of cycles by using different terms for them and for their phases and turning points. Labeling a period as a recession means that it is covered by all our generalizations about and measures of recessions and thus is definitely not just a matter of semantics. Whatever progress has been made at the NBER in the analysis of business cycles would have been impossible without Burns and Mitchell's insistence on the use and application of precisely defined concepts.

In this study economic fluctuations described by the revised definition are called growth cycles. The word is chosen for want of a better one and despite the disadvantage of its having served previously to designate certain long cycles. The growth cycle consists of a high-rate phase and a low-rate phase, terms suggested to me by Leonard H. Lempert. The endpoints of the phases are termed downturns and upturns, rather than peaks and troughs.

The Burns-Mitchell definition of business cycles[4] as adjusted for growth cycles is as follows: Growth cycles are fluctuations in aggregate economic activity. A growth cycle consists of a period of relatively high growth rates occurring at about the same time in many economic activities, followed by a period of similarly widespread low growth rates which merges into the high-growth phase of the next cycle.[5]

Two independent methods serve to distinguish between "high" and "low" growth rates. The long-run trend of economic activities is used as a criterion in the first method. Growth which is more rapid than the trend is classified as "relatively high." This method involves fitting a trend to the indicators and analyzing the deviations from this trend, the "deviation cycles."

The second method requires no trend fitting. It focuses directly on rates of change and distinguishes between high and low rates by comparing average rates of change in economic activities during successive time periods in a fashion which will be explained later on. The alternations between high- and low-rate periods are termed "step cycles."

[4] Arthur F. Burns and Wesley C. Mitchell, *Measuring Business Cycles*, New York, NBER, 1946, p. 3.

[5] It has been argued recently that what really matters are not fluctuations in aggregage activity but fluctuations in subdivisions of the economy, especially in "socially important" ones. However, it will hardly be denied that analysis of a part of the economy, say the construction industry, will not get far without relating that part to the whole.

The two-pronged approach provides a check on the reliability and stability of the growth cycle chronology which is most desirable in view of the exploratory nature of our undertaking. Since both methods refer to the same cycle concept they should, and actually do, yield approximately the same growth cycle turning dates.

An Objection to the New Concept

Problems of definition and measurement aside, the growth cycle concept encounters a serious objection: namely, its implications for economic policy. Recognition of growth cycles, it is argued, can impart an inflationary bias to economic policies. Labeling a period as a low-rate phase might be interpreted as a criticism of policy makers and as a recommendation of expansionary policies, but labeling it as a traditional expansion would not be interpreted this way.

Such an effect would, indeed, be unfortunate. But is it likely to occur? Classification of a period as one phase or the other involves no value judgment. Two observers who accept the same classification may hold opposite views regarding the desirability of a certain situation. It seems to me that it should be possible to make this clear and to prevent the new terms and new classification schema from affecting the judgment of policy makers and the public.

European reaction to the recognition of growth cycles is encouraging. Germany, for instance, has not experienced more inflation than other countries. Low-rate phases are not generally condemned. On the contrary, such phases are often termed "recovery of economic stability," or "cooling-off period," while high-rate phases may be designated as "imbalanced" and "overstraining."

Which of the phases of growth cycles is desirable depends, of course, on the attendant circumstances and on the observer's point of view. The situation is not really different from that encountered with classical cycles. Here too some recommend expansionary policies not only during recessions, but also during slow expansions; and others prefer mild recessions to the evils of inflation.

Computerized Cycle Dating

In addition to the development of the growth cycle chronology this study has a second purpose: to establish the feasibility of mechanical reference cycle dating.

Traditionally the determination of cycle turns by the NBER relies on a set of rules devised by Burns and Mitchell.[6] These rules, however, are meant to

[6] Burns and Mitchell, *Measuring Business Cycles*, Ch. 4.

aid, not to replace, the analysts' judgment. This goes for determination of "specific" turns in individual time series. But the role of judgment is very much greater when it comes to selecting reference dates. Decisions are required, for instance, on the weight to be attached to each economic class of indicators and then to each series within a class. Thus it takes the enormous expertise of members of the NBER staff to select the business cycle turns which have come to be accepted not only nationally but all over the globe.

The flexibility of the traditional method was virtually indispensable as long as detailed knowledge of business cycles was lacking; even today, it has great advantages over rigid mechanical procedures. Obviously, however, the necessity to rely on specialized experts and the consequent irreproducibility of the selections also has its disadvantages which critics have not failed to mention.

The large accumulation of knowledge about business cycles gained during many years of cycle dating and the possibility of using computer programs to simulate, in part at least, the traditional procedures have led Bry and Boschan of the NBER to experiment with a programed selection of indicator turns.[7] The results are most encouraging in the sense that the dates selected formerly by the NBER analysts are, in general, reproduced by the programed procedures.

The Bry-Boschan turning point program is basic to the present study, which carries the experiment further, to the dating of reference cycles. Reference cycle turns are defined as turns in composite indexes and diffusion indexes, and these indexes are derived by combining selected indicator series. As will be explained in detail in later sections, the composite index is an average of modified and standardized indicators, while the diffusion index is based on a count of the number of indicators rising and falling during a given month.

These methods are tested by applying them first to the dating of classical business cycles. They are successful beyond expectations. Each of the eight handpicked turns, 1948-61, can be exactly reproduced in this fashion.[8] This suggests that in growth cycles, too, the dates of our programed turns are those that would have been selected by traditional methods.

[7]Gerhard Bry and Charlotte Boschan, *Cyclical Analysis of Time Series: Selected Procedures and Computer Programs*, New York, NBER, 1971.

[8]With the indicator list used in this paper, one of the eight handpicked turns differs from its computerized counterpart. With the improved list that will be used in the final version of the study even this discrepancy disappears.

2. THE GROWTH CYCLE CONCEPT OF THIS STUDY
AND ALTERNATIVE CONCEPTS

The Definition of Growth Cycles Used in This Study

From the point of view of this study, the outstanding merit of the growth cycle concept chosen is its close resemblance to the Burns-Mitchell definition of business cycles which underlies the NBER business cycle analysis. This is important because it enables us to compare the insights gained in using the new chronology to the body of knowledge based on the traditional chronology.

The growth cycle definition given in the preceding section differs from the traditional one only in replacing the words "expansion" and "contraction" by "period of relatively high growth rates" and "period of relatively low growth rates."

Alternatively the Burns-Mitchell definition could be revised by inserting the words "adjusted for their long-run trends" after "economic activities." This version brings out the identity between classical cycles and growth cycles when long-run trends are horizontal. Establishment of growth cycle analysis means that Burns and Mitchell's old ideal——to have two sets of measures, "one as free as possible from trend factors, the other including intracycle trends"——will at long last have been attained. The realization of this ideal was prevented by the expensiveness of double analysis before the advent of the computer.[9]

One important implication of the use of the Burns-Mitchell definition is the rejection of the definition of reference cycles as cycles in a single comprehensive aggregate and retention of the idea of reference cycles as fluctuations occurring at about the same time in a broad variety of economic activities comprising inputs and outputs in physical and dollar units, measures of financial markets, prices, wages, interest rates, etc.

Concerning the duration of phases and cycles I adopt the rules used in the Bry-Boschan computer program: the minimum duration of a cycle phase is five months; of a full cycle, fifteen months. By comparison, the NBER rules used in the handpicking of turns are that a full business cycle must have a minimum duration of more than a year. (The shortest business cycle observed historically in the United States lasted seventeen months.) In specific series, cycles as short as fifteen months are recognized. No minimum length for a business cycle phase has been laid down in traditional cycle dating, but in practice no phase shorter than six months has been recognized.

[9] See Burns and Michell, *Measuring Business Cycles* p. 41; and Wesley C. Mitchell, *What Happens During Business Cycles*, New York, NBER, 1951, p. 14.

It may be noted that the relative length of the two phases of the classical cycle will differ from those of the growth cycle. In a growing economy high-rate phases must always coincide with expansions of classical cycles, while low-rate phases may coincide with either classical cycle phase. Conversely, classical expansions may be times of high or of low rates in growth cycles. Classical recessions, on the other hand, must be low-rate phases since negative rates of change are necessarily below the normal rising ones. High-rate phases thus will tend to be shorter than expansions, and low-rate phases longer than recessions. Or, downturns will tend to lead peaks and upturns will tend to lag troughs.

Regarding amplitudes and diffusion no specific requirements have been set up in the traditional NBER procedure, although the general requirement is imposed that cycles should be widely diffused and not be divisible into shorter cycles of similar character with amplitudes approximating their own.

Neither the Bry-Boschan program nor the method of this study specifies amplitude minima since such a criterion is very difficult to introduce. The degree of diffusion, on the contrary, is decisive in the computerized determination of reference cycles which relies on diffusion indexes and composite indexes.

Where the definition of growth cycles must differ from that of classical ones is in the criterion by which the two cycle phases are distinguished. In classical cycles this consists simply of the direction of change in economic activities. In growth cycles the criterion is the relation of a given rate of change in economic activities to a corresponding "average" or "normal" rate.

In this study, because of its exploratory character, two different definitions of a "normal" rate are used, each underlying a different statistical technique. In one concept the normal rate is the rate of a trend line fitted to the data. Growth cycles are here defined as deviations from the trends (deviation cycles), and are treated in the same fashion as are data unadjusted for trend in the analysis of classical cycles. This concept is as close as can be to the traditional one. It is, of course, open to the objection that the cycles depend on the selection of the trend.

Therefore the results are checked by those obtained with the second concept, which requires no trend fitting but deals directly with the rate of change rather than with the series proper. The "normal" rate is here the average rate in a full cycle. The cycle must comprise two parts: in one the average rate of change must be significantly higher than the cycle average and in the other it must be significantly lower. These alternations of periods of high growth rates with periods of low growth rates are termed step cycles.[10]

[10]I owe the idea and the name of step cycles to Milton Friedman and Anna J. Schwartz. Both cycle concepts will be explained in detail in a later section.

The reasons for defining growth cycles in terms of high and low rates as distinct from rising and falling rates will be explained in the chapter on step cycles.

Alternative Growth Cycle Concepts

Several alternative growth cycle concepts have been proposed in the literature or are being used in empirical work.

There is, first, the old idea of defining business cycles simply as cycles in a single comprehensive aggregate such as GNP. Correspondingly, growth cycles can be defined as cycles in the trend-adjusted GNP. This definition has been rejected by the NBER for classical cycles and is rejected in the present study because thorough investigations have shown how uncertainties in the measurement of GNP and the necessarily very frequent revisions, which often reach back a number of years, would increase the likelihood of selecting the wrong turns.[11] Moreover, GNP data are not available monthly, whereas a monthly reference chronology is required.

Rejection of the concept of reference cycles as cycles in the GNP implies a fortiori rejection of a definition which at first glance appears most appealing: a cycle in capacity utilization or in the gap between actual and potential output. The importance of the degree of capacity utilization makes this concept meaningful and hence attractive. However, the likelihood of error is even greater with this definition than when growth cycles are defined as cycles in the GNP. Potential output must be estimated with the help of estimates of potential inputs and of productivity. Clearly these estimates leave much room for the analyst's judgment. Thus the reference dates will be affected not only by the uncertainties of the basic GNP data but also by erroneous assumptions about the movements in potential GNP.[12]

[11] For an excellent study of the effects of dating reference cycles by GNP cycles, see two articles by Victor Zarnowitz, "On the Dating of Business Cycles," *Journal of Business of the University of Chicago*, April 1963, and "Cloos on Reference Dates and Leading Indicators: A Comment," *ibid.*, October 1963.

For a striking example of repeated back-and-forth shifts of a trough through GNP revisions, see Rendigs Fels and C. Elton Hinshaw, *Forecasting and Recognizing Business Cycle Turning Points*, New York, NBER, 1968, p. 29.

For general arguments against reliance upon a single measure, see Mitchell, *What Happens During Business Cycles*, p. 11, and Geoffrey H. Moore, "What Is a Recession?" *American Statistician*, October 1967.

For a contrary view, see George W. Cloos, "How Good Are the National Bureau's Reference Dates?" *Journal of Business*, January 1963.

[12] For an example of the application of this concept to the analysis of instability in twelve countries, see Lundberg, *Instability*. Lundberg comments (p. 102): "Obviously the suggested method involves a considerable degree of arbitrariness and subjective judgment."

Output gaps, it may be noted, can be regarded as deviations from a particularly meaningful trend line. They thus resemble the deviations from the trend-adjusted GNP which are among our indicators.

Another possible concept of growth cycles, which is being used in some countries as a basis for empirical research, should be considered. Its salient feature is that the direction of change is decisive, as in classical cycles. But, in contrast to the classical cycle concept, absolute declines observed in certain selected activities suffice for recognizing recessions. Indicators of especially high cyclical sensitivity may show absolute declines despite rising trends. Other indicators fail to participate in the general trend of the economy. Declines in indicators of this type constitute a recession by this definition, the continued growth in aggregate activity notwithstanding.

The switch from a widely diffused decline in aggregate activity to a decline in selected activities involves a more radical change in concept than may at first appear. The revised concept can be defended only on one of two assumptions: Either the activities selected for their absolute declines are more significant than those not declining; or else the absolute decline in selected activities coincides with reduced growth in the rest of the economy and is significant for this reason. Even if this last assumption should be warranted, preference for the use of absolute declines in selected activities would mean that such declines are deemed to be a better measure of retarded growth in aggregate activity than are growth rates in the majority of activities which show no absolute decline.

The concept of the business cycle described above has not been explicitly stated and advocated, as far as I know. Nor have the underlying assumptions been spelled out and investigated. Yet empirical business cycle research in some countries is based on it. The reason is probably that it retains the classical direction-of-change criterion, and, in contrast to our modified concept, requires no revision of statistical methods. However, this simplicity is more apparent than real in view of the crucial unanswered questions mentioned above.[13]

Another possible revision of the business cycle concept which deserves very serious consideration has recently been proposed by Solomon Fabricant.[14] Fabricant argues that "as everybody knows, the general price level has been rising more sharply in recent years than at any other time since the outbreak of the Korean War. Statistical series measuring economic

[13]It may be noted that in the United States at least, the series with absolute decline in periods of low growth in aggregate activity are mostly leading indicators rather than coincident ones. The former are, of course, not suited to the determination of a cycle chronology.

[14]See Fabricant's paper in this volume.

activity in terms of current-price values will be affected by these price changes to a greater degree now than in most earlier periods." He concludes that under today's conditions only indicators measured in real terms should be used in identifying business cycles. The customary pecuniary indicators should be replaced by their deflated counterparts.

Fabricant realizes, of course, that the concept of a deflated cycle is very different from the traditional business cycle concept. Changes in price-cost relationships and fluctuations in the rate of change of the general price level constitute major elements in the process by which a business expansion attains momentum and gradually develops the restrictive forces that tend to bring it to an end. Similarly, prices and costs play a part in the process by which recessions breed revivals. We cannot adequately describe what happens during business cycles, or adequately explain what happens, without referring to price changes. But this basic change is acceptable, Fabricant thinks, when we are concerned merely with identifying cycles and not with describing or explaning them.

To me this distinction appears questionable, since the only purpose of identifying cycles is to provide the framework for description and analysis. But be that as it may, the main question is whether the fundamentally changed concept is a significantly improved tool of cycle analysis.

There are various possible definitions of deflated cycles, and the chronology obtained depends on which one is chosen. One concept, which might be termed the deflated classical business cycle, differs from the traditional business cycle concept only in relying exclusively on indicators in physical units or in constant dollars. A recession is then an absolute fall in deflated indicators. A chronology based on this definition would add at most (we cannot tell yet in August 1970), one recession, in 1969-70, to those identified with the traditional definition. The 1961-69 expansion would remain unbroken.

Otherwise "the indicators based on pecuniary values, and the measurements free of price change, usually tell much the same story."[15] Some of the turning dates of earlier cycles would be shifted, however. Thus, the later part of expansions has typically been a period of rising prices and costs accompanied by relatively little or no growth in physical output. Hence, in deflated cycles, the last stage of some traditional expansions will be shifted into the contraction phase. Amplitudes also differ between real and pecuniary cycles, and the amplitude ranking of historical cycles is likely to change with the new concept.

Altogether then the use of the concept of deflated classical cycles means accepting a basic change in the definition of business cycles and a change in

[15] See Fabricant's paper in this volume, p. 99.

the traditional chronology in order (possibly) to reclassify the latest low growth period. Although it would be interesting to see how the deflated cycles differ from traditional ones, the benefits of this revision seem insufficient to justify it.

A second definition of deflated cycles, and the one Fabricant has in mind, refers to fluctuations in the deviations of the deflated series from their long-run trends. One might speak of deflated growth cycles. Again only physical unit or constant-dollar indicators are to be used. These indicators are to be fitted with trends, and the highs and lows of the deviations from these trends are the turning points.

This definition is quite similar to that of our deviation cycles. The main difference is the technicality that for deflated growth cycles pecuniary series are trend-adjusted in two steps (first for the price trend, then for the remaining trend), while for deviation cycles the adjustment is made in one step. A second possible difference between the two cycle concepts arises if not only the trend but also the cyclical movement of prices is eliminated in deflated growth cycles. If, however, deflation is defined as referring only to the price trend and not to the entire price movement——a possibility considered by Fabricant——then the results with deflated growth cycles should be essentially the same as those with deviation cycles.

Finally, an earlier method of analyzing mild economic fluctuations is to be mentioned here. In her work on cycles in consumption Ruth Mack identified minor waves occurring within business expansions or contractions of the interwar period.[16] Subcycles, as she called them, are shorter (their minimum duration is five months), and flatter (their minimum phase amplitude is zero), than regular business cycles. The subcycle concept proved a useful tool for the analysis of the interwar period. It was not designed, of course, for situations in which the predominance of negative rates of change is a rare exception.

3. CRITERIA FOR THE SELECTION OF INDICATORS

Does the change in the type of cycle to be dated affect the problem of selecting the indicators to be used? The answer for the present study is "no" and for the simple reason that without benchmarks for growth cycles there is no precise information on the behavior of individual indicators in these cycles. The general impression, confirmed by the study of German growth cycles, is that the timing of individual indicators in growth cycles tends to be similar to that in classical cycles. This rule may have important exceptions however. For instance, indicators with strong trends which for this reason are

[16] Ruth Mack, *Consumption and Business Fluctuations*, New York, NBER, 1956.

not useful in dating classical cycles may score high in the dating of growth cycles. Conversely, other indicators may fail to reflect the more subtle growth cycles although their sensitivity suffices for classical ones. Whatever such differences may emerge in the future, however, our best working hypothesis at present is to assume similarity in an indicator's relation to the two types of cycles. Thus we expect series which coincide with classical cycles to coincide also with growth cycles, and so on.

On this assumption we can accept the classification of indicators which underlies the NBER dating of classical cycles and choose indicators from the large collection of series whose cyclical properties have been thoroughly analyzed and evaluated at the NBER, especially by Geoffrey H. Moore and Julius Shiskin.[17]

It is not the new cycle concept but the new method of dating which creates a difficult problem in the selection of indicators. Because of the mechanical procedures it must be decided how many series to include, which ones to select, what weights to apply.

These questions did not arise when the traditional method was applied. Its flexibility enabled the analyst to vary the implied weight of a series as the situation required. He was free to disregard an otherwise reliable indicator if there was reason to believe that its movements in a particular case were due to special, noncyclical forces, as happens occasionally.[18]

In the mechanical determination of reference turns, on the contrary——and this is its greatest disadvantage——a fixed list of indicators must be used, at least at the present state of the experiment. Making up such a fixed list involves problems not heretofore encountered in cycle dating, but similar to problems met before in selecting so-called short lists of indicators. Actually these short lists can be regarded (and the latest ones are so regarded), as precursors of the fixed list.[19]

It is only by experimenting that the effect of the various choices to be made can be detected. Therefore the list on which most of the present study is based——and which is the fourth one tested——is still preliminary. We know

[17]See, e.g., Geoffrey H. Moore and Julius Shiskin, *Indicators of Business Expansions and Contractions*, New York, NBER, 1967, Occasional Paper 103, and Geoffrey H. Moore (ed.), *Business Cycle Indicators*, New York, NBER, 1961.

[18]"Indeed, one of the greatest hazards in forecasting is that a statistical series which is generally highly reliable may suddenly and without warning prove quite unreliable" (Alec Cairncross, "Economic Forecasting," *Economic Journal*, December 1969, p. 803).

[19]The "short list" is a "list of 25 series, drawn from the full 1966 list of 88 series. All . . . series on the short list have high scores and involve little duplication." A short list of indicators "is a step toward a summary, from which one may wish to go farther . . . " (Moore and Shiskin, *Indicators*, pp. 4 and 32).

that certain changes in it are desirable but have postponed them in the expectation that further ones will suggest themselves. Making all changes at one time saves the cost of repeated analysis.

The following are some of the required difficult choices: How many indicators should be included? Taking a small group has the advantage that the selection can be limited to the highest-scoring coincident indicators. But even the best indicators are imperfect, and this argues for a longer list which will reduce the effect of the vagaries of an individual series on the results. We have experimented with lists of 7, 12, and 19 indicators and settled tentatively on a 17-indicator list. The selections are described in section 4 and the series are shown in Table 3 (section 5).

The next question is whether to include only roughly coincident indicators or also leading and lagging ones.[20] Although the former are naturally the most important for cycle dating, leading and lagging series can also be helpful when they represent important aspects of the economy not represented by the coincident ones. In cases of double peaks and troughs, for instance, leading and lagging indicators may contribute to the decision.

Moreover, it would be wrong to assume that turns in averages of indicators classified as "roughly coincident" coincide exactly with the handpicked, classical reference turns. The truth is that the roughly coincident series lead far more often than they lag. This reflects the NBER principle of late dating, of which more below. If such series are used exclusively the combined index has a tendency to lead at reference dates. To compensate for this some lagging series must be included.

Further, the NBER timing classification is based on the record of a series during the full period for which it is available. In some instances this may differ from its record after 1947. An unclassified series may thus, in the period under review, coincide as regularly as a classified one. For these reasons the 17-indicator list includes, in addition to 12 coincident series, one leading, three lagging, and one unclassified series.

A third issue concerns the inclusion of quarterly series, which may be deemed inappropriate for determining monthly reference turns.[21] However, "it would not do ... to neglect quarterly series entirely. GNP, plant and equipment expenditures, new capital appropriations, changes in business inventories, and corporate profits, all of which are quarterly, are far too

[20] Rough coincidences include exact coincidences and leads and lags of three months or less.

[21] See e.g., Norman Trueblood, "The Dating of Postwar Business Cycles," American Statistical Association, *Proceedings of the Business and Economic Statistics Section*, 1961, p. 17.

important."[22] These séries are helpful in deciding the existence of a cycle in . doubtful cases and in determining the neighborhood of turns. Therefore, four quarterly series are included in the 17-indicator list.

However, the assumption that quarterly series turn in the center month of the quarter may impart a bias toward center-month turns to the reference dates. This can be avoided by constructing two alternative indexes in which turns are assumed to occur in the first and last months of the quarters respectively. Rules can be set up to decide the——relatively few——cases in which the reference turn varies among the three sets of indexes.[23]

How should one choose among all the possible indicator lists that would fit the : forementioned general considerations? Our main criterion in evaluating a list is its performance in dating classical business cycles. The chronology obtained when our mechanical methods are applied to the list in question should be as similar as possible to the generally accepted NBER chronology obtained by traditional subjective methods. The idea is that a list which yields the "right" classical turns will also yield the "right" growth cycle turns. This may certainly be questioned but, at present, it is the best working hypothesis. Moreover, use of such a list warrants the assumption that the relations found between classical and growth cycles are not attributable to the choice of indicators.

Should the currently used classical cycle chronology be the target to be duplicated or should we aim at slightly revised dates? The latter seems the preferable choice. The main reason is that some of the time series on which the chronology is based were revised substantially *after* the determination of the presently used dates. Since these revisions can, in some instances, affect the selection of a reference date, it is sensible to take them into account and to set up a slightly revised version of the customary NBER chronology as our target. The discussion of these revisions will be found in section 4.

The task is, then, to put together a list of indicators on the basis of which our mechanical methods reproduce the revised classical NBER cycle chronology. Outsiders may think that this is easy, that any combination of high-rated indicators will fill the bill. But this is not so. Due to the indicators' imperfections, the turns of indicator averages vary with the indicator mix. Considerable experimentation is thus needed to discover a list with which the computer program reproduces exactly each of the eight classical cycle turns, 1948-61. Our tentative 17-series list is still not perfect by this standard. On its basis the diffusion index misses one of the target turns and the composite index misses two.

[22]Moore and Shiskin, *Indicators*, p. 33.

[23] This procedure has been applied in Mintz, *Dating Postwar Business Cycles*, p. 21. In the present paper it has been used for one diffusion index without causing any change in turns. It will be applied to all indexes in the final version of the study.

Another criterion by which the quality of indicators should be judged has not been used so far, but will be used in the final version. It concerns the agreement between deviation cycles and step cycles. The higher the agreement between turns in the deviations of a series from its trend and turns in its rate of growth, the more suitable it is for the dating of growth cycles.

There are considerable discrepancies between deviation cycles and step cycles of some of our present indicators, as will be seen in later sections. These discrepancies are reflected in the resulting reference chronologies. In order to reduce the consequent uncertainty about growth cycle dates, indicators with large discrepancies will be eliminated from the final list as far as possible.

In the next section the classical reference dates obtained with different indicator lists will be discussed.

4. CLASSICAL BUSINESS CYCLES DATED BY COMPUTER METHODS

The Statistical Procedures

The procedures used in this study in adjusting and combining indicators are as follows:

Modification of Indicators. All indicators, except a few which show no seasonal fluctuations, are published in seasonally adjusted form in *Business Conditions Digest (BCD)*.[24] The adjustment is made either at the data source or at the Bureau of the Census by the X-11 seasonal adjustment program. We do not use the series in their published form, however, but in the modified version which is also produced by the X-11 program and is designed to eliminate extremes from the irregular component of the series.[25] Modification could be dispensed with in the analysis of classical cycles, but in the analysis of rates of change large erratic movements are so disturbing that this adjustment was found to be necessary. It is not to be denied that modification like seasonal adjustment may shift turns in undesirable ways at times, but this disadvantage is minor in comparison to some quite unacceptable results obtained with unmodified series in the analysis of growth cycles.

[24]*Business Conditions Digest* (formerly *Business Cycle Developments*), published monthly by the Bureau of the Census, U.S. Department of Commerce.

[25]The modification consists in replacing the extreme values of the series with the corresponding values of a smoothed version (a Henderson curve) of it. The method is described in Julius Shiskin, Allan H. Young, and John C. Musgrave, *The X-11 Variant of the Census Method II Seasonal Adjustment Program*, Bureau of the Census, Technical Paper No. 15, February 1967.

Turning Points in Indicators. The turning points of the adjusted and modified series are selected by the aforementioned Bry–Boschan computerized method.[26] This method consists, essentially, in first identifying major cyclical swings, then delineating the neighborhoods of their maxima and minima, and finally narrowing the search for turning points to specific calendar dates. All procedures are performed on the seasonally adjusted modified data.

This stepwise approach to the selection of turns is necessary because most time series are much too choppy for direct mechanical selection of cyclical maxima and minima. Such a procedure would, instead, give a large number of highs and lows most of which would indicate only a brief fluttering of the data rather than a cyclical turn. For this reason the existence of cycles must first be determined in a smoothed form of the series before the precise date can be selected in the unsmoothed data.

The first curve from which turning points are determined is a twelve-month moving average of the seasonally adjusted, modified data. This is a convenient means for eliminating fluctuations of subcyclical duration or of very shallow amplitudes. The rule for selecting turning points is: any month whose value is higher than those of the five preceding months and the five following months is regarded as the date of a tentative peak; analogously, the month whose value is lower than the five values on either side is regarded as the date of a tentative trough. These tentative turns are tested for compliance with a set of constraint rules concerning alternation of phases and duration of phases and cycles.

The next step in the process is the determination of tentative cyclical turns on the Spencer curve of the seasonally adjusted, modified data. The Spencer curve is selected as the next intermediary curve because its turns tend to be closer to those of the unsmoothed data than are those of the twelve-month moving average.[27]

In principle, the program searches, in the neighborhood (defined as plus or minus five months) of the turns established on the twelve-month moving average, for like turns on the Spencer curve. That is, in the neighborhood of peaks, it searches for the highest of the eleven points on the Spencer curve; in the neighborhood of troughs, for the lowest. The Spencer curve turns thus located are then subjected to several tests.

[26] Bry and Boschan, *Cyclical Analysis.*

[27] The Spencer curve is a complex fifteen-month graduation formula, a weighted moving average with the highest weights in the center and negative weights at either end. This ensures that the curve follows the data closely. It has approximately the flexibility of a five-month moving average but is much smoother.

They are rejected when they are (1) less than six months from either end of the series; (2) like turns and less than fifteen months apart; and (3) like turns without an intervening opposite turn.

The accepted turns in the Spencer curve provide the basis for the next step in the search for turns in the unsmoothed data. In this step the series is smoothed by a three- to six-month moving average. The exact number of months depends on the time it takes for the cyclical component to exceed the irregular component in the particular series analyzed.

The method of deriving turning points in this moving average is practically the same as that for the Spencer curve. The highest peaks on the moving average curve within a span of five months from the dates of the peaks on the Spencer curve are selected and, correspondingly, so are the troughs.

The last step of the procedure is to find the peak and trough values in the unsmoothed, seasonally adjusted, modified data which correspond to the short-term moving average turns previously established. This search is again analogous to the previous ones. The program establishes the highest values in the unsmoothed data within a span of plus or minus five months from the peak in the short-term moving average curve; correspondingly, the lowest value of the unsmoothed data in the neighborhood of moving average troughs is established.[28]

Having again eliminated any turns not complying to the rules, the remaining ones are the final programed turning points of the series.

It should be noted that the computer program does not utilize directly any information on the amplitude of cycles. The only way in which amplitude plays a role is that the moving averages, especially the initial twelve-month moving average, tend to iron out minor swings (though only if they are also brief). The program's disregard for amplitudes makes the good agreement between traditional and programed specific cycles even more remarkable.

Out of the 162 turns of nineteen indicators in classical business cycles, 1948-61, all but three have been accepted in this study. The three corrections are due to a minor shortcoming of the program.

Turning Points in Reference Cycles. One method of identifying reference cycle turns utilizes the indicator turns in the construction of a diffusion index. This index is constructed by counting, in each month covered, the number of indicators in their high-rate phase. The phase may be a classical expansion or a growth cycle phase. An indicator is classified as in high-rate phase during the months between its upturn and its downturn, exclusive of the upturn month and inclusive of the downturn month. (The low-rate phase is defined correspondingly.) The excess of the number of indicators in

---

[28]To be more precise, the span varies between four and six months, depending on the term of the moving average.

high-rate phase over the number in low-rate phase is expressed as a percentage of the total number of indicators covered. This percentage is termed the "historical diffusion index." A downturn in this index——the reference cycle downturn——is located in the month in which the number of indicators in the high phase exceeds the number in the low phase and which precedes a month in which indicators in the low phase outnumber those in the high phase. The index thus crosses the zero line between the downturn and the following

Chart 1
Classical U.S. Business Cycles, 1947—70
Seventeen Indicators

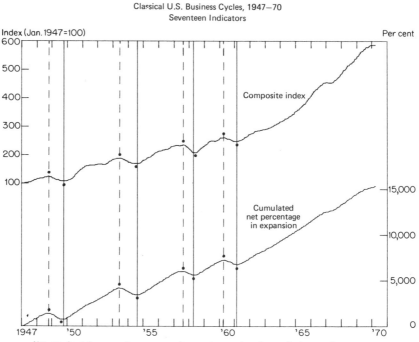

Net per cent in expansion: excess of percentage undergoing cyclical expansion over percentage undergoing contraction.

Composite index: average of amplitude — adjusted rates of change of 17 indicators. The average rate for January 1947 is set equal to 100.

Solid vertical lines indicate business cycle troughs, broken vertical lines, business cycle peaks based on the revised reference cycle chronology (see text).

month. The upturn is determined in corresponding fashion. In order to show cycle turns, as customary, at the highest and lowest points of cycle curves, rather than at the crossing of the zero line, the index is usually shown in cumulated form (Chart 1).[29]

[29] Some of the diffusion indexes in Table 1 and 2 are not "historical" indexes but "current" ones. The method of construction is the same in both. However, in the current index an indicator in a given month is defined as in upswing or downswing according to its change over a fixed span of months, instead of by its cyclical phase.

The second method of identifying reference cycle turns does not require identification of indicator turns. It uses composite indexes which are constructed as follows: First, the month-to-month percentage changes in each indicator are obtained, using as base the average of the two months rather than the initial month (to assure symmetrical treatment of increases and decreases). Second, these percentage changes are standardized so that their average, without regard to sign, is equal to unity (1.0 per cent per month) for each indicator, January 1947-March 1970. Third, the adjusted percentages for a given month are averaged over the several indicators, which are given equal weights. Fourth, these averages are adjusted so that they too will equal 1.0 per cent per month, January 1947-March 1970. Finally, the adjusted average percentage changes are cumulated into a monthly index.[30]

Turning points in composite indexes are selected by the same method by which turning points in individual indicators are determined.

Opinions will differ regarding the acceptance or rejection by the program of borderline cases, i.e., relatively mild cycles. Since drawing the line here is a matter of subjective judgment and since the turns selected by the program seem sensible to us, we have not attempted any modifications.

Comparison of Handpicked and Programed Chronologies of U.S. Classical Business Cycles

Chronologies Related to Traditional NBER Reference Cycle Turns. A number of diffusion indexes and composite indexes based on various lists of indicators have been constructed for the present study. The purpose was to find an index turning in the months previously selected as classical business cycle turns. The timing of turns in these indexes is shown in the lower part of Table 1.[31]

The smallest number of indicators is used in the composite index in line 9 and is based on the seven coincident indicators making up the NBER 1966 short list, which represents a well-rounded group of roughly coincident high-scoring series.

For the indexes in lines 10, 14, and 15 we have added five indicators to the original seven. Of the additions one is a leader and one a lagger, both from the short list; three are coincident but not on the short list.

The third group comprises seventeen indicators, of which six are coincident series from the short list, six are coincident series not from the short list, one is a leader and three are laggers from the short list, and one is an unclassified series (lines 11 and 16).

---

[30] Julius Shiskin and Geoffrey H. Moore, "Leading Indicator Indexes: Construction, Performance, and Uses" (mimeo), p. 9.

[31] The individual series covered are listed in Table A–1.

The fourth group differs from the third by including one more leader and one more lagger, both from the short list (lines 12, 13, and 17).

In addition to the indexes constructed for this study the table also shows indexes made up by others for various purposes other than the determination of business cycle turns (lines 4 to 8). Furthermore, the table includes for comparison the reference chronologies of Cloos and Trueblood, which are not based on mechanical methods but on judgment similar to that applied to the traditional NBER turning points (lines 2 and 3; see source note to table).

All indicators are monthly except for one quarterly series in the group of seven and three more quarterly series in the larger groups.

TABLE 1

Leads and Lags of Turns in 16 Chronologies of U.S.
Classical Business Cycles at NBER Reference Turns, 1948–61

(CI = composite index; DI = diffusion index)

Line No.	Type of Index	No. of Indicators	Lead (−) or Lag (+) in Months at the Following Peaks (P) and Troughs (T) in U.S. Business Cycles (Year and Month):								Total Discrepancies No.	Months	Author (See notes for full references.)
			P '48 11	T '49 10	P '53 7	T '54 8	P '57 7	T '58 4	P '60 5	T '61 2			
1													
2	No index used		−1	−3	0	−3	+1	0	0	0	4	8	Trueblood
3	Median	4	−1	−3	−1	−3	+1	0	0 or +2	0	5 or 6	9 or 11	Cloos
4	CI	5	−1	0	0	0	+1	0	−3	0	3	5	Shiskin-Moore
5	CI	6	−1	0	0	−3	+1	0	0	0	3	5	Shiskin
6	DI	8	−1	0	−2	−1	0	0	−1	0	4	5	Shiskin
7	DI	8	−2	+1	0	−4	+1	−1	0	0	5	9	Shiskin
8	DI	15	−2	0	−1	−2	−4	0	−1	0	5	10	Bry-Boschan
9	CI	7	−1	0	−2	−3	+1	0	−1	0	5	8	Mintz
10	CI	12	−1	0	−2	−3	−5	0	−1	0	5	12	Mintz
11	CI	17	−1	0	−1	−1	+1	+1	−1	0	6	6	Mintz
12	CI	19	−1	0	−2	−1	+1	+1	−1	0	6	7	Mintz
13	CI	19	−1	0	−1	0	+1	+1	−1	0	5	5	Mintz
14	DI	12	−2	0	−2	0	−4	−1	−1	0	5	10	Mintz
15	DI	12	−2	−2	−1	−3	−3	0	0	0	5	11	Mintz
16	DI	17	−1	−2	−1	0	+1	0	−1	0	5	6	Mintz
17	DI	19	−2	−2	−1	0	0	0	−1	0	4	6	Mintz

Notes to Table 1

P = peak.

T = trough.

Note: For a listing of the individual series included in each index, see Table A-1.

Line 1. The standard NBER business cycle chronology.

2. Source: Norman C. Trueblood, "The Dating of Postwar Business Cycles," *American Statistical Association, Proceedings of the Business and Economic Statistics Section,* 1961, pp. 17–19.

3. Source: George W. Cloos, "How Good are the National Bureau's Reference Dates?" *Journal of Business,* January 1963, pp. 14–32. Coverage: Roughly coincident indicators.

4. Source: Julius Shiskin and Geoffrey H. Moore, "Leading Indicator Indexes," draft prepared for a meeting of the International Statistical Institute, London, September 1969, p. 7. Also charted in U.S. Department of Commerce, Bureau of the Census, *Business Conditions Digest,* Monthly. Coverage: Roughly coincident indicators from the NBER 1966 Short List.

5. Source: Julius Shiskin, *Signals of Recession and Recovery,* New York, NBER, Occasional Paper, 66, 1961, p. 180. Coverage: Roughly coincident indicators from the NBER 1960 Short List.

6. Source: *ibid.,* p. 185. Coverage: Roughly coincident indicators from the NBER 1960 Short List. Diffusion index is current for one-month span.

7. Source and coverage same as for line 6. Diffusion index is current for three-month span.

8. Source: Gerhard Bry and Charlotte Boschan, *Cyclical Analysis of Time Series: Selected Procedures and Computer Programs,* New York, NBER, 1971. Coverage: Roughly coincident indicators from NBER 1966 Short List and Full List. Diffusion index is historical.

Lines 9 to 17. Indexes were constructed for this study.

9. Coverage: All roughly coincident indicators from the NBER 1966 Short List. Nonmodified series.

10. Coverage: Same indicators as in line 9, plus one leader and one lagger from the same list, plus three roughly coincident indicators from NBER 1966 Full List. Nonmodified series.

11. Coverage: From the NBER 1966 Short List: 6 roughly coincident indicators, 1 leader, 3 laggers. From the NBER 1966 Full List: 6 roughly coincident indicators and 1 unclassified series. Modified series.

12. Coverage: Same as in line 11, except that one leader and one lagger are added. Modified series.

13. Same as line 12, except that index is rounded.

Lines 14 to 17. All diffusion indexes are historical.

14. Coverage: Same as line 10. Nonmodified series.

15. Coverage: Same as line 10. Modified series.

16. Coverage: Same as line 11. Modified series.

17. Coverage: Same as line 12. Modified series.

The most striking feature of Table 1 is the stability of the dates. In not one instance do the measures suggest omission of a turn.[32]

But the table also reveals that all chronologies differ at some points from the traditional NBER dates. As indicated in the last columns such differences occur at from three to six of the eight turns covered and involve leads and lags adding up to from five to twelve months. Except for lags at the 1957 peak, almost all discrepancies are due to leads of the chronologies relative to the traditional NBER dates. We shall discuss this aspect presently.

The BCD composite index of five coincident indicators (line 4) differs "only" three times from the traditional chronology, but in one case (1960) the discrepancy amounts to as much as three months. The older composite index (line 5) agrees in 1960 but leads by three months in 1954. Even less agreement is shown by the diffusion indexes (lines 6, 7, 8).

Among indexes constructed for this study, the composite index based on the short list's seven coincident series (line 9) leads at 4 out of 8 traditional turns. This reflects the fact that more than half of the timing relationships of the individual indicators are leads and the average timing of every one of the seven is leading (measured by the median timing at the 8 turns).

There is no change in timing when the composite index is based on twelve indicators instead of on seven (line 10). The exception is the 1957 peak which is shifted from the end to the start of a flat ceiling by the addition of series with early downturns. This composite index thus leads at 5 out of 8 turns. Diffusion indexes derived from the same twelve indicators (lines 14, 15), also lead at the majority of turns and the leads are on the average longer than those of the composite indexes. Expanding the base of the indexes to seventeen or nineteen indicators reduces at least the average duration of the discrepancies if not their number (lines 11, 12, 13, 16, 17).

The evidence of Table 1 suggests that no otherwise satisfactory list of indicators will yield the exact dates constituting the traditional NBER chronology. This, of course, is not surprising. Quite the contrary, one must be impressed by the closeness of the programed turns based on the latest version of the indicators and the traditional turns based on earlier, yet unrevised versions.

Revision of Traditional NBER Reference Cycle Turns. However, the discrepancies are an argument for adjusting the traditional chronology. Not the only argument, of course. For years it has been recognized at the NBER

[32] There are also no additional turns in any of the indexes.

that the chronology should be reviewed in the light of the latest information.[33] This we have done and the revised chronology is shown at the top of Table 2.

The proposed adjustments shift three out of the four peaks covered to the month preceding the traditional peak and the fourth to the month following the traditional peak. The four troughs remain unchanged. The average shift is thus only half a month. (This may be compared to an average shift by 0.6 months for the cycles 1919-38.[34]

The adjustments reflect the long-recognized tendency of reference turns to lag relative to indicator turns.[35] Before World War II it occurred mainly at troughs, but afterward it became characteristic of the peaks. One cause of the lags is obvious: observance of the rule to place reference turns toward the end of flat turning zones. As troughs since 1948 have been far more sharply drawn than peaks, the late-dating rule affects only the latter.[36]

Another explanation of lateness of turns has been suggested, namely, that there is a systematic downward bias in unrevised data.[37] It is not clear why this should be the case. However, it would at any rate explain only lateness at troughs and have the contrary effect at peaks.

It has also been surmised that in the interwar period symptoms of economic upturns had to be viewed most cautiously, while in more recent cycles it is the downturn which is relatively unlikely. It is not impossible that considerations of this type affected the decisions of NBER analysts, but it appears much more likely to me that these decisions reflected simply the facts of each given situation: the concentrated sharp upturns of indicators at troughs, the scattered gradual decline of indicators at peaks.

The reasons for revising the traditional chronology will now be reviewed date by date, drawing on the views found in the literature and on the evidence shown in Table 1.

[33]"There is need for a review of the recent (postwar) business-cycle reference dates in the light of revised and new data now available. This has been clearly acknowledged by the National Bureau" (Zarnowitz, "Dating of Business Cycles," p. 189). Work in progress for this purpose was interrupted by the untimely death of Alexander Pitts.

[34]Geoffrey H. Moore, "Discussion," American Statistical Association, *Proceedings of the Business and Economic Statistics Section*, 1961, pp. 34–35.

[35]Moore (ed.), *Business Cycle Indicators*, p. 218.

[36]For discussion of the rule, see Zarnowitz, "Dating of Business Cycles," p. 194.

[37]Trueblood, "Dating of Postwar Business Cycles," p. 17.

The 1948 peak has been shifted from November to October. The two months were close rivals to begin with according to Moore ("Discussion," p. 34) and Fels (p. 25)[38] Trueblood is "persuaded that October is preferable to November as the cycle peak month" (p. 17) because revisions had lowered GNP, personal income, and industrial production in the very end months of 1948 relative to the autumn months.

The argument in favor of the earlier date is strongly supported by the evidence in Table 1, where all indexes without exception turn in September or October, rather than November.

The 1949 trough remains unchanged in October. In this case the NBER was faced with "a close decision because the trough was double-bottomed" (Fels, p. 5). This is confirmed by Moore who refers to uncertainty between October or "some earlier month" ("Discussion," p.34). Trueblood argues at length in favor of July as the correct date which, he maintains, was obscured by unrevised data and by the effects of major strikes (pp. 17, 18). Similarly Cloos finds that "July is a rather good reference month, and October is much too late" (p. 28). Zarnowitz discusses the difficulty of setting a reference date in a period of major strikes. He seems to be leaning more toward the later date (p. 187).

The evidence in Table 1 is mixed. The diffusion indexes give the earlier, the composite indexes the later, date. This means that while the majority of indicators rose in September and October, the amplitude of rises was on the average smaller than that of declines.

For this reason the case for August seems to me slightly stronger than that for October.

The 1953 peak has been shifted from July to June. This shift has not been suggested by others. Yet, most of the indexes suggest June, or even May, as the turning month. I conclude, therefore, that June is preferable to July.

The 1954 trough remains unchanged in August. Trueblood argues for a shift to May because the revised data show a "quite small" rise from May to August. But he also notes: "The question whether the period from the spring to late summer 1954 should be treated as a protracted 'bottoming out' period and part of the recession, or as the beginning of cyclical recovery, thus balances on a fairly narrow statistical margin" (p. 18). Zarnowitz does not make a choice but notes that "the uncertainty attaching to an earlier choice would have been considerably greater" (p. 198).

---

[38]Sources referred to in the discussion of individual turning points are as follows (figures in parentheses refer to footnote in which the full citation appears): Cloos, "National Bureau's Reference Dates" (11); Fels and Hinshaw, *Business Cycle Turning Points* (11); Moore (ed.), *Business Cycle Indicators* (17); Moore, "Discussion" (34); Trueblood, "Dating of Postwar Business Cycles" (21); and Zarnowitz, "Dating of Business Cycles" (11).

The timing of the indexes in Table 1 reflects the dilemma very well. Many turn before August, but those which we regard as the best ones do not and this is the basis for our decision.

The 1957 peak has been shifted from July to August. Moore found in 1958 that it was "difficult to say whether July or August should be considered the zenith" (*Indicators*, p. 146). Fels terms July "a close choice over August" (p. 30). Trueblood thinks that "a better case can be made for August than for July" (footnote 11).

The indexes in Table 1 show a mixed picture. But it is mixed between August and a much earlier month, April or even March, rather than between August and July. It is a clear case of a double peak with the later peak occurring definitely in August rather than in July.

The 1958 trough remains unchanged in April. According to Trueblood this is "the clearest monthly trough indicated for any of the recessions covered" (p. 19). Fels notes that no alternative has been suggested (p. 6).

Most of the indexes in Table 1 turn in April. There is thus no reason for an adjustment.

The 1960 peak has been shifted from May to April. This conflicts with the view of Trueblood that "May seems to be a reasonable choice for peak month although it does represent a compromise in a rather ambiguous period" (p. 19). It also conflicts with Cloos who regards July, if anything, as an alternative rather than April (p. 29).

Our decision is based on the evidence of the indexes which almost uniformly point to April as the peak date. The *BCD* composite index would select an even earlier month (February).

The 1961 trough remains unchanged in February. There is general agreement on this date and it is supported by every one of the indexes in Table 1.

Table 2 is the same as Table 1 except that the timing is now related to the revised reference turns. It may be noted that the revision reduces the discrepancies between the NBER dates, on the one hand, and the turns selected by Cloos, the Shiskin-Moore index, the Bry-Boschan index, and one of the Shiskin indexes, on the other. The revised dates are not closer, however, to the Trueblood dates, nor to two of the Shiskin indexes.

The indexes prepared for this study turn closer to the revised than to the standard dates, of course, since they have influenced the revision decision. Based on the 17-indicator list, the composite index and the diffusion index agree better with the reference dates than any chronology in Table 1. The composite index (line 11) coincides at six turns and differs by one month at each of two troughs. The diffusion index coincides at these same troughs, but leads by two months at the 1949 trough.

TABLE 2

Leads and Lags of Turns in 17 Chronologies of U.S. Classical Business Cycles at Revised Reference Turns, 1948–61

(CI = composite index; DI = diffusion index)

Line No.	Type of Index	No. of Indicators	Lead (−) or Lag (+) in Months at the Following Revised Peaks (P) and Troughs (T) in U.S. Business Cycles (Year and Month):								Total Discrepancies No. of Months		Author (See notes for full references.)
			P '48 10	T '49 10	P '53 6	T '54 8	P '57 8	T '58 4	P '60 4	T '61 2	No.	Months	
1	No index used		+1	0	+1	0	−1	0	+1	0	4	4	NBER
2	No index used		0	−3	+1	−3	0	0	+1	0	4	8	Trueblood
3	Median	4	0	−3	0	−3	0	0	+1 or +3	0	3	7 or 9	Cloos
4	CI	5	0	0	+1	0	0	0	−2	0	2	3	Shiskin-Moore
5	CI	6	0	0	+1	−3	0	0	+1	0	3	5	Shiskin
6	DI	8	0	0	−1	−1	−1	0	0	0	3	3	Shiskin
7	DI	8	−1	+1	+1	−4	0	−1	+1	0	6	9	Shiskin
8	DI	15	−1	0	0	−2	−5	0	0	0	3	8	Bry-Boschan
9	CI	7	0	0	−1	−3	0	0	0	0	2	4	Mintz
10	CI	12	0	0	−1	−3	−6	0	0	0	3	10	Mintz
11	CI	17	0	0	0	−1	0	+1	0	0	2	2	Mintz
12	CI	19	0	0	−1	−1	0	+1	0	0	3	3	Mintz
13	CI	19	0	0	0	0	0	+1	0	0	1	1	Mintz
14	DI	12	−1	0	−1	0	−5	−1	0	0	4	8	Mintz
15	DI	12	−1	−2	0	−3	−4	0	+1	0	5	11	Mintz
16	DI	17	0	−2	0	0	0	0	0	0	1	2	Mintz
17	DI	19	−1	−2	0	0	−1	0	0	0	3	4	Mintz

P = peak.
T = trough.
Note: For explanation of the revised reference turns, see text. For explanation of the indexes, see the notes to Table 1. Line 1 of Table 2 gives the lead (−) or lag (+) of the traditional NBER chronology shown on line 1 of Table 1.

The planned final revision of the 17-indicator list should remove even these small discrepancies. In the meantime the 17-indicator list is used in the remainder of this study as the currently best approximation to the desired one.

A further point to be noted in favor of the 17-indicator list is the extraordinary smoothness of the indexes based on it (see Chart 1). This greatly reduces the uncertainty of turning dates. The month-to-month percentage change of the irregular component of the composite index is only 0.26 as compared to 0.43 for the Moore-Shiskin index. The ratio of the irregular to the cyclical change is 0.27 for the 17-indicator index, compared to 0.57 for the Moore-Shiskin index.[39]

5. DEVIATION CYCLES AND STEP CYCLES IN INDIVIDUAL INDICATORS

Procedures for Deviation Cycles

The first of our two growth cycle definitions is: Growth cycles are cycles in a series' deviations from its long-run trend. The identification of deviation cycles and the dating of their turning points depends, of course, crucially on the selection of the trend curve. The unavoidable arbitrariness of this selection is a serious and valid objection to reliance on trend-adjusted data. It is the main reason for our use of a second growth cycle definition which is entirely independent of the choice of trends and thus provides a check on the deviation cycles.

It is also worth noting that the reference growth cycle is based on a composite of a number of indicators, each adjusted by its own trend. There is thus a chance for some offsetting of errors and the method is less dangerous than when an entire analysis relies on a single trend curve fitted to the GNP or to potential output.

As a check we have also recomputed several composite indexes by using indicators not adjusted for trend and, instead, adjusting the finished composite index. In most instances, the turns in deviations of this composite index from the 75-month moving average coincide with the turns in the corresponding composite index based on trend-adjusted indicators. But with most indicator lists one or two of the fourteen turns in each of two corresponding indexes differ by a month or two.

In order to reduce the arbitrariness of the trend adjustment as far as possible, we applied the same formula to all seventeen indicators. This could not have been done with fitted trends because of the diversity of long-run movements among indicators. In some instances the movements of a series have shifted over time, and two or more trends would have had to be fitted to a single indicator. Since it is inadvisable to fit several trends to a period of only twenty-three years and even more inadvisable to adjust different

[39]Measures for the Shiskin-Moore index are from *Business Conditions Digest*, June 1970, p. 101. For explanation of the measures and further examples, see Julius Shiskin, *Signals of Recession and Recovery*, New York, NBER, Occasional Paper 77, 1961, pp. 48, 49.

indicators in different ways, we decided on using a long-term moving average flexible enough to cope with the diversity of trends. In order to iron out cyclical swings a term of six to seven years is required. We chose a seventy-five-month moving average as a convenient figure that fits the requirement. The missing thirty-seven months at either end of the moving average are supplied with the help of its average rate of change during the first two years and last two years for which it is available. This method of extrapolation implies that the series proper is assumed to repeat, in the period not covered by the data, its pattern during the first and last years which are covered by the data. For two series the trends through March 1970 are shown in the top panels of Charts A-1 and A-2, in the appendix, below.

The percentage deviations of the series from their moving average trends represent the deviation cycles of the indicators (the second panels on Charts A-1 and A-2).[40] The turning points are selected by the computer program described in the preceding section.

Findings on Deviation Cycles

The analysis covers the period from November 1947 to March 1970. In this period the program identifies 15 turns in each of eight indicators; 13 turns in six more indicators; 12 turns in one and only 10 turns in the two remaining series. Of the 14 growth cycle phases delimited by these turns, 7 correspond to classical business cycle phases; 2 occur about 1951-53, the Korean war cycle; and 5 are phases of the 1960's. The phases skipped by those indicators which have fewer than 15 turns are most often those of the Korean cycle (seven indicators). The 1961-63 cycle is skipped by only one series, despite its mildness. Through March 1970, two series had not turned up since 1966 and two others had not turned down since 1967.[41]

Inspection of the charts shows that most trend-adjusted indicators move in clear-cut cyclical swings with unmistakable turning points.[42] (In the final version of the study charts like A-1 and A-2 will be provided for all indicators.) Sharply defined cycles of large amplitude are found in corporate profits, expenditures on plant and equipment, job openings, and imports. Cycles of smaller amplitude but of outstanding smoothness are characteristic

---

[40]The unemployment rate and the number of unfilled jobs show no rising trend. For some other indicators trends are debatable, at least for part of the period. However, for uniformity, all series have been expressed as deviations from the moving average.

[41]Of the 230 turning points recognized by the program I have changed three and omitted three. I have also added three turns not recognized by the program.

[42]In the final version of the study measures of amplitude and smoothness will be supplied.

of GNP in 1958 dollars, wages and salaries, the number of employees, and inventories. Deviation cycles are less clear, on the other hand, in series whose large erratic movements obscure to some extent the cyclical ones. This holds mainly for labor costs and interest rates. Prices have been stable over some periods so that the dating of their turning points is sometimes difficult.

In all series the amplitudes of deviation cycles which correspond to classical business cycles are much larger than the others. This implies that the amplitudes are smaller in the 1960's than in the 1950's. The flattest movements occur in most instances during the peak-to-peak cycle of 1951-53, and during the trough-to-trough cycle of 1961-63.

In these borderline cases existence of a deviation cycle may well be questioned. However, omitting flat cycles would require specificiation of amplitude minima. The thorny problems involved in setting amplitude standards have prevented their use in both the traditional NBER method and in the Bry-Boschan computer method. One main aspect of the problem is that amplitudes change over time; consequently, standards derived from an earlier period may be entirely inappropriate in a later one. For this and other reasons we have not attempted to introduce an amplitude constraint into the turning point program.[43]

Even the flattest cycle, however, represents a prolonged movement in one direction. And most importantly, there was remarkable consilience among indicators even in marginal cycles. This last point will be the topic of the following chapter.

Procedures for Step Cycles

Our second definition——growth cycles are alternations between periods with relatively high rates of change and periods with relatively low rates of change——has the advantage of focusing on that aspect of economic change which today attracts the greatest interest. Moreover, it is independent of subjective trend selections. However, the disadvantage of the approach, for our purposes, is that growth rates have to be analyzed by a technique different from the one applied to the original series.

The crucial point is that in the case of rates of change cycle phases cannot be defined by rises and falls but must be defined by high and low levels. This was found by Milton Friedman and Anna Schwartz in their work on money, and they termed the alternations of high and low rates "step cycles."[44] To avoid misunderstandings it should be noted that the special treatment of rates

[43]For a fuller explanation see Bry and Boschan, *Cyclical Analysis*, pp. 11–15, 16.

[44]Milton Friedman and Anna Schwartz, "Money and Business Cycles," *Review of Economics and Statistics: Supplement*, February 1963.

of change is not based on their exhibiting step patterns. The reason for the step cycle concept is, rather, that the timing of rises and falls in growth rates differs from their timing in the underlying series. Growth tends to be most rapid when it starts from a low base, i.e., shortly after the end of a period of low growth or decline. Conversely, rates tend to be lowest shortly after the termination of rapid-growth period and thus at the beginning rather than at the end of a low-growth period. This behavior of rates of change means that large parts of business expansions are characterized by falling rates and large parts of business contractions by rising ones, rather than the other way around.

This growth rate pattern is illustrated by the third curve on Charts A-1 and A-2, and there is ample evidence for it in the literature. For instance, the rate of increase of U.S. gross national product in constant dollars was 60 per cent higher, on the average, in the first halves of the seven expansions (1921-38, 1949-61) than in their second halves. The rate of fall in the corresponding seven contractions was twice as large in the earlier part than in the later one.

Furthermore, the average monthly rate of change of thirty-four comprehensive American series before 1938 was more than twice as high between business cycle troughs and the first third of expansions than in later expansion stages. The average rate of decline was largest in the first half of contractions.[45]

Thus, if cycle phases were defined by growth rate peaks and troughs, they would tend to lead business cycles by a half to nearly a full phase. Expansions, for instance, would usually include only the beginning of a high-growth period, while most of this period would be included in the contraction phase. Since this would run counter to generally accepted ideas on business cycles, peaks and troughs in growth rates cannot serve to delimit cycle phases. Instead, the downturn must be defined as the end of a period of relatively high growth and the upturn as the end of a period of relatively low growth.

Growth rates are classified as "high" or "low" by comparisons of average rates in each of three successive cycle phases. The average rate during a high step must exceed the average rates during the preceding and succeeding low steps. The main difference between deviation cycles and step cycles thus is in the definition of the "normal" growth rate which serves as standard for distinguishing high and low rates. In deviation cycles the normal rates are given by the long-run trend. In step cycles the normal rate in each cycle is the average rate for that cycle. For each cycle phase the average rate is measured

---

[45] See Mitchell, *What Happens During Business Cycles*, p. 299. For similar results regarding the rate of change of the money supply, see Phillip Cagan, *Determinants and Effects of Changes in the Stock of Money, 1875–1960,* New York, NBER, 1965, p. 271.

against two normal rates: the average rate of the cycle beginning with that phase and the average rate of the cycle ending with that phase.

Due to the basic similarity of both cycle concepts, the timing of step cycles is, in most instances, the same, or very close to, that of the trend-adjusted series proper. This will be shown below and agrees with the Friedman and Schwartz findings.

Analysis of rates of change also presents another problem, especially in monthly series. Month-to-month percentage changes are often highly jagged series with a sawtooth appearance and, at the first glance, reveal neither cycles nor cyclical turns. The rate of change of industrial production in Chart A-1 is a good illustration.[46] To deal with this problem, we first find the approximate dates when a period of high growth ended and low growth began, and vice versa, on a chart showing the twelve-month moving average of the rates of change. It is noteworthy how clearly the underlying cyclical movements stand out in the smoothed rates of change on curve *4* in Charts A-1 and A-2 even for rates as choppy as those for industrial production. Selecting the zone where a step turn occurred is thus not difficult in most instances. The exact month of the step turn is then tentatively identified by inspection of the chart of the unsmoothed rates.

At this point the computer program takes over.[47] Each tentative cycle, i.e., each period between two like tentative step turns is broken into two parts at every intervening month. For each of these possible breaking points the variance between the average rates of change in the two parts (the step means) is computed. The breaking point that yields the largest variance is selected as the turning point. For instance, if a tentative cycle had a duration of twenty-four months, the program would test the variance between the mean rates of change for partitions into six and eighteen months, seven and seventeen months, eight and sixteen months, etc.

One reason for maximizing the variance rather than the simple difference between alternative step means is that the latter neglects the influence of the step length. Doubtful months would be assigned to the longer step, because this would increase the difference between step means even if the standing of the series in the month in question were much closer to the average rate of the short step than to that of the long one.

If the computed turning point differs from the tentatively selected one, every analysis which used the latter must be repeated with the former. This

---

[46]One reason is that independent errors of measurement in the original series introduce a negative serial correlation into rates of change.

[47]The method used is essentially a computerized version of the Friedman and Schwartz method. Friedman and Schwartz decided by inspection, in most instances, and relied on calculation without use of computers in difficult cases.

procedure is continued until each upturn has been confirmed as the correct partition between the adjacent downturns and each downturn as the correct partition between the adjacent upturns. Each turn thus has to be confirmed by three computations. It must be valid (1) as the end of one cycle, (2) as the beginning of the next cycle, and (3) as the correct partition between two adjacent turns of the opposite type.[48]

All the step turns in the seventeen indicators have been confirmed in this manner. In the case of some quarterly indicators all tentative turns were validated at the first trial. For some very erratic series, on the other hand, up to fifty periods had to be partitioned before some twelve steps meeting the requirements could be identified.

It should be noted that this objective validation procedure eliminates most of the subjective element which adheres to the initial selection of the tentative turns. The only decision the computer program cannot handle is whether to treat a given period as part of a step phase or as a separate step cycle. In such borderline cases subjective judgment must be used.

[48]To illustrate: assume, first, that December 1955 has been confirmed, in the manner described below, as the date of a downturn and that January 1961 has been tentatively selected as the date of the next downturn. The computer program then finds the date of the upturn between these two downturns. For this purpose it divides the tentative cycle at each intervening month into two phases, the first, one of low growth and the second, one of high growth. For each of these partitions the variance is computed. Assume it is found that partition in April 1959 yields the largest variance between the two steps. (Partitions at points less than five months from the tentative turns are excluded by requiring a five-month minimum phase duration.)

Next, the computer-determined upturn in April 1959 is used together with the next tentative upturn in February 1963 in order to check whether the downturn in January 1961 (used previously for the selection of the upturn of April 1959) is the correct partition between April 1959 and February 1963. If the downturn in January 1961 is confirmed, we proceed to the checking of the following turn. If the downturn in January 1961 is rejected, however, and replaced by, say, March 1961, the analysis which used January 1961 as the cycle end, must be repeated with the new date, March 1961. This means that the period from December 1955 to March 1961 will be partitioned in the manner described above. This either may confirm the previously found upturn in April 1959 or may result in a different date, say, May 1959. In the latter case the April 1959–February 1963 analysis has to be replaced by one for the period May 1959–February 1963. And so on.

The first turns at either end of a series obviously cannot be confirmed in this fashion. All that can be done in order to identify the best possible turns at the ends is to experiment with several alternative dates. For each such date the maximum variance between the two following, or the two preceding, steps is computed. The alternative turn that yields the highest maximum variance is the one chosen.

Findings on Step Cycles

The timing of the step cycles agrees with that of the deviation cycles in the sense that nearly every turn in one type of cycle matches a turn in the other type (Table 3). (The steps are indicated in Charts A-1 and A-2 by horizontal lines drawn at the average level of the step.) Out of 230 deviation cycle turns, November 1947-March 1970, only 6 have no counterpart in step cycles, and 11 out of 241 step cycle turns do not match a turn in deviation cycles. Most of the nonmatching turns occur in the mild cycle 1951-53.[49]

Of the matching turns one-half coincide exactly and three-quarters coincide roughly. This correspondence is impressive when one considers the difference in methods used, the large erratic component of the movements analyzed, and the numerous borderline cases.

However, it must also be stressed that 58, or 26 per cent, of the turns in the two types of cycles occur more than three months apart. There are a number of reasons for these discrepancies. One is the occurrence of flat bottoms and ceilings or of double turns. In such instances it can easily happen that the two methods pick different dates. The 1951 downturn in industrial production provides a good illustration (Chart A-1). The downturn in the deviation cycle is the later, the step cycle downturn the earlier, of a pair of double peaks.

Other discrepancies reflect differences between the trend on which the deviation cycle is based and the trend implicit in the average growth rates on which the step cycles are based. The main case in point are the downturns 1955-57. In these years the 75-month moving average rises steeply enough in many series to produce early downturns while the rate of change remains––for nearly two years, in some instances––distinctly higher than in the low-rate phase of 1954 and 1958. Since this type of discrepancy is systematic it is reflected in the reference turns; the problem it creates will be taken up in the next chapter.

Another factor causing discrepancies between the two types of cycles are the deficiencies of some indicators. Agreement between deviation turns and step turns of some indicators is much better than that between turns of others. While 93 per cent of the turns in wages and salaries and 90 per cent of those in retail sales coincide roughly, only 46 per cent of the turns in the unemployment rate do so. In terms of exact coincidences the range is between 87 per cent of turns in wages and salaries and 23 per cent in (again) the unemployment rate.

[49] In 1951–53 a step cycle but no deviation cycle is identified in four indicators, while a deviation cycle but no step cycle is found in one indicator.

TABLE 3

Comparison of Turning Points in Deviation Cycles (DC) and Step Cycles (SC),
Seventeen U.S. Indicators, November 1947–March 1970

		Number of Turns					Per Cent of Turns		
		Covered		Matching	Coinciding		Differing 4 Months or More	Coinciding		Differing 4 Months or More
Ident No.ᵃ	Indicator Title:	DC	SC		Exactly	Roughly		Exactly	Roughly	
Summary:	**17 Indicators**	**230**	**241**	**224**	**109**	**166**	**58**	**49**	**74**	**26**
16	Corporate profits after taxes	13	13	11	7	7	4	64	64	36
41	Number of employees on nonagricultural payrolls, establishment survey	15	15	15	5	12	3	33	80	20
43	Unemployment rate, total	13	13	13	3	6	7	23	46	54
47	Index of industrial production	15	15	15	6	10	5	40	67	33
48	Man-hours in nonagricultural establishments	15	15	15	5	10	5	33	67	33
49	Nonagricultural job openings unfilled	10	13	9	5	6	3	56	67	33
52	Personal income	13	15	13	7	9	4	54	69	31
53	Wage and salary income in mining, manufacturing, and construction	15	15	15	13	14	1	87	93	7
54	Sales of retail stores	15	15	15	10	13	2	67	87	13
55	Index of wholesale prices, industrial commodities	10	12	10	4	8	2	40	80	20
61	Business expenditures for new plant and equipment, total	12	15	12	9	9	3	75	75	25
62	Index of labor cost per unit of output, total manufacturing	13	15	13	6	10	3	46	77	23
71	Manufacturing and trade inventories, total book value	15	15	15	6	12	3	40	80	20
114	Discount rate on new issues of 91-day Treasury bills	13	10	10	5	9	1	50	90	10
200	Gross national product in current dollars	15	15	15	5	11	4	33	73	27
205	Gross national product in 1958 dollars	15	15	15	5	9	6	33	60	40
512	General imports, total	13	15	13	8	11	2	62	85	15

ᵃThe series identification numbers used in the *Business Conditions Digest.*

A large irregular component may be one of the factors in an indicator's poor performance in this respect. That the unemployment rate has the largest irregular movement among our indicators seems to support this view.[50] But the evidence is mixed. Some series which are nearly as irregular as unemployment, e.g., the Treasury bill rate and imports, show good agreement between deviation and step turns.

Agreement between the step and deviation turns also is much better at certain dates than at others for most indicators. There are strong turns and weak turns, as will be brought out further in the discussion of the reference cycles. The greatest uncertainty surrounds the turns at either end of the period covered. The deviation cycles are here based on extrapolated trends which may differ widely from actual ones. Similarly the growth rate step averages cannot be compared to preceding ones at the beginning of the period or to following ones at the end. Hence turns close to the beginning or end of the series should be considered highly tentative.

As mentioned previously, we plan to replace indicators which are deficient for our purposes because of large disagreements between dates of turns in the two types of growth cycles by more satisfactory ones.

6. A CHRONOLOGY OF U.S. GROWTH CYCLES

Growth cycles in the general economy are determined on the basis of the growth cycles in the indicators. For this purpose the indicators are combined into two types of indexes: composite indexes and diffusion indexes.[51] Each

---

[50] The measure of irregularity referred to is the average month-to-month percentage change in the irregular component of the series. The irregular component is obtained by dividing a smooth, flexible moving average of the seasonally adjusted series, which represents the cyclical component, into the seasonally adjusted series.

[51] The indexes are constructed in the same fashion as those for classical cycles, described in Section 4, except as follows:

The *composite index for deviation cycles* uses the trend-adjusted indicators where the index for classical cycles uses non-trend-adjusted ones. The composite index for deviation cycles equalizes the month-to-month differences in the standing of the indicators, whereas the index for classical cycles equalizes month-to-month percentage changes. The latter are not used for deviation cycles because the trend-adjusted series are expressed as percentage ratios to the trend.

In addition to the main composite index for deviation cycles, described in the preceding paragraph, we constructed a short-cut composite index for deviation cycles. Instead of adjusting each indicator for its trend and then combining them into the composite index, we took the composite index for classical cycles and adjusted that for its trend as represented by the 75-month moving average. The turns in the short-cut composite index coincide with those in the main index except for slight differences in two instances.

The chronology in Table 4 is based on the main composite index which, however, has not been extended beyond June 1969. Therefore, the last downturn, April 1969, is taken temporarily from the short-cut index, which is also shown in Chart 3.

type of index is constructed for deviation cycles and for step cycles; consequently, with a given list of indicators, four reference chronologies are obtained.[52]

The basic features of the four sets of reference dates derived from the 17-indicator list are the same (Table 4). Each set consists of fifteen turning points, eight downturns and seven upturns, 1948-69. Eight of these turns correspond to classical peaks and troughs, 1948-61. Two turns mark the Korean war cycle, four the two growth cycles, 1961-67. We cannot tell at this writing (August 1970) whether the last downturn, in 1969, will or will not match a classical peak. Most observers would probably have expected the number and location of growth cycle turns to be approximately as we find them.

The seven cycles stand out as clearly as one might wish in the two diffusion indexes on Chart 2. The amplitudes of the cycles on this chart, it should be remembered, do not indicate amplitudes of indicator movements, but reflect the duration and degree of diffusion of these movements.

The seven cycles are clearly drawn also in the composite index based on deviation cycles, although this index is less smooth than the diffusion indexes and has a long, nearly horizontal stretch in 1963-64 (Chart 3). In the composite index based on rates of change the reference cycles are represented by the horizontal step lines (Chart 3, curve *B*). The cycle turns are at the ends of the steps, i.e., at the ends of periods of high or low rates.

Although the occurrence of the seven growth cycles is confirmed by each of the four chronologies: the exact turning dates differ in many instances. Hence, the choice among the four indexes is important and difficult. The choice is necessary because we aim at presenting a single growth cycle

---

The main *composite index for step cycles* is derived by using the month-to-month percentage changes of the indicators in the same fashion as the original series are used in the classical composite index. The amplitude adjustment is applied to month-to-month differences between rates of change instead of to month-to-month percentage changes. Step cycle turning points are obtained by partitioning the composite index by the same method by which individual indicators are partitioned.

Also, a short-cut composite index has been constructed for step cycles, analogous to the short-cut composite index for deviation cycles. A series of month-to-month percentage changes is derived from the composite index for classical cycles. This series is partitioned into step cycles. As in the case of deviation cycles, the turning dates are identical in the main and in the short-cut index, with two exceptions.

Because the main composite index for step cycles has not been updated, the chronology in Table 4 and the curve in Chart 3 are based on the short-cut index.

[52]The number of chronologies actually obtained in preparing this paper has been much greater, since we have experimented with several indicator lists.

TABLE 4

Leads and Lags of Upturns (U) and Downturns (D) in Classical Reference Cycles, in Three Growth Cycle Indexes, and in Leading Indicators at Growth Cycle Reference Turns, 17 U.S. Indicators, 1948–69

Date of Growth Cycle Reference Turns		Classical Cycles Composite Index[a]		Deviation Cycles Diffusion Index		Step Cycles Composite Index		Step Cycles Diffusion Index		Leading Indicators Composite Index[b]	
Upturns	Downturns	U	D	U	D	U	D	U	D	U	D
	Aug. 1948		+2		−2		+2		+1		−7
Nov. 1949		−1		0		0		0		−5	
	May 1951				+3		−1		−1		−4
July 1952				−1		0		−1		0	
	Dec. 1952		+6		+2		+3		+3		+1
Sept. 1954		−1		0		−2		−1		−6	
	Feb. 1957		+6		0		+6		+6		−14
May 1958		−1		0		0		−1		−1	
	Feb. 1960		+2		0		−9		−2		−10
Apr. 1961		−2		0		0		−2		−4	
	May 1962				0		−1		−3		−1
June 1964				−7		+3		+3		−20	
	Sept. 1966				−3		+1		+1		−6
Oct. 1967				0		−5		−4		−7	
	April 1969				+1		+4		+4		0

[a]Revised data; see Table 2.
[b]From *Business Conditions Digest*, March 1970, p. 102.

chronology. To work with two sets of dates, however similar to each other, would obviously be awkward and confining.[53]

Two Deviation Cycle Indexes Compared

Examination of agreements and disagreements among the four chronologies discloses, first, that turns in each pair of indexes for a given cycle type are very similar. Thus eight out of fifteen turns in the diffusion index and in the composite index based on deviation cycles coincide exactly, and all but one coincide at least roughly. The exception is the upturn occurring in November 1963 in the diffusion index and in June 1964 in the

[53]The NBER has always selected a single month as turning point even when the evidence did not point clearly to a single month. Otherwise it would be necessary to work with alternative turns or with turning zones, which would greatly reduce the usefulness of the chronology.

Chart 2
U.S. Growth Cycles, 1947–70
Diffusion Indexes, Seventeen Indicators

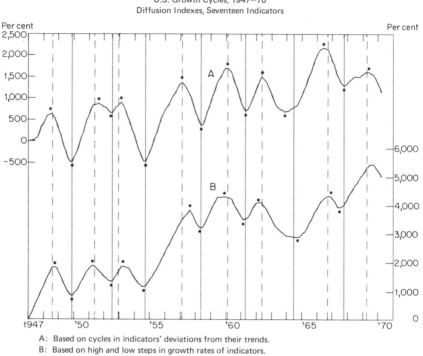

A: Based on cycles in indicators' deviations from their trends.
B: Based on high and low steps in growth rates of indicators.
  Diffusion indexes are constructed by cumulating the excess of the percentage of indica-
tors undergoing a cyclical speedup over the percentage undergoing a slowdown.
  Solid vertical lines indicate growth cycle upturns, broken vertical lines, growth cycle
downturns, based on Chart 3, Series A.

composite index. This upturn is the most difficult one to date because the
economy grew over many months at a nearly constant rate.

  In the center of the period, it should be noted, there is a sequence of six
turns which coincide exactly in the two indexes. As mentioned previously,
the turns in the center of the period covered are more reliable and thus
should agree better than those at the ends. A further noteworthy point is that
those turns which correspond to classical peaks and troughs agree much
better than the others. Of the former, 75 per cent coincide exactly, against 30
per cent of the latter. Another noteworthy feature is that upturns agree
better in the two indexes than downturns. Similarly, in classical cycles, since
World War II, troughs are much more sharply drawn than peaks.

Chart 3
U.S. Growth Cycles, 1947–70
Composite Indexes, Seventeen Indicators

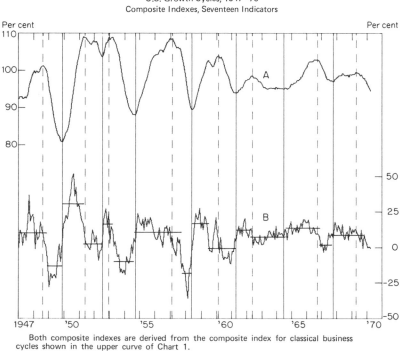

Both composite indexes are derived from the composite index for classical business cycles shown in the upper curve of Chart 1.

A: Classical composite index adjusted for trend (per cent deviations from trend).
B: Month to month per cent change in classical composite index (annual rates).

Solid vertical lines indicate growth cycle upturns, broken vertical lines, growth cycle downturns, based on Series A.

Two-Step Cycle Indexes Compared

The corresponding comparison between diffusion and composite indexes for step cycles shows similar results. Of the fifteen turns, seven coincide exactly, and all but one coincide roughly. The exception here is the 1959-60 downturn, which comes seven months earlier in the composite index than in the diffusion index.

Deviation Cycles and Step Cycles Compared

The differences between the dates of deviation cycle turns and step cycle turns are much greater than those between the two indexes for each type of cycle. Turns in the two composite indexes and the two diffusion indexes fail to coincide even roughly in four and five out of the fifteen instances. Exact coincidences are the exception (two in the diffusion indexes and four in the composite indexes). The median discrepancy is three months between the diffusion indexes and two and a half months between the composite indexes.

Most of the larger discrepancies are due to relatively flat movements of the indexes which make selection between two or more alternative dates depend on tiny differences between standings. For instance, the two diffusion indexes identify different turns in the flat bottom 1963-64 and at the rounded downturns in 1951 and 1966. The composite indexes disagree for the same reason at the double peak of 1960 and at the upturn in 1967. With an improved indicator list some or most of these discrepancies should be removed.

The 1957 downturn is a different case. Both diffusion indexes trace a sharp triangle here, and the six-month discrepancy reflects the difference in the two trend curves. The flatter trend implicit in the step cycles gives a later downturn. Since this lag occurs in nine of our indicators, including the most important ones, it will not be eliminated by a change in the indicator mix.

The difficult choice for the final growth cycle chronology is, thus, between deviation cycles and step cycles. The latter have the great advantage that they are independent of the subjective selection of a trend curve. The advantage of the deviation cycles, on the other hand, is that they are easily understood and quite similar in concept to classical business cycles.[54]

Other criteria to be considered in choosing among the indexes are their amplitude and smoothness. Judged by the smoothness of the composite indexes deviation cycles are far superior to step cycles, of course, since rates of change are always more erratic than the series from which they are drawn. The ratio of the irregular to the cyclical components of the indexes is nearly four times as large in the step cycle index as in the deviation cycle one.[55] The amplitudes of the composite indexes are not comparable because of the different definitions of the two types of cycles.[56]

[54]Chronologies based on German deviation cycles and German step cycles were quite similar, consequently, it made little difference which one was selected. I preferred the diffusion index for deviation cycles for its somewhat greater smoothness and amplitude. Composite indexes were not used for German growth cycles (see Mintz, *Dating Postwar Business Cycles*).

[55]This refers to the measure explained in footnote 50. The ratio of the irregular to the cyclical component is 0.4 for the deviation cycle index and 1.5 for the step cycle index.

[56]Measured by month-to-month change in the cyclical component, amplitudes of composite indexes always equal 1 by definition. Measuring amplitudes by differences in standings at turning points does not fit the step cycle concept. Step cycle amplitudes must be measured by differences between the levels of steps; these differences are not comparable to the amplitudes of deviation cycles.

The diffusion indexes hardly differ in either amplitude or smoothness (Chart 2). There is practically no countercyclical movement in either one. Although there are large differences in amplitudes of individual cycle phases, the average amplitude of the two indexes for the entire period is nearly the same. In both deviation and step cycles at least 15 out of the 17 indicators move in the same direction during some months. The exception is the 1951-53 downturn-to-downturn cycle in which this high degree of diffusion is not reached.

My tentative decision is to use the deviation cycles. Given this decision it does not make much difference whether the diffusion index or the composite index is used. I have tentatively chosen the composite index because it takes account of amplitudes of changes in the indicators, while the diffusion index registers only their direction.

From here on the comments and measurements refer to the composite index based on deviation cycles.

Description of U.S. Growth Cycles

The seven cycles vary greatly in amplitude as measured by the differences in index standings at turning points.[57] The largest cycle (1948-51, downturn to downturn) is more than five times as large as the two smallest ones (1966-69, downturn to downturn, and 1961-64, upturn to upturn). As expected, large amplitudes characterize cycles which match classical business cycles. On the average the swings of such growth cycles are twice as large as the swings of the others. This implies that the cycles of the 1950's are on the average larger than those of the 1960's.

Amplitudes of downturn-to-downturn cycles vary more than amplitudes of upturn-to-upturn cycles. This reflects the positive correlation of high rates and subsequent low rates and the absence of such correlation between high rates and preceding low rates.

As to phase amplitudes, a comparison of the seven high-rate phases shows that the 1958-60 amplitude was about average. Significantly, this phase matches the smallest of the classical expansions covered. The two large high-rate phases, 1949-51 and 1954-57, were very roughly twice the average. Among the four high-rate phases which were below average the largest, reaching two-thirds of the average, was in 1964-66, while 1967-69 was the

[57]The amplitudes referred to in the text are those of the short-cut composite index (see footnote 51). They are based on the ratios of the classical composite index to its trend and represent the differences between the standings of these ratios at turning points. The numerical values of the amplitudes are, therefore, not meaningful; that is why they are discussed in terms of their relative magnitudes only.

smallest, with only one-fourth of the average amplitude and one-ninth of the largest amplitude.

Amplitudes of low-rate phases vary much less than those of high-rate phases. Again the amplitude of the 1960-61 low-rate phase, which matches the smallest classical recession covered, is near average for the seven low-rate phases. The three phases 1948-49, 1952-54, and 1957-58 were about twice as large as the average, and the three phases 1951-52, 1962-64, and 1966-67 about half the average.

The latest low-rate phase can, at this writing, be measured only from April 1969 to March 1970, the last month covered. Within this period, its amplitude was somewhat smaller than the 1966-67 one and somewhat larger than the 1962-64 one.

Regarding acceptance of the proposed seven growth cycles, opinions may differ, of course. Does the flattest of the cycles deserve that name? Should not a minimum amplitude be stipulated in some fashion? The reasons for not setting such a rule are the same mentioned earlier with regard to cycles in the indicators: mainly the difficulty of setting standards suitable for a future different from the past. With the declining trend of amplitudes a lower limit set today may easily be obsolete tomorrow.

There are also other good arguments for acceptance of the seven cycles. One is their high degree of diffusion among the 17 indicators. At 11 of the 15 reference turns each of the indicators, with negligible exceptions, has a matching turn. One of the remaining four reference turns is the 1969 downturn, which is too recent for all indicator downturns to be identified as yet. (In fact, as of August 1970 downturns have been dated in 13 of the 17 series.) This leaves three turns at which diffusion is not high and which do mark a cycle whose elimination deserves serious consideration, namely, the one from the downturn in 1951 to the downturn in 1952. The deviation cycles of seven indicators skipped the 1952 upturn and either the 1951 downturn or the 1952 one. Diffusion was higher in terms of step cycles. A corresponding cycle was not identified in only four of the indicators.

Another objection to the 1951-52 cycle is its short duration. It lasted only 19 months as compared to 27 months (1960-62, downturn to downturn) for the next shortest cycle. The longest of the growth cycles lasted 52 months (1962-66) and their average length was three years.

But if the 1951-52 growth cycle is the shortest and the least diffused, there are also arguments in favor of its recognition. First, its amplitude ranks above that of the 1966-69 cycle. Second, it appears in each of the four growth cycle indexes and equally in every experimental index based on different indicator lists. Third, if this reference cycle were rejected, the majority of indicators would show a cycle not matched by a reference cycle.

Such "extra" cycles otherwise are rare exceptions. Last, but not least, the behavior of the leading indicators confirms the cycle. On balance, therefore, we deem it preferable to recognize the weakest of our cycles.

Relations of Growth Cycles to Classical Business Cycles

One important aspect of the growth cycles is their relation to classical cycles (Table 4). We expect classical troughs to lead growth cycle upturns and classical peaks to lag growth cycle downturns, and this is confirmed by the signs of the timing relation at all eight turns covered. The leads at the lower turning points are remarkably regular and also very short. Upturns were too sharp for the removal of the trend to have much effect. At the upper turning points there are two short (two months) lags in 1948 and 1960 and two long (six months) lags in 1953 and 1957. In the two latter instances the step cycle turns, too, lag behind the reference turns, reflecting the effect of a relatively steep trend curve on the latter.

The timing relations imply that high-rate phases are shorter than classical expansions and low-rate phases longer than contractions. In fact, the average duration of the two growth cycle phases is similar, 19 months for highs and 17 months for lows. The near-equal length is in accord with the definition of the phases as periods of above- and below-average growth. Also as expected, the average duration of growth cycles is much shorter——three years——than the average duration of classical business cycles, which was 46 months for the three peak-to-peak cycles, 1948-60, and would be much longer if an expansion, 1961-69, were included.

Assuming past timing relationships to continue into the future, one may conclude that once a growth cycle downturn has occurred, a classical peak should follow within six months at most or there will be no classical peak at all to match that particular downturn. This has an interesting implication for the current (July 1970) situation. If the date of the growth cycle downturn, April 1969, is correct, the classical peak should have followed by October 1969 at the latest, if at all. We find that no classical peak occurred through March 1970. Hence, on the basis of historical experience, such a peak should not be expected any longer which means there neither has been nor will be a classical recession matching the present slowdown.

If this conclusion should be wrong, if a classical peak should have occurred after March, this could signify either that the growth cycle downturn of April 1969 was placed much too early (which is quite possible in view of its tentative character), or that the lag of the peak behind the downturn was much longer this time than ever before.

Relations of Leading Indicators to Growth Cycles

How useful the growth cycle chronology can be in clarifying cyclical relationships is illustrated by its effect on the evaluation of the leading indicators. What we find is that the fifteen growth cycle turns match the turns in the composite index of the classical leading indicators one to one (Table 4).[58] This is important because one of the main objections to the usefulness of the leading indicators is that they give "false signals." It does not help us much, so the argument goes, that the leaders predict classical business cycle turns correctly, since they also predict turns which never occur. This argument is no longer valid when growth cycles are recognized and false signals become right signals.

The length of lead of the leaders differs, of course, between growth cycles and classical cycles. At upper turning points they are shorter, at lower ones they are longer, at growth cycle turns compared to classical turns.[59]

To cite just one more example of the uses of growth cycles we refer to the analysis of fluctuations in the quantity of money. From 1949 to 1970 cycles in the rate of change of the money supply match growth cycles one to one. And with one exception, where the two downturns coincide, the turns in money lead the growth cycle turns.[60]

Many other cyclical relationships may be expected to be clarified with the help of the growth cycle chronology.

7. CONCLUSION

This study demonstrates, first, that the traditional NBER business cycle chronology, 1948-61, can be reproduced exactly by computerized methods. One interesting implication of this finding is that the traditional NBER methods have all along been far more objective than one might have thought.

---

[58]The comparison refers to the Composite Index of 12 Leaders, Original Trend, published in *Business Conditions Digest*, March 1970, p. 102.

It should be noted that the leaders and the growth cycles have only one series in common, therefore, their agreement cannot be explained by an overlap of coverage.

[59]The variability of the lengths of leads is not smaller relative to growth cycles than to classical cycles. But this statement refers to the composite index of leaders without trend adjustment. In a later version our usual trend adjustment will be applied to this index, and this may reduce the variability of the leads. Julius Shiskin found a great reduction in variability of leads when he adjusted the composite index of the leaders to move along the same trend as the index representing classical cycles with which the leaders' index was being compared.

[60]This is based on step cycles in the rate of change of money as analyzed by Anna Schwartz.

The finding further suggests that after some more testing of the new methods they will be able to replace subjective cycle dating.

The second major result of the study is to give precision to a revised cycle concept, namely, growth cycles or cycles defined as alternating periods of above-and below-average economic growth. Growth cycles, it is found, can be identified as clearly and confidently as the traditional business cycles.

All our measurements lead to the recognition of seven growth cycles in the United States, 1948-69. These cycles were widely diffused. With very few exceptions, turns in every one of the seventeen indicators used match the growth cycle turns. The seven cycles vary greatly in amplitude and duration. Amplitudes of those growth cycles which match classical business cycles are, according to preliminary measures, about twice as large on the average as amplitudes of other growth cycles. Durations vary between 19 and 55 months. The average length of growth cycles was three years.

Turning now to the description of growth cycle phases, it is found that four low-rate phases match classical recessions but are three to seven months longer than the latter. Of the three remaining low-rate phases, one occurred after the Korean War, one from May 1962 to June 1964, and the third from September 1966 to October 1967. The amplitude of the largest low-rate phase was roughly four times that of the smallest one.

The low-rate phase which started in 1969 is not included above because its end cannot be ascertained on the basis of data through August 1970. At that date it had already lasted 17 months, which is longer than all but two of the preceding low-rate phases. The amplitude of the latest low-rate phase was, to August 1970, smaller than amplitudes of phases matching classical recessions but larger than amplitudes of the other three low-rate phases.

High-rate phases are, of course, much shorter than classical expansions. In the 1960's three such phases occurred within a single expansion and there were two high-rate phases during the 1949-53 expansion. The two high-rate phases which each correspond to a single classical expansion, viz., 1954-57 and 1958-60, are still seven months and three months shorter than their classical counterparts.

The range of amplitudes of high-rate phases is far greater than that of low-rate phases. The amplitude of the largest high-rate phase is about nine times as great as that of the smallest one (1967-69).

One example of the usefulness of the growth cycle chronology is the light it throws on the leading indicators. Turns in the composite of these indicators match the fifteen growth cycle turns one to one. It has always been regarded as the main weakness of the leading indicators that, while correctly predicting classical business cycle turns, they also falsely predict turns which never occur. However, these false signals become true ones once the existence of growth cycles is recognized and it is understood that the predictions of the indicators may be taken to refer not only to the classical cycles but to growth cycles as well.

POSTSCRIPT

The extension of the coverage through August 1970 has not changed the previous findings. The tentative downturn date of the growth cycle remains April 1969. The rise of the trend-adjusted composite index to this date and the subsequent fall stand out more sharply in the extended and revised data than in the previous ones.

In the composite index without trend adjustment, which represents the classical business cycle, no peak can be determined in the period covered. Although the index stands no higher in May 1970 than in December 1969 and thus identifies a period of stagnation, this does not suffice for classifying the period as a recession by traditional standards. The corresponding diffusion index also failed to cross the zero line through August 1970, since there was a majority of rising indicators in each month.

That the indexes which clearly identify each of the preceding recessions do not signalize a recession in the first half of 1970 is not surprising, since the behavior of the economy in the latter period was very different from that in the preceding four recessions. The contrast is fully described and discussed in Fabricant's essay in this volume (pp. 000-000 and Table 1).

I mention only a few of the striking differences Fabricant finds between classical recessions and the first half of 1970. First, in the latter period, but not in the former, most current-dollar indicators kept rising. But that is not all. When attention is restricted to deflated and physical volume series, the contrast persists. Thus the value of deflated retail sales kept rising in the first half of 1970, deflated personal income and the number of employees rose during the first quarter, and real GNP rose during the second quarter.

Where declines did take place in nonpecuniary indicators their mildness is again in contrast to those of previous recessions. In the first half of 1970 most declines amounted to no more than one-third to one-seventh of the corresponding ones in the recession of 1960-61 which itself is considered a borderline case because of its mildness. The unemployment rate is an exception because it rose almost as much in the first half of 1970 as in 1960-61. But even its rise was only half as much or less than those occurring in the three preceding recessions.

The foregoing comments, it should be noted, refer exclusively to the first half of 1970 and have no bearing on the possibility of a recession in the second half of the year.

APPENDIX

General Notes to Appendix Charts

Solid vertical lines indicate growth cycle upturns; broken vertical lines, growth cycle downturns.

Dots on curve 2 identify deviation cycle turning points.

Horizontal lines drawn through curve 3 indicate average rates of change during step phases. The last point of these lines is the step turn.

The slight oscillations of some curves in the charts occur because the computer plotting equipment plots a sloping line in small horizontal and vertical steps.

In the final version of this study there will be one chart for each indicator. In the August 1970 version there are only two charts for purposes of illustration. In these two charts curves 1 and 2 end in March 1970, but curves 3 and 4 are not extended beyond June 1969.

Chart A-1
Index of Industrial Production
(1957-59=100)

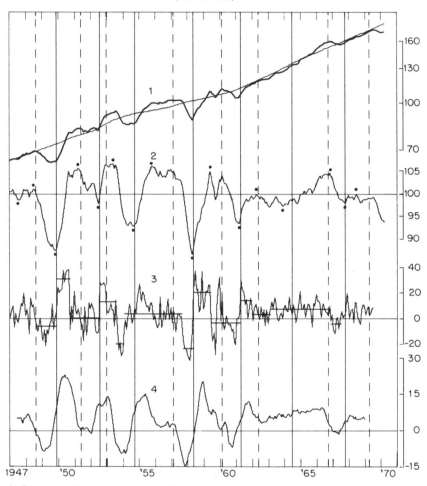

1: Seasonally adjusted data and seventy-five month moving average.
2: Deviations from seventy-five month moving average, per cent.
3: Change from month to month, per cent, annual rate.
4: Centered twelve-month moving average of line 3, per cent.

Chart A-2
Gross National Product in 1958 Dollars
(Annual rate, billion dollars)

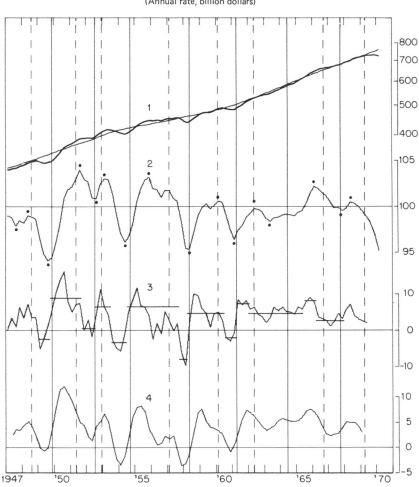

1: Seasonally adjusted data and twenty-five quarter moving average.
2: Deviations from twenty-five quarter moving average, per cent.
3: Change from quarter to quarter, per cent, annual rate.
4: Centered four-quarter moving average of line 3, per cent.

TABLE A–1

Listing of Indicators Used In Tables 1 and 2

(asterisk signifies that indicator was used)

Indicator No.	3	4	5	6	7	8	9	10	11	12	13	14	15	16	17
16								*	*	*	*	*	*	*	*
19										*	*				*
40						*									
41	*	*	*	*	*	*	*	*	*	*	*	*	*	*	*
42						*									
43		*	*	*	*	*	*	*	*	*	*	*	*	*	*
45						*									
46						*									
47	*	*	*	*	*	*	*	*	*	*	*	*	*	*	*
48								*	*	*	*	*	*	*	*
49								*	*	*	*	*	*	*	*
51			*	*	*										
52	*	*	*	*	*	*	*	*	*	*	*	*	*	*	*
53						*			*	*	*			*	*
54			*	*	*	*	*	*	*	*	*	*	*	*	*
55			*	*	*				*	*	*			*	*
56		*					*	*					*	*	
57	*					*									
61								*	*	*	*	*	*	*	*
62									*	*	*			*	*
71									*	*	*			*	*
72										*	*				*
114									*	*	*			*	*
200			*	*	*		*	*	*	*	*	*	*	*	*
205						*	*	*	*	*	*	*	*	*	*
512									*	*	*			*	*

Source: See Notes to Table 1. For indicator titles, see Table 3.

The "Recession" of 1969–1970

Solomon Fabricant

New York University and National Bureau of Economic Research

I

There can be no doubt that economic expansion came to a halt in the United States in the Autumn of 1969. What has been in question is this: Did the halt mark a pause in the expansion, or did it mark a peak in the business cycle and the onset of a recession?

The quotation marks in the title of this paper are intended to put the reader on prompt notice that no plain yes-or-no answer to the question can be given.

One reason is that most of the declines with which we are concerned when we ask the question have been small, counting to September 1970, the latest month for which much information is now (October) available——although not so small as to preclude the question.[1]

NOTE: This study was financed by grants from the Alfred P. Sloan Foundation and the Alex C. Walker Charitable and Educational Foundation. Grateful acknowledgement is also made of helpful comments by G. H. Moore; and of valuable secretarial and statistical assistance by Mildred Courtney, Chantal Dubrin, Dorothy M. O'Brien and Peggy Cahn. The charts were prepared under the direction of H. Irving Forman; Gnomi Schrift Gouldin edited the text.

[1] When the Colloquium was held on September 24, 1970, the latest month for which much information was available was August. [Note added in January 1971: Economic developments since September 1970 have erased what doubts economists might have had at the time on the identification of 1969–70 as a period of recession. The main thrust of this paper is unaffected, however, and I therefore let it stand as it was in October. Changes to the end of 1970 are discussed in my paper, "Recent Economic Changes and the Agenda of Business Cycle Research," a supplement to *National Bureau Report 8*, May 1971.]

There is another, more important, reason. The word, recession, means different things to different people. Not everyone has in mind the National Bureau's definition. But even that, as was recognized from the start, has its ragged edges. And it has, in any case, always been regarded as tentative, "subject to revision or abandonment if not borne out by observation."[2] The answer must depend on just what is meant by recession.

This is not to imply that every answer is equally valid. The burden of what I have to say is, in fact, that good grounds exist for choosing one answer, tentative though the answer must be. Studies of pre- and postwar business fluctuations by the National Bureau's staff and others, since the last revision of the Bureau's definition of business cycles in 1946, provide the basis for rethinking the concept of business cycles and of the recessions that constitute their downward phase. We need to take stock of what has been learned and put it to use.

A colloquium on "The Business Cycle Today," I hardly need mention, offers an exceptionally appropriate occasion to do this——to bring the knowledge to bear, as far as it will go, on the interpretation of a series of recent events of great public interest; and, at the same time, to pursue our scientific objectives by opening a discussion of the lines along which the National Bureau's definition of business cycles might best be revised.

II

The main lines in question may be briefly indicated by noting that whether or not economic developments like those of 1969–70 are identified as a business-cycle recession will depend upon:

Where the line is drawn between business-cycle recessions and pauses (or interruptions) in business-cycle expansions, with regard to extent of decline in aggregate economic activity, duration of decline, and degree of diffusion through the economy;

How aggregate economic activity is defined for this purpose——particularly, whether it is measured entirely in real terms, or in the mixture of real and pecuniary terms commonly used in the past——a difference of more than negligible importance in a period of rising price levels; and

Whether recessions are identified by their causes as well as by the course they run.

To be more specific about 1969–70: If a recession is defined as a sustained and widely diffused absolute contraction in aggregate economic activity, at

[2] Arthur F. Burns and Wesley C. Mitchell, *Measuring Business Cycles,* New York, NBER, 1946, p. 3.

least equal in intensity to one or more of the recessions already listed in the National Bureau's chronology of business cycles when intensity is measured in the same way and with the same kind of indicators as were those in previous years——that is, using measures of pecuniary as well as real economic activity——then the economic changes of 1969-70 do not, so far, appear to constitute a recession.

Continuing with the same concept, but measuring changes in aggregate economic activity exclusively in real terms——GNP in constant prices, deflated personal income, industrial production, employment, and the like——the economic changes in 1969-70 come closer to constituting a case of recession. In duration, the current decline already exceeds or is at least equal to the shortest recession in the record. In severity of decline and degree of diffusion measured in real terms, to judge by preliminary estimates, it is near if not actually within, the borders marking the limits implied by recessions listed in the National Bureau's chronology of business cycles.

If these limits are extended so that any sustained contraction in aggregate economic activity, measured in real terms, is accepted as a member of the species (even if the contraction is not as severe as in the mildest recession already recorded) then 1969-70 can more definitely be identified as a recession. Should the contraction have already come to an end (no one can be sure at this date) and should the statistical picture currently before us remain reasonably firm (some revisions are bound to be made later), the recession of 1969-70 would be the mildest on the list.

If, further, a business recession is defined as a sustained and widely diffused decline in the rate of growth of real aggregate economic activity relative to its long-term trend, or——what is not quite the same——in the proportion of available resources actually employed in production (measured, for example, by the relative gap between potential and actual GNP), the case for calling 1969-70 a recession is greatly strengthened. Here the likelihood of subsequent revisions of the currently available estimates is of very little moment. Revisions of the order of those in the past would not lead to a different conclusion.

Finally, during the expansion that stopped in 1969, signs appeared of the "restrictive forces that gradually but insistently come into play as a result of the expansion process itself."[3] If these are taken into account, along with the restrictive monetary and fiscal policies undertaken by the government to curb inflationary pressures——policies that may at least in part be viewed as one manifestation of the restrictive forces generated by the expansion——the case for identifying 1969-70 as a recession is even stronger.

[3] Arthur F. Burns, *The Business Cycle in a Changing World*, New York, NBER, 1969, p. 29.

Not all of these ways of characterizing the economic changes during 1969-70 are mutually exclusive, of course. Nor, as I have already suggested, are the several views equally valid. The one to be preferred, in my opinion, is the view based on the definition of a business-cycle recession as a sustained and widely diffused decline in the rate of growth of real economic activity, relative to its long-term trend. We have been experiencing a recession that, so far, is mild; but nevertheless it is, I believe, a member of the same species as the recessions already identified——without reference to a rate of growth criterion——in the National Bureau's chronology.

However, I add a reservation. Perhaps a subspecies needs to be distinguished, or a special label——"growth recession" or "slowdown"?—— attached to recessions that involve little or no absolute contraction in aggregate economic activity. But I also add that whatever the classification or the terminology, any persistently low rate of growth that widens the gap between potential and actual output is a matter for concern; as, indeed, is widely recognized in an age in which the standards by which the performance of the economy is judged are high, and the costs and benefits of every economic policy are subjected to close scrutiny and argument.

I should point out that if the definition I have just stated is accepted, far-reaching implications follow. Not only 1969-70, but also 1966-67 and perhaps even 1962, not to mention still other fluctuations in the rate of growth of aggregate economic activity listed by Mintz, Mack, and others, might be identified as recessions.[4]

The definition, then, requires testing, as would any modification of a definition found useful in the past. My application of the definition to 1969-70 should be viewed as a step in the essential task of acquiring experience in the use of the definition——a task to which Mintz has already made a substantial contribution.

Since identification of 1969-70, or of any of the earlier fluctuations I have mentioned, as a recession or even as a growth recession, may convey to some readers unwarranted political implications, as well as what I hope are warranted scientific implications, a further caveat is in order. Such an identification cannot, in and of itself, validly imply that government stabilization policy was mistaken either before, during, or after 1969 or 1966 or 1962. A slowdown in the rate of economic growth is a matter for concern, but it does not thereby follow that every slowdown must be avoided or

[4] Ilse Mintz, "Dating American Growth Cycles," in this volume; Ruth P. Mack, "Notes on Subcycles in Theory and Practice," *American Economic Review,* May 1957; Julius Shiskin, "The 1961–69 Economic Expansion in the United States: The Statistical Record," *Business Conditions Digest* (formerly *Business Cycle Developments*), January 1970; and G.H. Moore, Foreword to Ilse Mintz's *Dating Postwar Business Cycles: Methods and Their Application to Western Germany, 1950–67,* O.P. 107, New York, NBER, 1970.

promptly stopped at any price (that is, without any regard for the future stability of the economy or for the attainment of other national goals). What price is "required," and what price is "worth paying," are issues that extend well beyond the scope of the present discussion.

Maybe I had better be even more explicit. To identify 1969-1970 as a recession is not to say that the present Administration's anti-inflation policy is incorrect. Nor is it to say that the policy is correct. To judge the policy, one must weigh its benefits in dampening inflationary pressures and in improving the likelihood of sustainable rapid growth at high levels of employment in the future, against its current costs in lost production and unemployment. This would require estimating the trade-off between these competing objectives, and deciding what their relative social values are——taking into account also the risks involved in pursing or not pursuing the policy.

The 1969-70 episode, as well as the fundamental scientific question to which it leads, will be examined under the light shed by observation of a much broader experience. We shall be profiting from the studies undertaken with the aid of the National Bureau's definition and the research procedures adapted to it——however obsolete their features may now appear to be. The discussion may serve, therefore, to apprise or remind those concerned with current economic affairs of the practical value of scientific research on the problem of economic instability.

III

Before we take a close look at the economic changes of 1969-1970, it will be helpful to recall the main features of the broader experience against which we shall want to judge it. A first view is provided by the indicators of aggregate economic activity collected in Chart 1.

A variety of indicators is presented because no single indicator, even one as comprehensive as GNP, can provide a rounded view of aggregate economic activity. Nor can composites covering various kinds of activities be entirely free of doubts concerning the representativeness of the series covered, the weight given to each, and the method by which they were combined. It goes without saying, also, that no statistical series is so accurate that information from other sources is unnecessary.

The chart covers only the period beginning with 1948, but the series in the first panel suffice to remind us of two of the dominant characteristics of our country's economic development——its growth and its instability. In both these regards, there are many interesting similarities and differences among the various series and periods covered in the chart. All would repay careful

Chart 1
Indicators of Economic Activity in the United States, 1948–1970

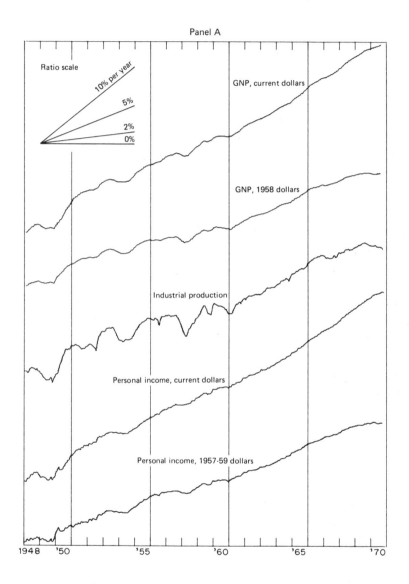

Panel A

Chart 1 (continued)

Panel A (concluded)

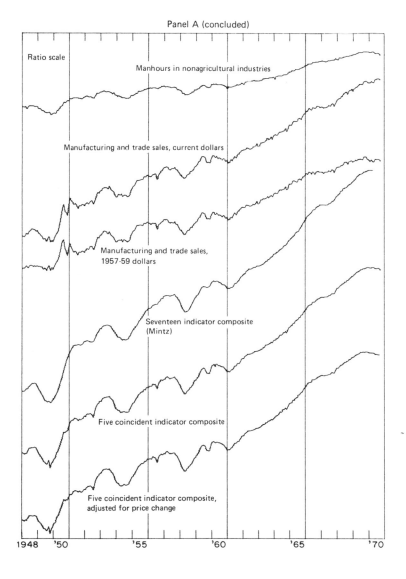

Chart 1 (continued)

Panel B1

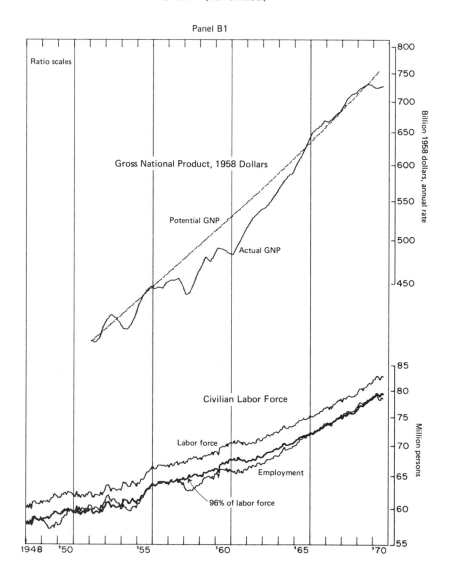

Chart 1 (concluded)

Panel B2

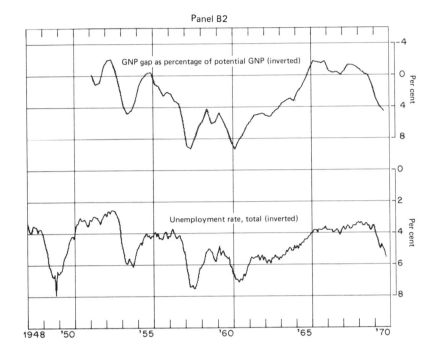

GNP gap as percentage of potential GNP (inverted)

Unemployment rate, total (inverted)

Panel C

Diffusion Indexes: Employment on Nonagricultural Payrolls — 30 Industries

6-mo. span
1-mo. span

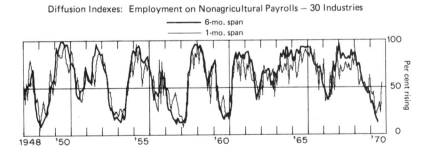

study but I take the time to note those of most importance for our present purpose.

First, the fluctuations are of all shapes and sizes, but even those common to the various series——the fluctuations of particular interest to us——range over a wide gamut. Nor is there any obvious clustering of these cycles into distinctly different groups, in terms of duration and amplitude. They fall into an array that seems to be fairly continuous, allowing for the limited size of the sample. To make the point more specific, any line drawn between the fluctuations that have been identified as business cycles in the past and those not so identified, would appear to be somewhat arbitrary. As those familiar with *Business Conditions Digest* (and various National Bureau publications) will have noticed, the usual vertical lines marking off business cycle peaks and troughs have been omitted from the chart. This was done deliberately, to encourage the reader to judge the matter for himself.

Second, there has been a tendency for the fluctuations to diminish in severity with the passage of time. This trend would be more pronounced were the chart to cover the pre-World War II period, but it is evident even over the past quarter-century. At any rate, fluctuations during the second half of the postwar period were clearly of smaller amplitude than those during the first half.

Third, even continued growth, when below the secular trend rate, could——and most often did——mean a widening gap between potential and actual performance. This is shown in the second panel of the chart by two overlapping sets of data: one, the difference between potential and actual GNP: the other, the difference between the number in the labor force and the number employed. Similar calculations that are (or could be made) available for other series in the chart would tell much the same story.[5] As we shall see, difficult questions can be raised about the meaning and measurement of "potential" output and "full" employment——and some also about actual output and actual employment——and therefore about the gaps. Nevertheless, these measurements provide a useful if rough way of judging the economy's performance.

Fourth, both growth and fluctuation in growth were widely diffused throughout the economy. In most years, as Panel C illustrates for employment, the number of persons at work in the great majority of industries generally rose from month to month or over longer spans, such as

[5] For industrial output, see Chart 2, below.

the six-month spans traced in the chart. During periods of slow growth in total employment, the majority fell or even tended to vanish. When total employment actually declined, the majority swung the other way: the fraction of industries with rising employment dropped well below the 50 per cent mark and remained there for months.

Fifth, the indicators based on pecuniary values, and the measurements free of price change, usually tell much the same story. But there are differences. Peaks usually come earlier and troughs later in the indicators of "real" economic activity, and declines are usually greater. These differences are not insignificant in the recent years and some earlier ones as well.

IV

Of the various fluctuations in aggregate economic activity noticeable in the chart, four are included in the National Bureau's chronology of business cycles. These are the general declines that began in 1948, 1953, 1957, and 1960. They are listed as recessions because they appeared to conform to the working definition of business cycles formulated to guide the National Bureau's researches, as it was revised in 1946.[6] (The date is important: the definition could not take into account the post-World War II experience.)

We can begin to understand this definition if we read it with an eye on the measured characteristics of the identified recessions listed in Table 1.

Business recessions were assumed, on the basis of the experience to 1946 (revealed by, or presumed from, business annals, statistical time-series analyses and business-cycle hypotheses) to be a distinct type of change in aggregate economic activity.[7] More specifically, recessions were taken to be a type of contraction in aggregate economic activity. So viewed, a recession is not a decline in the rate of growth of aggregate economic activity to a lower but still positive rate of growth; nor, more particularly, is it a decline to a rate

[6] There have been some shifts in terminology. "Recession" was formerly used to denote the downturn phase of the business cycles, that is, the peak or the zone surrounding the peak, and "contraction," to denote the declining phase. In recent years the declining phase has come to be labled "recession," perhaps with the connotation of a relatively mild contraction of the kind experienced in the post-World War II period. In the present discussion, the current usage is adopted. "Peak" or "downturn," then, takes the place of "recession" in denoting the phase during which expansion of aggregate economic activity is converted into decline.

[7] In what follows I have borrowed freely the language used by Burns and Mitchell, p. 3.

TABLE 1

Selected Measures of Duration, Depth, and Diffusion of Business-Cycle
Contractions, 1920—70
(by dates of contractions)

	1/20-7/21	5/23-7/24	10/26-11/27	8/29-3/33
1. Dates of Corresponding *Specific-Cycle Contractions*				
GNP, current dollars				
(quarterly)	IV21	I24-III24[*]	IV26-IV27[*]	III29-I33
GNP, constant dollars				
(quarterly)	IV21	II24-III24[*]	I26-II26[*]	III29-III32
Index of industrial production	2/20-4/21	5/23-7/24	3/27-11/27	7/29-7/32
Employees in nonagric. estab.				8/29-3/33
Man-hours in nonagric. estab.				
Personal income, current				
dollars		I24-II24	II26-IV26	8/29-3/33
Personal income, constant				
dollars		I24-II24	III26-IV26	4/29-3/33
Department store sales	7/20-3/22	**	**	9/29-3/33
Retail sales, current dollars				
Retail sales, constant dollars				
Mfg. & trade sales, current				
dollars				
Mfg. & trade sales, constant				
dollars				
Unemployment rate, civilian				
workers (inverted)				8/29-5/33*
Composite index [Shiskin] :				
6 coincident indicators				
unweighted	1/20-7/21	6/23-7/24	3/27-10/27[*]	8/29-3/33
weighted				
Composite index:				
5 coincident indicators				
weighted [BCD]				
weighted and deflated [NBER]				
Composite index [Mintz] :				
17 indicators, unweighted				

(Continued)

5/37-6/38	2/45-10/45	11/48-10/49	7/53-8/54	7/57-4/58	5/60-2/61	11/69-8/70[a]
III37-II38	II45-IV45	IV48-IV49	II53-II54	III57-I58	II60-IV60	**
III37-I38		IV48-II49	II53-II54	III57-I58	I60-I61	III69-I70
5/37-5/38	11/43-2/46	7/48-10/49	7/53-4/54	2/57-4/58	1/60-2/61	7/69-8/70
7/37-6/38	11/43-9/45	9/48-10/49	4/53-8/54	3/57-5/58	4/60-2/61	3/70-8/70
	11/43-12/45	7/48-10/49	3/53-9/54	12/56-4/58	4/60-12/60	12/69-8/70
6/37-5/38	6/45-9/45	10/48-7/49	10/53-4/54	8/57-12/57	**	**
6/37-5/38	2/45-9/45	11/48-7/49	5/53-1/54	8/57-4/58	**	3/70-6/70
10/37-10/38	**	10/48-7/49	5/53-1/54	8/57-2/58	**	
9/37-5/38	**	**	3/53-1/54	8/57-3/58	4/60-4/61	**
		**	3/53-12/53	8/57-3/58	4/60-4/61	2/69-12/69
	3/45-9/45	8/48-10/49	7/53-8/54	2/57-3/58	1/60-1/61	10/69-1/70
		7/48-10/49	4/53-12/53	2/57-4/58	1/60-1/61	9/69-4/70
7/37-6/38	10/44-5/46	12/47-10/49	6/53-9/54	3/57-7/58	6/59-5/61	2/69-8/70
7/37-5/38		10/48-10/49	7/53-5/54	8/57-4/58	5/60-2/61	
		10/48-10/49	7/53-5/54	8/57-4/58	4/60-2/61	
		10/48-10/49	7/53-8/54	8/57-4/58	2/60-2/61	12/69-8/70
		10/48-10/49	7/53-5/54	3/57-4/58	2/60-2/61	10/69-8/70
		10/48-10/49	6/53-7/54	8/57-5/58	4/60-2/61	

(Continued)

TABLE 1 (Continued)

	1/20-7/21	5/23-7/24	10/26-11/27	8/29-3/33
2. *Duration of Corresponding Specific-Cycle Contractions (in months)*				
Reference cycle	18	14	13	43
GNP, current dollars (quarterly)		6	12	42
GNP, constant dollars (quarterly)		3	3	36
Index of industrial production	14	14	8	36
Employees in nonagric. estab.				43
Man-hours in nonagric. estab.				
Personal income, current dollars		3	6	43
Personal income, constant dollars		3	3	47
Department store sales	20	**	**	42
Retail sales, current dollars				
Retail sales, constant dollars				
Mfg. & trade sales, current dollars				
Mfg. & trade sales, constant dollars				
Unemployment rate, civilian workers (inverted)				45
Composite index [Shiskin]:				
6 coincident indicators				
unweighted	18	13	7	43
weighted				
Composite index:				
5 coincident indicators				
weighted [BCD]				
weighted and deflated [NBER]				
Composite index [Mintz]:				
17 indicators, unweighted				

(Continued)

5/37-6/38	2/45-10/45	11/48-10/49	7/53-8/54	7/57-4/58	5/60-2/61	11/69-8/70[a]
13	8	11	13	9	9	9
9	6	12	12	6	6	**
6		6	12	6	12	6
12	27	15	9	14	13	13
11	22	13	16	14	10	5
	25	15	18	16	8	8
11	3	9	6	4	**	**
11	7	8	8	8	**	3
12	**	9	8	6	**	
8	**	**	10	7	12	**
		**	9	7	12	10
	6	14	13	13	12	3
		15	8	14	12	7
11	19	22	15	16	23	18
10		12	10	8	9	
		12	10	8	10	
		12	13	8	12	8
		12	10	13	12	10
		12	13	9	10	

(Continued)

TABLE 1 (Continued)

	1/20-7/21 Cycle		5/23-7/24 Cycle		10/26-11/27 Cycle		8/29-3/33 Cycle	
	Ref.	Spec.	Ref.	Spec.	Ref.	Spec.	Ref.	Spec.
3. Total Percentage Change[b]								
GNP, current dollars (quarterly)			-2.3	-4.9	+0.4	-3.0	-49.6	-49.6
GNP, constant dollars (quarterly)			-0.4	-4.1	+2.3	-2.0	-28.0	-32.6
Index of industrial production	-31.7	-32.4	-17.9	-17.9	-5.9	-7.0	-51.8	-53.4
Employees in nonagric. estab.							-31.6	-31.6
Man-hours in nonagric. estab.								
Personal income, current dollars			0.0	-3.6	+0.9	-2.5	-50.8	-50.8
Personal income, constant dollars			-0.5	-2.9	+1.7	-3.0	-32.1	-32.7
Department stores sales	-4.8	-17.4	-4.4	**	0.0	**	-44.0	-46.2
Retail sales, current dollars								
Retail sales, constant dollars								
Mfg. & trade sales, current dollars								
Mfg. & trade sales, constant dollars								
Unemployment rate, civilian workers[c]							+25.3	+25.6
Composite index [Shiskin]:								
6 coincident indicators								
unweighted	-42.3	-42.3	-14.3	-14.9	-1.2	-2.4	-67.0	-67.0
weighted								
Composite index:								
5 coincident indicators								
weighted [BCD]								
weighted and deflated [NBER]								
Composite index [Mintz]:								
17 indicators, unweighted								

(Continued)

5/37-6/38 Cycle		2/45-10/45 Cycle		11/48-10/49 Cycle		7/53-8/54 Cycle		7/57-4/58 Cycle		5/60-2/61 Cycle		11/69-8/70[a] Cycle	
Ref.	Spec.	Ref.	Spec.	Ref.	Spec.	Ref.	Spec.	Ref.	Spec.	Ref.	Spec.	Ref.	Spec.
-11.9	-16.2	-10.9	-11.9	-3.4	-3.4	-0.8	-1.9	-1.8	-2.6	-0.2	-0.3	+3.5	**
-8.9	-13.2			-1.6	-1.9	-2.2	-3.4	-3.4	-3.9	-1.4	-1.6	-0.2	-1.0
-31.7	-32.4	-31.4	-38.3	-8.5	-9.9	-9.0	-10.0	-14.1	-14.3	-5.7	-7.2	-1.5	-3.3
-10.4	-10.8	-7.9	-10.1	-5.1	-5.2	-3.4	-3.4	-4.0	-4.3	-1.8	-2.2	-0.6	-1.2
		-11.6	-15.3	-6.1	-6.6	-4.5	-5.2	-5.2	-6.1	-2.0	-3.2	-1.3	-1.5
-11.0	-12.6	-4.0	-6.8	-4.6	-5.7	0.0	-1.5	+0.4	-0.5	+1.0	**	+4.7	**
-9.3	-10.8	-5.6	-7.5	-2.7	-3.0	-0.2	-1.5	-1.8	-2.1	0.0	**	+0.5	-0.9
-12.5	-12.5	+6.7	**	-4.4	-12.3	0.0	-7.2	-1.0	-8.1	+1.0	**		
-15.0	-16.7	+9.9	**	0.0	**	-0.7	-4.9	-1.6	-3.8	-2.4	-4.6	+4.1	**
				+3.9	**	+0.5	-5.0	-3.5	-5.4	-3.1	-5.0	+1.1	-4.2
		-10.6	-16.5	-7.5	-8.7	-7.2	-7.2	-6.8	-8.2	-3.2	-5.2	+2.5	-1.6
				-2.8	-3.6	-7.0	-7.6	-7.9	-10.2	-3.6	-5.7	-0.2	-3.6
+8.8	+9.0	+2.2	+3.4	+4.1	+4.8	+3.4	+3.6	+3.2	+3.8	+1.8	+2.1	+1.6	+1.8
-23.8	-24.9			-9.4	-10.0	-8.0	-8.4	-8.5	-8.9	-4.7	-4.7		
				-10.7	-11.4	-8.1	-8.2	-8.9	-9.3	-3.7	-4.0		
				-13.5	-14.0	-11.0	-11.0	-11.2	-11.7	-4.8	-5.3	-0.7	-0.7
				-12.2	-12.6	-11.4	-11.6	-12.5	-13.4	-5.4	-6.1	-2.2	-2.3
				-12.9	-13.2	-9.5	-10.4	-11.4	-12.1	-5.0	-5.4		

(Continued)

TABLE 1 (Continued)

	1/20-7/21 Cycle		5/23-7/24 Cycle		10/26-11/27 Cycle		8/29-3/33 Cycle	
	Ref.	Spec.	Ref.	Spec.	Ref.	Spec.	Ref.	Spec.
4. Percentage Change per Month (at annual rate)								
GNP, current dollars (quarterly)			-1.8	-9.9	+0.3	-3.0	-14.2	-14.2
GNP, constant dollars (quarterly)			-0.3	-16.4	+1.8	-7.9	-8.0	-10.9
Index of industrial production	-21.1	-27.8	-15.3	-15.3	-5.4	-10.4	-14.4	-17.8
Employees in nonagric. estab.							-8.8	-8.8
Man-hours in nonagric. estab.								
Personal income, current dollars			0.0	-14.5	+0.7	-5.0	-14.2	-14.2
Personal income, constant dollars			-0.4	-11.4	-1.3	-12.1	-9.0	-8.3
Department store sales	-3.2	-10.4	-3.7	**	0.0	**	-12.8	-13.2
Retail sales, current dollars								
Retail sales, constant dollars								
Mfg. & trade sales, current dollars								
Mfg. & trade sales, constant dollars								
Unemployment rate, civilian workers[c]							+7.1	+6.8
Composite index [Shiskin]: 6 coincident indicators unweighted	-28.2	-28.2	-12.3	-13.8	-1.1	-4.0	-18.7	-18.7
weighted								
Composite index: 5 coincident indicators weighted [BCD]								
weighted and deflated [NBER]								
Composite index [Mintz]: 17 indicators, unweighted								

(Continued)

5/37-6/38 Cycle		2/45-10/45 Cycle		11/48-10/49 Cycle		7/53-8/54 Cycle		7/57-4/58 Cycle		5/60-2/61 Cycle		11/69-8/70 [a] Cycle	
Ref.	Spec.	Ref.	Spec.	Ref.	Spec.	Ref.	Spec.	Ref.	Spec.	Ref.	Spec.	Ref.	Spec.
-11.9	-21.5	-14.5	-23.8	-3.4	-3.4	-0.6	-1.9	-2.4	-5.2	-0.3	-0.6	+4.7	**
-8.9	-26.4			-1.6	-3.8	-1.8	-3.4	-4.6	-7.8	-1.9	-1.6	-0.3	-1.9
-29.2	-32.4	-47.1	-17.0	-9.3	-7.9	-8.4	-13.3	-18.8	-12.3	-7.6	-6.7	-1.9	-3.0
-9.6	-11.8	-11.9	-5.5	-5.5	-4.8	-3.1	-2.5	-5.3	-3.7	-2.4	-2.7	-0.8	-2.9
		-17.4	-7.3	-6.7	-5.3	-4.2	-3.4	-7.0	-4.5	-2.6	-4.7	-1.7	-2.2
-10.1	-13.8	-6.0	-27.2	-5.1	-7.6	0.0	-3.0	+0.5	-1.5	+1.3	**	+6.3	**
-8.6	-11.8	-8.3	-12.9	-2.9	-4.5	-0.2	-2.6	-2.4	-3.2	0.0	**	+0.6	-3.6
-11.5	-12.5	+10.0	**	-4.7	-16.4	0.0	-10.8	-1.4	-16.2	+1.3	**		
-13.9	-25.0	+14.9	**	0.0	**	-0.6	-5.9	-2.1	-6.5	-3.3	-4.6	+5.5	**
				+4.3	**	+0.4	-6.7	-4.7	-9.2	-4.1	-5.0	+1.5	-5.0
		-15.9	-32.9	-8.1	-7.5	-6.7	-6.7	-9.0	-7.6	-4.3	-5.2	+3.3	-6.2
				-3.0	-2.9	-6.5	-11.4	-10.5	-8.7	-4.8	-5.7	-0.3	-6.2
+8.1	+9.9	+3.3	+2.1	+4.5	+2.6	+3.1	+2.9	+4.3	+2.8	+2.4	+1.1	+2.1	+1.2
-22.0	-29.9			-10.2	-10.0	-7.4	-10.1	-11.4	-13.3	-6.3	-6.3		
				-11.7	-11.4	-7.5	-9.9	-11.8	-14.0	-4.9	-4.8		
				-14.7	-14.0	-10.1	-10.1	-14.9	-17.5	-6.5	-5.3	-1.0	-1.1
				-13.3	-12.6	-10.5	-13.9	-16.7	-12.4	-7.3	-6.1	-3.0	-3.4
				-14.1	-13.2	-8.8	-9.6	-15.3	-16.1	-6.7	-6.4		

(Continued)

Table 1 (Concluded)

	1/20-7/21	5/23-7/24	10/26-11/27	8/29-3/33
5. Diffusion				
Maximum % of industries declining (6-month span) nonfarm employment, 30 industries industrial production, 15-24 industries	88	78	72	100
Number of consecutive months when 75% or more of industries are declining (6-month span) nonfarm employment, 30 industries industrial production, 15-24 industries	2	1	0	27

Note: Blanks indicate data not available; *, not recognized as a specific cycle according to the standard NBER procedure; **, no specific cycle.

Source: Series are seasonally adjusted, except those series that appear to contain no seasonal movement. The table is based, with modifications and extensions, on a table prepared by G. H. Moore, "What is a Recession?," *The American Statistician,* October 1967.

GNP: H. Barger and L. R. Klein, 1921-29; Department of Commerce (OBE) 1929-70.

Index of industrial production; Federal Reserve Board.

Employees in nonagricultural establishments: Department of Labor, Bureau of Labor Statistics.

Manhours in nonagricultural establishments: Department of Labor, Bureau of Labor Statistics.

Personal income: H. Barger and L. R. Klein, 1923-29; Department of Commerce (OBE) 1929-70. Adjusted by the NBER for retroactive Social Security and federal pay increases. In constant dollars: NBER; deflated by the Consumer Price Index.

Index of department store sales: Federal Reserve Board. Discontinued January 1964.

5/37-6/38	2/45-10/45	11/48-10/49	7/53-8/54	7/57-4/58	5/60-2/61	11/69-8/70[a]
		90	87	88	83	88
	100	92	96	100	88	75
		8	10	10	7	3
	8	4	7	8	5	1

Retail sales: Department of Commerce, Bureau of the Census. In constant dollars: NBER; deflated by the CPI, all commodities (which excludes services). For 1937–55, the monthly deflator series is a straight-line interpolation of the quarterly series.

Manufacturing and trade sales: Department of Commerce, Office of Business Economics and Bureau of the Census. In constant dollars: NBER. Each of the major components was deflated separately by the appropriate BLS price index: retail trade sales, as above; wholesale trade sales – durable, by the WPI, all commodities, durable goods; wholesale trade sales – nondurable, by the WPI, all commodities, nondurable goods; and manufacturers' sales, by the WPI, total manufacturers.

Unemployment rate, all civilian workers (14 years old and over, 1929-46; 16 years old and over, 1947-70): NICB, 1929–40; Department of Commerce, Bureau of the Census, 1940–70.

Composite index (Shiskin), 6 coincident indicators (unweighted): Julius Shiskin, *Signals of Recession and Recovery: An Experiment with Monthly Reporting*, New York, NBER, 1961, and an unpublished table.

Composite index (Shiskin), 6 coincident indicators (weighted): Same as the preceding, but weighted by conformity score, Geoffrey H. Moore and Julius Shiskin, *Indicators of Business Expansions and Contractions*, New York, NBER, 1967; unpublished NBER table.

(Continued)

Notes to Table 1 (Concluded)

Composite index (BCD), 5 coincident indicators (weighted): BCD. Personal income is unadjusted for retroactive pay.

Composite index (NBER), 5 coincident indicators, (weighted and deflated): This is the BCD composite of 5 coincident indicators deflated by the NBER. The deflation applies to personal income and manufacturing and trade sales (see above). Deflated manufacturing and trade sales were not available for August 1970, when the computation was made.

Composite index (Mintz), 17 indicators (unweighted): See Mintz's paper, included in this volume. 12 of the indicators are "roughly coincident" indicators; one is a "leading" indicator; 3 are "lagging" indicators; and one is an indicator not classified by timing.

Diffusion index, nonfarm employment, 30 industries: BCD.

Diffusion index, industrial production, 15-24 industries: unpublished NBER table, 1919-38; *BCD*, 1948-70.

[a]Assumed.

[b]Based on one-month standings at peaks and troughs.

[c]In percentage points.

of growth still positive but inferior to the secular rate. A recession is characterized by a *negative* rate of growth in aggregate economic activity. No recession included in the chronology fails to have this characteristic.[8]

No specification of amplitude——severity of decline, either total or per month——is given in the definition. It is simply recognized that the amplitude is highly variable as, indeed, are many other business cycle characteristics. The measurements collected in Table 1 show that for the recessions recognized as having occurred between 1920 and 1961, the smallest decline in aggregate economic activity is no more than 2 or 3 per cent. During the recession of 1926–27, according to a composite made up of six "coinciding" series measuring both pecuniary and real activity, aggregate activity fell by

---

[8] It is barely possible——this is mere surmise——that one or two of the pre-World War I recessions included in the National Bureau's chronology involved no absolute decline. Some of the monthly data used in developing the earlier reference cycles related to trend-adjusted indexes of business activity. These indexes could show declines when, in fact, aggregate economic activity continued to rise, though less rapidly than the trend. (The same can obviously be said of the unemployment rate, one of the indicators used in identifying the more recent recessions.)

Contributing to this possibility may have been other deficiencies of the earlier data. In particular, the amplitude of fluctuations in the earlier periods may be overstated relative to the amplitude in recent periods, as a result of improvements in the data.

about 2.5 per cent; GNP in constant prices, by 2 per cent; and GNP in current prices, by 3 per cent. Industrial production declined by more, 7 per cent; and unemployment (omitted from the table because available only on an annual basis) rose by 2.2 percentage points. As I have already emphasized, the figures are very rough and not entirely consistent, but they seem sufficient to put 1926–27 at or close to the bottom of the list. The recession of 1960–61 is a close contender, however. In this recession, the six-series composite fell over 4.5 per cent, but GNP in constant prices declined only 1.5 per cent, and in current prices, less than a half per cent. In this recession, also, occurred the smallest rise in the unemployment rate (on a monthly basis)––somewhat more than 2 percentage points.

Further, a recession consists of contractions occurring at about the same time in many economic activities. That is, the declines are widely diffused throughout the economy. If only because the contractions in various economic activities occur at about the same time, not at exactly the same time, the scope of a recession is typically narrowest at its beginning and end, and widest between. In all recessions, of course, the minimum proportion of activities that join in the decline is in excess of 50 per cent; otherwise aggregate economic activity, measured in any reasonable way, could not be declining. But recessions vary also with regard to the maximum. Even in the most widely diffused recession, the fraction has never reached 100 per cent, for many new industries, and some old as well, continue to expand their markets even when business is generally shrinking[9]. The most narrowly diffused recession, according to the maximum percentage of industries with declining output, was 1926–27 with a maximum of 72 per cent. In the recession of 1960–61, next in this regard, the percentage was 88.

While milder in the other respects mentioned, in duration the 1926-27 recession, which lasted about thirteen months, was not greatly below average. In the full record, there are five recessions with a much shorter duration: the 1960–61 and 1957–58 recessions, nine months; and three with even shorter durations (the very shortest being the postwar recession of 1918–19 which lasted only seven months). Business recessions in the National Bureau's list have varied in duration from seven months to sixty-five months (1873–79),

[9]During the recessions of 1929–33 and 1937–38, production in every one of the fifteen to twenty-four mining and manufacturing industries distinguished declined over at least one six-month span. But this unanimity probably reflects only the gross character of the industrial classification. Were monthly records available for production in the many more narrowly defined industries distinguished in the SIC, it is very likely that there would be a significant number of industries with rising output.

with an average of about nineteen months over the period since 1854.[10] The recessions have usually been shorter than the expanding phases of business cycles, which have averaged about thirty months in the United States.

Moreover, business recessions are a phase of business cycles, a type of economic fluctuation in which recessions are followed by similarly general upturns, expansions, and downturns that merge into the recession phase of the next cycle. Implicit here is the notion——of which we shall make use later——that business recessions are identified not only by the characteristics already mentioned, but also by the developments that typically precede and follow them. While this sequence of changes is recurrent, it is not periodic, as the variety of durations has already made evident.

We shall have to come back, at a later point, also to another, related, part of the 1946 definition of business cycles: the requirement that they not be "divisible into shorter cycles of similar character with amplitudes approximating their own." For the moment, however, we concentrate on the three characteristics first mentioned. We ask how developments during 1969–70 compare, with respect to these characteristics, with the recessions already recognized.

V

The recession that began in 1969——if we may call it a recession——may or may not have ended. We should take this uncertainty into account when we compare the changes in aggregate economic activity during 1969–70 with the changes during past recessions. That is, we should not confine ourselves to a comparison of the changes during 1969–70 with the changes during the *full* run of past recessions. A useful supplement is a comparison of the average rates (or amounts) of change per month, over the period that has elapsed since the presumed peak in 1969, with the corresponding average monthly changes during the earlier recessions. There is evidence that after a recession or pause has run some six months or more, its characteristics will have been fairly firmly established.[11] We can therefore make a good, though hardly perfect, estimate of its eventual intensity and pervasiveness relative to series of events identified as recessions in the past.   There are several ways to

[10]G.H. Moore (ed.), *Business Cycle Indicators,* Princeton for NBER, 1961, vol. I, App. A; updated in *Business Conditions Digest.*
  Different indicators give somewhat different results, as is easily seen in the chart. The reference-cycle chronology may be thought of as representing the average values of these results.

[11]G.H. Moore, "Measuring Recessions," in *Business Cycle Indicators,* vol. I, pp. 120–161.

make this comparison. The results differ very little, however, so we limit our attention here to comparisons of changes over periods of identical length, counting from the peak (or assumed peak). We make the comparisons using about the same proportion of real and pecuniary series that were used in deciding on the past recessions.

A reference peak in 1969 must be assumed. Which month seems most appropriate? To answer this question we follow the procedure of studying the behavior of each of the indicators of aggregate economic activity and noting if and when it reached a high point, in 1969–70 (or earlier), from which it has receded (Table 2). We find, what is not surprising, that the real series generally peaked before the pecuniary series. Every one of the real series has already shown some decline from its high point. For industrial production and GNP in 1958 dollars, the peak was as early as July 1969 and the third quarter of 1969, respectively. For the five-coincider composite (with all components in real terms), it was October; and for employment and man-hours worked, it was around the turn of the year.[12] In contrast, some of the pecuniary series had not peaked as of September 1970 (GNP in current dollars, for example, and most of the price series) and those that did, peaked late.

This wide dispersion of turning points raises more than the usual difficulties in choosing a reference peak. My tentative choice is November 1969 although it so happens that none of the individual series in Table 2 actually reached a peak in that month. December seems to be an almost equally good candidate, but the declines from the peak are much the same whether one or the other of these (or of still other possible alternatives) is taken as the month of the turn.[13]

The latest quarter for which GNP and other quarterly series are available is the third quarter of 1970, which we may take as centered at August——nine months after November 1969. We therefore make our comparison of 1969–70 with changes over the first nine months of past recessions. As Chart 1 and Table 1 have already made clear, 1969–70 was so mild that the

[12]Inclusive of proprietors and unpaid family workers, man-hours worked in the private economy reached a peak in the third quarter of 1969; see the Bureau of Labor Statistics release on "Productivity, Wages, and Prices: Second Quarter, 1970," issued August 4, 1970. (However, the difference between the third and fourth quarters is very small, whether or not proprietors and family workers are included.) Inclusive also of government workers, man-hours reached a peak in the fourth quarter.

[13]According to the indicators of "real" economic activity, the turn would probably be dated October, or perhaps even September, 1969. Mintz's composite of seventeen real and pecuniary series reached its peak in April 1970 at the earliest; the *BCD* composite, in December 1969.

TABLE 2

"Roughly Coincident" Cyclical Indicators,
by Month of Most Recent Peak
(as of September 30, 1970)

Peak	BCD No.	Indicator Series	Type of Series "Pecuniary"	"Real"
May 1968	49	Nonagric. job openings unfilled		X
Feb. 1969	43	Unemployment rate, total		X
	*54d	Sales of retail stores, deflated		X
March 1969	40	Unemployment rate, married males		X
May 1969	45	Avg. wkly. insured unempl. rate, state programs		X
	96	Mfrs. unfilled orders, dur. goods indus.	X	
	*—	Merchant wholesalers' sales, deflated		X
July 1969	47	Index of industrial production		X
III/1969	205	GNP, in 1958 dollars		X
Sept. 1969	46	Index of help-wanted advertising in newspapers		X
Oct. 1969	*56d	*Mfg. and trade sales, deflated*		X
	*—	Mfrs. sales, deflated		X
	*—	Wage & salary personal income, commodity producing indus., deflated		X
	*820d	*Composite index, 5 coinciders, deflated*		X
IV/1969	97	Backlog of capital appropriations, mfg.	X	
Dec. 1969	48	Man-hours in nonagric. establishments		X
	820	*Composite index, 5 coinciders*	X	
Jan. 1970	42	Persons engaged in nonagric. activities, labor force survey		X
	114	Treasury bill rate	X	
March 1970	41	No. of employees on nonagric. payrolls, establishment survey		X
	*52d	Personal income, deflated (adjusted)		X
	53	Wages & salaries in mining, mfg. & construction	X	
May 1970	117	Municipal bond yields	X	
June 1970	116	Corporate bond yields	X	
	115	Treasury bond yields	X	
July 1970	93	Free reserves	X	

Series with latest available item the highest:

Table 2 (concluded)

II/1970	200	GNP, in current dollars	X
	57	Final sales	X
July 1970	54	Sales of retail stores	X
	56	Mfg. and trade sales	X
Aug. 1970	52	Personal income (adjusted)	X
	55	Index of wholesale prices, indus. comm.	X
	58	Index of wholesale prices, mfd. goods	X

Source: *Business Conditions Digest,* September 1970, with exceptions indic. .ed by an asterisk. Deflated pecuniary coinciding series were assumed to be coinciding series, in the absence of an analysis. Peak period is as given in *BCD,* or as determined by us. No. is the *BCD* number: with "d" added, it is the *BCD* series deflated by the NBER. Series not in *BCD* are unnumbered.

Interest rate series and the composite (#820), which includes two series in current prices, are treated as pecuniary series.

Composites and aggregates for which components are shown separately are italicized.

The personal income series, #52d, was adjusted for retroactive payments before deflation.

comparison need not extend beyond the recessions of 1926–27 and 1960–61. (Since the recession of 1960–61 lasted only nine months, the changes in Table 3 relate to its full run.) To these we add the "slowdown" in 1966–67.[14]

Of the series included in the comparison (Table 3) none declined between November 1969 and August 1970 more than during the 1960–61 recession. Industrial production, for example, fell by only 1.7 per cent after November 1969 as compared with the 5.6 per cent decline in 1960; GNP in constant dollars, by 0.2 per cent, as compared with 1.4 per cent; and man-hours worked in nonagricultural establishments, by 1.3 per cent as compared with 2.0. GNP in current prices rose by 3.5 per cent during the recent period, but fell minutely during 1960–61. Personal income, also in current prices, rose by over 4.5 per cent, but by only about 1 per cent during 1960–61. Retail sales rose during 1969–70, fell during 1960–61. The composite of five-coinciding indicators declined by little more than half a per cent, as

[14]GNP (in 1958 dollars) and industrial production declined from the fourth quarter of 1966, so we take November 1966 as the "peak." If the slowdown that dates from November 1966 is viewed as being over before August 1967, which is not unreasonable, the nine-month changes in Table 3 "bridge the valley" and therefore provide too favorable a picture of what happened during 1966–67. But any reasonable comparison of 1966–67 with 1969–70 would yield much the same conclusion.

TABLE 3

Changes in Selected Indicators of Economic Activity Between
November 1969 and August 1970, Compared with Corresponding
Nine-Month Changes during the Business Cycle Contractions
of 1926–27 and 1960–61 and the "Pause" of 1966–67

	Reference Peaks			
	Oct. 1926	May 1960	Nov. 1966	Nov. 1969
GNP, current dollars (quarterly)	+0.5	−0.2	+3.9	+3.5
GNP, constant dollars (quarterly)	+1.7	−1.4	+1.6	−0.2
Industrial production	−2.4	−5.6	−0.6	−1.7
Nonagricultural employment		−1.9	+1.6	−0.6
Man-hours in nonagric. establishments		−2.0	+0.9	−1.3
Personal income[a]		+1.1	+5.0	+4.6
Personal income, deflated [a]		+0.2	+3.0	+0.5
Retail sales		−2.9	+3.1	+4.3
Retail sales, deflated		−3.5	+1.6	+1.3
Manufacturing and trade sales		−3.6	+2.0	+2.3
Manufacturing and trade sales, deflated		−3.8	+1.3	−0.4
Unemployment rate (inverted)[b]		+1.7	+0.1	+1.5
Ampl. adj. composite index, 6 coin. series[c]	−0.9	−4.5		
Ampl. adj. composite index, 5 coin. series[d]		−4.8	+3.4	−0.8
Ampl. adj. composite index, 5 coin. series, deflated [d]		−5.4	+2.8	−2.1

Source: See Table 1. Blank spaces indicate data not available.

[a]Data adjusted for retroactive (Social Security and Federal) pay increases.

[b]Change in percentage points.

[c]Unweighted by score. Includes BCD series nos. 41, 43, 47, 51, 52, 54.

[d]Weighted by score. Includes BCD series nos. 41, 43, 47, 52, 56. Personal income unadjusted for retroactive (Social Security and Federal) pay increases. The deflated series does not include manufacturing and trade sales for August 1970.

compared with over 4.5 per cent in 1960–61. In fact, in these terms *none* of the aggregate activity series shows a decline greater than the least recorded in *any* postwar recession. The diffusion indexes are consistent with this picture. The only exception is deflated retail sales; this series rose, but not quite as much as it had during 1948–49.

We cannot be as definite about the comparison with the very mild recession of 1926–27. Industrial output fell a little more during the first nine months of the 1926–27 recession than during the 1969–70, and GNP in current prices rose less. On the other hand, GNP in constant prices fell in only one quarter during 1926–27, as Table 1 showed; over the nine months after the peak in October 1926, this series rose. However, prewar GNP data, in current or constant dollars, and even the other data, are far too rough for fine comparisons. About all we can say, even with the help of data not included in the tables here, is that 1969–70 may have been milder even than 1926–27.

To conclude: Measured in this way——using pecuniary as well as physical volume series——up to the latest date for which information is available (mainly August 1970), aggregate economic activity fell less from November 1969 than during the first nine months of any postwar recession. This can be said, but with less confidence, also of the 1969–70 record in comparison with the interwar recession of 1926–27. It is very clear, however, that 1969–70 has not been as mild as 1966–67, which was not recorded as a recession.

If such declines in aggregate pecuniary and real activity as occurred during 1969–70 came to an end during the summer of 1970, as some economists surmise, this conclusion about its mildness is strengthened. The decline from 1969 would then have lasted only about eight or nine months. The *total* decline during 1969–70, relative to the total decline during 1960–61 (which lasted nine months), would have been no greater and could have been less than the equal-period comparison made above. Relative to 1926–27, which lasted thirteen months, the total decline could also have been less (Table 1).

Two questions immediately arise. First, what would happen if we abandon the use of pecuniary series, or more correctly, deflate them before making our comparisons? Second, why accept 1960 (or 1926) as setting a lower bound? We consider these questions in turn.

VI

As everybody knows, the general price level has been rising more sharply in recent years than at any other time since the outbreak of the Korean war. Statistical series measuring economic activity in terms of current-price values will be affected by these price changes to a greater degree now than in most earlier periods.

As we expect, then, more of the indicators of activity declined during 1969—70, and the declines were greater, measured in real terms. The changes during 1969—70 bear a closer resemblance to those that occurred during the mildest of the recessions recorded since World War I than those during the pause of 1966—67, from which it differs sharply. The shift in relative position is small when measured in absolute terms, but not relative to the "distance" between 1969—70 and the mildest recorded recessions.

Further, the replacement of the pecuniary indicators by their deflated counterparts usually means a shift in the dating of the reference peaks, a shift that will be greater for some cycles than for others. Changes in reference dates, in turn, can alter the results of the comparisons we have been making. In particular, the decline in real aggregate economic activity during 1969—70 (from September 1969, rather than November 1969) would become slightly larger while the decline during 1960—61 would not be changed significantly.

But why should we deflate, when we ask whether a given series of events constitute a recession?

Consider an extreme case, when the price level is moving up very rapidly. If the inflation were ignored, recessions would never be found; not because a rising price level is always "good for business," but rather because many of the individual indexes of aggregate economic activity, and the indexes taken as a whole, are biased upward by the shrinking purchasing power of the monetary unit. Declines in the physical volume indicators would be offset or even swamped by rapid rises in the pecuniary indicators: an average of real and pecuniary indicators would not fall.[15]

Obviously, when price levels change but slowly or recessions are of considerable amplitude, as was usually the case before World War II, the deflation question is of small importance. Pecuniary indicators are only slightly affected by price level changes; they provide only slightly biased information on real changes. When price levels change rapidly and recession amplitudes are small, however, this is no longer true.

One can, of course, think of objections to concentrating on real indicators, when we ask whether a recession is under way and how severe it is. I do not find these objections convincing, but they deserve some discussion.

First, changes in price-cost relationships and fluctuations in the rate of change of the general price level constitute major elements in the process by

---

[15] The BCD type of composite involves a "standardization" adjustment to put each component "on an equal basis." So, in effect, does a cumulative diffusion index. But these adjustments cannot entirely avoid the problem caused by a rising price level.

which a business expansion attains momentum and gradually develops the restrictive forces that tend to bring it to an end. Similarly, prices and costs play a part in the process by which recessions breed revivals. We cannot adequately describe what happens during business cycles, or adequately explain what happens, without referring to price changes. However, it seems to me that neither of these is our present objective. We ask, only, whether a recession is under way and how severe it is.

True, we can reduce our uncertainty about the answer, when we are uncertain, by taking account of the developments that occurred in prices, costs, and profits (and other aspects of economic life) during the period prior to the slowdown in question, as well as those that occur during the recession itself. To take these into account in this way, however——as I do at a later point——does not preclude or argue against concentration on measures of real economic activity for our present purpose.

There is an alternative procedure that may go some distance towards taking care of the measurement problems created by inflation, and yet at the same time help meet the objection I have been describing. We could limit ourselves to "deflating out" only the *trend*, and particularly the trend in the general price level, and thus avoid deflating out the cyclical changes in prices, if these are believed essential to a proper judgment on the course of aggregate economic activity.[16] Applying such a procedure would yield a result that, roughly speaking, falls somewhere between the result obtained by following the full deflation procedure and that obtained by completely ignoring the deflation problem. However, I find this alternative more attractive when our question is what happens during business cycles.

It may be said, second, that when we worry about recessions, we worry about the changing distribution of real income and wealth, as well as about changes in the aggregate. When the general price level changes, large transfers of real income and wealth take place. Should not these changes in the general price level, therefore, be taken into account? There is good reason to worry, for these (and other) serious effects of recessions are not distributed evenly. It would probably be desirable, in fact, to include among the criteria used to determine the severity of a recession some series that are designed to measure

[16]Deflating out the trend in the general price level would also avoid deflating out the trends in relative prices, when the value or price series being deflated relate to sectors——not the whole——of the economy.

To deflate interest rates means, of course, to *subtract* the annual percentage trend rate of change in the general price level.

the distribution effects. However, the undeflated series do not serve this purpose. Nor do price indexes.[17,18]

Quite different is the objection that physical volume data, or data on the prices required for reducing pecuniary to volume series, are insufficient in quantity and quality for our purpose, even in an economy as rich in statistics as the United States is today. That is, we simply cannot afford to neglect pecuniary series. However, to measure aggregate economic activity in real terms hardly means to neglect undeflated series. Pecuniary series may and should be used, as has already been indicated, when price data are scarce and there is reason to believe that price changes are probably small in relation to the changes in the undeflated series. The latter will be good approximations to the deflated series. When price changes are large, however, and good price data are scarce, the use of a crude deflator tailored to the series, or even of an

[17]It might be desirable, also, to take account——somehow——of the fact that a given percentage decline in output or employment from a high level is, in a significant sense, less severe than the same percentage decline from a low level. The changes during the 1960–61 recession were worse than in 1969–70 because the rise in unemployment started from a peak in 1960 of 5 per cent, and in 1969, from a peak of only 3.5 per cent. Further, a given rate of unemployment in 1969–70 should not be considered "equal" to the same rate in 1960–61 because of the increased relative importance in the labor force of women and young people——"secondary" workers generally characterized by high rates of entry into and exit from the labor force, which are associated with high rates of umemployment. See J. Mincer, "Research in Labor Force and in Unemployment," *47th Annual Report* of the NBER, New York, June 1967, pp. 16–22.

[18]There is another objection to concentrating on real indicators that deserves a word, although it is of minor significance for the United States today. Consider an industry such as agriculture, the physical volume of whose output (apart from fluctuations due to the weather, pests, and similar factors) tends to be stable. Is this industry free of business cycles? To concentrate on its physical volume of output would be to overlook the effects of fluctuations in relative prices. Indeed, the major determinant of shifts between good and bad business in this industry will be change in its selling prices relative to its buying prices. The solution is simple: to deflate the industry's gross or net income by the prices it pays, not by the prices it receives.

When such an industry is dominant in a country that exports the industry's produce in order to obtain by import the goods and services it wants, the physical volume of production in the country as a whole will also tend to be stable. Fluctuations in business conditions will be largely caused by changes in export prices relative to import prices. The United States was not far from being such a country a century or more ago, as are many developing countries today. In this case, too, the solution offered in the preceding paragraph applies. In fact, real GNP is not——or should not be——measured by the physical volume of production. Real GNP is the aggregate of real consumption and real investment; and these, on the assumptions made, are largely dependent on the volume of exports and the foreign terms of trade. In effect, current dollar GNP is, or should be, deflated by import prices, not by export prices.

index of the general price level such as the GNP implicit price index, would be better than no deflation at all. (This kind of approximation is more often used in production indexes than their consumers realize.)

To return to the main point: with any reasonable deflation, there appears to have been a sustained and absolute, though slight, contraction in real aggregate economic activity during 1969–70. To judge by data currently available, then, 1969–70 was not a case of a decline to a low but still positive rate of growth.[19]

But if 1969–70 is taken to be a recession, it will be the mildest in the list, at least as far as the information available through August 1970 indicates. Does this argue against identifying 1969–70 as a recession?

VII

The 1946 definition requires that business cycles not be "divisible into shorter cycles of similar character with amplitudes approximating their own." In a comment on this, Burns and Mitchell mention that the "expansion and contraction of many cycles seem to be interrupted by movements in the opposite direction. . .When the irregularities are slight they do not seriously

[19]Revisions of currently available data are bound to occur. Whether and how much they will alter the above conclusion remains to be seen. In the meantime, it is well to keep in mind that some of the declines during 1969–70 were very small. The rather minute changes in real GNP are especially noteworthy; a later revision could conceivably change even the signs of these changes.

In this connection, see Rosanne Cole, *Errors in Provisional Estimates of Gross National Product,* New York, NBER, 1970, p. 70. The current-dollar estimates of change in GNP during each of the four postwar contractions (1948–49, 1953–54, 1957–58, and 1960–61) were later revised upward; that is, the later estimates of the declines from peak to trough were smaller than the earlier estimates. This was true also of the estimates of change in constant dollar GNP for 1957–58 and 1960–61, for which I have made a comparison similar to Cole's. The initial estimate of the decline during 1957–58, was 5.7 per cent; the final estimate, 3.9 per cent. For 1960–61, the two estimates were 2.3 and 1.6, respectively.

Another qualification on the GNP series is worth noting. The GNP series based largely on expenditures (the "official" estimate) differs from the GNP series based largely on income, by the amount of the "statistical discrepancy" between the two sides of the account. The income-side estimate in real terms declined (very slightly) between the first and second quarters of 1970, while the expenditure-side estimate rose (very slightly).

Further, alternatives to the usual GNP implicit price deflator prepared in the Department of Commerce, when applied to either of the two estimates of current–dollar GNP, yield constant-dollar estimates of GNP that decline between the first and second quarters of 1970. See A.H. Young and C. Harkins, "Alternative Measures of Price Change for GNP," *Survey of Current Business,* March 1969, and the later "Alternative Measures of Price Change for GNP, 1967–1970," in *Survey of Current Business,* August 1970.

complicate the task of identifying business cycles; but in some instances, notably in this country since 1930, they attain considerable proportions. Hence the need of criteria for deciding what reversals in direction mark the end of a cyclical phase. Most brief movements are excluded by the clause that business cycles " 'cover more than one year'." By adding the clause concerning amplitudes, "a rule is laid down for deciding when to treat movements lasting several years as a single cycle and when to recognize two or more cycles," But, they note, "this rule cannot be applied without knowing at least approximately what tamplitudes are characteristic of business cycles."[20]

This point is made with reference to the amplitude of the cycle as a whole and not separately to the amplitude of the recession of expansion. But it implies an upper limit to the amplitude and duration of the expansion phase when recessions are of small amplitude or duration. Specifically, it suggests that if the expansion that has been taking place since the last previously recognized trough has exceeded the amplitude of the largest expansion on the record, and this expansion was interrupted by one or more "movements in the opposite direction," or pauses, not recognized as recessions, there is reason to reconsider the earlier decisions. If this does not lead to a revision, it indicates the action of an extraordinary "exogenous" factor or factors that have stretched out the expansion (a great war, for example); or the need to ask whether a mutation in the character of business cycles should be recognized.

The expansion that stopped in 1969 was, in fact, the longest expansion included in the U.S. record. Dating it from February 1961 to November 1969, it lasted 105 months. The longest previous expansion was that of June 1938–February 1945, eighty months. The longest previous peacetime expansion was that of March 1933–May 1937, fifty months. The expansion that began in 1961, even if we date its end in 1969, then, had already been so long that it probably exceeds that of any previous expansion. Since aggregate economic activity did show a decline during 1969–70, slight though it was, this exceptionally large amplitude provides a ground for accepting 1969 as the end of the expansion, and thereby accepting 1969–70 as a recession. Put a little differently, if one is willing to accept 1961–69 as a single expansion, despite the fact that it falls outside the historical range of amplitude and duration, why should one not accept 1969–70 as a reccession, despite the

[20] Burns and Mitchell, pp. 3 and 7–8.

fact that it falls on the other side of the historical range of amplitudes (though not of duration)?[21]

But this argument is not yet very persuasive. It is necessary to pursue it further, as we shall now do, by going to the restrictive forces bred by the process of expansion——forces that tend to grow stronger the longer an expansion persists.

VIII

I have been backing into the question that might perhaps have been better faced directly and at the very outset: what our conception of "the business cycle today" contributes to the interpretation of 1969–70. If what happened during 1969–70 constitutes a recession, it is a phase in a recurrent sequence of changes in which expansions occurring at about the same time in many economic activities are followed by similarly general downturns, recessions, and revivals that merge into the next expansion phase. Any doubts about the nature of the economic changes during 1969–70 can therefore be resolved, or at least lessened, by considering what came before the pause in 1969, as well as whether changes typical of a recession have been occurring since.

Following Mitchell and Burns, we may usefully conceive of business cycles as resulting from economic processes "that of themselves tend to generate cyclical movements"; and these, however, can be strengthened or opposed, speeded up or slowed down (sometimes even reversed) by episodic or erratic disturbances. This conception is consistent with the repetitive features of business cycles, as well as with the variations among business cycles, uncovered by many years of quantitative research. Economists differ in the relative importance of the roles they assign to particular economic processes and particular external factors when they think of business cycles generally or when they try to explain differences among business cycles. But I expect that all or most of us here would find the general conception congenial to our thinking. Any of its variants provides a basis on which the economic changes since 1969 can reasonably be characterized as a recession.

[21] It might be argued that the expansion that began in 1961 did not, in fact, continue until 1969, and thus did not reach 105 months in length. This would be to suppose that, for example, 1966 marked the end of the expansion that began in 1961, not merely an interruption in the expansion. The expansion that paused in 1969 would then be only about thirty months long and the question of its amplitude would no longer be disturbing. But by the same token, we would be counting 1966–67 as a recession. We would have to count 1969–70 as a recession also. There are indeed grounds for regarding 1966–67 as a recession, but this too involves a discussion of the causes of recession.

Consider, first, the accumulation of restrictive forces generated by the expansion prior to the pause of 1969. Output, we may recall, had risen to levels that exceeded even "potential" output, as it is measured by the index shown in Chart 1. The unemployment rate had dropped below the 4 per cent level usually supposed to indicate "full" employment. It is not surprising, therefore, that——as in other, less exuberant, expansions——signs appeared of these restrictive forces. One such sign was the narrowing of the scope and reduction in the pace of expansion. Another was the rise in costs, which eventually exceeded the rise in selling prices and reduced profits per unit of sales and then, also, aggregate profits. A third was the increase in construction costs and interest rates, which sharply depressed home building and dampened state and local government construction plans. Coupled with the slowdown in expected profits, these increases eventually led also, and on a widening front, to a reduction in the establishment of new businesses and the postponement of ambitious plans for investment by existing firms in business plant and equipment, measured in real terms. A fourth was the depressant effect of these developments on the stock market; the decline in stock prices became, in turn, another restrictive force on business investment, home building, and the purchase of large items of durable consumer goods. In time, as we now know, these and other developments, many of which are summarized in the composite of leading indicators,[22] led to further retardation in the rate of growth, and then to actual decline of aggregate production, and to a widening gap between a continually growing number in the labor force and a stable or declining number employed.

Too many people, I suspect, have been ignoring the fact that these restrictive forces had been gathering strength in our economy for some time before 1969. It is reasonable to suppose that even by themselves, had subsequent policy been neutral, they would eventually have caused a substantial decline in the rate of growth, if not an absolute contraction, of aggregate economic activity.

Contributing to such an eventuality——to the extent that it has not already been counted among the restrictive factors generated by the expansion——was the halt to further increase, and then the sharp cut, in the rate of expansion of the money supply (defined broadly or narrowly) that came in 1968 and early 1969. The halt would of itself have probably served sooner or later to bring about a reduction in the rate of growth of aggregate economic activity, even apart from the sharp decline in the rate of growth of money supply that

[22]This composite, like the composite of coincident indicators, should be adjusted for the rise in the general price level. And if a "reverse-trend adjustment" is applied to it, the trend used should be the trend of the adjusted coincider composite.

followed it. With the tightening of monetary policy the restrictive forces already pressing on the rate of growth of aggregate economic activity were strengthened. Much the same can be said of the federal government's budgetary policy, as it is reflected in the federal surplus on the national accounts basis.

What I concluded from the survey of changes in aggregate economic activity during 1969–70——that these do constitute a recession——is, then, supported by this brief review of antecedent developments.

IX

It may be asked whether the conception of business cycles outlined above is consistent with just a decline in the rate of growth of aggregate economic activity to a level below its trend level. Does it not require, or imply, an absolute contraction?

As I have already indicated, such a decline, measured in real terms——though very modest by historical standards——did in fact occur during 1969–70. However, the statistics are admittedly rough and subject to revision. It is possible, though I believe rather unlikely, that at a later date when all the information is finally available, we shall find that aggregate economic activity during 1969–70 did not actually decline; that what happened was a decline in the rate of economic growth during this period to a level of about zero. If so, will this mean that 1969–70 was not a recession; that it was not the declining phase of a business cycle?

I can find nothing in the conception of business cycles that requires an absolute contraction in aggregate economic activity as an invariant feature of a business-cycle recession. The National Bureau's 1946 definition of business cycles does speak of a contraction. But I have already noted that it was formulated in the light of observations on pre-World War II business cycles and that Burns and Mitchell took pains to emphasize that the definition was tentative, subject to revision if not borne out by further observation. What is essential in the conception of the business cycle as an endogenous process is a tendency for expansion to gather momentum and "for a time become a self-reinforcing process," but eventually to generate restrictive forces that finally push down the rate of increase of aggregate activity to a low or even negative level; and for recession, when it comes, to spread at first, but then to release corrective forces that "combine with the more persistent forces of growth"[23] to bring the recession to a halt.

I have expressed the process in terms of rates of change because the corrective forces can be released, it seems to me, even when aggregate

[23]The quoted phrases are from Burns, p. 41.

economic activity does not decline absolutely. A decline in the rate of growth of aggregate activity, for example, is inevitably accompanied by an absolute decline in the business of many enterprises, as the diffusion indexes make clear. These enterprises, and also those still growing but making smaller rates of return, will be impelled to seek ways to restore efficiency and cut costs.

As for the conception of the business cycle that stresses external factors, it may be sufficient to mention that in his latest publication Friedman sketches the adjustment process following a "monetary disturbance" entirely in terms of rates of change. Indeed, he is quite explicit in saying that "there must. . . be a cyclical reaction, an overshooting, in the rates of change in nominal [money] income and prices, though not necessarily in their levels."[24]

X

A number of questions have been accumulated during our discussion of how the definition of a recession might be revised. These questions will have to be dealt with in the tests to which any revised definition should be subjected. I take a moment, therefore, to pose two of the questions explicitly.

One concerns the determination of the long-term trend. If a recession is defined as a sustained decline in the rate of growth of aggregate economic activity relative to its long-term trend, then to recognize a recession one must know what the trend is. When the decline is sharp, the difficulty is minor; any rough estimate of the trend based on any reasonable rationale will serve. But not so when the decline is slight.

Further, the usual method gives the trend at a moment in time essentially as some sort of moving average of rates of change subsequent to the moment as well as prior to it. But when we wish to determine the *current* trend, we do not know just what subsequent changes will be. These have to be assumed. In addition to the methods discussed by Mintz, consideration might be given to measuring the trend by some average of past rates of changes——perhaps adjusted (or qualified) by reference to current and prospective developments in the factors that determine changes in the trend——as in essence is done in measuring potential GNP.[25]

[24]M. Friedman, "A Theoretical Framework for Monetary Analysis," *Journal of Political Economy,* March/April 1970, p. 232; reprinted as O.P. 112, New York, NBER, 1971.

[25]On the question of trends, it is still worth referring to the studies by Edwin Frickey, *Economic Fluctuations in the United States,* Harvard, 1942. See also Burns and Mitchell, p. 38. The use of a moving average of variable span is described in Gerhard Tintner's *Prices in the Trade Cycle,* Vienna, Julius Springer, 1935, pp. 22-24. Important among more recent discussions is Simon Kuznets' *Capital in the American Economy: Its Formation and Financing,* Princeton for NBER, 1961, Ch. 2.

This brings us to the second question: Why would it not be better to define a recession as a decline in the proportion of available resources employed in production, or as a widening of the gap between potential and actual output, rather than as a decline in aggregate economic activity relative to its trend? The idea is attractive.[26] The difficulty arises in measuring the volume of available resources, or alternatively, the volume of potential GNP, over which there has been some controversy.[27] Estimation of the trend of potential GNP is difficult enough; the gap estimate requires, in addition, an estimate of the *level* of potential GNP, which is another matter. What is involved, of course, is an old and very difficult problem: How to determine the "optimum" rate of unemployment (of all resources, not only labor), or the optimum volume of output; and this shades into the problem of the optimum rate of economic growth.

For the present, it may be of some comfort (to economic diagnosticians) to note that the slowdown during 1969–70 was in fact sufficiently sharp and sustained so that various ways of determining the long-term trend yield not altogether inconsistent results. This is illustrated by the trends and deviations from trend in GNP and industrial production traced in Chart 2 and summarized in Table 4. Although there are striking differences among the trends, for our present purposes the resemblances are more important than the differences. The turning points in the growth cycles agree closely. Also, differences among the several "growth recessions," measured relative to any of the trends, are much the same. The coefficients of rank correlation between alternative measurements of duration, or total decline, or rate of decline, are high: of the order of 0.8 or even 0.9. Specifically, the decline relative to trend during 1968–70 was more severe than during 1966–67, and 1966–67 was more severe than 1962–63, according to any of the measurements in Table 4.

[26] A subsidiary question (and answer) is implied here, and has been implied elsewhere in the paper. Explicitly, to define a recession, for the present purpose, in terms of an output gap or a rate of unemployment of resources is to define aggregate economic activity more narrowly than it usually has been in the National Bureau's business cycle studies. The objective, in these studies, has been broader: to describe what happens during business cycles and why.

[27] See, for example, the discussion between Burns and the Council of Economic Advisers headed by W.W. Heller, in *The Morgan Guaranty Survey,* May and August, 1961; and Burns' 1936 review (reprinted in *The Frontiers of Economic Knowledge,* NBER, 1954) of the Brookings study by E.G. Nourse and associates, *America's Capacity to Produce.* The CEA gap analysis originated in the 1961 study by Arthur Okun, "Potential GNP: Its Measurement and Significance," reprinted in his *The Political Economy of Prosperity* New York, 1969, Appendix. See also J.W. Knowles, *The Potential Economic Growth in the United States,* Study Paper No. 20, Joint Economic Committee, Washington, D.C., Government Printing Office, 1960.

TABLE 4

Selected Measures of Duration and Depth of Specific
"Growth-Cycle" Expansions and Contractions, 1948–70

	1948–49	1949–52		1952–54	
	Contraction	Exp.	Contr.	Exp.	Contr.

GNP in 1958 Dollars

*1. Deviation from moving-
   average trend (Mintz)*

Dates	II/48–IV/49	IV/49–III/51	III/51–III/52	III/52–I/53	I/53–II/54
Duration (months)	18	21	12	6	15
Rate of change (% per year)					
trend	4.3	4.4	4.5	4.9	3.6
actual	0.1	11.6	1.3	9.2	−1.9
deviation	−4.2	7.2	−3.2	4.3	−5.5
Total change (%)					
trend	6.5	7.6	4.5	2.5	4.5
actual	0.1	20.2	1.3	4.6	−2.4
deviation	−6.4	12.6	−3.2	2.1	−6.9

*2. Deviation from trend in
   potential GNP*

Dates	n.a.	n.a.	n.a.	II/52–II/53	II/53–II/54
Duration (months)				12	12
Rate of change (% per year)					
trend				3.5	3.5
actual				6.9	−3.4
deviation				3.4	−6.9
Total change (%)					
trend				3.5	3.5
actual				6.9	−3.4
deviation				3.4	−6.9

(Continued)

1954–58		1958–61		1961–63		1963–67		1967–70	a
Exp.	Contr.	Exp.	Contr.	Exp.	Contr.	Exp.	Contr.	Exp.	Contr.
II/54–	IV/55–	II/58–	II/59–	I/61–	II/62–	II/63–	I/66–	IV/67–	II/68–
IV/55	II/58	II/59	I/61	II/62	II/63	I/66	IV/67	II/68	III/70
18	30	12	21	15	12	33	21	6	27
2.3	2.6	2.6	3.4	4.5	4.9	5.3	4.6	4.6	4.8
7.3	−0.6	9.2	0.3	7.5	3.5	6.9	3.0	6.4	1.4
5.0	−3.2	6.6	−3.1	3.0	−1.4	1.6	−1.6	1.8	−3.4
3.4	6.5	2.6	5.9	5.7	4.9	14.5	8.1	2.3	10.8
11.0	−1.5	9.2	0.6	9.3	3.5	18.9	5.3	3.2	3.1
7.6	−8.0	6.6	−5.3	3.6	−1.4	4.4	−2.8	0.9	−7.7
II/54–	IV/55–	II/58–	II/59–	I/61–	IV/62–	II/63–	IV/66–	IV/67–	III/68–
IV/55	II/58	II/59	I/61	IV/62	II/63	IV/66	IV/67	III/68	III/70
18	30	12	21	21	6	42	12	9	24
3.5	3.5	3.5	3.5	3.5	3.8	3.8	4.0	4.0	4.2
7.3	−0.6	9.2	0.3	6.6	2.9	6.4	2.3	5.7	1.0
3.8	−4.1	5.7	−3.2	3.1	−0.9	2.6	−1.7	1.7	−3.2
5.3	9.0	3.5	6.2	6.2	1.9	14.0	4.0	3.0	8.4
11.0	−1.5	9.2	0.6	11.5	1.4	22.4	2.3	4.2	2.1
5.7	−10.5	5.7	−5.6	5.3	−0.5	8.4	−1.7	1.2	−6.3

(Continued)

TABLE 4 (Concluded)

	1948–49 Contraction	1949–52		1952–54	
		Exp.	Contr.	Exp.	Contr.

Industrial Production

1. Deviation from moving-average trend (Mintz)

Dates	6/48–10/49	10/49–3/51	3/51–6/52	6/52–5/53	5/53–8/54
Duration (months)	16	17	15	11	15
Rate of change (% per year)					
trend	4.7	4.9	4.6	6.6	4.0
actual	−7.3	22.2	−1.6	17.0	−6.8
deviation	−12.0	17.3	−6.2	10.4	−10.8
Total change (%)					
trend	6.3	7.0	5.8	6.1	5.0
actual	−9.8	31.5	−1.9	15.6	−8.5
deviation	−16.1	24.5	−7.7	9.5	−13.5

2. Deviation from AT&T trend

Dates	6/48–10/49	10/49–3/51	3/51–7/52	7/52–7/53	7/53–8/54
Duration (months)	16	17	16	12	13
Rate of change (% per year)					
trend	4.2	4.2	4.3	4.1	4.2
actual	−7.3	22.2	−2.9	18.7	−8.4
deviation	−11.5	18.0	−7.2	14.6	−12.6
Total change (%)					
trend	5.6	5.9	5.7	4.1	4.6
actual	−9.8	31.5	−3.9	18.7	−9.1
deviation	−15.4	25.6	−9.6	14.6	−13.7

3. Deviation from trend in Wharton estimate of "capacity"

Dates		10/49–8/50	8/50–7/52	7/52–5/53	5/53–8/54
Duration (months)		10	23	10	15
Rate of change (% per year)					
trend		5.3	6.9	3.4	3.9
actual		33.4	−0.6	21.5	−6.8
deviation		28.1	−7.5	18.1	−10.7
Total change (%)					
trend		4.4	13.2	2.9	4.9
actual		27.8	−1.1	18.0	−8.5
deviation		23.4	−14.3	15.1	−13.5

1954–58		1958–61		1961–63		1963–67		1967–70	
Exp.	Contr.	Exp.	Contr.	Exp.	Contr.	Exp.	Contr.	Exp.	Contr.[a]
8/54–	10/55–	4/58–	5/59–	3/61–	3/62–	1/63–	10/66–	10/67–	6/68–
10/55	4/58	5/59	3/61	3/62	1/63	10/66	10/67	6/68	9/70
14	30	13	22	12	10	45	12	8	27
2.1	3.1	2.7	3.6	6.0	5.4	6.3	5.2	5.3	5.5
14.7	−4.9	22.7	−2.7	13.0	2.3	8.8	−1.4	8.4	0.0
12.6	−8.0	20.0	−6.3	7.0	−3.1	2.5	−6.6	3.1	−5.5
2.5	7.6	3.0	6.6	6.0	4.5	23.7	5.2	3.5	12.4
17.1	−12.2	24.6	−4.9	13.0	2.0	33.1	−1.4	5.6	0.0
14.6	−19.8	21.6	−11.5	7.0	−2.5	9.4	−6.6	2.1	−12.4
8/54–	10/55–	4/58–	6/59–	2/61–	4/62–	1/63–	10/66–	10/67–	7/69–
10/55	4/58	6/59	2/61	4/62	1/63	10/66	10/67	7/69	9/70
14	30	14	20	14	9	45	12	21	14
4.3	4.4	4.1	4.5	4.1	4.0	3.9	3.5	3.6	3.5
14.7	−4.9	21.6	−3.4	11.9	2.0	8.8	−1.4	6.3	−4.2
10.4	−9.3	17.5	−7.9	7.8	−2.0	4.9	−4.9	2.7	−7.7
5.1	11.0	4.7	7.5	4.7	3.0	14.8	3.5	6.2	4.1
17.1	−12.2	25.2	−5.7	13.9	1.5	33.1	−1.4	11.1	−4.9
12.0	−23.2	20.5	−13.2	9.2	−1.5	18.3	−4.9	4.9	−9.0
8/54–	10/55–	4/58–	5/59–	2/61–	4/62–	12/62–	10/66–	10/67–	7/69–
10/55	4/58	5/59	2/61	4/62	12/62	10/66	10/67	7/69	9/70
14	30	13	21	14	8	46	12	21	14
3.2	4.7	3.2	5.2	3.5	4.0	3.8	4.5	3.6	3.8
14.7	−4.9	22.7	−3.0	11.9	1.8	8.7	−1.4	6.3	−4.2
11.5	−9.6	19.5	−8.2	8.4	−2.2	4.9	−5.9	2.7	−8.0
3.7	11.7	3.5	9.0	4.1	2.7	14.6	4.5	6.4	4.4
17.1	−12.2	24.6	−5.3	13.9	1.2	33.5	−1.4	11.1	−4.9
13.4	−23.9	21.1	−14.3	9.8	−1.5	18.9	−5.9	4.7	−9.3

Notes to Table 4

Source: The Mintz moving-average trends are based on a 25-quarter moving average of actual GNP in 1958 dollars, and a 75-month moving average of the FRB index of industrial production – see Mintz's paper in this volume. Mrs. Mintz's series were extended from the first quarter of 1970 (in the case of GNP) or March 1970 (in the case of industrial production) to August 1970 on the assumption of a continuation of the trend in the immediately preceding period.

Potential GNP is based on a trend line of 3.5 per cent per year (intersecting actual line in middle of 1955) from 1st quarter 1952 to 4th quarter 1962, 3.75 per cent from 4th quarter 1962 to 4th quarter 1965, 4 per cent from 4th quarter 1965 to 4th quarter 1969, and 4.3 per cent from 4th quarter 1969 to 3rd quarter 1970 – see *Economic Report of the President*, 1965 and current issues of BCD.

The AT&T trend in industrial production is based on an exponential trend fitted to the per capita data, for 1869 through 1968, and then multiplied by population – see Supplement to *Business Conditions*, Economic Analysis Section, American Telephone and Telegraph Company, New York, February 1970.

The Wharton estimate of industrial production "capacity" was derived from the Wharton quarterly index of rate of utilization of industrial capacity divided into the FRB index of industrial production. The monthly series is a straight-line interpolation of the quarterly data. See *The Wharton Index of Capacity Utilization*, Lawrence R. Klein and Robert Summers, Economics Research Unit, Department of Economics, Wharton School of Finance and Commerce, University of Pennsylvania, 1966, and the quarterly *Wharton Economic Newsletter*. The peak in the growth cycle of 1948-1949 in industrial production, measured as a deviation from the Wharton index of industrial capacity, apparently came before 1947, the first year for which the Wharton series is available.

[a]Through fourth quarter or December 1970.

To repeat an earlier warning, however, these comparisons should not be taken as measuring the relative social "costs" of the growth recessions. In judging the "cost" of a recession, whether absolute or relative to trend, it is desirable to take account (among other things) of the level from which the recession began. While the growth recession of 1968–70 is more severe than that of 1959–61, in terms of amount of decline in real GNP relative to the trends, given in Table 4, the latter decline started from a lower level, if the estimates are anywhere near the mark. Indeed, if the initial phase of the decline relative to trend during 1968–70 is taken as a movement towards rather than away from the optimum level of output––as it would be, on the basis of the gap estimates used––the social "cost" of the initial decline (between the second quarter of 1968 and the third quarter of 1969) was offset or more than offset by a "benefit." But there are questions about the gap measurements, and these must therefore also appear on our list of questions requiring further study. Whatever our doubts about them, however, the gap measurements help to remind us that there is no simple one-to-one

Chart 2
Alternative Measure of Trend and Deviation from Trend, National and Industrial Output, 1947–1970

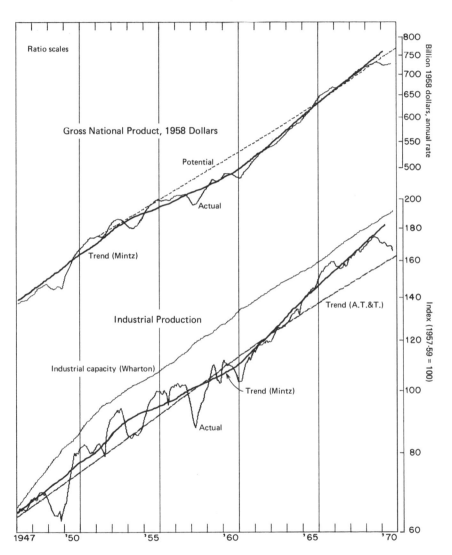

relationship between the measurements given in the table, and measurements of change in the performance of the economy or the economic welfare of our people.

XI

It is now almost sixty years since Wesley Mitchell closed his book on *Business Cycles* with a discussion of the "wider aspects of business cycles." The cumulative changes that take place in economic organization, he saw, must react upon the character of business cycles and make for changes in the phenomena of business cycles——changes that stand out clearly "in the lapse of years." "Hence, " he concluded, "economists of each generation will probably see reason to recast the theory of business cycles they learned in their youth."[28]

There is little doubt that our generation has good reason to recast the theory of business cycles "we learned in our youth."

On the basis of "further observations" made after 1946, Burns pointed to the progress that had been made towards stabilizing the economy.[29] The many changes, planned and unplanned, that had occurred in the structure, organization and institutions of the economy now tend to limit the spread of the forces making for recession. The greater importance of the relatively stable service industries is an example. So is our improved financial system, with bank-deposit insurance among other things. The unemployment and social security systems now act as "built-in stabilizers" by helping to maintain incomes. So does the progressive income tax, since the tax authorities absorb part of every rise or decline in income. Not least in importance is the widely accepted governmental responsibility for supporting stable economic growth at high levels of employment. With a stronger role by government recognized, government policy can now join——as it already did, earlier this year——with the corrective forces generated by the recession, and the persistent forces of growth present in the private economy, to prevent a decline in the rate of growth from continuing until a serious absolute contraction occurs in aggregate economic activity. As a consequence, expansions have tended to become longer and recessions shorter and milder.

On this view of the business cycle today, recessions may sometimes turn out to be only declines in the rate of economic growth and not absolute contractions.

[28]W. C. Mitchell, *Business Cycles,* University of California, 1913, pp. 582–583; reprinted in *Business Cycles and Their Causes,* University of California, 1941, p. 168.

[29]A. F. Burns, Presidential Address before the American Economic Association, 1959, *American Economic Review,* March 1960, reprinted in *The Business Cycle in a Changing World,* New York, NBER, 1969, Ch. 3.

What has been seen since Burns gave his address on "Progress Towards Economic Stability" in 1959——further changes in the structure and organization and institutions of our economy, a still wider acceptance of governmental responsibility for supporting stable economic growth at high levels ef employment, and even more, a rate of economic growth remarkably stable by historical standards——has provided additional support for this view. There is little doubt, therefore, that the business cycle of today differs in important respects from the business cycle of the pre-World War II period.

It is for this reason that in my introductory remarks I added a reservation: that the recession of 1969–70 may perhaps equally well be viewed as a member of a subspecies different in several important respects from the parent species indentified in the National Bureau's chronology of business cycles, and that this subspecies may deserve a name of its own.

Whether we should designate the developments of 1969–70 as something other than a recession is, from a scientific point of view, a matter of convenience. The causes of business cycles have not vanished. The fact that today's business cycles may run a course different from the course business cycles ran in the economy of earlier days does not of itself compel us to stop thinking of them as members of the same species. A tiger caged is not the same as a tiger loose in the streets, but neither is it a paper tiger. There are good reasons for not forgetting that important fact.

On the other hand, it may help to avoid misunderstanding on the part of the public if a distinction is drawn between the business cycles and recessions of yesterday and those of today, and a distinctive terminology applied to the latter. Perhaps the terms "growth cycle," and "growth recession" (or "slowdown"), may serve.

What we economists must be sure to convey to the public is that it would be foolish to forget all that has been learned in studies of prewar business cycles. Whatever changes we may choose to make in the language in which we address them, we must remind our listeners that while the business cycle of today is not quite the same as the business cycle of yesterday, it is by the same token not altogether different. We and they need to keep in mind the admonition with which Arthur Burns closed his *Encyclopedia* article on business cycles: "It would, nevertheless, be premature to conclude that the older hazards of the business cycle belong to the past. . . . It is possible that in the future a 'recession' will mean merely a reduced rate of growth or aggregate activity instead of an actual and sustained decline, but there is as yet insufficient ground for believing that economic developments will generally conform to this model in the near future.

"Hence," Burns went on to say, "the wise course for economists is to continue basic research on the nature and causes of business cycles, to remain watchful of developments that seem likely to bring on a slump in activity, and to extend the search for acceptable pathways to prosperity without inflation."[30]   Close study of the 1969–70 "recession"——or "growth recession" or "slowdown"——and of the expansion and pauses preceding it, when more of the facts are in, should provide a valuable addition to the empirical information essential for a sound theory of the business cycle of today.

[30] Arthur F. Burns, "Business Cycles: General," in David L. Sills (ed.), *International Encyclopedia of the Social Sciences,* Vol. 2, New York, 1968, p. 244; and reprinted as "The Nature and Causes of Business Cycles," in Arthur F. Burns, *The Business Cycle in a Changing World,* New York, NBER, 1969.

The Cyclical Behavior of Prices

Geoffrey H. Moore
Bureau of Labor Statistics

INTRODUCTION

The National Bureau of Economic Research celebrated its fiftieth anniversary in 1970. In those fifty productive years, the National Bureau has generated a large number of studies bearing upon the cyclical behavior of prices. The work of Wesley C. Mitchell, Frederick C. Mills, Arthur F. Burns, Thor Hultgren, Daniel Creamer, George Stigler, Solomon Fabricant, Milton Friedman, Irving Kravis, Robert Lipsey, and many others has provided new statistical information or better organized data about the price system, findings about its internal structure and network of relationships, and generalizations pertaining to the monetary, competitive, cost, and other economic factors that influence prices and are in turn shaped by them. The general tendency for the price level to move with, rather than against, changes in the level of output; the lags of retail prices behind wholesale prices; the lags in wage rates and in unit labor costs; the marked inverse influence of changes in unit costs upon profit margins——all these and many additional findings have stemmed from National Bureau studies.

On the statistical side, we are indebted to Mills for the development of price indexes for various classifications of commodities; to Hultgren for carefully matched price and cost indexes; to Creamer for indexes of wage changes in the 1920's and 1930's; to Fabricant and to Kendrick for

Note: I am indebted to John Layng, Nancy Leach, and Mildred Tweedy of the Bureau of Labor Statistics staff for their assistance in the preparation of materials for this report.

comparable price and productivity indexes; to Kravis and Lipsey for prices of goods bought and sold in foreign commerce; to Stigler and Kindahl, most recently, for indexes of transaction prices at wholesale; and so on. These new statistics have not only illuminated the past; they have led to the continuing provision of and improvement in current statistics on prices, wages, costs, and productivity. For these and other reasons, our debt to the work of the National Bureau is not only large, but growing. It is not my purpose, however, to review and evaluate the work that has already been done. Rather, I shall set forth a few additional results, particularly with reference to the period since 1946.

Inflation is characterized by a general and widely diffused rise in prices and costs. However, all prices and factors affecting prices do not begin to rise or fall at the same time. In part, this is due to the existence of more or less regular sequences in the movement of different prices. Prices in some markets almost always begin to rise more promptly than in other markets. Similarly, some prices typically begin to fall sooner than others.

Moreover, prices do not all move at the same pace, and in particular they do not necessarily move at the same pace as wages or costs of production. Prices of some types of assets, such as common stocks or land, rise or fall, while the money price of other assets, such as savings accounts or debt instruments, may not change at all. These differences in price behavior have significant consequences. Real wages——money wages adjusted for price changes——may rise or fall, with vital effects on the wage earner and his family. Profit margins, dependent on the difference between prices and costs, may rise or fall, thereby encouraging or discouraging expansion of production, development of investment plans, or shifts of resources from one activity to another.

This paper sets forth the results of a recent study of the cyclical behavior of prices. It describes a chronology of fluctuations in the rate of change in the price level (particularly since 1946); considers the relationship between these fluctuations and those in economic activity in general; examines how price increases and decreases are diffused through the price system; measures the tendencies of some prices to lead and others to lag; shows how the rates of change in costs and prices alter their relationship to one another during a cyclical swing; and finally, examines the current price situation in the light of these historical findings.

A REFERENCE CHRONOLOGY FOR PRICES

The National Bureau's reference chronology of peaks and troughs, created by Wesley Mitchell, is one of the simplest yet most effective devices for studying business cycles. It has become widely used. Nowadays almost every economic statistician knows what the "shaded areas" on charts of monthly time series represent. A similar device may be employed for studying movements in the price system. To do so, a number of questions must be faced. Should the chronology represent peaks and troughs in the level of prices or in their rate of change? If the latter, how should the rate of change be measured? What index or set of indexes of prices should be used to establish the chronology? What criteria should be set up to define the chronology and identify its turning points?

The business cycle chronology is based on the working definition of business cycles set forth by Mitchell in his 1927 volume, *Business Cycles--The Problem and Its Setting,* and later refined by Burns and Mitchell in their 1946 monograph, *Measuring Business Cycles.* In brief, the definition applied three criteria to the problem: the magnitude, the duration, and the diffusion of fluctuations in economic activity. One inquired how large the fall or rise in total activity was, how long it lasted, and how widely it was diffused over different economic sectors. Turning points were identified not by a single aggregate, such as gross national product, but by determining the consensus among a number of series, each of which had some claim to represent or reflect total economic activity.

A business cycle chronology was constructed not only for the United States, but also for Great Britain, France, and Germany. Still other countries, such as Canada, Japan, and Italy, have constructed business cycle chronologies along similar lines. Much is to be said for developing a price chronology in a similar manner. Whether it is the level of prices or their rate of change that is selected as the ultimate variable, attention should be focused upon swings that are of substantial size, last more than just a few months, and are widely diffused throughout the price system. A single general price index is most convenient for this purpose. Although the idea of an index of the general price level is an ancient one, today no single widely accepted measure exists. The three leading candidates would be the Consumer Price Index, the Wholesale Price Index, and the Implicit Price Deflator for Gross National Product. Each of these has its merits and deficiencies for the purpose.

The deflator is quarterly, and the other two indexes are monthly; other things equal, a monthly chronology is to be preferred. The deflator has the largest economic coverage, but that also means it includes some dubious elements, notably "prices" in the government sector which--lacking good information on the price of government purchases--are really wage rates. For this reason, many consider the Private GNP Deflator a better price index. The deflator is affected not only by changing prices but also by changes in the composition of output, whereas the other two indexes use fixed weights and hence reflect price changes alone.

The Wholesale Price Index, of course, does not cover one part of the price system, namely, services. Also, it has some gaps in its industrial coverage and depends in part upon list prices rather than actual transaction prices. The Consumer Price Index is the closest approximation of the three to an actual transaction price index, but is limited to prices paid by urban wage earner and clerical worker families. Unlike the other two, it includes prices for existing goods, such as houses and used cars, as well as for currently produced goods and services.

These considerations do not point to a clear-cut conclusion, except to suggest a real need for a monthly general price index. Lacking this, I have based the chronology in this paper upon the rate of change in the Consumer Price Index, using the GNP Deflator and the Wholesale Price Index, and some of their principal components (e.g., the Private Deflator and the WPI for industrial commodities) to provide supplementary evidence. The CPI has risen almost continuously since 1954, but there have been sizable fluctuations in its rate of increase, and the chronology identifies these fluctuations. The rate of inflation is, of course, a matter of major concern. The chronology shows when this rate, as measured by the CPI, reached high points and low points since 1947.

For the identification of turning points, we are fortunate to have, again thanks to the National Bureau, a computer program recently developed by Charlotte Boschan and Gerhard Bry. This essentially reproduces, in an objective and mechanical fashion, most of the choices of "specific cycle" turning points that used to be entirely dependent upon the judgment of National Bureau staff. Of course, it uses criteria that are similar to those used by the staff. It bases its choices upon whether the fluctuations in the data are large enough and long enough to be reflected in various moving averages, but does not explicitly use any criterion as to the size of a swing. Despite this, it is rather uncanny in its ability to detect and identify turning points independently selected by experts––and, I might add, to uncover inconsistencies in judgment by the less expert. We have used the turns selected by the computer program in a large majority of instances. The exceptions are due to the occasional failure of the program to select a large movement because it is too short, or (more frequently) to select very small movements simply because they last quite long. I dare say our entire analysis could have been carried out strictly in terms of the turning points identified by the computer program, without major effect upon our conclusions.

After deciding upon the rate of change in prices as the variable that the chronology would represent, several other decisions remain. First, the rates of change must be seasonally adjusted or derived from seasonally adjusted indexes. During the past year the Bureau of Labor Statistics has been reporting the seasonally adjusted rate of change in the CPI. The seasonal pattern has a relatively small effect upon the level of the index (currently the largest and the smallest seasonal factors are, respectively, 100.12 in July and 99.83 in January and February). Nevertheless, it has a substantial effect upon rates of change over short periods. For example, the rate of change from July 1969 to January 1970 is raised from an annual rate of 5.7 per cent to 6.3 per cent after seasonal adjustment, which is equivalent to dividing a seasonal index of 90 into the unadjusted rate. This seasonal effect has been powerful enough to cause the unadjusted July-to-January rates to be lower than either the preceding or the following January-to-July rates in four out of the past five years.[1]

Next, precisely how the rate of change is to be measured must be determined. The range of possibilities is wide. The interval over which a change is measured can be as short as one month or as long as twelve months

[1] The magnification of the seasonal effect on the rate of change compared with the level can be illustrated as follows. The increase in the seasonal factor from 99.83 in January to 100.12 in July is 0.6 per cent at an annual rate. If the increase in the unadjusted index is at a 6 per cent annual rate, the seasonal factor is accounting for about one-tenth of the rise. Of course, it has an equal and opposite effect on the increase from July to January. The ups and downs in the rate of increase that are attributable to seasonal factors can be quite misleading in judging trends in the rate of inflation. For example, the unadjusted rate of increase during the six months ending in July 1965 showed a sharp acceleration, but by January 1966 the rate had declined sharply again, largely for seasonal reasons. There was a similar acceleration in July 1966, and then a retardation again in January 1967. This time, however, the decline was reflecting both seasonal factors and the 1967 minirecession. In short, as the figures given below indicate, the seasonally adjusted rates show the onset of inflation in 1965, its interruption in 1967, and its continuation thereafter.

Per Cent Change at Annual Rate, CPI, All Items

	Unadjusted	Seasonally Adjusted
1964--January–July	1.1	0.6
July–January	1.1	1.6
1965--January–July	2.4	1.9
July–January	1.5	2.0
1966--January–July	4.2	3.7
July–January	2.5	3.1
1967--January–July	3.2	2.6
July–January	3.6	4.2
1968--January–July	5.0	4.4
July–January	4.3	5.0
1969--January–July	6.7	6.1
July–January	5.7	6.3
1970--January–July	6.0	5.4

Chart 1. Rates of Change in Comprehensive Price Indexes (Centered)

(Measured over six-month or quarter-to-quarter span, seasonally adjusted, at annual rate.)

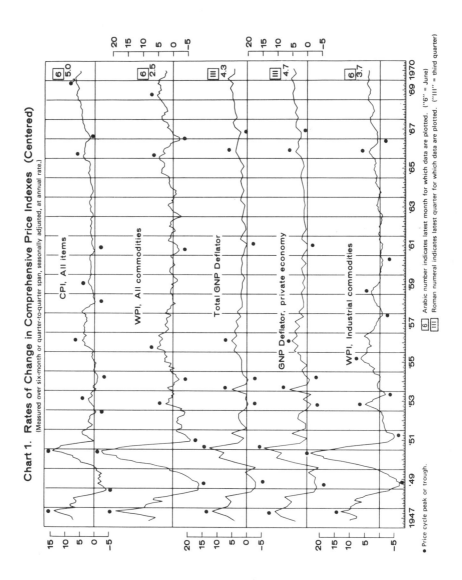

CPI, All items

WPI, All commodities

Total GNP Deflator

GNP Deflator, private economy

WPI, Industrial commodities

• Price cycle peak or trough.

6 Arabic number indicates latest month for which data are plotted. ("6" = June)

III Roman numeral indicates latest quarter for which data are plotted. ("III" = third quarter)

or more. Monthly indexes can be averaged over calendar quarters, or over moving three-month intervals, and rates of change measured between these averages. More complicated smoothing formulas can be applied. Generally, month-to-month changes are highly erratic, so some form of smoothing is desirable. On the other hand, smoothing formulas can twist and distort cyclical patterns and timing relationships. After some experimentation I have concluded that the rate of change over a six-month span meets reasonably well such criteria as smoothness, simplicity, and limited distorting effects, for the CPI and most other price and wage series. For series that are available only in quarterly form, quarter-to-quarter changes are used. (Although the interval between two adjacent quarters is only three months, the averaging over a quarter offsets the shorter interval, so the smoothing effect is similar to a six-month change.) Occasionally, I use changes over twelve-month or four-quarter spans, when these are the only data available or when the six-month or one-quarter rates are unduly erratic.[2]

Taking into account the foregoing considerations, Chart 1 presents the reference chronology, based upon the rate of change in the Consumer Price Index, together with the rates of change in the other comprehensive indexes mentioned above. Six contractions in the rate of change are identified: in 1947-48, 1950-52, 1953-54, 1956-58, 1959-61, and 1966-67. We have marked a tentative peak in February 1970. If confirmed, this will mark the beginning of the seventh contraction since 1947 (see below). Taking the 23 year period between the 1947 and 1970 peaks, we find that expansions in the rate of change lasted 162 months in the aggregate, while contractions covered 106 months (see Table 1). That is, although the level of the Consumer Price Index has been generally rising during this period, the rate of increase has declined over long stretches——aggregating nearly nine years.

The other indexes show broadly similar fluctuations, but with exceptions, especially in the period 1959-64. In terms of these comprehensive indexes, therefore, the chronology seems to represent fluctuations that are spread widely throughout the price system. This matter will be examined more directly in the section on diffusion indexes.

[2] A question related to the length of span is whether the rates of change should be centered within the interval they cover or placed at the terminal month. Placing at the terminal month, while convenient for current analysis, tends to make the dates of historical peaks or troughs later the longer the interval over which change is measured. Thus, six-month rates of change will typically turn down after month-to-month changes do, and twelve-month changes still later. Centering eliminates this bias, and is especially important when different spans are being used for different series. In this paper we shall follow the convention of centering, and since we generally use a six-month span this means that dates are three months earlier than they would be had they been set at the terminal month.

TABLE 1

Reference Chronology for the Rate of Change in Prices, Based on the
Consumer Price Index, 1947–70

Peaks and Troughs	Dates	Per Cent Rate of Change[a]		Change in Rate from		Number of Months from	
		At Peak	At Trough	Peak to Trough	Trough to Peak	Peak to Trough	Trough to Peak
Peak	Oct. 1947	13.8	–	–	–	–	–
Trough	Nov. 1948	–	–4.3	–18.1	–	13	–
Peak	Nov. 1950	14.3	–	–	+18.6	–	24
Trough	Nov. 1952	–	–.6	–14.9	–	24	–
Peak	July 1953	2.1	–	–	+2.7	–	8
Trough	Aug. 1954	–	–1.2	–3.3	–	13	–
Peak	July 1956	4.3	–	–	+5.5	–	23
Trough	July 1958	–	–0.2	–4.5	–	24	–
Peak	July 1959	2.3	–	–	+2.5	–	12
Trough	March 1961	–	0	–2.3	–	20	–
Peak	Jan. 1966	4.1	–	–	+4.1	–	58
Trough	Jan. 1967	–	1.6	–2.5	–	12	–
Peak	Feb. 1970[b]	6.7	–	–	+5.1	–	37
Average	1947–70	6.8	–0.8	–7.6	+6.4	18	27
	1952–67	3.2	–0.1	–3.2	+3.7	17	26

[a]Change over six-month span, centered, seasonally adjusted at an annual rate.
[b]Tentative. The latest figure centered on July 1970 is 5.0 per cent.

Some interesting points emerge from Table 1. During the first three contractions in the rate of change in the CPI, the rate fell below zero, that is, the index declined. But the rate barely reached zero in the next two contractions (1958 and 1961), and did not do so at all in the last one (1967). Indeed, the level of the rate at its successive low points becomes progressively higher throughout the period. There is a related tendency for the declines in the rate to become progressively smaller. In the first two contractions the rate dropped 18 and 15 percentage points; in the next two, 3 and 4½ percentage points; and in the last two, 2 and 2½ percentage points. However, the high points in the rate have not become progressively higher, nor have the expansions become progressively larger. If there has been a rising floor under the rate, there has not been a rising ceiling also. One possible explanation, which needs further exploration, is that the rising importance of services, and the diminishing importance of foods, in family budgets has had the effect of preventing declines in the rate of change of the CPI from reaching as low a level in recent years as they did earlier in the postwar period.

PRICE CYCLES AND BUSINESS CYCLES

How does the price chronology compare with the business cycle chronology? Four of the price contractions correspond with the four business contractions of 1948-49, 1953-54, 1957-58, and 1960-61. But the business expansion of 1949-53 was interrupted by the price contraction of 1950-52 during the Korean War, and the long business expansion that began in 1961 was interrupted by the price contraction of 1966-67. Both of these interruptions were also characterized by some hesitancy in business as well. Hence there is a notable degree of correspondence between the behavior of the rate of change in the Consumer Price Index and general economic activity. Since World War II, every economic slowdown or actual recession has been accompanied by a cyclical contraction in the rate of change in the price level, and cyclical contractions in the rate of change in the price level have not occurred at other times.

This does not mean, however, that a business recession as defined by the National Bureau of Economic Research is a necessary condition for a reduction in the rate of inflation. As already noted, two such reductions since 1947 have occurred at times when the economy merely slowed down. Moreover, several of the declines in the rate of price rise that were associated with business cycle contractions began well before the contraction in business activity got underway. The 1947 and 1956 peaks in the rate of change in the Consumer Price Index both came about a year before the business cycle peak, and the 1959 price peak came ten months before the business peak. In fact, in 1948, all of the decline in the rate of change in prices——and it was substantial——took place before the recession began. In 1953, the two peaks coincided. More often than not, then, the CPI has begun to decelerate while business activity was still expanding.

On the other hand, low points in the rate of price change have coincided rather closely with business cycle troughs, at least on three out of four occasions. The 1948 upturn in the rate of price change (from a level of −4 per cent) came eleven months before the business upturn, but the 1954 price upturn coincided with the business upturn, while the 1958 and 1961 price upturns followed the business turn by three months and one month, respectively. In short, declines in the rate of price change have typically started earlier and hence have continued somewhat longer than business cycle contractions.

However, the rate of price change has usually persisted at a low level, even a negative level, beyond the point of upturn. These tendencies are illustrated in Chart 2. Perhaps the most striking showing is that about a year after the business peak the rates of price change have all been in the vicinity of zero,

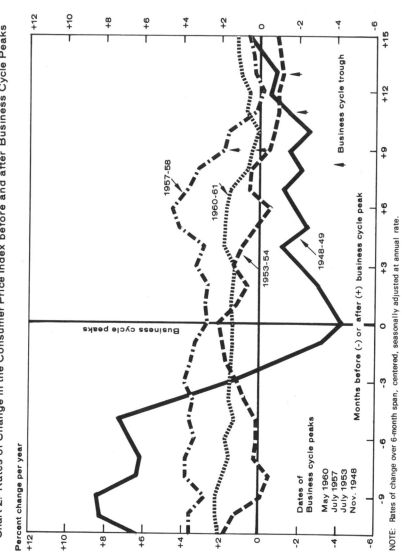

Chart 2. Rates of Change in the Consumer Price Index before and after Business Cycle Peaks

Percent change per year

Business cycle peaks

1957-58

1960-61

1953-54

1948-49

Business cycle trough

Dates of
Business cycle peaks

May 1960
July 1957
July 1953
Nov. 1948

Months before (-) or after (+) business cycle peak

NOTE: Rates of change over 6-month span, centered, seasonally adjusted at annual rate.

plus or minus 1 per cent. The food price component of the CPI, highly sensitive to economic demand, is largely responsible for this result.

DIFFUSION OF PRICE CHANGES

One of the characteristics of business cycles that Wesley Mitchell deemed important, and which he demonstrated empirically time and again, was their generality. "A business cycle consists of expansions occurring at about the same time in many economic activities, followed by similarly general recessions, contractions, and revivals . . . ," says the definition formulated by Burns and Mitchell in 1946. Among the many activities are prices, and we have just seen that the rate of change in the price level is clearly one of the participants in the ebb and flow of business cycles.

This observation does not, however, directly answer the question whether the price chronology we have constructed reflects widespread similar movements among different prices. We can get at this question by examining diffusion indexes of prices, for such indexes report how many out of a given population of prices are rising at a particular time and how many are falling. In terms of the popular conception of whether or not the economy is experiencing inflation, or whether inflation is getting worse or better, variations in the degree of generality of price increases are perhaps more significant than variations in the rate of change in a price index.

Chart 3 brings together several price diffusion indexes and illustrates several propositions. First, at all times some prices are falling and some are rising, but the proportions that are in the one category or the other vary greatly. Second, the most widespread increases in prices generally have occurred during the periods marked off as expansions in our price chronology; and the most widespread reductions, during the contractions. That is to say, the reason why the consumer price index increases more rapidly at some times than at others is not only that price increases at those times are larger but also that they are more widespread.

Third, there are discernible sequences in the process whereby price changes spread through the economy. Prices of industrial materials take an early position, wholesale prices of manufactured goods move somewhat later, and retail prices of consumer goods and services come still later. The sequences among those parts of the price system that are shown in the chart are so long drawnout, in fact, that on several occasions (notably during 1957-58) the most widespread declines in the early-moving prices came almost at the same time as the most widespread increases in consumer prices. Unless the sequences in the price system are taken into account, one could be misled into thinking that the cyclical swings in prices are less general than they are in fact.

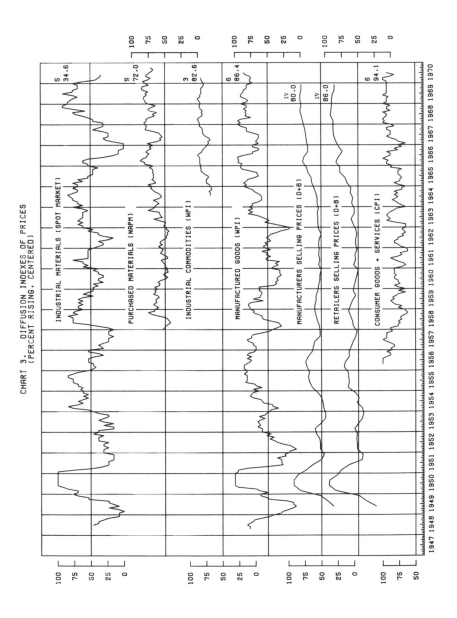

CHART 3. DIFFUSION INDEXES OF PRICES
(PERCENT RISING, CENTERED)

LEADS AND LAGS IN PRICES

The diffusion indexes in Chart 3 depict some of the sequences in the price system. But we can examine the matter more thoroughly by referring to the rates of change in a larger array of price indexes, using the price chronology as a reference frame in the same way that the business cycle chronology has been used to study leads and lags in economic activities generally. In this manner we can observe not only the leads and lags of other prices vis-à-vis the Consumer Price Index, but also their leads and lags with respect to one another.[3]

Looking first at certain major components of the Consumer Price Index we find that the turns in the commodity component match those in the total index very closely (see Table 2). On five occasions since 1956 (when the commodity-service grouping first becomes available) the turns in the rate of change in the commodity index and in the total index came in exactly the same month, while on the remaining occasion the commodity turn was one month earlier. This correspondence is due more to food prices, whose volatile movements have a marked effect on both the commodities component and the total, than to commodities other than food. As for prices of services, their well-known tendency to lag is apparent. Perhaps less well known is that the rate of change in service prices undergoes cyclical movements that correspond closely, except for the lag, to those in commodity prices. The lag of service prices behind commodity prices averages about three months. These relations are shown by Chart 4.

Turning to wholesale prices, we find that the total WPI exhibits a slight tendency to lead the total CPI (see Table 3). That is, it leads on five occasions, exactly coincides four times, and lags only once. The lead appears to derive more from the industrial commodities in the WPI than from the farm products, processed foods, and feeds component. The latter component, however, matches the CPI quite closely, and of course compares most directly with the food price component of the CPI, which, as we have seen, itself has a dominant effect on the CPI. The behavior of consumer prices depends, to an extent most city dwellers are probably unaware of, on the behavior of farm prices.

The industrial commodities component of the WPI has turned before the CPI nine times since 1948, coincided once, and lagged twice. The tendency to lead is imparted primarily by the prices for crude and intermediate materials

[3] This is possible, and efficient, only when a large portion of the cyclical turns in the other price series can be matched with those in the CPI. This is generally, but not always, the case.

TABLE 2
Leads and Lags in Rates of Change of Major Components of the Consumer Price Index, 1947−70

Item	Dates of Corresponding Peaks and Troughs					Lead (−) or Lag (+) in Months, at Turns in CPI, All Items			
	All Terms	Commod-ities[a]	Food	Other Commod-ities[a]	Ser-vices[a]	Commod-ities[a]	Food	Other Commod-ities[a]	Ser-vices[a]
Peak	10/47	−	10/47	−	−	−	0	−	−
Trough	11/48	−	11/48	−	−	−	0	−	−
Peak	11/50	−	11/50	−	−	−	0	−	−
Trough	11/52	−	2/53	−	−	−	+3	−	−
Peak	7/53	−	2/54	−	−	−	+7	−	−
Trough	8/54	−	10/54	−	−	−	+2	−	−
Peak	7/56	7/56	4/56	12/56	2/57	0	−3	+5	+7
Trough	7/58	7/58	7/58	7/58	9/58	0	0	0	+2
Peak	7/59	7/59	5/60	4/59	6/59	0	+10	−3	−1
Trough	3/61	3/61	3/61	5/60	5/61	0	0	−10	+2
Peak	1/66	1/66	12/65	−	6/66	0	−1	−	+5
Trough	1/67	12/66	1/67	−	4/67	−1	0	−	+3
Peak	2/70[b]	3/69	11/69	−	−	−	−	−	−

DATES OF EXTRA PEAKS AND TROUGHS[c]

	Food	Other Commod-ities	Ser-vices
Peak	9/63	−	7/61
Trough	4/64	10/56	10/62
Peak	−	1/58	8/63
Trough	−	−	4/65

Item	Summary of Leads and Lags in Turns in CPI, All Items			
	Commod-ities[a]	CPI, Food	Other Commod-ities[a]	Ser-vices[a]
Number of:				
Leads	1	2	2	1
Exact coincidences	5	6	1	0
Lags	0	4	1	5
Total timing comparisons	6	12	4	6
Rough coincidences[d]	6	10	2	4
Median lead (−) or lag(+), in months:				
At peaks	0	0	+1	+5
At troughs	0	0	−5	+2
At all turns	0	0	−1.5	+2.5

Note: Dashes indicate no timing comparison. Per cent changes are computed over 6-month spans, centered, and seasonally adjusted at annual rate.

[a]Data are not available before 1956.

[b]Tentative.

[c]Extra peaks and troughs are those that do not match turns in the CPI, all items.

[d]Rough coincidences include exact coincidences and leads or lags of 3 months or less.

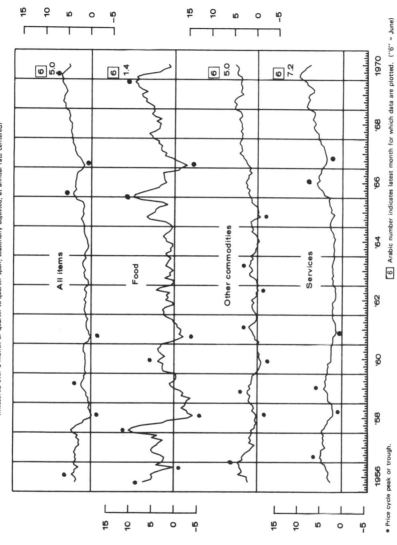

Chart 4. Rates of Change in the Consumer Price Index and its Major Components

(Measured over 6-month or quarter-to-quarter span, seasonally adjusted, at annual rate centered)

All items

Food

Other commodities

Services

6 5.0

6 1.4

6 5.0

6 7.2

• Price cycle peak or trough.

6 Arabic number indicates latest month for which data are plotted. ("6" = June)

TABLE 3
Leads and Lags in Rates of Change of Wholesale Price Indexes, 1947–70

Peaks and Troughs	CPI, All Terms	WPI, All Commodities	WPI, Industrial Commodities	WPI, Farm Products, Processed Foods and Feeds	WPI, Crude Materials	WPI, Crude Materials Less Food	Spot Market Price Index, Industrial Materials[a]	WPI, Intermediate Materials	WPI, Consumer Finished Goods	WPI, Consumer Foods	WPI, Other Consumer Consumer Goods	WPI, Producer Finished Goods
(1)	(2)	(3)	(4)	(5)	(6)	(7)	(8)	(9)	(10)	(11)	(12)	(13)
Peak	10/47	10/47	10/47	10/47	10/47	8/47	—	10/47	10/47	10/47	10/47	8/48
Trough	11/48	2/49	4/49	11/48	11/48	4/49	—	2/49	11/48	11/48	2/49	7/49
Peak	11/50	11/50	10/50	11/50	11/50	7/50	8/50	10/50	9/50	9/50	10/50	10/50
Trough	11/52	6/51	8/51	11/52	5/51	8/51	6/51	7/51	11/52	1/53	10/51	9/52
Peak	7/53	4/53	4/53	2/54	2/54	4/53	3/54	4/53	2/54	2/54	4/53	—
Trough	8/54	7/54	10/53	9/55	9/55	10/53	—	7/54	7/54	7/55	10/53	—
Peak	7/56	2/56	8/55	3/56	2/56	9/55	—	7/55	12/57	12/57	11/56	8/56
Trough	7/58	—	11/57	12/58	7/59	—	9/57	11/57	8/58	12/58	3/58	5/58
Peak	7/59	—	2/59	2/60	—	—	8/58	2/59	2/60	2/60	2/59	12/58
Trough	3/61	3/61	9/60	3/61	~	8/60	9/60	7/61	2/61	3/61	2/61	6/60
Peak	1/66	1/66	4/66	11/65	11/65	12/65	8/64	4/66	12/65	12/65	—	10/66
Trough	1/67	12/66	10/66	12/66	12/66	10/66	11/66	11/66	12/66	12/66	—	4/67
Peak	2/70[b]	3/69		3/69	3/69	5/69	6/69		12/69	12/69	—	None
				DATES OF EXTRA PEAKS AND TROUGHS[c]								
Peak		None	None	2/57	2/57	10/57					None	None
Trough				12/57	2/58	7/58	2/61	7/63	10/61	12/62		
Peak				9/61			4/62	3/64	12/62	12/63		
Trough				12/62								
Peak					9/61	4/61						
Trough					12/62	4/62						

LEADS (−) AND LAGS (+) IN MONTHS, AT TURNS IN CPI, ALL ITEMS

Turn											
Peak 10/47	0	0	0	0	—	−2	0	0	0	0	+10
Trough 11/48	+3	+5	0	+3	—	+5	0	0	+5	+3	+8
Peak 11/50	0	−1	0	−1	−3	−4	0	0	−1	−1	−1
Trough 11/52	−17	−15	−18	−16	−17	−15	−18	0	−15	−13	−2
Peak 7/53	−3	−3	+7	−3	+8	−3	+7	+7	−3	−3	—
Trough 8/54	−7	−10	+13	−1	—	−10	+13	+13	−10	−10	+1
Peak 7/56	−5	−11	−5	−12	−10	−10	−5	−4	−11	+4	−2
Trough 7/58	—	−8	+12	−8	−11	—	+12	+5	−8	−4	−7
Peak 7/59	—	−5	—	−5	−6	—	—	+7	−5	−5	−9
Trough 3/61	0	−6	—	+4	−17	−7	—	0	−6	−1	+9
Peak 1/66	0	+3	−2	+3	−2	−1	−2	−2	+3	−1	+3
Trough 1/67	−1	−3	−1	−2	—	−3	−1	−1	−3	−1	+3

SUMMARY OF LEADS AND LAGS AT TURNS IN CPI, ALL ITEMS

Number of:											
Leads	5	9	3	4	9	7	8	5	3	7	5
Exact coincidences	4	1	5	3	0	0	1	3	3	1	0
Lags	1	2	4	3	1	—	3	4	6	2	5
Total timing comparisons	10	12	12	10	10	—	12	12	12	10	10
Rough coincidences[c]	8	5	7	5	4	2	7	9	7	5	5
Median lead (−) or lag (+), in months:											
At peaks	0	−2	0	0	−3	−7	−2	+.5	3	−1	+1
At troughs	−1	−7	0	0	−7	−8	−1.5	−.5	3	−4	−2
At all turns	−5	−4	0	0	−3.5	−8	−1.5	−.5	6	−2	0

Note: Dashes indicate no timing comparison. Percentage changes are computed over 6-month spans, centered, and seasonally adjusted at annual rate.

a Weekly index, not a component of the WPI.

b Tentative.

c Extra peaks and troughs are those that do not match turns in the CPI, all items.

d Rough coincidences include exact coincidences and leads or lags of 3 months or less.

other than foods, rather than for finished goods. Prices for crude materials other than food have led nine out of ten turns in the CPI since 1947, an average lead of about four months. This index is similar in its movements and timing to the weekly index of spot market prices of industrial materials prices. On most occasions the turns in the rates of change in these two materials price indexes have occurred within a month or two of each other. Prices for producer finished goods——i.e., machinery, equipment, trucks, office furniture, etc.——show about as much tendency to lag behind as to lead the movements in the CPI. Many of these relationships as well as others are depicted in Charts 5 and 6.[4]

The rate of change in the GNP Deflator is a lagging indicator relative to the rate of change in the CPI (see Table 4). This is true also of the Private Deflator, since its turns usually coincide with those of the total. The deflators have lagged behind the turns in the CPI far more frequently than they have led or coincided with it, and the average lag has been about three months.

---

[4]The recent study by Stigler and Kindahl (*The Behavior of Industrial Prices*, New York, NBER, 1970) indicates that the substitution of an index of transaction prices for the present BLS index, which is based in large part on list prices, would, if anything, reduce the length of the leads of industrial commodity prices relative to the CPI. Their index of industrial prices covers about 19 per cent of the content of the BLS industrial commodities index, and they construct an index of comparable coverage from BLS data. The turning points in the rates of change (over six-month spans, centered) correspond as follows with those in the Consumer Price Index:

	Trough	*Peak*	*Trough*
CPI, all items	7/58	7/59	3/61
WPI, industrials			
Restricted coverage			
NBER	3/58	10/58	7/61
BLS	1/58	8/58	2/61
Total, BLS	11/57	2/59	9/60

WPI, industrials	*Lead (−) or Lag (+) in Months, at Turns in CPI*		
Restricted coverage			
NBER	−4	−9	+4
BLS	−6	−11	−1
Total, BLS	−8	−5	−6

The NBER index lags behind the comparable BLS index at each turn, apparently because of the inclusion in the former of long-term contract prices at the dates when deliveries were made rather than when the contracts were consummated. Otherwise, the transaction price index might be expected to lead.

Chart 5. Rates of Change in Wholesale Price Indexes, by Stage of Process

(Measured over 6-month span, seasonally adjusted, at annual rate, centered)

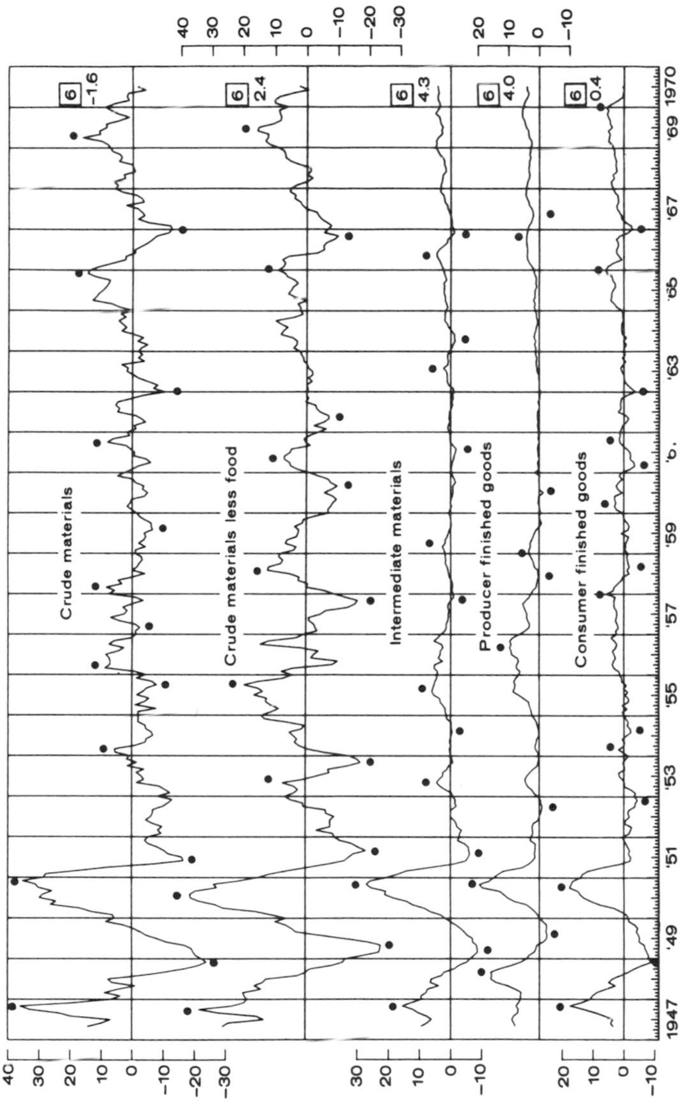
Crude materials
Crude materials less food
Intermediate materials
Producer finished goods
Consumer finished goods
6 -1.6
6 2.4
6 4.3
6 4.0
6 0.4
1947
'49
'51
'53
'55
'57
'59
'61
'63
'65
'67
'69
1970

• Price cycle peak or trough.

[6] Arabic number indicates latest month for which data are plotted. ("6" = June)

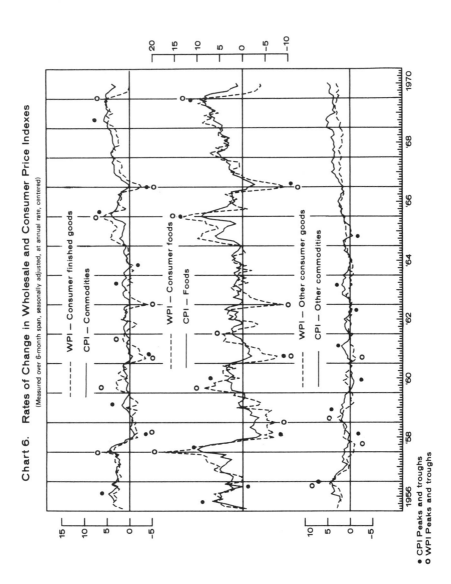

Chart 6.   Rates of Change in Wholesale and Consumer Price Indexes

(Measured over 6-month span, seasonally adjusted, at annual rate, centered)

--- WPI – Consumer finished goods
——— CPI – Commodities

--- WPI – Consumer foods
——— CPI – Foods

--- WPI – Other consumer goods
——— CPI – Other commodities

• CPI Peaks and troughs
O WPI Peaks and troughs

TABLE 4

Leads and Lags in Rates of Change of GNP Implicit Price Deflators, 1947–70

Peaks and Troughs	CPI, All Items	Dates of Corresponding Peaks and Troughs GNP deflator		Lead (−) or Lag (+), in Months, all Turns in CPI, All Items GNP deflator	
		Total	Private Sector	Total	Private Sector
Peak	10/47	10/47	10/47	0	0
Trough	11/48	4/49	1/49	+5	+2
Peak	11/50	1/51	1/51	+2	+2
Trough	11/52	4/53	4/53	+5	+5
Peak	7/53	1/54	1/54	+6	+6
Trough	8/54	7/54	7/54	−1	−1
Peak	7/56	7/56	7/56	0	0
Trough	7/58	−	−	−	−
Peak	7/59	−	−	−	−
Trough	3/61	7/61	7/61	+4	+4
Peak	1/66	4/66	4/66	+3	+3
Trough	1/67	4/67	4/67	+3	+3
Peak	2/70[a]	−	−	−	−

Item	Summary of Leads and Lags at Turns in CPI, All Items, (GNP deflator)	
	Total	Private Sector
Number of:		
Leads	1	1
Exact coincidences	2	2
Lags	7	7
Total timing comparisons	10	10
Rough coincidences[b]	6	7
Median lead (−) or lag (+), in months:		
At Peaks	+2	+2
At troughs	+4	+3
At all turns	+3	+2.5

Note: Dashes indicate no timing comparison.
[a]Tentative.
[b]Rough coincidences include exact coincidences and leads or lags of 3 months or less.

The reason for the lag may be that personal consumption expenditures——i.e., the type of expenditure reflected in the CPI——constitute less than two-thirds of total GNP, and prices for the two largest elements in the remainder——fixed investment goods and government services——are relatively sticky. The fluctuating weights in the GNP Deflator may be a factor, also. When the Deflator is computed with fixed (1958) weights, as the Department of Commerce has done since 1962, the 1966 peak and the 1967 trough in the rate of change are reached one quarter earlier, and the most recent high is two quarters earlier.

In this brief review we have, of course, only scratched the surface of the complex structure of leads and lags in the price system. In the vanguard are the wholesale prices of raw and semifabricated materials. At the rear are the retail prices of services. In between are the wholesale and retail prices of foods and many other commodities. We have dealt with fairly large groups of prices of goods and services, and have not touched upon the prices of fixed assets, such as land or buildings, or the price of labor, or interest rates. There is a large amount of room for further investigation.

PRICES, COSTS OF PRODUCTION, AND PROFITS

During the past few years a systematic body of statistics has been built up that connects the rate of change in the price level with rates of change in compensation per man-hour, output per man-hour, labor costs per unit of output, profits, and other costs per unit of output. The data are available quarterly for the private sector as a whole, as well as for certain major elements of the private sector. They tell us some things about the cyclical behavior of prices and the factors affecting them that hitherto could be inferred only indirectly, if at all.

The year-to-year rates of change in these data since 1947 for the total private economy are shown in Charts 7 and 8. They reveal that output per man-hour has risen in every year and that hourly compensation has done likewise. In most years, the increase in compensation has exceeded the increase in productivity, so labor costs per unit of output have also risen. But the fluctuations in unit labor costs are wider than in productivity or compensation, and they also bear a closer relationship to price. The remaining costs (depreciation, interest, and indirect taxes) also fluctuate considerably per unit of output, in part no doubt because of their relatively fixed nature; but they have been generally increasing relative to output in the postwar period. The fluctuations in profits per unit of output are wider still, and for the most part they move inversely with unit labor costs and with total unit costs.

Chart 7. Annual Percent Change in Prices, Productivity, Labor Compensation
and Unit Labor Costs, Total Private Economy, 1948-1970

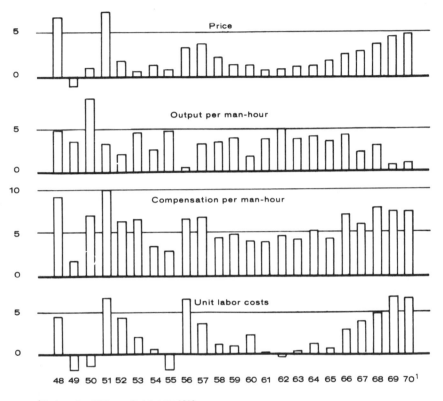

[1] 2nd quarter 1970 over 2nd quarter 1969.

Compensation and labor costs include wages and salaries and supplemental
payments for employees and an estimate of the salaries and supplements
for the self-employed. Other (nonlabor) costs include depreciation, interest
and indirect taxes. Profits include corporate profits, estimated profits of
unincorporated enterprises, and net rental earnings of owner-occupied
dwellings.

Unit costs and unit profits are total costs and profits divided by total
output.

Chart 8. Annual Percent Change in Prices and Unit Costs
Total Private Economy, 1948-1970

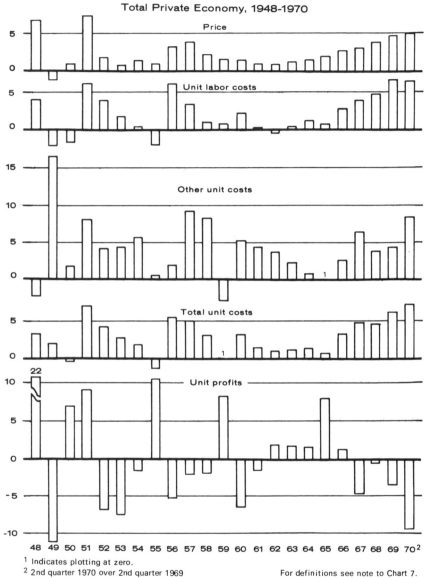

¹ Indicates plotting at zero.
² 2nd quarter 1970 over 2nd quarter 1969   For definitions see note to Chart 7.

The relationships of costs and profits to price depend not only on how they fluctuate but also on their magnitude. The data enable us to take the magnitude into account and thereby decompose the change in price into its constituent cost and profit components (see Chart 9). Thus in 1968-69, for example, when the price index rose 4.5 per cent, the share absorbed by increased unit labor costs was 4.0 percentage points; the share that went to meet increases in other unit costs was equivalent to 0.9 percentage points, while the decline in unit profits offset the rise in costs to the extent of 0.4 percentage points. In general, since payments for labor constitute the largest single cost and since unit labor costs have generally been rising, the share of unit labor costs usually has been positive and closely related to the change in price. The share of other costs is smaller, though usually positive, and less well correlated with the change in price. As often as not, the share of price change absorbed by unit profits has partly offset the increases in other costs.

A fairly characteristic picture of the behavior of costs and profits during a cyclical rise and fall in the rate of change in prices emerges from these data, particularly when use is made of the quarterly figures. At the bottom of the price cycle, with prices relatively stable or declining, the rate of increase in output per man-hour is high, but after prices start rising it diminishes as the upswing in prices continues. Rates of increase in hourly compensation, on the other hand, are usually at a moderate level during the initial phase of the upswing in prices, but soon begin to rise, partly in response to the price movement. As a joint result of the changing discrepancy between the rates of change in compensation and productivity, the rate of change in unit labor costs diminishes during the initial phase of the price expansion, but rises sharply in the later phase. Other unit costs follow somewhat the same path; so, at the start of the price expansion, costs are rising less rapidly than prices while at its close they are rising more rapidly than prices, even though the price rise has in the meantime accelerated. Unit profits, therefore, typically rise rapidly at the start of a price expansion, but decline at the end.

As the downswing in the rate of price increase begins, output per man-hour usually continues to show lower growth rates for a time, but shortly a recovery sets in. This reduction in physical costs is no doubt partly a consequence of the downswing in prices, as producers react to the profit squeeze, but it also serves to support it. Further support is provided by a decline in the rate of increase in hourly compensation. Both factors generate a decline in the rate of increase in unit labor costs. Other unit costs also show lower rates of growth as the price contraction continues. The upshot is that while the increase in total unit costs exceeds that of prices at the start of the price contraction and unit profits are therefore declining, this situation is reversed before the end of the price contraction. Cost increases become

Chart 9. Decomposition of Annual Rates of Change in Prices into Cost and Profit Components, Total Private Economy, 1948-1970

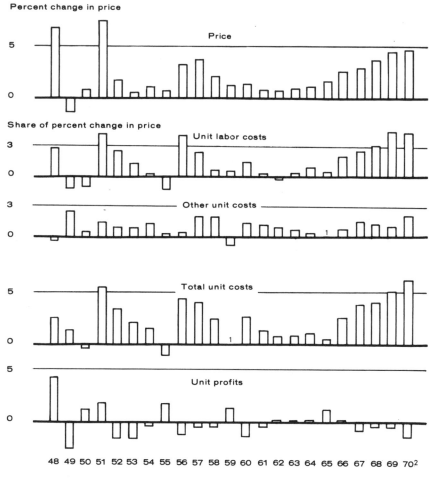

1 Indicates plotting at zero.

2 2nd quarter 1970 over 2nd quarter 1969

For definitions see note to Chart 7.

sharply lower or actual cost reductions take place, the downswing in costs exceeds that in prices, and unit profits begin rising again.

This description of the interplay of costs and profits during a cycle in the rate of change in prices is, of course, highly generalized. Although it is based on recent data, it follows fairly closely the process that Wesley Mitchell described nearly sixty years ago in his classic treatise, *Business Cycles,* whereby costs rise relative to prices and encroach upon profits during an economic boom. I believe it can still help us to comprehend and to anticipate the developments experienced both when inflationary pressures build up and when they subside.

THE CURRENT SITUATION

One of the purposes of the National Bureau's studies of business cycles was to make possible better judgments about the current economic situation. Improved statistical data, more precise knowledge of economic relationships, and better understanding of the changing nature of these relationships all serve this end. There is a reverse effect as well. The unfolding situation may, by adding one more observation, so to speak, help to confirm, to contradict, or to modify what we thought we had learned from the past. It is well, therefore, to consider some recent developments in the cyclical behavior of prices to see whether they are illuminated by, or help to illuminate, our historical findings.

Our tentative peak date for the reference chronology of prices, based upon the rate of change in the Consumer Price Index, is February 1970. This is the date when the seasonally adjusted rate of change over a six-month interval reached its highest level in the current upswing, 6.7 per cent per year, and began to decline. February is simply the central month of that interval, which runs from November 1969 to May 1970. Several factors persuade me to call this a tentative rather than a definite peak. The most important, of course, is that the subsequent decline to 6.0 per cent in March, 5.4 per cent in April, 4.8 per cent in May, and 5.0 per cent in June and July has been brief, but at present writing the July figure (representing the change from April to October) is the latest we have. The decline to date is shorter than any previous contraction in our chronology——the shortest was 12 months in 1966-67. In magnitude, the decline (1.7 percentage points) is smaller than in 1966-67 (2.4 points). Unless the decline continues, therefore, it will not qualify as a contraction in our chronology.

Although we cannot, therefore, at this time consider the peak to be firmly established, there are a number of bits of evidence pointing in that direction. First, the rates of change in the CPI over shorter spans than six months show peaks around the turn of the year, with much larger declines thereafter. Next, our observations upon leads and lags suggest that a peak in the rate of change in the CPI is apt to be matched closely by one in food prices and to be followed by one in service prices. In fact, food prices reached their highest rate of increase over a six-period interval, nearly 9 per cent per year, in November 1969. The decline to the latest figure, about 1 per cent at an annual rate, has been precipitous. As for services, their high point to date, about 9½ per cent, occurred in February 1970, some three months after the turn in food prices.

Third, corroboration is to be found in the behavior of other price indexes, notably the WPI, where we now have data through November. The total index reached its peak rate of increase (over a six-month span, seasonally adjusted at annual rate) in March 1969 at 5 per cent, and has declined since then to about 2 per cent. The decisive drop occurred in the farm products, processed foods, and feeds component, from 8½ per cent in December 1969[5] to a negative figure currently (September 1970). Industrial commodity prices, as usual, have shown a much milder movement but nevertheless did decline from a 4 per cent rate in October 1969 to about 3 per cent currently. The drop in the rate of change in food prices at wholesale has been sharper than at retail, as has usually been the case in the past. The high month was December 1969, at 10 per cent, and the latest figure is −2 per cent.

The prices of crude materials at wholesale have played their traditional role by declining early and sharply. Their peak rate of increase, 16 per cent per year, was attained in March 1969. The latest, and lowest, rate is −3 per cent. The weekly industrial materials index has behaved in a similar, though more extreme, fashion, by declining from a peak rate of increase of 25 per cent per year in January 1969 to a current low of −14 per cent, a drop of 39 percentage points in the past year and a half. The GNP Deflator reached its fastest rate of increase between the fourth quarter of 1969 and the first quarter of 1970, namely, 6.4 per cent. The latest figure, for the second to the third quarter, is 4.6 per cent.

Finally, all the diffusion indexes of Chart 3 have receded from their highs, which were reached during 1968 and 1969. The decline to date has been largest in the index that has typically moved earliest: industrial materials prices. In general, the rise in prices is no longer as widespread as it was, and price reductions are now somewhat more common.

All these developments are consistent with what has happened during past economic slowdowns. Although we must await further evidence to be confident that a decline of substantial dimensions in the rate of change in prices is under way, if this welcome development does take place it will mark

[5] The cyclical peak is March 1969, at 9 per cent.

one more occasion when the price system has reacted to a reduction in demand pressures.

The long-continued upswing in the rate of change in prices, and its recent subsidence, have been accompanied by changes in costs and profits that bear a striking resemblance to earlier episodes. Table 5 tells the story. Between 1964 and 1969 unit labor costs accelerated steadily, partly as a result of the acceleration in compensation rates per hour, partly because of the retardation in output per man-hour. Other costs also accelerated, but the big contributor to the advance in the rate of increase in total costs was labor cost. By 1966 costs were rising faster than prices, and they have continued to do so every year since. At the same time, unit profits began to decline, and they have

TABLE 5

Percentage Change in Prices, Costs, and Profits,
Total Private Economy, 1965–70

Year	Price	Output	Output per Man-hour	Compensa- tion per Man-hour	Unit Labor Costs	Other Unit Costs[a]	Total Unit Costs	Unit Profit[b]
Change from preceding year								
1965	1.7	6.6	3.4	4.1	0.7	0.0	0.5	8.0
1966	2.5	6.4	4.0	6.9	2.8	2.5	2.8	1.3
1967	2.9	2.3	2.1	5.8	3.7	6.2	4.4	−4.5
1968	3.6	4.9	2.9	7.6	4.6	3.7	4.3	−0.4
1969	4.5	2.9	0.7	7.2	6.5	4.1	5.8	−3.3
1970[c]	4.6	−0.2	0.9	7.3	6.3	9.2	7.1	−10.8
Change from preceding quarter at annual rate								
1969								
Third	4.5	2.5	1.6	8.2	6.5	5.5	6.2	−5.9
Fourth	4.7	−1.0	0.8	8.8	7.9	10.1	8.5	−17.5
1970								
First	5.3	−3.0	−2.5	6.8	9.6	9.0	9.4	−20.0
Second	4.1	0.7	3.7	5.3	1.5	12.3	4.4	1.8
Third	4.5	1.6	4.6	7.7	3.0	9.6	4.8	2.4

Source: U.S. Department of Labor, Bureau of Labor Statistics, September 1970.
[a]Includes depreciation, interest, and indirect taxes.
[b]Includes corporate profits, estimated profits of unincorporated enterprises, and set rental earnings of owner-occupied dwellings.
[c]Second quarter 1969 to second quarter 1970.

declined each year also. Mitchell himself could not have asked for a better illustration of the process he described.

The annual time unit used in Table 5 is too crude to show changes during the past few months, but the quarterly data reveal an important shift. Between the first and second quarters of this year the rate of change in the price index for the private sector fell to 4 per cent, the lowest rate since 1968. Output per man-hour advanced at an annual rate of about 3 per cent, also the best showing since 1968. Coupled with a decline in the rate of increase in hourly compensation to about 5 per cent, this produced a sharp decline in the rate of increase in unit labor costs to around 2 per cent. Quarter-to-quarter changes are, of course, erratic, but the directions these changes began to take in the second quarter and continued in the third are in line with what previous experience suggests is likely when an inflationary boom comes to an orderly end and a downswing in the price cycle begins.

THE NEED FOR FURTHER WORK

In my former capacity at the National Bureau of Economic Research, one of my favorite pieces of advice to authors was to close their reports with suggestions for further research and for improved statistics. To follow my own advice on this occasion is surely fitting.

I shall confine myself to a single general admonition, which is, to pay more attention to the price side of economics. Over the past twenty-five years or so, this aspect has been relatively neglected. It is time, I think, for a change. A great concern has developed over the problem of inflation in this country, and not only in this country but around the world. Our ability to cope with it depends on our ability to understand it, and the starting point for understanding is statistical information and research.

Statistical information and research has helped to resolve the problem of the business cycle. The cyclical behavior of prices is ripe for an equally thorough probing. The National Bureau of Economic Research and the Bureau of Labor Statistics, continuing a long and fruitful cooperative relationship, might well devote themselves to this end.

DISCUSSION—MORNING SESSION

Includes comments by Paul Samuelson, of the Massachusetts Institute of Technology, who was chairman of this session; Otto Eckstein, of Harvard University, and Henry Wallich, of Yale University, who acted as program discussants; and Bert Hickman, of Stanford University, who offered additional observations; also, comments by Moore on the papers by Fabricant and Mintz and a reply by Mintz. The recorded oral presentations were edited by, or with the cooperation of, the speakers. Remarks made during the open discussion period are not included.

Introductory Remarks by Paul Samuelson

Now that the National Bureau is fifty years old, it has worked itself out of one of its first jobs, namely, the business cycle. I don't know when the American Cancer Society was founded, but by similar reasoning fifty years after that date some optimist could hope to cross cancer off his list. The Bureau was thus in danger of becoming just a museum of fossils; but nobody likes to work himself out of a job, so you naturally redefine the field of study. I predicted some time ago that this would happen, and Ilse Mintz this morning has confirmed my prediction.

I am not sure whether it is a healthy sign in a science when you have experts quoting what some expert said back in 1946, and some other expert said even earlier—however appropriate reminiscing may be for a fiftieth birthday party. The discussion then becomes very academic— almost that of the medieval schoolmen, almost talmudic. Substantively, I would like to make three brief observations. The first relates to the story told by our President Meyer about his being told on a visit to Japan that during what they call a recession real output does not decline but rather grows only by 5 and 12 per cent. I suggest that this is not a joke, but deserves really very serious consideration. Second, I'd like to add a similar observation: If our president would go to Latin America, he might hear some Brazilian or Chilean economists speak about a recession in the sense that the rate of growth of the price level has gone from 70 per cent per year down to only 30 per cent per year. That, too, suggests the importance of both the study of price growth cycles, Geoffrey Moore's subject, and the use of deflators. And finally, for the non-academic members of this group, I might mention that there is a third facet of life that some people consider important. I have in mind a recent interview with Sidney Homer, of Salomon Brothers and Hutzler. He said that this may seem like a mild recession to academics, but from the standpoint of Wall Street and the capital markets it has been quite a serious situation. I invite you to recall 1953–54 from this viewpoint. Everybody agrees it represented both a growth cycle and an old-fashioned recession. But from the standpoint of the financial market it probably was hardly noticed at all, whereas the present experience which Homer made reference to has been very important in the financial area, as was the nonrecession of 1961–62.

*   *   *

Otto Eckstein: I am very pleased to be able to participate in this Fiftieth Anniversary celebration of the Bureau. My own ties to the Bureau are fairly tenuous; I am only a director. You know what that means!

I learned my National Bureau methodology not at the feet of Wesley Mitchell or Arthur Burns, but from Gottfried Haberler, when he was president of the Bureau. So if I say anything unsound you will have to blame it on Gottfried.

The fact that you asked outsiders to comment was an open invitation to be a bit broad-minded about the subject, to be a bit of a gadfly, and I will oblige. Let me start with the final question. Are we in a recession, or are we not? We really don't have trouble with the facts; we only have trouble with fitting them into the National Bureau definition. All through the postwar period, we have had genuine business cycles with all the proper absolute declines, and the slowdowns of '52 and '62. There is no ambiguity about these cases, and the growth cycle definition picks them up very easily. I don't think there are any close decisions. The current episode is on the margin of recession, and the growth recession clearly covers the case. So it appears to be useful.

How do we move from here? What do we do with the National Bureau cycle methodology now that we move to the growth cycle concept? First, we have to draw a clear distinction between measuring the economic process and measuring economic performance. Performance focuses on advancement of economic goals, full employment, growth, price stability, etc. The Bureau, on the other hand, measures process, which is the basic building block of the theory of Wesley Mitchell. It is the theory in Arthur Burns's more modern statement. It is what the leading indicators try to measure—some things happen before others. It is usually intuitively obvious what precedes what, and the National Bureau has made an enormous contribution in trying to develop this sequence of processes. This has really been the substructure of the subsequent definitions of cycles. On the other hand, when people are interested whether there is a recession or not, the process definition can get in the way. One of the things that is odd about it, compared to the man-in-the street's notion, is that recession is defined to be the period of contraction; it begins at the peak, when nobody feels in a recession. It ends at the lower turning point, and yet three months after that turning point people are out of a job, profits are down; it still feels like recession. The reason is that the public thinks about performance, and the definition is in terms of process. What is it we wish to measure? Do we wish to continue to focus only on process, or do we also wish to measure performance? Your *Annual Report* shows various projects on measuring social indicators, and there the same problem appears. Are we going to measure process, or are we going to measure performance? Most people assume that there will be performance measures—performance in the sense of how well we are achieving our goal.

Let me make a few specific points on the papers. The paper by Ilse Mintz moves the subject forward in a very significant substantive way, and I think it contains in it the foundation for where one should go. Let me put out a few warning signs early in the game before it becomes official Bureau dogma. First, the seventeen indicators in her paper are still a hodgepodge of different things. There are real magnitudes, such as production, employment, and unemployment. There are money magnitudes, such as personal income and profits, among others. And there are interest rates. We are having an inflationary recession in which the price level has not slowed down as quickly as real activity, so a blend of money and real indicators becomes confused and measures nothing.

Sol Fabricant has faced up to that question very clearly and has come to a conclusion. I have come to the same conclusion. We don't want a single composite indicator. What, then, would we want? First, we should switch to the growth cycle idea because, given the values of society, the probability of a traditional recession with unemployment of 7 per cent is fairly low; and in every meaningful episode you do have a growth cycle.

Second, we don't want to lose the idea of process. However, once we accept it, we have to go back to the distinction of leading, coincident, and lagging indicators—but focused around growth rather than just the cycle.

Third, I would give up the idea of an all-in-one leading indicator (God forbid, weighted equally). At the very least—and here Julie Shiskin and BCD [*Business Conditions Digest*] have led the way—we do need subindexes, and we need to emphasize that it is in the subindexes in which the truth resides, not in a composite. We definitely need a growth index which is a real measure based on production, payroll data, perhaps unemployment data, perhaps income data as well, but the income had better be deflated. We need another set of indexes—which Geoff Moore has started—on prices and costs; here, particularly, the process is important, and we hope that the BLS will move ahead and produce leading, coincident, and lagging indexes of prices and costs.

Fourth, we probably need some kind of a subindex on the financial sector, though I have not thought through its conceptual foundations.

Finally, I would hope that the Bureau would apply its expertise more explicitly to develop the social indicators. I would hope that the social indicator project will benefit from the long history of the Bureau on the traditional economic indicators, and that you will attempt to develop the same kind of work carefully. This might include such factors as income distribution, minority unemployment, etc. I am tempted to urge leading, coincident, and lagging social indicators. How does social progress happen? What are the early signs of social disintegration? There is a need for indicators of process and of performance.

Henry Wallich: The principal topic to which I would like to address myself is the shift in definitions, from an absolute cycle to a growth cycle.

As a general proposition it seems to me that when ancient definitions cease to reflect current reality it is a good thing to shift gears and get it over as quickly as possible. There is so much inertia in every system that whatever one can do to move things ahead will probably be to the good. I am also impressed by the usefulness of a change in definitions in terms of the self-preservation of the cyclical analyst. As Paul Samuelson pointed out—when by traditional measures the cycle seems to disappear, we have to redefine it so as to be able to earn our daily bread.

The change that is being proposed here is a particularly brilliant one because, while updating definitions, it also recaptures the cycle. As you will remember, the cycle has twice deserted the analysts. It deserted them first when it ceased to be periodic. Periodicity, after all, is implicit in the term "cycle"; but that aspect somehow got lost in the course of time. It deserted the analysts a second time when it refused to turn down in an absolute sense. Now, by shifting to a growth cycle, all is recovered. Not only are there downturns. There is also again periodicity, because we have a rather plain pattern of, I think, four growth recessions during each of the postwar decades; the soaring sixties and the fumbling fifties suddenly look alike in the number of recessions, and they look alike in periodicity.

This much said in favor of a change in definition, I nevertheless become a little ill at ease when I observe the policy implications. Here I must apologize to the two speakers. I realize that they do not draw policy implications from their scholarly findings. Unfortunately, one cannot put fine print into headlines, and people sometimes do not read fine print. If they see a headline "National Bureau Declares Recession" it does not help a great deal to have it said somewhere in the paper that this really is no call for an easier monetary policy or a budget deficit.

It is my fear that, in going to a growth cycle definition for income and for prices, we are doing a bad thing in terms of policy making. In the area where we have done relatively well, the area of income stabilization, we are now raising our standards. In the area where we have done relatively badly, in the area of price stability, we seem to be lowering our standards. With apologies to Geoff Moore, one hardly can blame a reader of his excellent paper for failing to note the difference between reducing the rate of inflation and achieving stability. Thus we establish a lower performance test on inflation and a tougher performance test on income. Hence, as Mrs. Mintz points out at the beginning of her paper, there is a clear danger of inviting more inflationary policies.

My final caution on the definition of the cycle is this: Any definition of an economic pattern ought to allow for the possibility of its non-existence. If we define the cycle in such a way that it must necessarily exist, because fluctuations in the rate of growth are inevitable, we have lost some of the interest inherent in the analysis of business cycles. These are the misgivings I have about the principle of the redefinition.

As for the timing of the proposed redefinition, clearly this must be done in the light of experience. Mrs. Mintz cites some of the elder statesmen of the National Bureau to the effect that we have to keep observing how the definitions stand up in the light of developments. On the other hand, there is a danger of tailoring new definitions too closely to a single event—acting too much under the impression, for instance, of the disappearance of the traditional cycle during the 1960's. We may be in danger of doing that now.

The conclusion that I would draw, as far as analysis and policy action are concerned, is this: The new definition, if it is to be accepted, ought to be "defused." It should be defused in the sense that any current policy implications should be removed as clearly as possible. That means, for instance, to maintain the old definition along with the new. It might mean to differentiate among different degrees of severity of the new cycle. We could say, for instance, that a given move was a very slight one, or a more severe one, or that a growth cycle had changed into the old traditional cycle. It would be very unfortunate if publication of a monthly GNP index, as Geoff Moore suggests, were to give rise to demands for expansionary policies each time the rate of growth turned down, which could happen several times a year.

On the question of whether we have been in a recession, I agree with President Meyer that this is not the subject of today's session, and it is, in any event, an irrelevant question. By the narrowest of margins, if one takes a couple of billion very seriously, one could say that there were two successive quarters of downturn. I was impressed by the complete absence from today's discussion of this popular conception of National Bureau theology, namely, two successive quarters of downturn. But that is the popular conception, and seventeen indicators will not eradicate it. By that popular test, one can argue there was or that there was not a recession. I would not put enough weight on the fourth quarter of 1969 to say that there was. What I would stress is that, by this test, an expansion started, in the second quarter, because the trough of the movement evidently was in the first. The upturn, therefore, is substantially behind us. If the automobile strike causes a drop in the fourth quarter somebody will undoubtedly say that this was the year in which we managed to have two recessions.

In conclusion, we have on one side the "new cycle," which seems to argue for more hectic policy activity, while on the other side there is the New New Economics, which argues against fine tuning and instead for very stable policies, both monetary and fiscal. I would urge that we combine these two novelties and do the best we can flexibly but not hectically.

*   *   *

Bert Hickman: I am in the enviable position of having the opportunity without having had the responsibility—I think I really ought to take advantage of that. As I've been sitting here I've been thinking of some historical and doctrinal comments I want to make. I hope they're not particularly dull, and don't take us too far back into history. There are some names I would have thought might have come up in this discussion but have not. These names, long associated with the National Bureau, include Kuznets and Abramovitz. And the reason I think of them is that they talked about something called growth cycles too—the long swings in the rate of economic growth. This concept was originally coined by Kuznets, and also by Arthur Burns, who worked on it in the 1930's. In more recent years Moses Abramovitz has spent a great deal of time and effort investigating, dating, and analyzing long swings in the rate of growth. There may be some awkwardness developed if we start talking about growth cycles in this new sense that Mrs. Mintz has proposed, because that terminology is also sometimes used in connection with the long swings in the rate of growth—sometimes called growth cycles, also sometimes called Kuznets cycles.

Another name which I thought might have come up is that of Ruth Mack, because Ruth Mack for many years was interested in something she called the subcycle.[1] This included the concept of a possible cycle consisting not of an absolute decline but a retardation in the rate of growth. Of course, for Ruth Mack this was primarily connected with the question of inventory phenomena; and the endogenous component, if any, of these subcycles, was thought to have something to do with the inventory investment process.

So, I would think, it might be very interesting to try to review some of that earlier work in the context of this present chronology. Given the fact that you have the long swings or long growth cycles, it might be useful to think in terms of a parallel to the major and minor business cycle concept, which was also popular for many years. The distinction between major contractions and minor contractions was primarily associated with Alvin Hansen's and R. A. Gordon's work on business cycles. We might have major and minor growth cycles now—that's a possibility, I suppose.

All this suggests a more basic point I want to stress: I would hope that to the extent that this new method of looking at changes in aggregate economic activity does become rooted in study, there will be an effort made to distinguish among different kinds of so-called growth cycles, instead of treating it as all one phenomenon, because I don't really think it is all one phenomenon. I think that's a very important point. The distinction between major and minor business cycles is con-

[1] As presented at the colloquium, the paper by Mrs. Mintz did not include the discussion of the subcycle concept which appears in the final version included in this volume. [Ed.]

cerned not only with amplitude characteristics, but also with the notion that there were different causal factors at work. Similarly, Ruth Mack's subcycle distinction was getting at the notion that there were different causal factors at work. So one would hope that this new chronology will not be used in such a way that everything becomes averaged into one set of turning point comparisons, one set of reference cycle and specific cycle patterns, and so forth, instead of taking the opportunity of perhaps thinking of some of these growth retardations (I would prefer that term to growth recession) as being due to different causes and having different implications than others.

I was struck by some of these differences in looking at some of the charts that have been presented, and one in particular strikes me as important and I would like to mention that specifically. (Oh, by the way, one more thing on terminology. One way around this terminological problem is to use Schumpeter's device. You remember he made the distinction between Kondratieff, Juglar, and Kitchin cycles. And later we had the Kuznets cycle, or major growth cycle. We could think of a Mintz or a Mack cycle, or perhaps Mack-Mintz might turn out to be the proper term; it depends on what correlation there is between Ruth Mack's work and Ilse Mintz's work, and I just don't know that at this point, but I suspect there may well be a high correlation in their chronologies.) The thing that strikes me is a chart that appeared in Sol Fabricant's paper. It's a chart on the relation of GNP in 1958 dollars to potential GNP. There's a corresponding chart on the inverted unemployment rate and the GNP gap as a percentage of potential GNP. These are panels B1 and B2 of Chart 1 in the paper. And the thing that strikes me is this, that the most recent growth cycle distinguished by Ilse Mintz before the present one was in 1962–64. And that looks to me very different from this present one in one particular respect. The retardation of growth in 1962–64 carried only to the potential output line if you regard that as the one drawn on this particular chart, and correspondingly, the unemployment rate stayed at slightly less than 4 per cent and was stable throughout that period. If you look at the recent period, according to this chart we've been carried a considerable distance below potential output and the unemployment rate has risen considerably above 4 per cent—in fact it's recently reached 5 per cent. Now you might want to call both of these things growth retardations or growth recessions, but I think it makes a lot of difference to have a deceleration that does not carry unemployment above that which is regarded as the full employment level and one which does. In somewhat the same vein, there's the very old story that we might remind ourselves of—if you go back to the period between 1960 and 1965, there are certainly periods there of an upswing in the growth cycle, an increase in the rate of increase of GNP, but it's still not carried up to full employment. What I wish to do here is simply to reinforce those remarks that have already been made about the need to be careful in drawing policy implications from this kind of chronology. One has to look at what's happening in these different episodes to the performance of unemployment, to actual GNP in relation to potential, to rates of price increases, and so forth, so as to try to distinguish among these episodes to understand why some of them are mild and some severe.

*   *   *

Paul Samuelson: In connection with the last point made, I was a little disappointed, when Otto spoke about performance, that he immediately began to talk about social indicators, because that sounds as if it's a shift from the hard economics to a soft noneconomics. And he may have intended only that, although he did indicate inequality and so forth. But he didn't use the word "gap." Now the whole Keynesian thrust for two decades, which rather pointed away from an interest in National Bureau matters, was: *It's the level of unemployment and how well we do with respect to our potential that is the most important thing.* I remember as a student that I couldn't care less whether 1924 or 1927 were regarded as bona fide National Bureau cycles. There were some disputes among the scholastics of that day. Well, similarly, a decade from now nobody will be interested *really* in similar nice questions. Going back to how you create work for yourself, if we think of a man who is an expert in dinosaurs—let's say in a university or in a museum—and he runs out of dinosaurs, well, he can, of course, redefine a lizard to be a dinosaur and keep up his budget. But you can't really interest people in lizards— because they're really *not* dinosaurs, and they're not as interesting. The reason that we used to be so desperately interested in the Wesley Mitchell process was because in the bad old days that conventional business cycle process was unmistakably associated with very bad performance. And so a humanitarian like Wesley Mitchell could take the oath of pure science knowing that the things he did in pure science would be extremely interesting. However, what really has happened, it seems to me, is not that the cycle has disappeared but that its spectrum has shifted; namely, it used to be a cycle that went from high unemployment to low unemployment at reasonably stable prices, and now it's a cycle that goes through a somewhat similar unemployment range but with prices moving cyclically around an average that represents creeping inflation. The amplitude of the movement, if you can define something that consists of different dimensions, might not be all that different. Also, in respect to Japanese and German cycles, I understand that the amplitude of their growth cycles in terms of GNP behavior was approximately the same as that of the American cycle only over a different spectrum of average real growth rates.

*   *   *

Geoffrey H. Moore: Both Fabricant and Mintz agree, and I agree with them, that the recent economic slowdown has been an exceedingly mild affair compared with the business cycle contractions experienced in the past. Gross national product in constant dollars declined from the third quarter of 1969 to the first quarter of 1970 by about 1 per cent, which is much smaller than the declines in two of the mildest recessions in the National Bureau's hundred-year chronology, those of 1926–27 and 1960–61. Furthermore, one must always remember that GNP figures are revised, and that in each of the past four recessions, including 1960–61, the revised figures showed a smaller drop than the preliminary. Since the current figures have not yet been revised, the chances are that when they have been, the current slowdown will look even milder than it does now. Other measures of aggregate activity, however, confirm the finding that the recent dip has been exceptionally small.

What is more controversial in the two papers are the attempts at a new definition. Fabricant seems ready to adopt a definition that has not been thoroughly tested. Mintz tests rather thoroughly two types of definition, neither of which Fabricant accepts. In my paper, I use still another method of developing a cyclical chronology, which seems to me particularly appropriate in studying prices. So we have a variety of approaches, but no consensus. In view of this, I believe that Fabricant's conclusion, namely, that a new and untested method be adopted now, and used to characterize the current situation, is premature.

Fabricant does not tell us how the method he proposes, which depends upon trend-fitting, would have worked in the past—how reasonable or unreasonable its specific results would be. He concentrates most of his attention on how it would have worked in 1969–70.

Methods of cyclical analysis that depend on trend-fitting have been notoriously weak, because the cycles defined by a fitted trend depend significantly on the type of trend that is fitted, what period is used in fitting it, how it is extrapolated, and how deviations from it are measured and analyzed.

For example, the growth trend used in measuring potential GNP has been raised in steps from 3.5 per cent in 1952–62, to 3.75 per cent in 1962–65, to 4.0 per cent in 1965–69 and to 4.3 per cent in 1969–70. If, instead, the 3.75 percent rate had been used from the start and extrapolated through 1970, GNP would have been below "potential" ever since 1955. Cycles defined in terms of deviations from a trend line are highly sensitive to the particular trend that is used.

Fabricant suggests, however, that trends be used in a different manner. A recession would be defined as a "sustained and widely diffused decline in the rate of growth of real aggregate economic activity, relative to its long-term trend." If we adopt his definition, he says, 1966–67 and perhaps 1962 as well as other periods might be identified as recessions. In the case of 1966–67, if we take the 4 per cent rate of growth in potential GNP as the criterion, the quarterly rates fell below this from QII–1966 to QI–1968 with the exception of two isolated quarters. That is, there was a "recession" lasting almost two years. Would anyone accept this as a reasonable definition? Furthermore, since rates of growth of real GNP remained above 4 per cent only for the next three quarters, the implication is that since the beginning of 1966 we have been in a "recession" more than 80 per cent of the time. During most of this period, of course, the unemployment rate was well below 4 per cent, and the price level was climbing at a rapid rate. The term "recession," or even "growth recession" just does not seem to fit.

Fabricant indicates he would not be willing to depend upon a single series, say, real GNP. If not, what method of trend determination is to be applied to other series, and what would the results look like? Since such trend-adjusted series are not in common use today—and even the GNP gap measurement has suffered some diminution in attention, partly because it seems to require rather arbitrary shifts in the rate of trend growth—is it wise to adopt a method of defining the business cycle that depends upon data that are not widely used and accepted? This is my principal criticism of Ilse Mintz's trend-deviation method.

It is not quite so obvious as it may first appear that deflated aggregates should be the desideratum, as Fabricant argues. The price level does reflect what is happening to the state of demand. Suppose the physical volume of sales has been declining, but begins to rise at a rate of 3 per cent per year. Suppose the price level has been falling, and continues to fall for a time, say, at a rate of 4 per cent per year. Has an expansion in economic activity begun, or not? That is, if sales are rising, but the aggregate *value* of what is being sold is falling, is "economic activity" rising or falling? To put it another way, should not the severity of a recession (or a possible recession) be judged in part by what is happening to demand, including prices? If one of our goals is stability in the price level, should not the price level be considered in judging the degree of instability? Exclusive emphasis on the physical volume of activity or the utilization of capacity in defining the business cycle, it seems to me, means paying less attention to the behavior of the price level. This does not, of course, mean that current-dollar aggregates or price indexes should be used exclusively either. I do think they have a bearing on how we should define a recession, and when it starts or ends.

Although Fabricant does pay some attention to the concept of diffusion, he does not deal with the idea that business cycle turning points have in the past been chosen to represent the consensus among a large number of economic activities. A peak in a broad aggregate can generally be depended upon to represent the consensus of peaks in its components. This concept of consensus has great advantages in analyzing a large number of different economic series, since comparisons of each with the consensus is a short-cut way of getting at direct comparisons of one series with another. If series A leads the business cycle and series B lags, we can usually infer that series A leads series B. It is not clear what happens to this idea when business cycles are defined in terms of growth rates. They will certainly no longer represent the consensus of up-and-down movements in individual series. Should all series be converted to growth rates? If not, how does one use the business cycle chronology in analyzing individual series?

Finally, a word about "step cycles." Mrs. Mintz's use of this idea for defining a cycle in rates of growth is ingenious, and carefully executed. The principal question I have about it is that the rates of growth to which the steps are fitted do not look much like steps. Without smoothing, as she points out, most rates of change are jagged, irregular, randomlike series. After smoothing, it seems to me, they look much like other series, and they do not proceed in steps. The step-fitting operation, therefore, seems to be imposing on the data something that is not obviously there. This is the reason why, in my chronology of the rate of change in prices, I simply identified peaks and troughs in rates of change measured over a long enough span so that most of the irregularities were erased and cyclical movements exposed.

To sum up, a number of empirical and theoretical matters need to be considered in adopting or changing the definition of business cycles. I'm all for considering them, but it seems to me premature to adopt them without further empirical testing. Ilse Mintz has begun this work, and I hope that others, including Fabricant, will take it up.

Reply by Ilse Mintz

Terminology

The terms that I use—growth cycles, speedups, slowdowns—leave much to be desired, and I would be glad to drop them if better ones were suggested. (Lempert suggests "high-rate phase," "low-rate phase," which is correct but very awkward.)

But however deficient they may be, using new terms is a great deal better than using old terms with a new meaning. Fabricant uses "recession" for periods which differ in dates, durations, amplitudes, etc., from traditional recessions. My objection to this has absolutely nothing to do with whether the new definition is or is not in the spirit of the old one. As long as measures of duration, amplitude, and so on, based on the new concept differ from their counterparts based on the old concept, separate terms are needed for clarity and simplicity. If both types of measures are described as measures of "recessions" it becomes necessary to add to each statement or table a note saying which concept of recession is being referred to.

Even now, Fabricant's use of "recession" has given the misleading impression that his and my conclusions about 1969–70 are different. In fact, they are very nearly the same, except that he calls "recession" what I call "slowdown."

The Alternative Revised Concepts

A decline in selected indicators: Moore has suggested (orally) that a slowdown could be defined as a decline in those indicators which still do show absolute falls.

My objection to this proposal is that most indicators of this type are leaders and thus not usable for a chronology. When we look at

1966–67 as a good example of the type of episode we want to define, we find that only the following coincident indicators declined: some (not all) measures of the labor market, interest rates, and the industrial production index. Determination of a cycle would thus rest on very thin evidence, which might easily dwindle further in the near future so that another revision might soon be required. The concept of a widely diffused decline in aggregate activity would, of course, be abandoned by this definition.

Peaks and troughs in rates of change: Moore's method for price cycles is to identify turns in the rate of change measured over six-month spans and centered in the middle month. This method is very useful for interprice comparisons, but it is not suitable (and has not been proposed by Moore) for reference cycle dating.

The main reason for not using growth rate turns is explained below. In addition it should be noted that the method is not as simple and familiar as one might think from inspection of Moore's charts. How many readers realize that a peak in, say, February 1970 has nothing to do with what happened in that month, but signifies that the rise from November to December 1969 was greater than the rise from May to June 1970? Also, the turning date depends on the choice of the span. For instance, the peak in the rate of change of the CPI is in March 1969, with a three-month span, and in February 1970 with a six-month span.

Deflated indicators: This method (Fabricant's) is discussed in Moore's comments. I will add only that the main difference between it and my deviation cycles is in the type of trend removed. While I remove the total trend, Fabricant removes only that part of the trend which is due to inflation. He classifies a period as expansion as long as real growth is positive. Alternation of a period of 10 per cent real growth with one of 1 per cent real growth is not regarded as a cycle. The years 1961–69 remain an unbroken expansion.

It will be very interesting to see the results obtained with this method, but I doubt that it goes far enough in adjusting the cycle concept to current needs. Since the absence of traditional recessions is not solely due to inflation, we will not obtain by deflation the distinction between cycle phases that is needed as an analytic tool and that corresponds to the general views on current fluctuations.

Cycles in deviations from trends: Moore's principal criticisms of this method are the arbitrariness of trend adjustment and the unfamiliarity of trend-adjusted data. Both objections are justified. The question is whether they outweigh the objections to the use of data that are not trend-adjusted.

Since my reference cycle is based on a number of indicators, each adjusted by its own trend, the choice of the trend line is not as crucial as in the GNP-gap approach, cited by Moore, where *everything* depends on one trend. Furthermore, the deviation cycles are not accepted unless they are confirmed by the step-cycle method.

As to the unusual form of the data, I think the public will quickly get used to detrended series just as it got used to deseasonalized, deflated, and rates-of-change series.

Step cycles: Evidently the explanation of step cycles in my colloquium paper is insufficient and greatly in need of improvement. The step-cycle concept does not rest on the assumption that growth rates are a peculiar type of series moving stepwise. Moore is right in finding that growth rate curves, except for choppiness, look like curves of other series. The reason for the step-cycle treatment of rates of change is that they must be interpreted differently from other series. What is commonly regarded as a period of expansion is not a period of rising growth rates, but a period of high growth rates.

Growth rate peaks typically occur shortly after cyclical upturns, so that expansions of the economy are characterized largely by falling, not by rising, growth rates. In terms of growth rates, a business cycle is an alternation between high and low rates, not between rising and falling rates. In traditional business cycles "low" rates must be negative; in growth cycles they may be either positive or negative. The month in which high growth ends is the downturn. Usually this is also the month in which above-trend growth ends, the date of downturn of the deviation cycle.

The turning points are selected by our efficient computer program, which partitions the interval between two upturns into a high-rate and a low-rate period in such a way that the variance between the two steps is maximized. It enables us to distinguish between periods of above-average and below-average rates independently of any arbitrarily imposed trend line.

In answer to Moore's questions, near the end of his comment, there is high consensus among individual growth rate series. Except for one cycle, sixteen out of the seventeen indicators agree in some months of each cycle phase. All series are converted into growth rates or first differences.

The Urgency of Choosing a Revised Business Cycle Definition

Moore thinks that further testing is required. Juster believes it will be a long time for a decision to be made.

In my view the decision should be made right now. The need for a reference frame is so great that, in the absence of leadership from the NBER, every analyst is driven to devise his own method. This is what is happening today, and the various methods used are, of course, short-cuts and inferior to NBER methods. As the responses to my colloquium paper suggest, a tower-of-Babel confusion has replaced the former uniform NBER concepts.

Forecasting Economic Conditions: The Record and the Prospect

Victor Zarnowitz

University of Chicago and National Bureau of Economic Research

1. Introduction: Uses, Sources, and Collection of Forecasts

To men who must plan and act——in government, business, even in such private affairs as personal finance——economic forecasts are tools for reducing uncertainty and inputs into the process of making decisions. To persons in positions of authority, they may serve as a means of communicating intentions or influencing opinion. To professional economists, they are important as products of theories, judgments, and estimating procedures, which can be used in testing the underlying hypotheses, models, and methods. Forecasts of business conditions can be sampled to examine their consensus and dispersion at any time and also continuous revisions over time: this may provide the observer of the economic scene with useful information about what the prevailing climate of opinion is and how it is changing. By analyzing the relations between predictions and subsequent realizations, the accuracy of the former, which interests both makers and users of forecasts, can be assessed. By analyzing the relations between current predictions and earlier predictions and actual events, some understanding can be gained of the genesis of those forecasts that are not based on specific, reproducible methods, and this is of particular concern to the student of the formation and economics of expectations.

The recent and current studies of short-term economic forecasting by the National Bureau of Economic Research, which supply much material for this

Note: I wish to thank Messrs. Mervin A. Daub and James C. Ellert and Mrs. Josephine Su for their valuable statistical assistance. I am also grateful to Mrs. Ester Moskowitz, who edited the manuscript.

paper, are directly or indirectly concerned with all of these different uses of forecasts. The reports by Moore and Shiskin, Zarnowitz, Fels and Hinshaw, Mincer, Cole, and others, produced in the first phase of this project and published during 1967–69,[1] focus on the accuracy of general economic forecasts and on several related topics, including factors that affect forecasting procedures and performance; properties and quality of forecasting tools and targets (indicator series, anticipatory data, national aggregates of income and output); and the dependence of forecasts and their errors on types of economic change, in particular cyclical developments and turning points. This work is, as usual, in many ways a continuation of previous efforts: from the early (1929) report of Cox [6], through the NBER conference volumes of 1951 and 1955 [27], [5], to the subsequent studies by Christ [2], Okun [20], [21], Stekler [23], Suits [24], Theil [25], [26], and others, much has been done to develop and apply methods of evaluating various types of economic forecasts. But the recent National Bureau studies have put research in this area on a more comprehensive and systematic basis by collecting and analyzing a substantial body of data on economic forecasts of various types. The availability of these relatively rich and authenticated quantitative materials reflects the great proliferation of forecasting activity in the last two decades.

The materials analyzed in the early stages of the project consist in large part of predictions by business economists, who are in fact the source of the great majority of economic forecasts in the United States. The demand for forecasts of economic conditions increased greatly in the last two decades, judging from the expansion of the corresponding output, and business management clearly had a very large share in that demand. The preference of business has been for unconditional and, increasingly, for specific and numerical predictions. Forecasts by company economists are for the most part unaccompanied by explicit specifications of the methods or models used. In aiming at the comprehensive economic aggregates, such as gross national product (GNP) and its major components, they are presumably motivated by the working hypothesis that forecasts of these macrovariables are needed for predicting the microvariables of direct interest to a company (notably its own sales). The microforecasts, however, are generally not available and were not studied.

[1] These publications include [18], [29], [11], [15], and [4] (see References at end of this paper). These are reports of a study of short-term economic forecasting that was supported by grants to the National Bureau from the Whirlpool Corporation, General Electric Company, Ford Motor Company Fund, Relm Foundation, and the U.S. Steel Corporation, as well as by other funds of the National Bureau. A grant of electronic computer time to the National Bureau by the International Business Machines Corporation was used for some of the statistical analysis.

A continuing quarterly survey of general economic forecasts, based on a new questionnaire designed by the NBER, was initiated in November 1968 by the American Statistical Association; since then, its results are being regularly processed and analyzed by the National Bureau.[2] In the past year, steps were also taken to start a systematic collection of quarterly forecasts and related statistics for several major econometric models of the United States economy. In this second, current phase of the NBER research on forecasting, econometric models are a major subject for study, with primary attention being given to their short-term forecasting qualities and related properties, such as the ability to simulate cyclical developments in the economy and the effects of policy changes. Two products of this work are forthcoming. One, by Evans, Haitovsky, and Treyz [9], deals with the predictive performance of the quarterly Wharton and OBE models; the other, by Zarnowitz, Boschan, and Moore [34], with the cyclical and other properties of these models and the FRB-MIT-PENN model as revealed by various nonstochastic and stochastic simulations.[3] Further studies in this area are in progress.

In the next section of this report, I attempt to identify and review the main lines of investigation pursued in the National Bureau studies of economic forecasting and related topics. In the third section, some results of these studies are brought up to date and evaluated. In the last section plans for future research are discussed.

2. Directions of Recent and Current Research

2.1 Measures of the Accuracy and Structure of Forecasts

Whatever services the forecasts are expected to render to the user, they vary greatly, and are not easily defined by an outside observer; but the usefulness of most forecasts is surely in the first place a positive function of their accuracy. We therefore began by working on methods of assessing the

[2]Mrs. Charlotte Boschan and I share the responsibility for this work. The results are reported quarterly in press releases published in each successive issue of *The American Statistician* beginning in April 1969. The survey is carried out among members of the Business and Economic Statistics (B & E) Section of the ASA, with nationwide coverage; the participants are business, government, and academic economists whose professional work involves regular forecasting of the course of the economy. Ten major economic indicators are predicted for each of the four quarterly periods ahead, the base levels of the forecasts are specified, and questions are answered regarding the major assumptions and methods used and the probabilities attached to the expected changes in some key variables. For a description of the survey, see [32]; for an appraisal of the predictions for the first three quarters covered, see [33].

[3]For descriptions of the Wharton-EFU (Economic Forecasting Unit), OBE (Office of Business Economics, U.S. Department of Commerce), and FRB-MIT-PENN models, see [10], [14], and [22], respectively.

degree of predictive accuracy and applying them to the collected "judgmental" forecasts ([29] and [16]).

Accuracy is evaluated first with the aid of a battery of statistical measures of the closeness with which predictions approximate realizations. Arithmetic and absolute averages and standard deviations of forecast errors are employed as simple descriptive devices. Regressions of actual on predicted values and the decomposition of mean square errors provide estimates of bias and inefficiency. The measurement of accuracy in this absolute sense is followed by comparisons of actual forecast errors with errors resulting from alternative extrapolations of the time series concerned. There is a progression of these benchmark extrapolations from the simplest "naive models" to technically rather sophisticated autoregressive forms; but even the best of them make little or no use of economic theory and pose relatively few requirements in terms of data and computational operations. Thus, these comparisons with the benchmark models show what, if any, is the net contribution of the forecasts to the information about the future that can be obtained from other quicker and cheaper methods.

Besides being useful as yardsticks of predictive performance, extrapolations can help explain the implicit structure of judgmental forecasts on the plausible assumption that most of these (and other) forecasts rely, to some extent, on various types of extrapolation. In [16, sec. III], methods are developed to decompose forecasts and forecast errors into extrapolative and other (autonomous) components. Application to a few sets of business forecasts shows how this approach can be used to evaluate the relative importance of extrapolations in generating such forecasts, and the effects of extrapolation error on forecasting error. In [17], further efforts are made to infer from the available forecast data, and particularly their estimated extrapolative components, how forecasters may be revising their expectations in the light of their past errors. Of the linear models of adaptive behavior examined, the one that receives most support and attention involves forecast revisions which are a fraction of the current observed forecast error, the fraction being smaller for longer-term than for near-term predictions. This analysis is extended in [8] and applied to the problem of how forecasts of future spot rates of interest are formed in the market (the working hypothesis here being that these market forecasts are given by the forward rates implicit in the term structure).

2.2 The Effects of Data Errors and of the Time Span of Prediction

In [29] several factors are shown to affect strongly the absolute and relative accuracy of the forecasts assembled there. One is the lack of accurate information about the conditions prevailing at the time the forecast is made. The initial level from which the predicted change is measured must itself be predicted; and although these base values are estimated at a close range, they often contain significant erors which contribute to the errors of forecast.

This is closely related to the broader subject of the effects of errors in current and past data on forecasting accuracy. In [4], successive revisions of provisional GNP estimates are found to reduce the GNP data errors on most occasions, mainly by reducing errors arising from extrapolations of past benchmark values. The provisional estimates are themselves partly near-term predictions, and they have some characteristics frequently observed in "true" forecasts such as the tendency to underestimate increases and levels of GNP. The estimates for a year just ended are on the average substantially more accurate than the forecasts for a year ahead, but they are not much better than the forecasters' own estimates of the current or base levels (which are typically made about three to four months earlier). The use of preliminary rather than revised GNP data appears to account for more than one-third of the observed average errors of the annual GNP forecasts [3].

Accuracy tends to diminish steadily as the forecast span increases [29]. Business economists' forecasts of GNP and industrial production, for example, are typically better than various types of extrapolation over periods from one to three quarters ahead. Forecasts for four quarters or more ahead, however, are generally not superior to simple extrapolations of the recent trend. Year-to-year forecasts are on the whole more accurate than even the more refined autoregressive projections, but they can be viewed as having mean spans of little more than six months.[4] Decomposition of relative mean square errors, in [16], shows that the contribution to predictive efficiency of the nonextrapolative (autonomous) component of the forecast typically declines as the span lengthens. At the same time, trend projections become potentially more useful, but forecasts fail to take sufficient advantage of them and consequently deteriorate faster than the best of the extrapolations as the predictive span is extended beyond a few quarters. However, marginal errors of multiperiod forecasts show no systematic rise, so average errors increase less than in proportion to the lengthening of the span. They also increase much less than the errors in simple naive models (see [29]).

Consideration of ingredients of general economic forecasts helps to explain these findings. In addition to extrapolations of some kind, forecasters use relations between the series to be predicted and known lagged values or estimated current values of other variables; various indicators of major changes in aggregate economic activity and in anticipatory data such as surveys of consumer and investment intentions and government budget estimates; and, finally, their own judgments. Each of these potential sources of forecast is likely to deteriorate as the span of prediction increases. The

---

[4]The annual forecasts are generally made in the late autumn for the calendar year that is about to begin; if they score well in the first two quarters, their record will be moderately good for the year as a whole.

forecasting relations between time series involve various lags, but typically the relations weaken as the lags are increased. Most of the leading business cycle indicators have relatively short effective forecasting leads beyond which their usefulness declines (see [18] and [19]). The same appears to apply to anticipatory data and probably to informed judgments and estimates generally.[5]

2.3 Errors in Predicting Economic Growth

Other studies have suggested that forecasters tend to underestimate changes in the predicted series.[6] This would not be a type of systematic error that forecasters could or should avoid if it merely resulted from failure to predict random variations in the actual values. Indeed, forecasts that captured all but the random component of the change can be viewed as optimal, and they would necessarily be underestimates in the sense of having a smaller variance than that of the actual values. (This last property applies more generally to all unbiased and efficient predictions of change; see [16, p. 18]). However, underestimation becomes undesirable if it applies to longer cyclical movements, not just to short irregular variations; predictions that systematically understate high values and overstate low values of the series are inefficient (being correlated with their own errors) and can be corrected (potentially) (see [16] and [29]). Finally, forecasts with a tendency either to under- or overestimate the actual values of the given series (its "levels") contain a bias, which is usually regarded as a very objectionable error that should be eliminated as far as possible. But all this refers to population or "long-run" characteristics. In the limited samples of comparable predictions and realizations that are typically available, bias and inefficiency are difficult to ascertain, let alone measure and project with sufficient confidence; hence attempts to remove or at least drastically reduce such errors are often frustrated.

[5] Most data for business and consumer anticipations represent single-span forecasts or expectations, but the OBE-SEC quarterly surveys of investment intentions produce two series of anticipated business expenditures for new plant and equipment: the "first anticipations" (A_1) reported early each quarter for the next quarter and the "second anticipations" (A_2) reported at the same time for the current quarter. A_2 is on the average substantially more accurate than A_1 (see Okun in [28, p. 436], with references). Also, in regressions of purchase rates for new automobiles on consumer buying intentions and attitudes (Bureau of the Census and University of Michigan Survey Research Center data) better results are obtained in most cases with a six-month lag of purchases than with nine- or twelve-month lags (see Table 5-2 and text in [13]).

[6] See Franco Modigliani and Owen H. Sauerlander in [5, pp. 288–289] and H. Theil in [25, Chap. III–VI], among others.

Most forecasts examined do underestimate on the average the growth of the economy as measured by GNP. About two-thirds of the annual increases in GNP during the period 1952–63 were underpredicted; and the same applies to the concurrent changes in personal consumption expenditures, a still more smoothly growing aggregate which experienced no year-to-year decreases. The declines in GNP were less frequently underestimated. Changes in series that fluctuated more and grew less vigorously (e.g., gross private domestic investment in 1952–63) have been overestimated about as often as they have been underestimated. The same applies to decreases in all the major GNP expenditure components taken together; but these were just as frequently missed (though the proportion of these turning-point errors varies greatly among forecasts from different sources). As for increases, in this set of predictions they were underestimated nearly half the time and overestimated more than one-third of the time, while turning-point errors accounted for the remaining one-sixth of the observations [29, pp. 45–51].

These findings suggest that the observed "underestimation of changes" reflects principally a conservative prediction of growth rates in series dominated by upward trends. As this implies, the levels of such series also are generally underpredicted [16, p. 19].

2.4 Predicting Cyclical Movements and Turning Points

Predictive errors appear to be affected by the cyclical characteristics of the forecast period [29, pp. 27–30]. Thus, the underestimation of the increases in GNP is typically largest for the beginning of a recovery from a business recession, when the growth rates are particularly high. Later in the expansion, the increases are usually smaller, at least in relative terms, and the amount of underestimation is on the whole much less (and the same applies, consequently, to the associated target levels of the forecasts). Indeed, overestimation prevailed in one period of retardation (1962) and was frequent in another (1967). In contractions, the predicted levels are often too high, sometimes because the decline turned out to be larger than expected but mainly because the downturn was missed.

Annual forecasts of GNP had some success in predicting both the frequency and the timing of the turning points [29, pp. 51–59; 19, pp. 3–5].[7] They are certainly superior in this respect to extrapolations, which are by and large incapable of *signalizing* the business cycle turns and are instead apt either to "smooth" them out of existence or to reproduce them with lags. It is true that forecasts can and occasionally do predict turns which

[7]Much of the detailed information underlying the discussion in this and the three following paragraphs has not yet been published; it is contained in Victor Zarnowitz, "The Record of Turning Point Forecasts of GNP and Other Major Aggregates," NBER (draft manuscript).

then fail to occur, while trend projections avoid giving such "false warnings"; but the latter errors are infrequent and this disadvantage of forecasts is outweighed by their advantage of missing fewer actual turning points. A naive assumption that next year will always produce a turning point would avoid all errors of missed turns, but it would of course be a very poor one for predicting comprehensive aggregates such as GNP in an economy that tends to grow most of the time; the forecasts are far better than this benchmark model in that they make fewer errors of the false-signal type. They are also much better than the almost equally naive assumption that GNP is a series of random numbers and also better than the somewhat less naive model that would treat the annual *change* in GNP as random [19, p. 4].

However, these comparisons do *not* imply that the forecasters were able to predict the turns in the months ahead; they indicate only an ability to recognize the turns with relative promptness. Consider the forecasts for 1954 made in November or December of 1953: They showed 1954 as lower than 1953 in terms of GNP, i.e., 1953 to be a peak year. But by this time the midyear at which the turning point in annual data is conventionally dated was long over. Actually, the peak in the business cycle occurred in or near July 1953, and late in the year (at the height of the "forecasting season") the decline was widely recognized, though not necessarily as a cyclical contraction or recession.[8] In 1957 the peak again occurred shortly after midyear and forecasts made in late autumn or early winter had only to recognize a contraction then in process; in 1960, the peak probably came still earlier (the NBER reference month is May), but the recognition process was generally slower, reflecting the disturbing effects of the 1959 steel strike and the shallowness of the contraction. In each of these three episodes, the task of predicting annual changes was also made easier by the widespread expectation (which proved largely correct) that the contraction would be short and mild. Furthermore, the timing of the troughs was early enough for the forecasts made late in 1954, 1958, and 1961 to benefit from many indications that each of the respective contractions had already ended or was about to.

Forecasts made near the middle of the year for the next calendar year account only for one-tenth of all annual GNP predictions collected in [29]. Their record is a great deal worse than that of the end-of-year forecasts and not much better than guesswork as far as turning-point errors are concerned [19].

Forecasts made two or four times in a year for sequences of four to six quarters ahead are more relevant for an appraisal of turning-point errors. The

---

[8] See Rendigs Fels, "The Recognition Patterns of Business Analysts," in [11, Part I, p. 28].

reason is that there are more turns in quarterly than in annual series, and they can be dated with greater precision. There are relatively few directional errors associated with increases, but many associated with decreases (that is, missed peaks). Of 194 predicted quarter-to-quarter rises in GNP, 155, or nearly 80 per cent, coincided with actual rises; of 19 predicted declines, only 4, or 21 per cent, did so.[9] As this shows, forecasters know very well that increases prevail heavily among the quarterly changes of GNP, and they make increases similarly dominant in their predictions (in fact, somewhat more so). What the forecasters evidently do *not* know is how to anticipate correctly when the declines are coming. Predictions for sequences of two semiannual periods ahead (from different sources) have a slightly better record, but they too are consistent with the general conclusion that there is little evidence of forecasters' ability to detect the major cyclical reversals in the economy well in advance of the event.

Statements about the business outlook in the leading business and financial publications show a pattern in the neighborhood of business cycle peaks and troughs. The analysts "become increasingly aware of first the possibility, then the probability, and finally the certainty of a turning point" [11, Part I, p. 47]. In the three months preceding the event, expectations of a turn become slowly but clearly stronger and more definite, and the process of increasing recognition continues for several months after the actual turn (as dated *ex post* in the NBER reference cycle chronology). The recognition of the four business cycle troughs in the period 1948–61 has been on the whole faster than the recognition of the four peaks. Evidently, the analysts, like the majority of forecasters, were basically optimistic about the growth prospects of the economy and the short-lived nature of the contractions. Given this prevalent attitude and the historical course of events, the downturns proved to be more difficult to predict and recognize than the upturns.

The system of scoring reports on the economic outlook developed in [11, Part I] was applied in a companion study to the appropriate statements in the minutes of the regular meetings of the Federal Reserve Board's Open Market Committee (FOMC) in 1948–60.[10] The results are of major interest in view of the importance of the FOMC in determining the nation's monetary policy. They indicate that the Committee was a little more successful than the

---

[9] An alternative way of describing this property of the quarterly forecasts is this: of 43 actual declines in GNP, 39 or nearly 91 per cent were missed. It may also be noted that most of the predicted declines relate to the first two quarters ahead; beyond that, for the third to sixth quarters ahead, very few declines were anticipated and none at the right times.

[10] C. Elton Hinshaw, "The Recognition Pattern of the Federal Open Market Committee," in [11, Part II].

average of the published business outlook reports in recognizing and confirming (not in predicting ahead of the event) the cyclical peaks and troughs of the economy. The FOMC definitely avoided false signals more successfully than did the business analysts.

Before the date of a business cycle peak or trough, the estimated probability of the occurrence of a turning point was typically below 50 (on a 0 to 100 scoring scale) for both the business analysts and the FOMC [11, Parts I and II]. Only one or two months *after* the turn would the odds begin to favor slightly the affirmation of a cyclical reversal over its negation. The odds would then reach 3 to 1 (probability of 75) about three or four months after the turn and odds of 9 to 1 (probability of 90) about five or six months after. This record is in most cases somewhat worse than that of the quantitative business forecasts [11, Part I, pp. 45–46]. It confirms the general lack of demonstrated ability to predict major turning points in aggregate economic activity ahead of the event.

2.5 Forecasts of the Major Expenditure Components of GNP

Forecasts of total GNP are often substantially better, in the sense of having smaller percentage change errors, than the forecasts of most major GNP expenditure components from the same source [29]. The over-all predictions apparently benefit from partial cancellation of errors in predictions of the components. While this is definitely preferable to the opposite case of positively correlated and mutually reinforcing errors, any gross inaccuracies in the components must of course be seen as detracting from the quality of the forecaster's product, even if these errors happen to be largely compensating. However, there are some systematic factors that are likely to confer a relative advantage on the GNP forecasts. Certain methods of forecasting, such as the use of business cycle indicators or monetary variables, are concerned directly with measures of aggregate economic activity rather than with any component expenditures or sectors of the economy, and hence may yield better forecasts for total GNP. Moreover, there are strong equilibrating or shock-absorbing forces at work in the economy, which effectively localize many disturbances that impinge upon the different processes or sectors. As a consequence, GNP is a rather smooth series dominated by a pronounced growth tendency, and it is therefore easier to predict than most of its components, which are much more volatile.[11]

[11] This rule has important exceptions, however: the massive aggregate of personal consumption expenditures, which accounts presently for over 60 per cent of GNP, follows a smoother course than total GNP, owing to the stability of personal outlays on nondurable goods and services and despite the volatility of spending on automobiles and other durables. The total of state and local governments' purchases of goods and services also shows fewer and smaller relative deviations from trend than does GNP.

There is strong evidence that the more volatile a series, the more difficult is the prediction of its relative changes and the greater the probable forecast error [29, Chap. 4]. Thus, only total and nondurables consumption and state and local expenditures are predicted about as well as, or better than, total GNP, according to the business forecasts for 1953–63 (see footnote 11). The errors in predicting percentage changes in personal consumption are far smaller than those in forecasts of gross private domestic investment, whereas the errors for total government spending are intermediate: larger than those in consumption but much smaller than those in investment. Within aggregate consumption, the errors for durable goods exceed greatly those for either the nondurables or services. Within aggregate investment, the record for producers' durable equipment turns out to be worse than that for total new construction.[12]

Although the errors of consumption forecasts are smaller than those for the other major GNP components when measured in deviations of percentage changes, they are large relative to the errors of appropriate extrapolations. The consumption aggregates (except for durable goods) are smoothly growing series that could have been predicted very well by simple trend projections; and, indeed, the average errors of the latter have often been smaller than those of recorded consumption forecasts. It would seem, then, that there is much scope for potential improvement in these forecasts, through better utilization of the historical content of the series.[13]

Improvement appears to be much more difficult to come by, but is probably even more necessary, in forecasts of components of investment, particularly residential structures, changes in inventories, and net exports. Even though these series have relatively weak trends and strong cyclical and irregular movements, and hence cannot be very effectively extrapolated by any simple means, their forecasts have on the whole proved to be either just slightly better or worse than mere extrapolations of last levels or average

[12]Expenditures on producers' durables have been less stable than those on structures in the period here covered. Expenditures on housing, however, have fluctuated widely and behaved quite differently from other major expenditure categories, reflecting the countercyclical effects of financial factors (mortgage credit was scarce in several periods of advanced expansion and relatively abundant in some periods of late contraction and recovery).

[13]The more volatile the series to be predicted, the less can the forecast in general gain from extrapolation. It is quite reasonable that forecasters should make greater use of extrapolation where this promises to be more efficient. Apparently, such distinctions are in fact made, for we observe that, e.g., forecasts of plant and equipment outlays have relatively smaller extrapolative components than forecasts of consumption [16, pp. 30–31]. However, the latter forecasts are still deficient in their use of the extrapolative potential of the consumption series.

changes. The predictions of net inventory change are particularly important for an appraisal of the business outlook in times of mild economic fluctuations, during which the "inventory cycle" is widely believed to play a major role; but these predictions are also particularly unsatisfactory. [14]

Aggregation of short-term expectations of business concerns about their expenditures on plant and equipment results in better predictions of the total of such capital outlays than are available from the independently made global forecasts of business fixed investment. This can be inferred from the markedly lower accuracy of the annual investment forecasts collected in [29] that were made before the McGraw-Hill Survey of Investment Intentions compared to those made after it. Also, the OBE-SEC investment anticipations series show not only very high simple correlations with actual plant and equipment expenditures but also high partial correlations, holding the investment forecasts constant. In contrast, the investment forecasts add very little or nothing to the statistical explanation of the variance of actual expenditures after allowing for the high correlation of expenditures with anticipations: the partial correlations here are small and as often negative as positive. This applies to quarterly as well as annual predictions [30, pp. 30–33].

2.6 Forecasts of Production and the Price Level

Among variables other than GNP and its major components, the FRB index of industrial production represents a favorite target of business economists' forecasts. It is generally predicted with a degree of accuracy similar to that of the GNP forecasts from the same sources, at least for the annual and shorter forecasts: comparisons in terms of index numbers on a common base somewhat favor GNP; comparisons with benchmark extrapolations in most cases favor industrial production [29]. For longer spans, predictions of the FRB index often come out better than those of GNP, according to the yardstick of simple trend projections. Monthly data provide more current information than quarterly data, which gives an advantage to the industrial production forecasts. The latter suffer less from the underestimation-of-growth bias than the GNP forecasts do, but they are more adversely affected by turning-point errors. In terms of correlation of actual with predicted changes, the forecasts of both GNP and industrial production are definitely superior to all examined types of extrapolation,

[14]For example, in business predictions for 1953–63, the absolute average error of forecasts (in current dollars) was greater for net inventory change than for total government expenditures and the major components of fixed investment, even though the average magnitude of the inventory change is very small compared with the typical levels of these other variables [29, pp. 39–40].

including the relatively accurate trend projections and autoregressive models. This advantage of greater efficiency appears to be widespread, and it is by and large not offset by the disadvantage of greater bias that the forecasts often have relative to the best of the benchmark extrapolations [29, Chap. 6]. The advantage can be traced to the contribution of the autonomous components of the forecasts [16, sec. II].

Forecasts of general price movements, although still much less numerous than those of GNP and related variables, attract increasing attention in these times of strong inflationary tendencies. Forecasts of the Consumer Price Index in recent years (mainly 1957–67, though some sets go back to 1953 and before) have on the average been more accurate than the naive model predictions. Some but not all of them were also better than simple trend (average historical change) extrapolations. Forecasts of the Wholesale Price Index were on the whole considerably weaker, but this is partly due to the extraordinary stability of this index in the years 1958–64 (which favored the naive "same-level" model). Both the CPI and the WPI forecasts show generally small average absolute errors, relative to the levels of the indexes and to the errors of forecasts of other comprehensive series such as GNP; but the changes in the indexes were also relatively small and less than their counterparts for these other variables. Forecasters have tended to underestimate the large changes and to overestimate the small changes in the price indexes, which suggests a certain inertia of expectations; there is more uniformity and predictability in the predicted than in the actual price-level behavior. However, here too, there are definite positive correlations between the forecast and the realized changes, and mechanical extrapolations of past price levels or changes could not have done as well in this respect [31].

The effects of the price errors on the GNP forecasts are not always adverse. For several forecast sets, these errors were negatively correlated with the errors of the implicit quantity component of GNP.[15] As a consequence of partial offsets between the errors of the quantity and price components, forecasts of GNP in current dollars have been on the average more accurate than the implicit forecasts of GNP in constant dollars for most of the private sources of the CPI and WPI predictions assembled in [31].

[15]Since there are no predictions of the GNP price deflator from these sources, a weighted combination of CPI and WPI forecasts had to be used as a rough approximation. The resulting composite price-level forecasts were applied to the GNP forecasts from the same source to obtain the implicit predictions of GNP in constant dollars. Expressing all figures as forecasts of percentage changes, additive quantity and price components were then computed. As an outcome of this decomposition, three series of predictions are available for each of the forecast sets covered, relating to GNP in constant dollars, the composite price level, and GNP in current dollars.

Materials on business forecasts of different variables suggest that turning points in lagging indicators such as plant and equipment expenditures and consumer prices are on the whole more accurately predicted than turning points in leading or coincident indicators such as inventory change and wholesale prices. Forecasts of the laggers benefit from observation of related series that move earlier in the course of the business cycle [19, p. 5].

2.7 Econometric Model Forecasts and Simulations

Moore [19, pp. 12–14] presents an analysis of predictions of annual percentage changes in GNP in constant dollars, based on an econometric model that grew out of the early work by Lawrence Klein and Arthur Goldberger and was developed by Daniel Suits [24]. The forecasts are prepared by the Research Seminar in Quantitative Economics, and they are usually presented in the November preceding the target year at the Conference on the Economic Outlook, both at the University of Michigan.[16] Sixteen forecasts, for 1953–68, are evaluated in [19]. Their mean absolute error is about 1.5 percentage points, less than half of the corresponding mean of actual changes (3.8 percentage points). The results for 1953–63 are almost identical, and they resemble closely those obtained for one of the judgmental forecast sets in [29], which also refers to changes in real GNP during the same period.[17] These comparisons suggest that, in predicting changes in GNP excluding the price movements, forecasts with this econometric model "appear to stand up comparatively well" [19, p. 14]. Similarly, Cunnyngham's analysis of GNP predictions in current and constant dollars led to the conclusion that these forecasts "have been about as accurate as the better business forecasts" [7, p. 60].

[16]The predicted percentage changes used in [19] were computed from published reports of the Michigan Conference and data supplied by the Research Seminar. The forecasts were not produced by a single model, but rather by a whole family of models plus judgments about not only the inputs of exogenous variables but also various adjustments of the constants in some of the equations (assumptions of nonzero residuals). The models themselves were modified (mostly elaborated) almost from year to year. Sometimes alternative forecasts for a given year were made, based upon different data or policy assumptions; see [19, Table 5, p. 13] for the numerical identification of such forecasts and the selections made.

[17]The other forecasts in that collection (also covering the years 1953–63) are not directly comparable because they refer to GNP in current dollars and are therefore affected by errors in predicting the price levels. The mean absolute errors of forecasts of annual rates of change in current-dollar GNP varied from 1.4 to 3.0 and averaged 2.0 percentage points for the eight sets concerned (only one of these sets, however, had a mean error of more than 2.3 per cent). The mean of the coefficients of correlation between the predicted and actual percentage changes in GNP is 0.78 for this sample; the correlation for the Suits model is 0.72.

However, it is very important to keep in mind that these are *ex ante* predictions that involve judgmental forecast of the exogenous inputs, recurrent revisions of the model, and frequent adjustments of the constant terms ("fine tuning")——all of these decisions being subject to modifications in the light of the preliminary and other information available to the econometric forecaster. Such results, therefore, tell us something about how well the latter forecasts rather than about how well the econometric model forecasts. To answer questions about the forecasting quality of both the models and the econometrician's judgments, and about how these elements interact, it is necessary to analyze not only the *ex ante* but also the *ex post* forecasts (which use the actual historical values for the exogencous inputs) and to take into account the adjustments of the constant terms.

A systematic analysis of this kind was made recently for the quarterly Wharton-EFU and OBE models in [9]. Its principal findings are very revealing. The true *ex ante* forecasts are superior to the *ex post* forecasts with the same constant-term adjustments and lagged values of the endogenous variables. Thus, surprisingly, the forecasts made with the model-builders' estimates for the exogenous variables are here better (mostly by substantial margins) than the forecasts with the correct values of these variables. The true *ex ante* forecasts (with subjective adjustments of constant terms) are generally much better than forecasts that use the same estimated exogenous inputs but either without adjustments or with only mechanical adjustments of constant terms. The *"ex ante"* forecasts in the latter category tend to be more accurate than the *ex post* forecasts of the OBE model with the same mechanical adjustments or with none, but this result is reversed for the Wharton model.[18]

It is clear that the intercept adjustments must have often improved these forecasts considerably, which speaks well for the econometrician's judgment qua forecaster. But the poor showing of the *ex post* forecasts indicates that "econometric models cannot generate good forecasts if they are used only in a mechanical fashion" [9, p. 160]. Indeed, such forecasts are in a great many cases worse than the simplest naive models of the "same change" or even of the "no change" variety, when made over the shortest spans (of one or two quarters) and without any adjustments. The accuracy of the forecasts relative to the naive models improves with the lengthening of the span to three to six quarters, which reflects the fact that the forecast errors (1) have relatively small systematic components, and (2) are mainly due to "imperfect

[18]The period covered by the Wharton model forecasts is I-1965–IV-1968; that covered by the OBE model forecasts is II-1967–IV-1968. The forecasts are quarterly, and each consists of a sequence of predictions for either one to six quarters ahead (Wharton) or for one to four quarters ahead (OBE).

covariation" [25, pp. 35–37], one can also say that the forecasts track the longer movements better than the shortest changes over the next quarters. However, since the errors of the *ex post* predictions are significantly large for the longer spans, and the naive models represent quite weak standards for such forecasts, none of these results can be viewed as really satisfactory.

Three different possible reasons are suggested in [9] for the finding that *ex ante* forecasts are better than *ex post* ones: (a) the *original* (subjective) adjustments succeeded in offsetting "bad guesses" about the exogenous inputs; (b) the actual data are at fault; and (c) errors in forecasts of exogenous variables tend to cancel the misspecification errors in the models. The authors dismiss (a) on the ground that, in almost half the cases, the *ex ante* forecasts retain their superiority even when no adjustments or the same *mechanical* adjustments are used in these and the corresponding *ex post* forecasts. They treat (b) rather more seriously, though viewing only the figures for government expenditures as likely to be distorted in reporting.[19] Finally, (c) is discussed in the form of the offsetting effects of underestimation of government spending and overstatement of fiscal multipliers.

Of these factors, (c) is most disturbing and (b) is not damaging at all as far as the predictive quality of a model is concerned. My own conjecture is that the role of (b) is likely to prove rather limited and that of (c) principal, while (a) could well be considerably more important than implied by its treatment in [9]. But certainly this whole subject is exceedingly interesting, and it deserves much further investigation.

Sample-period simulations of the Wharton model for I-1953–IV-1964 and of the OBE model for III-1955–IV-1966 are also presented and discussed in [9]. These are calculated for six quarters ahead from each starting date, that is, from each consecutive quarter in the sample period.[20] They use actual data for the initial conditions and the exogenous variables but model-generated lagged values of endogenous variables after the starting date

---

[19]The reason is that these expenditures and, in particular, defense spending may be entered in the national income accounts as inventory investment while the goods are being produced and as government purchases only when they are ready for delivery and paid for [9, pp. 138–139].

[20]For the **Wharton-EFU model**, the sample period actually starts in 1948, but the earlier years were excluded from these simulations because of the difficulties with the solution program encountered for some of the six-quarter intervals during the Korean War years. Toward the end of the period covered, in 1963–64, the intervals were gradually reduced to 5, 4, . . . , 1 quarters so that they would not reach beyond the sample period. For the OBE model, however, this was not done: the simulations do not stop in IV-1966 but continue for six quarters regardless of the originating date. This is said to be unlikely to affect the main conclusions more than slightly [9, pp. 34-35, 72].

over each simulation period. Their average errors increase steadily as the prediction span lengthens from one to six quarters, but they tend strongly to decline with the span when taken relative to the average errors of the naive model of last-known level projections. For the one-quarter span, the Wharton simulations are not much better than the extrapolations with this naive model. The simulations of the OBE model tend to have smaller errors than the simulations of the Wharton-EFU model for the shortest spans, but the differences narrow and become minor for the longest spans.

The results for the sample-period simulations are generally very different from those for the *ex post* forecasts beyond the sample period. The latter have much larger errors (which for the shortest spans are often greater than the naive-model errors, as noted before). Also, the constant-term adjustments, which are essential for obtaining reasonable *ex post* predictions in the forecast period, have little effect on the accuracy of the sample-period simulations.

Different types of simulations are examined in [34]: nonstochastic model solutions for the entire sample period and for six-quarter intervals around business cycle turns, and stochastic simulations for long (hundred-quarter) spans starting at the end of the sample period and extending into the future. The main concern in compiling this study is with the dynamic properties of the models (Wharton, OBE, and FRB-MIT-PENN) and their relation to the observed cyclical characteristics of the U.S. economy. This lies largely outside the boundaries of the subject of forecasting and is treated in a separate paper.[21] However, it should be stated here that the analysis in [34], like that in [9], indicates that the models, even though concerned largely with short movements over a few quarters, do not track such movements very well (judging, in [34], from the record of six-quarter simulations in the vicinity of business cycle peaks and troughs).

2.8 Standards of Predictive Performance

Even the least "naive" of the extrapolative models utilize only the past history (and usually only recent history) of the forecast series; they leave out much information of potential predictive value and should not represent very demanding standards for the short-term aggregate forecasts. Sets of past predictions that have proved superior to the benchmark extrapolations themselves provide a higher and more realistic standard. However, the future period may be either more or less difficult to forecast than the past, and it should be desirable to improve upon, not just match, the historical record.

---

[21] See Victor Zarnowitz, "Econometric Model Simulations and the Cyclical Characteristics of the U.S. Economy," another paper prepared for this colloquium.

Moreover, comparisons with what happened may over- or undervalue conditional forecasts, depending on the degree to which the conditions have or have not been met. For these stated reasons, a different standard is proposed and experimentally applied in [19, sec. IV]. A composite index of indicators that have generally led at business cycle peaks and troughs appears to anticipate GNP by six months: percentage changes between *fiscal-year* averages of that index are well correlated with percentage changes between the *subsequent calendar-year* values of GNP. This relation would yield predictions that are mechanically quite accurate but also late and of short range; to get a benchmark model that would match actual forecasts made, say, in October-November, the percentage changes in the index are calculated from the preceding fiscal-year average to the third quarter of the year preceding the calendar year being forecast.

The method yields the following mean absolute errors of relative change in GNP (in percentage points): 1.8 for 1953–63, 0.7 for 1962–67. The corresponding error figures are higher for both an average of eight sets of business forecasts from [29] (2.0 for 1953–63) and the forecasts prepared by the Council of Economic Advisers and published each year, beginning with January 1962, in the *Economic Report of the President* (1.3 for 1962–67). According to analogous measures for GNP in constant dollars, forecasts with indicators were slightly less accurate than forecasts with Suits' econometric model in 1953–67 and slightly more accurate than Suits' and the *Economic Report* forecasts in 1962–67.[22]

Benchmark forecasts with leading indicators are similar to *ex post* forecasts with econometric models, and particularly to predictions of GNP made from reduced forms of larger systems, where the coefficients represent weights applied to the predetermined variables so as to measure the net direct or indirect effects of these variables on GNP. Still better, they are analogous to forecasts from single equations which include only known exogenous variables as predictors. They share the general advantages and disadvantages

---

[22] The mean absolute errors (in percentage points) are: Indicators: 1.6 for 1953–67, 0.9 for 1962–67; Suits' model: 1.5 for 1953–67, 1.1 for 1962–67; *Economic Report:* 1.1 for 1962–67. It should be noted that the forecasts of the indicator model for 1962–67 are based on regression equations fitted to data for the prior period, 1949–61. The forecasts for 1953–63, however, benefit from being based on regression equations fitted to concurrent data (for 1952–67).

of such predictive equations vis-à-vis the larger systems.[23] Their specific source of strength is the selection of variables with strong anticipatory elements; but, let us recall, the leading indicators were chosen, not with regard to their correlation with subsequent GNP movements, but mainly for the consistency of their timing in the business cycle. The theoretical rationale for including some of the indicators in this particular synthetic form of relationship seems weak, and problems of various kinds arise at this point, notably with respect to differences in the aggregation levels, the timing and area of impact, the distribution of the lags involved, etc.; but it is not at all clear what effects these factors have on the proposed method and what can be done to reduce any difficulties they may cause.[24]

The single-equation and reduced-form approaches to forecasting have, of course, a great many different applications. The relative effectiveness of the

[23] Large models can accomodate more predictors, which is an advantage if the latter are properly selected and related to each other; but the chances of misspecification and propagation of errors are by the same token large, too. Advances in technical ability to handle such models have accelerated enormously with the progress in computer hardware and software, outstripping the growth in both the required theoretical knowledge and the availability of proper data. Smaller models suffer correspondingly less from such discrepancies, being simpler, more easily surveyed, and less demanding of the knowledge of economic relationships and the data needed to estimate them; but they may not be comprehensive enough to do the job well. Single-equation models represent an extreme class in this ranking by size and simplicity and are strictly applicable only to one-way cause-and-effect relationships, not to mutual dependencies. For *ex ante* predictions, they must employ known lagged values or outside forecasts of the independent (exogenous) variables; otherwise they can provide only *ex post* predictions conditional on the knowledge of the exogenous inputs.

[24] It is possible to establish by experimentation what is the best simple lag in the relation between the changes in the composite of the indicators and the subsequent changes in GNP (for some work along these lines, see [19, pp. 16–17]), and this could be extended to distributed lags. But what is optimal in the sample period need not be so in the forecast period, and the stability of the lag may be especially problematic here because we are dealing with composites of series with different timing properties.

It may also be instructive to experiment with indexes that differ in the number and identity of the indicators included (again, some results on this are reported in [19]), and likewise with different dependent variables (for example, with employment or industrial production instead of GNP). In short, the procedure is quite flexible and it is easily kept up to date, too. But these advantages derive from its basically mechanical nature. It is because of the latter that the method is treated as another benchmark model, though one that may not be easy to beat. This implies the expectation that, over time, skilled judgmental use of the indicators should yield better forecasts. (Analogously, judgmental adjustments are viewed in [9] as necessary means for obtaining good-quality forecasts from econometric models.)

leading indicators model clearly suggests a simple but important generalization: that in this comprehensive class of applied economic forecasts the use of predictors with early timing ("leading" series, "anticipations" data) has a comparatively high probability of success. Such predictors should therefore be in strong demand, and one might expect to see much effort spent on increasing their limited supply by data compilation, experimentation, and testing. The leading indicators and the anticipations data, although for the most part a by-product of more basic research, have indeed long been a subject of much scientific interest in their own right, in recent years primarily at the National Bureau and at the IFO-Institute in Munich; and there is little doubt that practicing forecasters use such materials widely. But such data are still not fully and systematically incorporated in formal econometric models, even where forecasting of short-term movements of the economy is a major objective. One probable reason for this is that their use imposes limitations upon the model. When an aggregate anticipations variable is included, which is based on microdata obtained from surveys of the relevant decision-making units, it is difficult to extrapolate the model successfully beyond the time span covered by the survey because the anticipations themselves cannot be well predicted. A similar problem exists for the leading indicators.[25] Nevertheless, there is surely both need and scope for making more and better use of such data in forecasting with econometric models (and indeed in short-term economic forecasting generally).[26]

3. Forecasts of the U.S. Economy: A Review of the Updated Record

In this section that follows, several standards of predictive performance are applied to updated materials on forecasts of various types, from "purely" judgmental to those made by or with econometric models, including comparisons between forecasts from the same sources for different periods; between forecasts by different persons and methods made for the same

---

[25] At least some of these early-moving series make much better tools than targets of forecasts. Thus, as shown in detail in Victor Zarnowitz, *Orders, Production, and Investment —— A Cyclical and Structural Analysis* (New York, NBER, forthcoming), new orders precede output and shipments in manufacturing industries in which production to order is important, and they predict these activities as well as possible. However, such orders contain a large element of "autonomous" expectations and are themselves poorly predicted. (This is shown, in particular, by microdata on business forecasts of new orders for nonelectrical machinery in Machinery and Allied Products Institute, *Capital Goods Review*, December 1965.) In fact, it is where new orders cannot be predicted sufficiently well at acceptable costs that production will be largely "to order"; where they can be so predicted and supplying them appears profitable, production will be "to stock."

[26] Further remarks on this point are made in section 4 of this paper.

periods; between *ex ante* and *ex post* forecasts for some econometric models; and between forecasts and benchmark predictions or extrapolations.

3.1 Private Judgmental Forecasts of GNP, 1953–69

The record of business and other private judgmental forecasts presented in [29] ends in 1963. Since then some of these forecasts were discontinued or excluded, while a few new sets were added to our collection. The amounts of continuous data from the same sources are now sufficient for compiling a record of forecasts through 1969 and for attempting to answer the question: How does the forecasters' performance in the most recent years (1964–69) compare with their performance in the earlier postwar period (1953–1963 or parts thereof)?

Table 1 shows some summary measures of accuracy for eight different sets of annual forecasts of GNP relating to the years 1953–69. The sources are: a group of economists from various industries, government, and academic institutions; a graduate faculty group; the economic staffs of three large business firms in insurance, banking, and manufacturing; a business publication; an individual university researcher; and a business consulting service. Five of the sets were included in [29], three (K, L, and M) were not.

For the two groups (A and M), which are relatively small, averages of separate forecasts made by the members are used, and it should be noted that such averages tend to be more accurate over time than most of the forecasts by the individual participants in the given group because of compensating errors among the member forecasters [29, pp. 123–126]. Furthermore, comparability of the different forecasts sets is impaired by differences in the periods covered and in the dates of issue (late forecasts can take advantage of recent information not available for earlier forecasts). However, it is not the question of who the best forecasters are that concerns us here but rather the over-all accuracy and some other interesting properties of the forecasters' products.

Since the initial level from which a change is predicted is itself as a rule unknown and must be estimated, the error in forecasting the change typically differs from the error in forecasting the future level, the difference being equal to the error in the estimated current position or "base" of the forecast. This base estimate should always be reported by a forecaster but only too often it is not; however, in recent forecasts this deficiency seems to be much less frequent, perhaps because the need to remove it, stressed in the literature reviewed in this paper, is being increasingly recognized.[27]

[27]Where the base forecasts are not reported, they must be imputed to make possible an analysis of the forecasts of change. Such imputations were made for this study by extrapolative methods selected so as to approximate as closely as possible any base estimates for other periods made by the given source (clues of this sort are often available; where they are not, methods approximating the results for other, similar forecasts were used). Compare [29, pp. 32-35].

TABLE 1

Annual Forecasts of GNP: Average Errors of Prediction of Base Values,
Changes, and Levels and Comparisons with Three Extrapolative Models,
Eight Sets of Private Judgmental Forecasts, 1953-69

| Forecast Set[a] | Period Covered | Mean Error (ME)[b] | | | Mean Absolute Error (MAE)[b] | | | Root Mean Square Error (M_P)[b] | Ratios of Root Mean Square Errors: Forecast to Extrapolation[c] | | |
		Base[d] (1)	Change (2)	Level (3)	Base[d] (4)	Change (5)	Level (6)	(7)	R_1 (8)	R_2 (9)	R_2^* (10)
A	1954–69	−3.7	−6.4	−10.2	4.4	10.6	12.7	14.9	.391	.761	.602
B	1953–69	−2.8	−3.2	−6.0	3.4	9.2	11.1	12.5	.328	.641	.504
C	1958–69	−3.4	−3.8	−7.2	3.7	8.7	10.7	11.8	.271	.642	.432
F	1953–69	−3.2	−4.4	−7.6	3.5	6.9	9.7	11.1	.290	.570	.448
G	1953–69	−2.9	−0.5	−3.4	3.4	7.7	9.6	11.9	.312	.614	.481
K	1957–69	−5.2	−1.2	−6.4	5.2	7.0	8.8	10.9	.261	.612	.413
L	1956–69	−4.5	−3.3	−7.8	4.5	7.4	9.6	12.1	.281	.699	.478
M	1953–69	−2.5	−6.8	−9.3	3.1	10.4	11.8	14.0	.374	.723	.562

[a]For a brief description of forecasts, see text.

[b]A forecast error (E) is defined as the predicted value minus the corresponding actual value (P − A). The actual values are the first estimates of the U.S. Department of Commerce for the preceding year, which appear in January. All entries in these columns are in billions of dollars. The formulas for the averages are: $ME = (1/n) \sum (P_t - A_t)$; $MAE = (1/n) \sum |P_t - A_t|$; and $M_P = \sqrt{(1/n) \sum (P_t - A_t)^2}$, where the summation is over all n periods covered by the given set of forecasts. The M_P measures (column 7) refer to level errors.

[c]The ratios are: $R_1 = M_P/M_{N1}$; $R_2 = M_P/M_{N2}$; and $R_2^* = M_P/M_{N2}^*$. The denominators, M_N, are the root mean square errors of three types of extrapolation: $N1$ refers to the projection of the last known level, $N2$ to that of the last known change, and $N2^*$ to that of the average historical change. See text for more detail.

[d]Errors in the estimated positon or base of the forecasts. The base values are the forecasters' own estimates, except for sets A (before 1957), K, and L.

For the GNP forecasts, base errors all have, on the average, negative signs, as do the errors of change; accordingly, the mean errors of level, which equal the algebraic sums of the corresponding mean errors of base and of change, are also all negative and, when signs are disregarded, the errors of level are largest of the three (Table 1, columns 1–3). The errors are computed by substracting the actual from the predicted values; thus, given the upward trend in GNP, the negative signs of the mean errors indicate the forecasters' tendency to underestimate the increases and hence also the target levels of this variable. The minus signs of the base errors also are related to this tendency, which apparently prevailed for the preliminary official estimates of GNP as well.[28]

In terms of absolute averages, the level errors are in each case larger than the change errors, (the weighted means for all sets are $10.5 billion and $8.5 billion, respectively) and the base errors are the smallest (columns 4–6). The latter result accords with expectation, since the present or the recent past should be better known than the future. However, the base errors are certainly significant, amounting on the average to more than one-third of the corresponding level errors.

Comparisons of the forecasts (P) with benchmark extrapolations (N) were made in terms of the level errors only, by calculating the ratios of the root mean square errors (M_P/M_N). These measures involve squaring the individual forecast errors, so that greater weight is attached to large than to small deviations of predictions from actual values.[29] Three extrapolative models are used: $N1$, which projects forward the current level of the given variable (here, the base-year value of GNP); $N2$, which projects the last change; and $N2^*$, which projects an average historical change.[30] The ratios are labeled R and bear the subscript of the model used in computing the denominator, e.g., $R_1 = M_P/M_{N1}$.

[28] See section 2.2 above on the effects of data errors on forecasting errors, with references to [3] and [4].

[29] See Table 1, footnote b, on the definitions of the root mean square error of forecast M_P, and the other averages used: mean error (ME) and mean absolute error (MAE). Except in the trivial case where all errors are equal, $M_P > MAE > ME$ (compare the corresponding measures for the level errors in columns 3, 6, and 7 of Table 1).

[30] The assumption of $N1$ is that $A_{t+1} = A_t + u_{t+1}$, where A is an actual value and u is a random error. Hence the forecast here is $P_{N1} = A_t^*$ (the preliminary estimate of the current value of the series). $N2$ specifies that $A_{t+1} = A_t + \triangle A_t + u_{t+1}$, and the corresponding forecast is $P_{N2} = A_t^* + \triangle A_t^*$. The assumption of $N2^*$ is that $A_{t+1} = A_t + \triangle A + u_{t+1}$ where $\triangle A$ is the average value of past changes in the given series as available to the forecaster from the historical record (for GNP, the starting date of that record is 1947). Hence, the forecast $P_{N2^*} = A_t^* + \triangle A$.

As shown in the three last columns of the table, the ratios M_P/M_N are definitely less than 1 in all cases; that is, the root mean square errors are smaller for the forecasts than for any of the three extrapolative or naive models ($M_P < M_N$). For each of the forecast sets, R_1 is the smallest and R_2 the largest of the ratios, with R_2^* ranking in the middle; simple averages of the ratios for the eight sets are 0.32 for R_1, 0.49 for R_2^* and 0.66 for R_2^*. This means that, of these models, $N1$ gives the weakest and $N2$ the strongest results for GNP in the years from 1953 through 1969. But these are all exceedingly simple models, which ought to be viewed generally as providing only minimal standards of predictive accuracy. Although models such as $N2$ and $N2^*$ can be relatively effective for series with pronounced trends which are approximately linear over the periods covered, it will be desirable in further work to confront the GNP forecasts with more stringent yardsticks such as autoregressive predictions with certain optimal properties.

3.2 Forecasts Before and Since 1964

In Table 2, the GNP forecast records summarized in the preceding section are analyzed for two separate subperiods: one beginning in 1953 or later and ending in 1963, the other including the years 1964–69. The table shows that the root mean square errors of the level forecasts for the latter period exceeded their counterparts for the former period in each case and often by relatively large margins (columns 1 and 5). For all eight sets, these M_P figures average about $10 billion in the periods through 1963, $15 billion in the years 1964–69, and $12 billion in all years covered.

However, larger absolute errors do not necessarily denote worse forecasts. The size of errors depends on the size (as well as dispersion) of the values to be predicted. In forecasts of two series with similar behavior, the errors for the series that has lower levels are likely to be smaller on the average (e.g., GNP in 1958 dollars is predicted with smaller absolute errors than GNP in current dollars). GNP measured in current dollars rose from $365 billion to $589 billion between 1953 and 1963 and from $629 billion to $932 billion between 1964 and 1969; the observed increase in the average forecast errors appears rather moderate when compared to the contrast between the average levels of GNP in the two periods. Indeed, the ratios R_1 are on the whole much smaller for the GNP forecasts relating to 1964–69 than for those relating to the pre-1964 years (Table 2, columns 2 and 6). Thus, comparisons with the naive "same-level" projections show the more recent predictions in better light than the earlier ones.

The ratios R_2^* also are decidedly lower for the 1964–69 forecasts than for the pre-1964 ones (columns 4 and 8). It can be said, then, that the GNP forecast errors increased on the average less between the two periods than did

TABLE 2

Annual Forecasts of GNP: Comparisons with Three Extrapolative Models,
for Periods Before 1964 and 1964–69, Eight Sets of Private Judgmental Forecasts

Forecast Set	Forecast Periods Through 1963[a]				Forecast Period 1964–69			
	Root Mean Square Error $(M_p)^b$ (1)	Ratios of Root Mean Square Errors: Forecast to Extrapolation[c]			Root Mean Square Error $(M_p)^b$ (5)	Ratios of Root Mean Square Errors: Forecast to Extrapolation[c]		
		R_1 (2)	R_2 (3)	R_2^* (4)		R_1 (6)	R_2 (7)	R_2^* (8)
A	12.5	.506	.651	.781	18.2	.331	1.219	.497
B	10.7	.435	.553	.699	15.2	.276	1.024	.421
C	11.0	.424	.534	.797	12.5	.226	0.840	.343
F	8.8	.359	.457	.578	14.3	.258	0.959	.394
G	7.9	.322	.410	.518	17.0	.306	1.140	.467
K	8.5	.342	.453	.656	13.2	.238	0.882	.363
L	7.2	.283	.359	.591	16.6	.299	1.114	.456
M	12.8	.531	.839	.841	15.8	.294	1.061	.436

[a]For B, F, G, and M: 1953–63; for A: 1954–63; C: 1958–63; K: 1957–63; L: 1956–63.

[b]In billions of dollars. All means refer to level errors. See Table 1, footnote b.

[c]See Table 1, footnote c.

the mean annual change in GNP measured cumulatively over the postwar years.

In contrast, the R_2 ratios present a picture that is clearly unfavorable to the more recent forecasts in all but two sets (columns 3 and 7). For 1953–63, these ratios are concentrated in the 0.4 to 0.6 range; for 1964–69, in the 0.8 to 1.1 range. In periods of steady growth without turning points and major retardations, such as the middle and late sixties, the N_2 extrapolations of last change in GNP have a great advantage; in times of weaker trends and stronger cyclical movements, such as the post-Korean decade, this model performs much worse.

Inspection of the underlying series of individual forecasts and their errors shows that underestimation of growth was much more pronounced in 1964–69 than in the earlier period. The average year-to-year change in GNP (disregarding sign) was, $22.2 billion in 1953–63 and $55.6 billion in 1964–69; the corresponding averages for the predicted change are $21.7 billion and $46.5 billion.[31] The annual forecasts of GNP for 1953–63 include 43 underestimates, 25 overestimates, and 7 turning-point or directional errors (among the 75 forecasts included, six relate to declines in actual values, and they include three under- and three overestimates). The forecasts for 1964–69 include 41 underestimates and 7 overestimates; no actual declines occurred, and none were predicted, so the class of turning-point errors is here empty. These results are consistent with those obtained from a different sample of pre-1964 forecasts in [29]: as reported in section 2.3 above, underestimation has been related primarily to increases in series with dominant upward trends.

The rankings of the forecasters according to the average size of errors as measured by M_P and according to any of the R ratios are very different in the two subperiods. The rank correlations based on the entries in the corresponding columns (1 and 5, 2 and 6, etc.) of Table 2 are all virtually zero.[32] In terms of these ranks, sets A, G, and L have slipped, the last two considerably, and sets K and (especially) C and M have gained better relative positions (for B and F, no determinate shifts in ranks are observed). These

---

[31] These averages cover all eight forecast sets included in Table 2 and are weighted by the numbers of observations in each set. The averages for the actual change include the actual values that correspond to all these predictions and are analogously weighted.

[32] The ratios M_P/M_N have a common denominator for all the forecasts in a given period (it is a certain specific value of M_{N1} for the ratios R_1, of M_{N2} for the ratios R_2, etc.). Ranking the forecasts according to any of the ratios must, therefore, yield the same results as ranking according to M_P if the periods covered are the same. In the present case, however, the periods differ, and hence the rank correlations also differ slightly. The Spearman rank correlation coefficients are as follows (the subscripts refer to the columns of Table 2): $\rho 15 = -0.047$; $\rho 26 = +0.024$; $\rho 37 = +0.024$; and $\rho 48 = -0.190$.

findings tend to agree with those reported previously on the apparent lack of consistency in forecasters' performance from year to year [29, pp. 130–132].

Table 3 shows some measures of absolute and relative accuracy for selected forecasts of the major expenditure components of GNP, using errors computed by taking differences between the predicted and the actual percentage changes. The dollar levels of these series differ greatly and errors of forecasts relating to these levels, or to the corresponding dollar changes, lack all comparability between such variables. An analysis in terms of relative change errors is more appropriate.

Although the level errors are on the average larger for the 1964–69 GNP forecasts than for the pre-1964 forecasts, as shown in Table 2, the opposite applies to the relative change errors (Table 3, forecast sets B, C, and F for GNP, columns 1 and 4). For the investment and government expenditure forecasts, too, the relative-change errors in the earlier years tend to exceed those in 1964–69, while for the consumption forecasts the errors in the two subperiods differ little (columns 1 and 4).

The average errors in predicting year-to-year percentage changes are much smaller in forecasts of personal consumption expenditures than in forecasts of gross private domestic investment (GPDI) in either subperiod and in the total period covered. The errors for the residential construction component are even larger than those for total GPDI, while the errors for government expenditures tend to exceed the errors for consumption but are also much smaller than those for investment (columns 1, 4, and 7). These results parallel the findings in [29, pp. 36-40].

With a few exceptions, the R_1 and R_2 ratios in Table 3 fall below unity, indicating that these forecasts are more accurate than the corresponding naive-model projections.[33] For consumption and government expenditures, the $N1$ model generally works worse than the $N2$ model (i.e., $R_1 < R_2$), while for GPDI the contrary is true. For residential construction, $R_1 > R_2$ in the earlier years and $R_1 < R_2$ in 1964-69, but the differences are relatively small. The ratios, R_1 are in virtually all cases larger for the investment variables (particularly residential construction) than for consumption and government expenditures; the R_2 ratios are in nearly two-thirds of the comparisons larger for the investment variables.

From the evidence of the R_1 ratios one would infer that these forecasts have on the whole improved in recent years, but the R_2 ratios present a mixed picture: for consumption and GPDI, they are higher in 1964-69 than in earlier years; for the housing and government expenditures, they are lower.

[33]Three ratios for residential construction forecasts and one for a government expenditures forecast are larger than 1. These cases include two R_1 and two R_2 ratios (see Table 3, lines 10 and 15).

TABLE 3

Annual Forecasts of Relative Changes in GNP and Four of its Major Expenditure Components: Comparisons with Two Extrapolative Models for Periods Before 1964 and 1964–69, Three Sets of Private Judgmental Forecasts

Forecast Set	Forecast Periods Through 1963[a]			Forecast Period, 1964–69			Total Forecast Period		
	(M_P)[b] (1)	R_1 (2)	R_2 (3)	(M_P)[b] (4)	R_1 (5)	R_2 (6)	(M_P)[b] (7)	R_1 (8)	R_2 (9)
Gross National Product									
B	2.15	0.395	0.531	1.70	.225	0.804	2.00	0.320	.576
C	2.04	0.374	0.505	1.31	.173	0.618	1.71	0.442	.531
F	1.70	0.312	0.419	1.28	.169	0.604	1.54	0.246	.443
Personal Consumption Expenditures									
B	1.52	0.318	0.528	1.49	.205	0.785	1.51	0.263	.583
C	1.44	0.310	0.528	1.44	.198	0.759	1.44	0.236	.612
F	1.69	0.354	0.588	1.14	.156	0.601	1.52	0.264	.592
Gross Private Domestic Investment									
B	12.83	0.901	0.569	5.90	.620	0.607	10.93	0.789	.582
C	8.50	0.570	0.313	3.98	.419	0.410	6.64	0.532	.637
F	7.20	0.506	0.318	2.95	.311	0.304	5.95	0.430	.314

Table 3 (concluded)

Forecast Set	Forecast Periods Through 1963[a]			Forecast Period, 1964–69			Total Forecast Period		
	(M_P)[b] (1)	R_1 (2)	R_2 (3)	(M_P)[b] (4)	R_1 (5)	R_2 (6)	(M_P)[b] (7)	R_1 (8)	R_2 (9)
Residential Construction									
B	14.12	1.229	1.049	6.14	.538	0.593	11.92	1.032	.958
C	9.04	0.865	0.770	6.55	.575	0.632	7.89	0.714	.711
F	9.15	0.931	0.832	6.45	.556	0.623	8.10	0.762	.757
Total Government Expenditures									
B	2.82	0.406	0.467	1.40	.150	0.397	2.45	0.279	.464
C	2.17	0.319	0.690	1.30	.140	0.368	1.79	0.219	.535
F	2.15	0.309	0.355	4.56	.489	1.292	3.21	0.364	.609

[a]For B and F: 1953–63; for C: 1958–63.

[b]In percentage points. All measures refer to relative change errors. See Table 1, footnotes b and c, for the general definitions of the root mean square error M_P and the ratios $R_1 = M_P / M_{N1}$ and $R_2 = M_P / M_{N2}$.

In sum, the record does not show that the assembled forecasts generally have either improved or deteriorated in the recent years. Comparisons of level forecasts limited to some of the benchmark models ($N1, N2^*$) would have suggested improvement, but this merely reflects the fact that these models themselves are less effective for GNP in the mid- and late sixties than in the preceding decade; the opposite applies to $N2$ and when this model is used as a yardstick the forecasts appear to have worsened. The average errors in predicting annual percentage changes have become smaller for the forecasts of GNP and some of its major expenditure components, both absolutely and relative to the corresponding errors of the $N1$ model; but again the comparisons with $N2$ suggest in large part the opposite. Thus the results vary for the different forecast sets, variables, and criteria. One can merely speculate about why a more general and definite improvement has not been achieved.[34]

3.3 Some Comparisons with Governmental Forecasts of GNP, 1962–69.

Forecasts of annual percentage changes in GNP and the general price level prepared by the Council of Economic Advisers (CEA) can be taken or inferred from the *Economic Report of the President* for the years since 1962. Moore has reconstructed these important predictions in [19]. In Table 4, the CEA forecasts of GNP are compared with the actual values and with some selected private predictions for each of the successive years 1962–69.[35]

The CEA forecasts underestimate the actual percentage changes of GNP in each year except 1962 and 1967, and so do the average private forecasts (represented by mean predictions for the eight sets used in Tables 1 and 2). The underestimation errors are smaller in the CEA forecasts than in the

[34]The expectation that forecasts should improve is based in the first place on the general view of forecasting as a cumulative learning process. However, some practitioners take the skeptical position that changes in the economy are often such as to make the experience gained in the period past a weak guide to the future. Since the economy followed a more stable upward course in 1964–69 than in the preceding decade, which included three business recessions, one might contend that the recent years were easier to predict. But it can also be argued that excessive reliance on lessons of the previous period of economic hesitancy has contributed to the conservativeness of so many forecasts in the more recent years of stronger growth and inflation.

[35]The CEA forecasts listed in Table 4, line 2, are updated figures from [19]. The actual values in line 1 are computed from the first Commerce estimates that are also used elsewhere in my analysis of the accuracy of GNP forecasts. They differ but slightly from the actual values used by Moore in [19], which are the first official estimates given in the President's *Economic Report*. The divergencies never exceed ± 0.1 percentage points, and the mean of the actual percentage changes, disregarding sign, is the same according to either set of figures.

TABLE 4

Forecasts of Annual Percentage Change in Gross National Product, President's Economic Report and Some Selected Private Sources, 1962–69

	1961–62 (1)	1962–63 (2)	1963–64 (3)	1964–65 (4)	1965–66 (5)	1966–67 (6)	1967–68 (7)	1968–69 (8)	Mean 1962–69 (9)	Absolute Mean 1962–69 (10)
Actual and Predicted Percentage Change										
1. Actual[a]	6.8	5.5	6.6	7.6	8.6	5.5	9.0	7.6	7.2	7.2
2. CEA[b]	9.4	4.4	6.5	6.1	6.9	6.4	7.8	7.0	6.8	6.8
3. Average, 8 forecast sets[c]	8.0	4.1	5.8	5.7	7.0	6.4	7.6	6.8	6.4	6.4
Errors in Forecasts of Percentage Change[d]										
4. CEA[e]	+2.6	−1.1	−0.1	−1.5	−1.7	+0.9	−1.2	−0.6	−0.34	1.21
5. Average, 8 sets[f]	+1.2	−1.4	−0.8	−1.9	−1.6	+0.9	−1.4	−0.8	−0.72	1.25
6. Set K	−1.0	+0.6	−0.7	−1.6	−0.7	+2.3	−0.5	−0.8	−0.30	1.02
7. Set F	+1.9	−1.5	−0.8	−1.4	−2.2	+0.0	−0.8	−1.3	−0.76	1.24
8. Set C	+1.9	−2.0	−1.9	−2.1	−0.5	+0.5	−0.7	−1.1	−0.74	1.34

[a] Based on the first estimates of the U.S. Department of Commerce for the preceding year, which appear in January.

[b] Forecasts by the Council of Economic Advisers. Source: *Economic Report of the President*, January 1962 through February 1969 (based on figures on dollar levels, dollar changes, or percentage changes as given in the *Report*).

[c] Includes forecast sets A, B, C, F, G, K, L, and M, each of which provides a full coverage of the years 1962–69. Each entry in columns 1–8 represents the mean of the eight forecasts for the given year.

[d] Errors equal predicted minus actual percentage change, in percentage points.

[e] Errors of the CEA forecasts that are listed in line 2. See footnote b, above.

[f] Errors of the average forecasts that are listed in line 3. See footnote c.

average private forecasts in all but one year; on the other hand, the overestimate for 1962 is considerably larger in the CEA forecast (Table 4, lines 1–3). The average errors disregarding sign show only a minute difference in favor of the CEA predictions, which may or may not be significant (lines 4 and 5, with the summary figures in column 10).

Of the eight private forecast sets, K has a somewhat lower mean absolute error than the CEA forecasts, and two sets F and C show errors that are on the average not much larger (lines 6–8). Set K also underestimates the rates of growth in GNP a trifle less than the CEA forecasts, but the other two sets show stronger underestimation tendencies (as shown by the size of the negative mean errors in column 9). Of the five sets not individually included in Table 4, all have larger mean absolute errors (ranging from 1.4 to 1.8 percentage points), and in only one is the underestimation lower than that of the forecasts that are included.[36]

Comparisons with the three simple benchmark models, $N1$, $N2$, and $N2*$, indicate that the forecasts represented in Table 4 are all definitely superior to such extrapolations. The average errors disregarding sign are 7.1, 1.9, and 3.6 percentage points for the $N1$, $N2$, and $N2*$ projections, respectively.[37]

Finally, the examination of all available annual forecasts of GNP suggests that the variability of predictions from year to year tends to be greater than the variability of predictions by different forecasters in a given period. I suspect that this is indeed often so and not confined to this particular variable and period, for the following reasons (which, although plausible, are also difficult to test): For all their diversity, which is considerable, forecasts for a given macroeconomic variable in a given period must have much in common because competent forecasters use to a large extent the same data and similar methods, are exposed to the same major current events and prevailing expectations, and possibly influence each other directly. Hence one might expect many forecasters to share at one time in a common success and at

[36]The predictions in set G consist of four overestimates and four underestimates (in 1965–69) and have a mean error of −0.21 and a mean absolute error of 1.38 percentage points.

[37]The mean errors, listed in the same order, are −7.1, −0.6, and −3.6 percentage points. The $N1$ criterion is, of course, an extremely weak one for a series growing as fast and as steadily as GNP in the 1960's, and it is merely noted here as one of the conventional yardsticks. The $N2*$ benchmark model used to be rather effective for the earlier postwar period; when applied to forecasts concentrated in the years 1953–63 this model produced generally more accurate projections than either $N1$ or $N2$ [29, pp. 83–90]. The deterioration in the performance of $N2*$ in the more recent years is clearly due to the increased growth rates in GNP as compared with the earlier postwar period. The relative stability of the growth rates in the period covered naturally works strongly in favor of the $N2$ model.

another in a common failure (using these terms in a broad and relative sense). As for the variability over time of economic forecasts and their errors, this reflects mainly economic instability which has many forms and causes; some types of economic change are more difficult to predict than others and different types prevail at different times.

3.4 Some Multiperiod Forecasts by Business Economists

Some of the collected forecast sets provide chains of predictions made at a given date for two or more successive periods. Thus set A includes forecasts made annually for two and four quarters ahead; set C, forecasts made at somewhat irregular intervals four times per year for spans ranging from one to five quarters; and set G, forecasts made semiannually for spans varying from one to six quarters. Table 5 shows the root mean square errors of the GNP predictions from two of these sources and also the ratios of these M_p figures to the corresponding statistics for the naive models $N1$ and $N2$.

The M_p figures virtually always increase with the span of the predictions in any of the periods covered, i.e., since 1964 and before (there are no exceptions of this rule in the cases illustrated in Table 5, columns 1, 4, and 7). The *increments* of M_p in the successive quarters vary considerably, however, and show no tendency either to rise or fall; so the marginal errors are not necessarily larger for the more distant quarters than for those in the nearest future and may even be occasionally smaller. To put it differently, the increase in the average errors is typically less than proportional to the increase in the forecast span.

The R_1 ratios are all smaller than 1 and are concentrated in the range between 0.4 and 0.6 for any of the spans and periods covered (but they are, in most cases, somewhat larger in the period since 1964 than before; see columns 2, 5, and 8). This means that all these forecasts are better (approximately twice as accurate on the average, in terms of the root mean square errors of the level forecasts) than the same-level projections of the benchmark model $N1$.

The R_2 ratios also are smaller than 1 for all included forecasts that refer to the periods before 1964 and the total periods covered, but they are throughout appreciably larger than 1 for the forecasts relating to the 1964–69 period (columns 3, 6, and 9). This confirms that the last-change projections with the naive model $N2$ present a rather difficult standard of comparison for the GNP forecasts in the second half of the 1960's (see the high R_2 ratios for the annual GNP predictions of 1964–69 in Table 2, column 7).

As the span of forecast is extended, the ratios R_1 and R_2 decrease more often than increase, but the relationships are not very strong or regular. For

TABLE 5

Two Sets of Forecasts of GNP over Spans of from One to Five Quarters,
Comparisons with two Extrapolative Models for Periods Before 1964 and 1964–69

Span of Forecast (no. of quarters)	Forecast Periods Through 1963[a]			Forecast Period 1964–69			Total Forecast Period [b]		
	(M_P)[c] (1)	R_1 (2)	R_2 (3)	(M_P)[c] (4)	R_1 (5)	R_2 (6)	(M_P)[c] (7)	R_1 (8)	R_2 (9)
				Set C (1958–69)[d]					
1	7.5	.412	.547	10.9	.732	1.361	9.0	.539	.767
2	10.8	.456	.507	17.9	.585	1.910	14.2	.531	.811
3	12.3	.413	.413	22.5	.512	1.668	17.2	.488	.702
4	15.0	.417	.414	27.1	.431	1.569	20.5	.425	.672
5	19.5	.428	.368	28.9	.358	1.312	24.3	.379	.588
				Set G (1953–69)[e]					
1	9.4	.507	.497	9.3	.502	1.371	9.4	.505	.606
2	10.2	.402	.366	14.0	.460	1.638	11.3	.431	.520
3	12.4	.418	.372	21.8	.466	1.440	16.4	.448	.566
4	13.8	.389	.324	25.6	.411	1.428	18.9	.409	.554

[a]For C: 1958–63; for G: 1953–63.

[b]For C: 1958–69; for G: 1953–69.

[c]In billions of current dollars. All measures refer to level errors. See Table 1, footnotes b and c, for the general definitions of the root mean square error M_P and the ratios $R_1 = M_P/M_{N1}$ and $R_2 = M_P/M_{N2}$.

[d]Includes 22, 20, 19, 13, and 7 forecasts for spans of one to five quarters, respectively, in the period 1958–63; 19, 14, 13, 8, and 6 forecasts for the same spans in the period 1964–69.

[e]Includes 20 forecasts per span for 1953–64. In the period 1964–69, includes 12 forecasts for spans of one or two quarters and 11 forecasts for spans of three or four quarters.

all observations in Table 5, declines in the ratios prevail over rises 30 to 12, and for the largest samples (total forecast periods) the dominance of the declines is even more marked (11 to 3). Hence it appears that the forecasts tend to *improve* relative to both naive models as the span lengthens.

The quarterly and multiperiod forecasts for the recent years, like the annual forecasts, make a better showing when evaluated in terms of errors of relative change instead of level errors (compare the measures for the annual GNP predictions in Tables 2 and 3). In the course of the present study, the absolute and relative accuracy of the updated multiperiod forecasts of relative changes in the major expenditure components of GNP was examined, but only a brief statement about the general results of this analysis is warranted here.[38]

The average errors of forecasts of consumption expenditures, gross private domestic investment, government spending, and several components of these categories, are all found to increase with the span of prediction, for the most part monotonically. However, the marginal errors of these forecasts do not increase systematically, that is, the average errors do not increase as fast as the span of forecast. The R_1 and R_2 ratios become in most cases lower as the forecasts reach further out into the future, indicating that the longer-range predictions are more accurate relative to the naive models than the short ones.[39] All of this agrees with, and amplifies, the findings obtained for the GNP forecasts, as summarized above.

Relatively few of the percentage change forecasts examined have root mean square errors exceeding those of the naive models (i.e., R_1, $R_2 > 1$), even in the 1964–69 period. Exceptions are the forecasts of residential construction and net change in inventories, for which a large proportion of the R_1 ratios are larger than unity. Generally, $N1$ is more effective than $N2$ for these variables and gross private domestic investment as a whole (that is, R_1 tends to exceed R_2 here), while the opposite applies to consumption and government expenditures.

---

[38]The reason is that this material comes largely from one forecast set that is rather unlike the others in our collection of private judgmental forecasts, namely, set C, which evolved from a more informal forecast toward one that relies importantly on relationships estimated with an econometric model. These results, though interesting, are therefore somewhat limited in scope; yet it would take considerable space to present them in a more specific form.

[39]Changes in the R_1 ratios associated with successive one-quarter increases in the forecast spans consist of decreases in nearly two-thirds of the observations, while for the R_2 ratios the over-all proportion of decreases is over three-fourths. This includes the results for both the subperiods and the total forecast periods; when only the latter are considered, the connection of increasing spans with declining R ratios becomes more pronounced, particularly for R_2.

3.5 *Ex Ante* and *Ex Post* Forecasts with Two Econometric Models

Recently, Haitovsky and Treyz have brought up to date and extended the analysis of the forecasting properties of two econometric models, Wharton-EFU and OBE, which was first presented in [9]. I owe the data used in Table 6 to their courtesy.

The mean absolute errors of the *ex ante* forecasts *(MAE-XA)* for eight selected variables show the usual tendency to increase with the predictive span, from one to four quarters. There are only a few exceptions to this rule among the measures for the Wharton model (column 1), and none among those for the OBE model (column 4). However, the successive increments in these errors do not increase systematically, that is, the errors in predicting the first quarter are not always smaller on the average than the errors in predicting the second quarter, etc. In other words, the errors do not double and triple as the span of forecasts doubles and triples; in fact, they most often increase less than in proportion to the span, although no uniform and regular relationships emerge between these variables. All this agrees qualitatively with the findings for the judgmental forecasts as noted in [29, Chap. 5] and earlier in this paper.

The forecasts in question are the authentic *ex ante* predictions that involve judgmental adjustments of the constant terms by the Wharton and OBE forecasters. Several alternative mechanical adjustments were applied to the two models in [9] and again the updated version of [9]. The forecasts obtained with these reproducible adjustments tend to be less accurate than the true *ex ante* forecasts, often by substantial margins. Without any adjustments at all, the forecasts turn out to be still worse.

Ratios of the *MAE-XA* figures to the mean absolute errors of the simplest naive-model projections ($N1$ or $N2$, whichever proved more effective for the given variable) are listed in Table 6, columns 2 (Wharton-EFU) and 5 (OBE). For GNP in current and constant dollars, the implicit price deflator, and consumption expenditures on durable goods other than automobiles, $N2$ gave better predictions, hence the ratio shown is *MAE-XA/MAE-N2*. For the other four variables——expenditures on automobiles and on plant and equipment, net change in inventories, and the unemployment rate——$N1$ worked better and the entries correspondingly refer to the ratio *MAE-XA/MAE-N1*.

For both Wharton and OBE, the ratios for the forecasts of GNP in constant dollars are generally lower than those for current-dollar GNP (lines 1–10). The Wharton forecasts for GNP had larger errors than $N2$ (i.e., the ratios exceed 1) for the two shortest spans; the OBE forecasts had the larger errors for all but the shortest span. These poor results are apparently to a large extent due to very unsatisfactory price-level forecasts. Most of the ratios for GNP in 1958 dollars are smaller than 1 but several are not much smaller

TABLE 6

Wharton and OBE Model *Ex Ante* Forecasts of Eight Selected Variables over
Varying Spans, Comparisons with Naive Model Extrapolations
and *Ex Post* Model Forecasts, 1966–69

Span of Forecast (no. of quarters)	Wharton-EFU Model[a]			OBE Model[b]		
	$MAE\text{-}XA^c$ (1)	$\dfrac{MAE\text{-}XA^d}{MAE\text{-}N}$ (2)	$\dfrac{MAE\text{-}XA^e}{MAE\text{-}XP}$ (3)	$MAE\text{-}XA^c$ (4)	$\dfrac{MAE\text{-}XA^d}{MAE\text{-}N}$ (5)	$\dfrac{MAE\text{-}XA^e}{MAE\text{-}XP}$ (6)
GNP (N2; billions of current dollars)						
1. One	3.8	1.05	0.63	2.1	0.68	0.49
2. Two	7.8	1.04	0.78	7.8	1.07	0.89
3. Three	10.4	0.82	0.89	12.7	0.99	0.93
4. Four	12.6	0.71	0.89	19.4	1.21	1.01
5. Next year	6.6	0.61	0.76	11.5	1.21	1.03
GNP (N2; billions of 1958 dollars)						
6. One	2.8	0.91	0.56	1.8	0.64	0.77
7. Two	5.7	0.96	0.68	4.8	0.83	1.04
8. Three	7.2	0.71	0.68	7.0	0.64	0.95
9. Four	6.7	0.46	0.55	9.4	0.66	0.93
10. Next year	5.3	0.62	0.66	6.1	0.78	1.06
GNP Implicit Price Deflator (N2; 1958 = 100)						
11. One	0.7	1.14	1.07	0.3	1.65	1.22
12. Two	1.0	1.17	1.27	0.6	1.78	1.33
13. Three	1.3	1.21	1.49	1.1	1.68	1.36
14. Four	1.8	1.40	1.62	1.5	1.89	1.30
15. Next year	1.1	1.22	1.38	0.9	1.91	1.41
Consumption Expenditures–Automobiles (N1; billions of current dollars)						
16. One	1.5	1.13	0.89	1.6	1.23	0.91
17. Two	2.0	0.94	1.00	2.3	0.96	0.87
18. Three	2.8	0.96	1.00	3.2	0.88	0.84
19. Four	2.9	0.71	0.86	4.5	0.88	0.86
20. Next year	2.0	0.82	0.98	3.0	0.89	0.85

(continued)

Table 6 (concluded)

Span of Forecast (no. of quarters)	Wharton EFU Model[a]			OBE Model[b]		
	$MAE\text{-}XA^c$ (1)	$\dfrac{MAE\text{-}XA^d}{MAE\text{-}N}$ (2)	$\dfrac{MAE\text{-}XA^e}{MAE\text{-}XP}$ (3)	$MAE\text{-}XA^c$ (4)	$\dfrac{MAE\text{-}XA^d}{MAE\text{-}N}$ (5)	$\dfrac{MAE\text{-}XA^e}{MAE\text{-}XP}$ (6)
Consumption Expenditures–Durables, Nonautomotive (N2; billions of current dollars)						
21. One	1.4	1.36	1.07	0.7	0.83	1.00
22. Two	1.6	1.07	1.10	0.7	0.53	0.99
23. Three	2.2	1.47	1.15	1.1	0.86	1.09
24. Four	2.6	1.04	1.03	1.7	0.84	1.15
25. Next year	1.9	1.30	1.21	0.8	0.72	1.19
Investment in Plant and Equipment (N1; billions of current dollars)						
26. One	1.9	0.87	0.91	1.6	0.66	0.93
27. Two	3.8	1.13	0.84	2.6	0.68	0.87
28. Three	4.2	0.97	0.84	2.9	0.52	0.80
29. Four	3.8	0.70	0.91	4.2	0.56	0.82
30. Next year	2.8	0.87	0.89	2.1	0.47	0.84
Net Change in Inventories (N1; billions of current dollars)						
31. One	3.7	0.74	0.93	2.7	0.65	0.98
32. Two	4.8	1.13	0.92	3.2	1.02	1.05
33. Three	4.1	0.94	0.78	3.6	1.47	0.92
34. Four	3.8	0.70	0.71	4.3	1.31	0.85
35. Next year	3.5	0.87	0.88	2.3	0.80	1.02
Unemployment Rate (N1; per cent of labor force)						
36. One	0.2	2.09	0.68	0.1	0.92	0.92
37. Two	0.4	2.05	0.69	0.2	1.15	0.80
38. Three	0.5	2.00	0.52	0.3	1.16	0.64
39. Four	0.5	2.38	0.52	0.5	1.71	0.73
40. Next year	0.4	2.47	0.60	0.3	1.58	0.77

[a]For III-1966–III-1969. The number of forecasts included in the averages for this model, for all the variables covered and all three forecasts (*ex ante, XA; ex post, XP,* and naive, *N*) varies with the predictive span as follows: one quarter, 13; two quarters, 12; three quarters, 11; four quarters, 10; next year, 10.

[b]For II-1967–III-1969. The numbers of *XA* and *N* forecasts included in the averages for this model vary with the predictive span as follows: one quarter, 10; two quarters, 9; three quarters, 8; four quarters, 7; next year, 7. These samples of observations are used for the

Notes to Table 6 (concluded)

entries in columns 4 and 5. The number of *XP* forecasts are the same, with these exceptions: four quarters, 6; next year, 6. These somewhat smaller samples are used for the entries in column 6.

[c]*MAE-XA* denotes the mean absolute error of the *ex ante* forecasts.

[d]Ratio of *MAE-XA* to the mean absolute error of a naive model (*MAE-N*). *N*1 projections are used in the ratios for some variables and *N*2 projections for others, depending on which of the two naive models worked better in the given case. The selected model is identified in parentheses after the subtitle for each variable.

[e]Ratio of *MAE-XA* to the mean absolute error of the *ex post* forecasts (*MAE-XP*). The *ex post* forecasts use the same adjustments of constant terms that were made by the model builders in the corresponding *ex ante* forecasts. See text.

and two are larger (the poor results include the two shortest Wharton forecasts and the OBE forecasts beyond one quarter). The ratios for the predictions of the price deflator all exceed unity and are particularly large for the OBE model (lines 11−15).

The results are also poor (in the sense of "less accurate than the better of the naive models") for the shortest forecasts of spending on automobiles and for the Wharton forecasts of spending on other durables, while the other predictions for these two variables pass these tests with more success (lines 16−25). The comparisons for the two investment variables (lines 26−35) are on the whole more favorable to the forecasts, although some of the ratios, here too, are high, as, for example, the OBE predictions of the inventory change over longer spans. The worst results (highest ratios) are for the unemployment forecasts, especially in the Wharton model (lines 36−40).

It is disappointing that these forecasts, based as they are on well-known and rather elaborate econometric models, do not score better in comparison with simple naive-model projections; but this outcome must be seen in its proper historical context, and its importance must not be exaggerated. The forecast periods are short (III-1966−III-1969 for Wharton, I-1967−III-1969 for OBE) and they cover no declines in such variables as GNP in current and constant dollars and the price deflator but only strong and fairly steady upward trends. The growth trend was not much less dominant even in the expenditures for consumer durables excluding automobiles. It is not surprising that the *N*2 model gave relatively good results for these series in this particular period, and it is clear that at some other times this model would not perform nearly as well. Probably more significant is the failure of these econometric forecasts to achieve better scores relative to the *N*1 benchmark for the more volatile series: the expenditures on automobiles, investment in plant and equipment, net change in inventories, and the unemployment rate.

Table 6 also includes comparisons of *ex ante* with *ex post* forecasts in the form of ratios of the corresponding mean absolute errors, *MAE-XA/MAE-XP* (columns 3 and 6). The *ex post* forecasts incorporate the same original constant-term adjustment as the *ex ante* ones. This makes the comparisons more meaningful; moreover, the *ex post* forecasts are, on the whole, more accurate with these adjustments than with the mechanical adjustments or, a fortiori, without any adjustments at all.

Most of the ratios *MAE-XA/MAE-XP* in Table 6 are smaller than 1, particularly for the Wharton model, indicating that the *ex ante* forecasts tend to be more accurate than the *ex post* ones with the same original adjustments. However, the ratios exceed unity for the Wharton and the OBE predictions of the price deflator and of expenditures on consumer durables other than automobiles (lines 11−15 and 21−25).

The Wharton *ex post* forecasts are less accurate than the selected naive models in half of the cases examined, including most of those relating to GNP in 1958 dollars, expenditures on durables excluding automobiles, and the unemployment rate.[40] The OBE *ex post* forecasts also have larger *MAE*'s than the naive models in about half of the forty cases covered in Table 6. It is interesting to note that among the OBE predictions those of nominal GNP, expenditures on automobiles, and unemployment compare unfavorably, while virtually all others compare favorably, with the benchmark extrapolations.

3.6 The Relative Accuracy of Econometric Model Forecasts and Judgmental Forecasts

It is difficult to get meaningful comparisons of errors for these two classes of predictions. On the one hand, forecasts made without an explicitly formulated econometric model are much more numerous than forecasts made with such a model, and they also cover longer periods of time than the *ex ante* model predictions (this applies particularly to quarterly forecasts). On the other hand, for the short periods they do cover, the econometric model forecasts are generally much more regular and complete than the others. All in all, there are not very many forecasts in the two categories that are "strictly" comparable in the sense of having been made at about the same time for the same target period.

[40]Ratios of *MAE-XP* to *MAE-N* for the Wharton model can be obtained by dividing the entries in column 2 by the corresponding entries in column 3 of Table 6. "Less accurate" forecasts are those for which the ratio is greater than 1 (column 2 greater than column 3). Similarly, by taking the ratios of the corresponding entries in columns 5 and 6 of the table, *MAE-XP* can be compared with *MAE-N* for the OBE model.

Table 7 collects such forecasts for the Wharton model and four sets of business economists' forecasts and compares their mean absolute errors over spans of from one to four quarters. The forecasts refer to GNP in current and constant dollars and include both *ex ante* and *ex post* model forecasts (with the original judgmental adjustments).

The errors of the Wharton *ex ante* forecasts of GNP are on the average smaller than those of the judgmental forecasts in sets A, G, and S; in only two of these comparisons are the ratios *MAE-XA/MAE-P* larger than 1, though the ratios for set S are all high, exceeding 0.8 (Table 7, lines 1–4, 9–16). The forecasts of set C, however, tend to produce somewhat smaller errors than the Wharton model (as shown by the ratios in lines 5–8, column 5, only one of which falls below unity). But the set C forecasts themselves are in the recent years based largely on an econometric model used flexibly by the economic staff of the company that formulated it; hence these comparisons are not so much between forecasts with econometric models and judgmental forecasts as between academic and private business forecasts both of which exemplify the model-cum-judgment approach.

The Wharton *ex post* forecasts of GNP score on the whole less well relative to the judgmental forecasts. They appear to be in most cases less accurate than forecasts C and not much more accurate than forecasts G and S, while the comparisons with set A produce a very mixed picture (columns 3, 4, and 6).

For GNP in constant dollars, both the *ex ante* and the *ex post* forecasts with the Wharton model tend to have larger mean absolute errors than the predictions from sets C and S and smaller *MAE*'s than the predictions from set G (Table 7, lines 17–27).

In Table 8, which has exactly the same format as Table 7, the relative accuracy of the OBE model and the judgmental forecasts is analyzed. The *ex ante* predictions of GNP with the OBE model are better than the corresponding predictions of sets A and G (lines 1–3, 8–11, columns 2, 4, and 5). In comparisons with sets C and S, however, only the shortest OBE forecasts come out ahead (lines 4–7, 12–15).

The OBE *ex post* forecasts of GNP likewise present a mixed picture. The *MAE* ratios are here larger than 1 in most comparisons with forecasts C and S, but smaller than 1 in virtually all comparisons with sets A and G (Table 8, columns 3, 4, and 6).

Similarly to the Wharton forecasts, the OBE forecasts of real GNP, both *ex ante* and *ex post,* have for the most part larger average errors than sets C and S (but the opposite applies to some of the shortest forecasts), while set G is here definitely inferior (Table 8, lines 16–26).

TABLE 7

Comparisons of Average Errors of Wharton Model and Judgmental
Forecasts over Span of from One to Four Quarters, 1966–69
*(GNP is in current dollars in lines 1–16; in constant dollars
in lines 17–27)*

Span of Forecast (no. of quarters)	No. of Forecasts in Each Average[a] (1)	Mean Absolute Errors (*MAE*) for the				
		Ex Ante Model Forecasts (*MAE-XA*) (2)	*Ex Post* Model Forecasts (*MAE-XP*) (3)	Forecasts in Sets A. . .S (*MAE-P*)[b] (4)	*MAE* Ratios	
					$\frac{MAE\text{-}XA}{MAE\text{-}P}$[c] (5)	$\frac{MAE\text{-}XP}{MAE\text{-}P}$[d] (6)
Set A (I-1967–III-1969)						
1. One	3	5.1	12.5	6.6	0.77	1.90
2. Two	3	6.9	10.0	11.9	0.58	0.84
3. Three	3	8.8	5.3	13.5	0.65	0.39
4. Four	2	14.8	14.4	14.0	1.06	1.03
Set C (III-1966–III-1969)						
5. One	6	4.8	8.1	3.4	1.41	2.38
6. Two	6	7.1	8.4	7.0	1.01	1.20
7. Three	6	9.8	9.5	10.9	0.90	0.87
8. Four	5	15.2	15.8	11.8	1.29	1.34
Set G (I-1967–III-1969)						
9. One	6	5.2	8.4	7.5	0.69	1.12
10. Two	5	8.0	8.3	15.2	0.53	0.84
11. Three	5	10.3	7.1	21.2	0.49	0.87
12. Four	4	17.1	12.6	29.8	0.57	0.94
Set S (III-1968–III-1969)						
13. One	5	4.9	5.6	5.7	0.86	0.98
14. Two	4	10.5	8.9	10.6	0.99	0.84
15. Three	3	18.2	15.0	17.2	1.06	0.87
16. Four	2	19.1	22.6	24.0	0.80	0.94
Set C (III-1966–III-1969)						
17. One	6	4.2	6.8	2.8	1.50	2.43
18. Two	6	5.6	6.9	4.9	1.14	1.41
19. Three	6	6.3	9.2	6.0	1.05	1.53
20. Four	5	7.4	14.2	4.8	1.54	2.96

Table 7 (concluded)

		Set G (I-1967–III-1969)				
21. One	6	4.1	7.1	5.6	0.73	1.27
22. Two	5	5.9	6.2	11.2	0.53	0.55
23. Three	5	5.6	6.2	16.0	0.35	0.49
24. Four	4	6.6	10.0	22.5	0.29	0.44
		Set S (III-1968–III-1969)[e]				
25. One	4	1.9	4.7	1.9	1.00	2.47
26. Two	3	3.8	6.3	1.1	3.45	5.73
27. Three	2	4.9	7.6	0.8	6.12	9.50

[a]Refers to the corresponding entries in each of columns 2, 3, and 4.

[b]P denotes predictions in one of the sets identified in the subtitles below (set A, C, G, or S). Set S represents the American Statistical Association–NBER quarterly Business Outlook Survey (group median forecasts). For a brief description of the other forecast sets, see text.

[c]Ratio of column 2 to column 4.

[d]Ratio of column 3 to column 4.

[e]The four-quarter forecasts could be compared for a single period only and are therefore omitted.

The *MAE* ratios for either model show no general and systematic tendency either to increase or decrease with the span of the forecast. However, the ratios do increase markedly with the span in some cases, notably for the OBE *ex ante* forecasts in comparisons with set C and all the model forecasts in comparisons with set S (Table 7, lines 25–27, and Table 8, lines 16–19 and 24–26). Thus, possibly with the above exceptions, these groups of forecasts apparently do not possess any strong differential advantages or disadvantages that would depend specifically on the span of forecast.

To sum up these findings, the *ex ante* forecasts with Wharton and OBE models hold a slight edge over the judgmental forecasts, their average errors being the smaller ones in 58.5 per cent of the cases.[41] The *ex post* forecasts with these models are on balance only about as accurate as the forecasts in the other four sets (the two models show smaller errors in 50.9 per cent of the cases).[42]

These results should not be used for any extensive generalizations and must indeed be interpreted very cautiously because they are based on small samples limited (as already noted) by the scarcity of data for different

[41]For the Wharton model alone, the percentage is 55.6; for the OBE model, 61.5.

[42]Again, to quote the corresponding percentages separately for the two models: Wharton, 48.1 per cent; OBE, 53.8 per cent.

TABLE 8

Comparisons of Average Errors of OBE Model and
Judgmental Forecasts over Spans of from One to Four Quarters, 1967–69
*(GNP is in current dollars in lines 1–15; in constant dollars
in lines 16–26)*

		Mean Absolute Errors *(MAE)* for the			*MAE* Ratios	
		Ex Ante Model	*Ex Post* Model			
Span of Forecast (no. of quarters)	No. of Forecasts in Each Average[a]	Forecasts *(MAE-XA)*	Forecasts *(MAE-XP)*	Forecasts in Sets A. . .S *(MAE-P)*[b]	$\frac{MAE\text{-}XA^c}{MAE\text{-}P}$	$\frac{MAE\text{-}XP^d}{MAE\text{-}P}$
	(1)	(2)	(3)	(4)	(5)	(6)
		Set A (I-1968–III-1969)[e]				
1. One	2	1.8	6.9	6.8	0.26	1.01
2. Two	2	11.0	2.7	13.4	0.82	0.20
3. Three	2	14.8	4.9	17.8	0.83	0.28
		Set C (III-1967–III-1969)				
4. One	4	2.9	7.1	3.9	0.75	1.82
5. Two	4	10.6	9.4	7.1	1.49	1.32
6. Three	4	15.5	13.7	14.6	1.06	0.94
7. Four	3	21.3	19.9	18.4	1.18	1.08
		Set G (III-1967–III-1969)				
8. One	5	2.4	5.8	8.7	0.28	0.67
9. Two	4	10.6	9.4	17.0	0.62	0.55
10. Three	4	15.5	13.7	21.8	0.71	0.63
11. Four	3	21.3	19.9	31.7	0.67	0.63
		Set S (III-1968–III-1969)				
12. One	5	2.9	4.8	5.6	0.52	0.86
13. Two	4	9.7	12.7	10.6	0.92	1.20
14. Three	3	17.3	21.2	17.1	1.01	1.24
15. Four	2	24.2	30.6	23.7	1.02	1.29
		Set C (III-1967–III-1969)				
16. One	4	2.3	4.2	3.4	0.68	1.24
17. Two	4	6.5	4.3	5.5	1.18	0.78
18. Three	4	9.8	7.5	7.4	1.32	1.01
19. Four	3	12.8	11.6	5.7	2.25	2.04

Table 8 (concluded)

		Set G (III-1967–III-1969)				
20. One	5	2.0	3.7	6.5	0.31	0.57
21. Two	4	6.5	4.3	13.3	0.49	0.32
22. Three	4	9.8	7.5	17.4	0.56	0.43
23. Four	3	12.8	11.6	25.5	0.50	0.45
		Set S (III-1968–III-1969)[e]				
24. One	4	1.3	1.5	1.9	0.68	0.79
25. Two	3	2.0	3.0	1.2	1.67	2.50
26. Three	2.	2.5	3.0	1.2	2.08	2.50

[a]Refers to the corresponding entries in each of the columns 2, 3, and 4.

[b]P denotes predictions in one of the sets identified in the subtitles below (set A, C, G, or S). Set S represents the American Statistical Association–NBER quarterly Business Outlook Survey (group median forecasts). For a brief description of the other forecast sets, see text.

[c]Ratio of column 2 to column 4.

[d]Ratio of column 3 to column 4.

[e]The four-quarter forecasts could be compared for a single period only and are therefore omitted.

forecasts that can be matched by span and target period. Since intertemporal variations in errors of predictions from a given source are often large, it is possible that at least some of the details in the picture presented by these comparisons reflect strongly the particularities of the periods covered and would not be upheld by the evidence from larger samples.[43]

4. Suggested Agenda for Future Research

4.1 Focus and Feasibility of the New Studies

The results of past and current studies summarized in the two preceding sections of this report, and the experience and materials accumulated in the

[43]Comparisons of the *MAE-XA* figures in Table 6, columns 1 and 4, with those in Tables 7 and 8, columns 2, show that the average errors in GNP forecasts with both the Wharton and the OBE model have been for the most part larger in the selected periods than in the total forecast periods. Of the other GNP forecasts, set C appears to be favored by the selection, in the sense of having a smaller *MAE* in the periods covered in Tables 7 and 8 than at other times, whereas the opposite applies to set G. If average errors of all GNP predictions available from each of these sources were used, that is, if all differences in the periods covered were disregarded, the comparisons with some of the other forecasts, notably those of set C, would be definitely more favorable to the *ex ante* forecasts with the two econometric models. For the *ex post* forecasts and the real GNP predictions, the results of a similar analysis are mixed.

process of this research, indicate both the need for and the promise of further work on short-term economic forecasts and forecasting models. They also provide a good basis for planning and executing such work.

The planned research consists of several related projects that share a focus on the problem of how predictive accuracy is related to the method and structure of the forecasts. This presupposes (a) that the accuracy of predictions of different types and from different sources can be measured and compared, and (b) that the methods used by forecasters and the ingredients of forecasts can be ascertained and analyzed. No doubt, neither of these conditions is fully met, but, here as elsewhere, it is necessary to do the best one can with unavoidably incomplete information and imperfect knowledge. I am prepared to argue that, as a consequence of previous and current work, it is now possible to undertake studies so oriented with a fair chance of making a significant contribution.

Thus, regarding (a), recent studies (including those reviewed in section 2) have achieved considerable progress in developing criteria of forecasting accuracy and applying them to diverse forecasting data. There is much less success to report on matters relating to (b), but it has been shown that useful information about "judgmental" forecasts (defined as those that are not based on an explicit forecasting "model") can be gained from comparisons of such forecasts with predictions derived by a known, replicable method.[44] Moreover, direct information is now being systematically collected about the forecasting methods used by the participants in the new ASA-NBER Quarterly Survey of the Economic Outlook.[45] These data, then, permit a cross-classification by both accuracy and method of a sample of business forecasts for any particular period surveyed and over time. When sufficient material from the successive surveys becomes available, it should be possible to learn from it whether the quality of forecasts varies systematically with the method used, and if so how. In seeking an answer to this question, one will be able to control for several factors: the date of issue of the forecasts (the survey questionnaires are collected at certain fixed times), the recent and base-period estimates (they are given or reported), and the key assumptions about tax and monetary policy, defense posture, government spending, and so on (the forecasters are asked to specify them and most do).

The econometric forecasts, of course, do rely on explicitly formulated models and certain more or less standardized methods of statistical estimation. However, the *ex ante* forecasts with econometric models must use judgmental predictions or estimates of the exogenous inputs, and they

[44] See [16], [17], and [29], *passim*.

[45] See [32] and [33].

typically use various adjustments of the constant terms, which likewise involve judgment and cannot as a rule be reproduced by extrapolative or other mechanical procedures.[46] In the past, such operations were frequently not well recorded, and experience shows that it is difficult and sometimes impossible to reconstruct econometricians' forecasts without this vital documentation. It is therefore indispensable for the studies here contemplated that a systematic collection of forecasts from several selected econometric models be carried out in such a way as to include not only the predictions that were made but also the judgmental inputs and adjustments which, along with the known structure of the model, produced these predictions. Full information of this type is necessary for independent replication of the forecasts, to ensure that the appropriate models and data (inputs and outputs) are being recorded. Steps have already been taken at the National Bureau to initiate such a collection of quarterly econometric forecasts and related statistics. The Wharton-EFU and the Commerce-OBE models are being processed, as is the new quarterly Michigan model, and it is hoped that other models will be added. Of course, the cooperation of the model builders is essential for this effort and its success.[47]

4.2 Comparisons of Types and Methods of Forecasting

Economic forecasts can be classified by several different criteria such as (a) the degree to which they use formalized methods vis-à-vis informal judgment; (b) the degree to which they rely on relationships among different variables vis-à-vis projections of past behavior of the variable to be predicted; and (c) the degree to which they are based on averages of macropredictions or aggregations of micropredictions from different sources vis-à-vis global forecasts from a single source. According to (a), a whole gradation could be established, from forecasts that are "purely judgmental" to those produced by fully specified and strictly implemented econometric models. According to (b), similarly, there is, at least in principle, an ordering of forecasts from pure extrapolations of past values of the given variable (inferring X_{t+i} from X_{t-j}, where i and j denote the various discrete or distributed lags that may be involved) to outputs of equations in which X_{t+i} is related to other variables only, say Y_{t-j}. According to (c), finally, forecasts would be divided into predictions by individuals and small teams, weighted or unweighted averages

---

[46]For a description and evaluation of such adjustments, see [9, section III and IV] and [12, section 3.1].

[47]This may involve some restrictions on the scope or timing of the release of the resulting information, but arrangements of this sort have already been made in some cases and they should not pose any critical problems.

of such predictions (including small group forecasts and large opinion polls), aggregates based on surveys of businessmen's or consumers' anticipations, and so on.

These various classes of forecasts overlap and can be combined in diverse ways; the pure or extreme forms are generally used only as benchmarks of predictive preformance, not as forecasts proper. For example, a forecast of GNP and its major components may combine extrapolation, relationship of the target series to known or estimated values of some other variables, external information such as a survey of investment intentions and government budget estimates, and the judgment of the forecaster. This can be and often is true of a "judgmental" forecast by a business economist as well as of a "model" forecast by an econometrician. The main difference between the two would be that the econometrician's model is explicitly formulated in quantitative terms, whereas the business economist's is not. Mechanical methods of extrapolating the series to be predicted and of relating it to other series would then serve to provide standards against which to measure the performance of the bona fide forecasts made by identifiable sources prior to the event. Where such forecasts relate to variables covered by the surveys of anticipations or intentions, the aggregated results of these surveys furnish another important yardstick of predictive accuracy.

The currently relevant forecasting procedures can be broadly classified as (a) extrapolative techniques; (b) surveys of intentions or anticipations by economic decision-making units; (c) business cycle indicators; and (d) econometric models. Each of the four methods furnishes data that constitute ingredients of actual forecasts of the course of the economy; and each of these four classes of data, too, can be used to construct mechanically reproducible predictions that represent appropriate benchmarks for forecast evaluation. In large part, the proposed research strategy consists in confronting forecasts of different types with an array of these benchmark predictions in such a way as to extract from the comparisons as much information as possible about both the accuracy and structure of the forecasts.

To use for illustration a case particularly rich in opportunities for such comparisons, consider an econometric model's equation for business expenditures on plant and equipment. Forecasts of this variable produced by the econometrician armed with this model can be confronted by: (a) corresponding extrapolations from different "naive models," including some relatively sophisticated and effective types of autoregression; (b) aggregated business anticipations of plant and equipment outlays (based, say, on the OBE-SEC surveys); (c) forecasts from regressions including some appropriate "leading indicators" such as new orders and contracts for plant and equipment or new capital appropriations; and (d) *ex post* forecasts based on the model as a whole, or alternatively, on the single equation concerned, with actual values used for the exogenous inputs and no judgmental adjustments of the constant terms.[48] The model may, of course, incorporate one or more of these elements in some form and may also have other ingredients of net predictive value, in which case it should prove superior to the benchmark(s) in question; e.g., if the investment equation includes a lagged value of the dependent variable along with other significant explanatory factors, then the forecasts based on it will be better than the standard offered by predictions from the corresponding autoregressive model. But such an outcome is by no means always to be expected, for the model may not use fully or optimally the information embodied in the extrapolative, anticipatory, or indicator benchmark models, and it may contain other misspecifications. Where the comparisons indicate such weaknesses, it is a logical next step to try to improve the model by adding to it the elements that seem promising and removing those that seem disturbing in the light of these tests.

Such studies, then, should not only contribute to our knowledge of the relative accuracy of different forecasts and forecasting models (including the benchmark models), but they should also help locate some of the areas of strength and weakness in the underlying methods and specifications. An analysis of this kind is likely to yield the highest returns for the forecasts based on explicit models, but even where such models are lacking the payoff may be considerable. For example, suppose one can demonstrate that business forecasts from a particular source would have gained in the past by being combined with extrapolations of some specific type (say, by means of weights derived from a regression of the actual values on both the forecasts and the extrapolations). If this is a sufficiently stable relationship, it may be indicative of a systematic and correctable deficiency of the forecast.

Clearly, there are many examples in the literature of such comparisons as are here proposed, and some useful lessons can be drawn from them. The advantage of the suggested approach is that it combines these familiar elements into a framework for a more comprehensive and systematic analysis of economic forecasting than has been hitherto attempted.

[48] Alternatively, certain mechanical adjustments could also be employed. In systems with lagged terms of the endogenous variables, model-generated values for these factors must be used to generate multiperiod forecasts (in single-equation models, such inputs are of course limited to the values of one dependent variable). The use of anticipatory data tends to limit the time span over which a model can be successfully extrapolated into the future because such data are themselves difficult to predict well, as noted at the end of section 2.8.

4.3 The Qualities of Short-Term Econometric Model Forecasts

In continuation of new and significant research undertakings in this area,[49] *ex ante* and *ex post* forecasts of the principal endogenous variables need to be compared for each of the major quarterly models of the U.S. economy listed at the end of section 4.1. It is necessary to have several different variants of this analysis: with and without such judgmental adjustments as were made by the model builders for their forecasts, and also with the most promising of the mechanical adjustments of the constant terms. The results will permit assessments of (a) the magnitude and effects of errors in the projections of the exogenous variables; (b) the quantitative impact and relative efficiency of the different types of adjustments; and (c) the magnitude of forecast inaccuracies that are attributable to errors in construction and solution of the given model. It will then also be possible to make certain inferences about the interaction of errors from these different sources.

Both *ex ante* and *ex post* model forecasts should then be confronted by various "naive" and autoregressive extrapolations, a sample of judgmental forecasts, single-equation predictions, and (if appropriate) aggregated micro-anticipations data from surveys. Efforts should be made to standardize at least the sample period used, so that meaningful intermodel comparisons can be made of the accuracy and other properties of the forecasts.

This analysis is expected to help provide answers to several interesting questions about the relative merits and demerits of different models and forecasts. To list some that seem particularly important: (a) What are the desirable properties of measures of goodness of predictions? (b) Are predictions from econometric systems superior to noneconometric predictions? (c) Do large-scale models perform better than small-scale models in forecasting GNP and its major components? (d) Insofar as they yield to our measurement efforts, how do the benefits and costs of econometric-system forecasts compare with those of single-equation predictions? (e) With what success for future prediction can technical adjustments be made on the basis of the prediction record?

Some of these questions, such as (b) and (e), have already received partial and tentative answers in [9] and in section 3 of this report, but the analysis needs to be extended to materials for other model and nonmodel forecasts and to the remaining and related questions. The most basic and penetrating ones among the latter deal with misspecification errors in the models covered: (f) Where do the most serious errors of this kind originate in each of the

---

[49]See references to [9] and to related ongoing research mentioned in earlier parts of this report.

models? (g) How do they affect the forecasting qualities of the models? (h) What changes in the models would be likely to reduce such errors and improve the forecasts? (i) What are the properties of a sound short-term predictive model—do they differ from those of a good structural model and, if so, how?

Even a very comprehensive evaluation of the forecasting aspects of the models will not be sufficient to settle questions of this type, but some contributions to the answers should be forthcoming from this work when combined with the simulation analyses that are discussed below. However, a more effective treatment of misspecification problems presumably requires a thorough review of a model, by individual structural equations and by blocks of closely related equations for a given economic sector or process. Re-estimation of a given block, with the variables in other blocks being taken as exogenous, would be desirable, so as to detect those results that are in conflict with theoretical expectations (the latter refer generally to such conditional predictions). This examination of block simulations and predictions could at least help isolate those instances in which the signs of the model-generated statistics appear objectionable; the theory has less to say about the magnitudes of the various coefficients, multipliers, and elasticities involved, but the procedure should be able to spotlight any estimates that are grossly out of line. In this way, one might hope to trace the misspecifications to the individual equations, which should then be revised; after which the "corrected" model should be subjected to new exercises in simulation and prediction designed to test its performance. There is a very wide range of variation on this general theme, and a number of approaches appear promising; e.g., separate estimates for periods of cyclical expansions and contractions could be computed and examined in an effort to test the effects of nonlinearities in the models. The need for all such tests has been emphasized, and there are some notable initiatives in this direction in recent literature.[50] However, these are limited critical articles by individuals, and what is required here is clearly a comprehensive and systematic study by a group of researchers.[51]

[50]Two papers on the Brookings model should be noted in this context: Zvi Griliches, "The Brookings Model Volume: A Review Article," *Review of Economics and Statistics,* May 1968, pp. 215–234 (see also "Comment" on this article by Gary Fromm and Lawrence R. Klein, *ibid.*, pp. 235–240); and Robert J. Gordon, "The Brookings Model in Action: A Review Article," *Journal of Political Economy,* May–June 1970, pp. 489–525.

[51]It would of course be highly desirable for such a project to secure the cooperation of the model builders, but the latter should preferably not be included in the research group itself.

4.4 Business Cycle Analysis of Econometric Model Simulations

Simulation studies of the quarterly U.S. models can help answer some of the questions formulated above (a, c, e, f, g, h, and i) and others such as these: (j) Do the models under review generate cyclical behavior as defined and observed in the empirical business cycle studies, notably those of the NBER? (k) If so, to what extent are such fluctuations in the estimated series produced endogenously by the models, and to what extent are they attributable to external impulses? In the process, much can be learned from the models about the qualities of the *ex post* or conditional predictions, e.g., about the sensitivity of the simulations to the initial conditions and the length of the predictive span. Such findings are likely to lead to inferences about the structural properties of the models; thus, a tendency for nonstochastic simulations to produce strongly *damped* fluctuations in projected GNP would suggest that the model in question is dynamically stable. Last but not least, insofar as the models provide valid representations of the economy, simulation studies hold out a promise of contributing to the knowledge of business cycles "in the real world," the question here being, Do the cycles consist mainly of endogenous or exogenous movements?

As an outgrowth of the 1969 Harvard conference and owing to the cooperation of the builders of several models, there now exists a very large volume of rich statistical materials bearing on these problems. A cyclical analysis of some of these data was undertaken in [34]. This study was seriously limited by the resources available, including time, but its results met with considerable interest and a consensus that further work in this area was definitely desirable.[52]

To produce any cyclical movements, the models examined so far apparently require perturbations in either the exogenous variables or the relationships with endogenous variables or both. In experimenting with 100-quarter stochastic simulations that start at very recent dates and extend into the future, smooth trend projections for the exogenous variables were used in [34], but the absence of shocks or fluctuations in these projections is an unrealistic feature which could be at least partly responsible for the weakness of the cyclical elements in the simulations analyzed. Further tests are needed to determine whether this weakness can be remedied or reduced by imposing more or less sporadic disturbances on the exogenous factors.

Only small samples of the stochastic simulations have as yet been studied for most of the endogenous variables selected for this investigation. The

[52]This conclusion is based on the discussions at the Conference on Econometric Models of Cyclical Behavior cosponsored by the Social Science Research Council and the National Bureau of Economic Research, Cambridge, Mass., November 14, 1969, and at the follow-up meeting to that conference at the NBER, New York, February 27, 1970.

analysis needs to be extended to larger samples and to models other than those included in [34].

4.5 Interaction of Economic Developments and Policy Changes

Another important use of simulation techniques is for the study of the effects upon the economy of alternative changes in the exogenous policy variables. All full-scale models have variables of this kind, which are specified as being determined by the actions of fiscal or monetary authorities. However, the choice of these policy factors varies between the different models, and some factors, particularly in the monetary area, have only recently begun to receive explicit attention; the resulting discrepancies impair intermodel comparisons of policy sensitivity.

Moreover, there are feedback effects of developments in the economy upon the policy variables, which are very much in need of being explored. For example, Federal Reserve policy is not necessarily exogenous in the sense that it cannot be explained by other parts of the system; that policy might be assumed to respond to the behavior of prices or unemployment or the balance of payments (or to all of these and to still other factors), and is exogenous only in the sense that the monetary authorities are not constrained to take specified actions because of competitive or other kinds of market forces. A systematic relation capable of being described in the model could exist between, say, the changes in national output and the price level and the reaction of the monetary and fiscal authorities as reflected by movements in the so-called exogenous policy variables.

In a paper prepared for this colloquium, Yoel Haitovsky and Neil Wallace discuss the results of experimental work with stochastic simulations designed to reveal the effects of such interactions. They impose upon a model some alternative fixed "policy rules," which involve certain quantified monetary and fiscal responses to changes in the unemployment rate and the implicit price deflator for GNP. The model includes autoregressive equations for the noninstrumental exogenous variables, and the parameters and additive disturbances are chosen randomly for each run or from quarter to quarter. The experience gained in this pilot study should prove highly valuable for future research in this area, which would probably involve extensions of the analysis to a variety of models, policy rules, and instruments.

4.6 Feedback Effects of Major Macroeconomic Forecasts

A closely related problem concerns the feedback effect attributable to publication of the forecast. Certain influential forecasts may significantly affect the behavior of economic agents; the resulting changes in the economy might in turn lead to revisions of the policies, which would alter the general economic development, and so on.

Published official forecasts (such as those of the Council of Economic Advisers in the *Economic Report of the President*) are of particular interest here, since they may well carry special weight as expressions or instruments of the government's economic policies. The accuracy of such forecasts should be compared not only with the accuracy of reputable private forecasts but also with that of government agency forecasts that are made ahead of the event but are not published or released until some later time. Both the relative accuracy of the official forecasts and their influence on private forecasts and expectations are matters of very considerable interest. There is also need to study government forecasts in the context of concurrent and subsequent economic policies, so as to learn more about how these factors interact.

In some countries (Holland, Sweden, France), highly authoritative and influential forecasts, based to a substantial extent on econometric models, are prepared by agencies of governments that assume very active roles in macroeconomic planning and policies. (In the United States, there is much less centralization in these affairs.) In such situations, publication of the government forecast may be interpreted to mean that steps will be taken to change policy variables in the event that private actions are inconsistent with the forecast results. In effect, under some circumstances the forecast might be more accurately described as a plan to be implemented. Private reactions are likely to be different if the forecast is viewed as a plan that can influence policies rather than if no such connection between prediction and the policy-making power is perceived. For these reasons, the feedback effects of forecasts would probably lend themselves best to study by means of selected international comparisons of forecasts and policies.

How effective are forecasts in influencing policies and general expectations, and thereby their own accuracy? Are forecasts frequently and significantly validated when the predicted developments appear desirable to those whose decisions count and are they, analogously, invalidated when they predict changes that are deemed undesirable? Of the interesting but limited theoretical work on such problems, some is highly abstract and speculative, and little is conclusive.[53] Yet, with the presently available models and data,

[53]The main contributions are: Emile Grunberg and Franco Modigliani, "The Predictability of Social Events," *Journal of Political Economy,* December 1954, pp. 465–478; Murray Kemp, "Economic Forecasting When the Subject of the Forecast Is Influenced by the Forecast," *American Economic Review,* June 1962, pp. 492-496; and the Communications on the latter paper by A. C. Chiang, Grunberg and Modigliani, and Kemp, *American Economic Review,* September 1963, pp. 730–740.

better results should be obtainable, and considerable interest apparently exists in international comparisons of economic forecasts generally and in the specific questions raised here.[54]

4.7 Other Proposals and Concluding Remarks

Other related projects in this general area of research are being planned at the National Bureau, and some of them appear to be as important and as promising as those discussed above; but this report is long already and must be kept within reasonable bounds, so only brief references can be made to these proposals. One of the potentially most useful undertakings, as far as improvement of the short-term predictive accuracy of econometric models is concerned, is to revise the models in the direction of making more and better use of survey data on business and consumer anticipations, governmental budget estimates, leading indicators, and other similarly forward-looking information. Besides enhancing the forecasting ability of the models, this work may also yield returns in increased understanding of the economic processes involved and in the feedback on the surveys, which could suggest ways of obtaining more useful expectational data.

Another newly opened field of study that deserves much attention would combine estimation of monthly aggregative series, where only quarterly data now exist, with construction and examination of a monthly econometric forecasting model of the U.S. economy. The feasibility of constructing a monthly recursive macromodel was recently tested by T. C. Liu, with generally positive results.[55] Monthly series for GNP and its major components can be estimated indirectly by the method of interpolation by related series for which monthly observations are available, although much remains to be done to establish how best to implement this approach. Once a monthly model, similar in size, structure, and estimation procedure to an existing quarterly model, is constructed, the relative predictive performance of the two could be compared by means of an analysis of corresponding *ex post* forecasts and simulations. The dynamic properties of the monthly model could be examined by spectral analysis and by business cycle analysis of model simulations. This research, too, could provide some insights into the consequences of aggregating an econometric model over time. It would

[54]This opinion is based on exploratory discussions that the author had with several prospective suppliers of statistical data and other information pertinent to such a study: the directors or officers in charge of forecasting at the leading economic research institutes and planning agencies in London, Stockholm, Paris, and the OECD.

[55]See Ta-Chung Liu, "A Monthly Recursive Econometric Model of United States: A Test of Feasibility," *Review of Economics and Statistics,* February 1969, pp. 1–13.

probably be sufficient to use small-scale models, at least in the pilot studies contemplated here.

In the nature of things, *plans* for future research permit no *conclusions*, so only a few general remarks are offered to conclude this report. The investment in research resources embodied in the past and current National Bureau studies on economic forecasting is believed to have paid off well in the results which are partly and briefly summarized in sections 2 and 3 above; but the verdict on this must be left to the reader and the user of these studies and, ultimately, to those who will judge their influence on and usefulness for future scientific inquiry. The last part of my paper will have accomplished much of its purpose if it showed how much remains still to be done, while also conveying the sense that ambitious efforts in this field are now both needed and promising.

REFERENCES

1. Christ, Carl F. "A Test of an Econometric Model of the United States, 1921–1947." In [26, pp. 35 – 107].
2. ––– . "Aggregative Econometric Models: A Review Article," *American Economic Review,* June 1956, pp. 385–408.
3. Cole, Rosanne. "Data Errors and Forecasting Accuracy." In [15, pp. 47–82].
4. ––– . *Errors in Provisional Estimates of Gross National Product.* New York, National Bureau of Economic Research, 1969.
5. Conference on Research in Income and Wealth. *Short-term Economic Forecasting.* Studies in Income and Wealth, Vol. 17. Princeton University Press for NBER, 1955.
6. Cox, Garfield V. *An Appraisal of American Business Forecasts.* Rev. ed. Chicago, University of Chicago Press, 1930.
7. Cunnyngham, Jon. "Econometric Model Forecasts." *Forty-fifth Annual Report of the National Bureau of Economic Research.* New York, June 1965, pp. 60–64.
8. Diller, Stanley. "Expectations in the Term Structure of Interest Rates." In [15, pp. 112–116].
9. Evans, Michael K.; Haitovsky, Yoel; and Treyz, George I.; assisted by Vincent Su. "An Analysis of the Forecasting Properties of U.S. Econometric Models," In *Econometric Models of Cyclical Behavior.* Studies in Income and Wealth, Vol. 36, New York, NBER, 1972.
10. Evans, Michael K., and Klein, Lawrence R. *The Wharton Econometric Model.* Studies in Quantitative Economics No. 2. Philadelphia, Economics Research Unit, University of Pennsylvania, 1967.
11. Fels, Rendigs, and Hinshaw, C. Elton. *Forecasting and Recognizing Business Cycle Turning Points.* New York, NBER, 1968.
12. Green, George R., in association with Maurice Liebenberg, and Albert A. Hirsch. "Short- and Long-Term Simulations with the OBE Econometric Model." In *Econometric Models,* (see [9]).
13. Juster, F. Thomas. "Consumer Anticipations and Models of Durable Goods Demand." In [15, pp. 167–242].

REFERENCES (continued)

14. Liebenberg, Maurice; Hirsch, Albert A.; and Popkin, Joel. "A Quarterly Econometric Model of the United States: A Progress Report." *Survey of Current Business,* May 1966, pp. 13–39.
15. Mincer, Jacob, ed. *Economic Forecasts and Expectations: Analyses of Forecasting Behavior and Performance.* New York, NBER, 1969.
16. Mincer, Jacob, and Zarnowitz, Victor. "The Evaluation of Economic Forecasts." In [15, pp. 3–46].
17. Mincer, Jacob. "Models of Adaptive Forecasting." In [15, pp. 83–111].
18. Moore, Geoffrey H., and Shiskin, Julius. *Indicators of Business Expansions and Contractions.* New York, NBER, 1967.
19. ——— . "Forecasting Short-Term Economic Change," *Journal of the American Statistical Association,* March 1969, pp. 1–22.
20. Okun, Arthur M. "A Review of Some Economic Forecasts for 1955–1957." *Journal of Business,* July 1959, pp. 199–211.
21. ——— . "On the Appraisal of Cyclical Turning-point Predictions." *Journal of Business,* April 1960, pp. 101–120.
22. Rasche, Robert H., and Shapiro, Harold T. "The FRB-MIT Econometric Model: Its Special Features." *American Economic Review,* May 1968, pp. 123–149.
23. Stekler, Herman O. *Economic Forecasting.* New York, Praeger, 1970.
24. Suits, Daniel B. "Forecasting and Analysis with an Econometric Model." *American Economic Review, March 1962,* pp. 104–132.
25. Theil, Henri. *Economic Forecasts and Policy.* 2nd ed. Amsterdam, North-Holland, 1961.
26. ——— . Applied Economic Forecasting. *Chicago, Rand-McNally, 1966.*
27. Universities–National Bureau Committee for Economic Research. *Conference on Business Cycles.* New York, NBER, 1951.
28. ——— . The Quality and Economic Significance of Anticipations Data. *Princeton University Press for NBER, 1960.*
29. Zarnowitz, Victor. *An Appraisal of Short-Term Economic Forecasts.* New York, NBER, 1967.
30. ——— . "Eine Auswertung von Kurzfristigen Wirtschaftsvoraussagen in den USA." *IFO-Studien,* 1966, pp. 1–41.
31. ——— . "An Evaluation of Price-Level Forecasts." *1968 Proceedings of the Business and Economic Statistics Section.* American Statistical Association. Washington, D.C., 1968, pp. 284–289.
32. ——— . "The New ASA-NBER Survey of Forecasts by Economic Statisticians." *The American Statistician,* Februrary 1969, pp. 12–16.
33. ——— . "The ASA-NBER Quarterly Survey of the Economic Outlook: An Early Appraisal." *1969 Proceedings of the Business and Economic Statistics Section.* American Statistical Association. Washington, D.C., 1969, pp. 241–249.
34. Zarnowitz, Victor; Boschan, Charlotte; and Moore, Geoffrey H.; with the assistance of Josephine Su. "Business-Cycle Analysis of Econometric Model Simulations." In *Econometric Models* (see [9]).

Econometric Model Simulations and the Cyclical Characteristics of the U.S. Economy

Victor Zarnowitz

University of Chicago and National Bureau of Economic Research

1. QUESTIONS, METHODS, AND DATA

This paper grows out of a comprehensive study which addresses some old but unsolved questions to several of the newest econometric models.[1] The major substantive issue that is involved here has been raised early in the literature: Do business cycles consist mainly of endogenous or exogenous movements? This is presumably an empirical problem, in the usual sense of being amenable to scientific treatment through formulation of suitable hypotheses that can be tested against the data. There is no dearth of either endogenous or exogenous or "mixed" theories, some of which can be and have been tested, though not always adequately or persuasively. Over the years, the subject of business cycles attracted much systematic research and

[1] Victor Zarnowitz, Charlotte Boschan, and Geoffrey H. Moore, with the assistance of Josephine Su, "Business Cycle Analysis of Econometric Model Simulations," report prepared for the Conference on Econometric Models of Cyclical Behavior, Cambridge, Mass., November 1969; and published in Bert G. Hickman (ed.), *Econometric Models of Cyclical Behavior,* Studies in Income and Wealth 36, New York, NBER, 1971. I am greatly indebted to Mrs. Boschan for helpful comments, to Mrs. Su for valuable statistical assistance, to Mr. H. Irving Forman for the preparation of the chart, and to Mrs. Gnomi Schrift Gouldin for editorial improvements.

observation, which resulted in considerable growth of factual knowledge in this broad area. Nonetheless, the issue still resists a solution, and perhaps not surprisingly so; it might well be argued that the required degree of understanding the modern economy in motion is not yet achieved.

It seems quite natural that a close connection should exist between the problem of how business cycles are generated and the method of studying the economy through building and analyzing econometric macromodels. Indeed, interest in testing various cyclical hypotheses first motivated Tinbergen to construct such models.[2] However, even now, more than three decades and several generations of aggregative econometric models later, disagreement abounds on how best to scale, specify, and estimate such models. The great gains in theory, information, and computational techniques and capacities have yet to be fully reflected in comprehensive systems of proved superiority. This presents a grave problem since what an econometric model suggests about the nature of business cycles may not be dependable if the model itself is not.

The study on which I report is, therefore, more properly described as a search for answers to these questions: Do the models under review generate cyclical behavior as defined and observed in the empirical business cycle studies, notably those of the National Bureau of Economic Research (NBER), which provide the main documentation on the subject? If so, to what extent are such fluctuations in the estimated series produced endogenously by the models, and to what extent are they attributable to external impulses? The aims of the study, then, will be recognized as very similar to those of the 1959 analysis of the annual Klein-Goldberger model by Irma and Frank Adelman.[3] Its scope, however, is substantially larger as the materials now available are much richer. Four different quarterly models are examined, to be labeled Wharton, OBE, FMP, and Brookings.[4] It is generally recognized that quarterly data are far more adequate in business cycle analysis than are annual data.

[2] Jan Tinbergen, *Statistical Testing of Business Cycle Theories, II, Business Cycles in the United States of America, 1919-1932,* Geneva, 1939.

[3] "The Dynamic Properties of the Klein-Goldberger Model," *Econometrica,* October 1959, pp. 596-625.

[4] The abbreviations refer, respectively, to: the Wharton-Econometric Forecasting Unit model; the Office of Business Economics of the U.S. Department of Commerce model; the Federal Reserve Board-MIT-PENN model; and the Brookings-SSRC model. The model variants on which this analysis is based are those developed by the summer of 1969 and explained in several papers prepared for the Harvard Conference of November 1969 (see note 1).

The methods employed also parallel largely the techniques used in the pioneering study by the Adelmans. Three types of complete-model simulations are analyzed, namely:

(a) Nonstochastic simulations over six-quarter periods beginning, alternatively, one, two, and three quarters before each of the business cycle turns that occurred during the model's sample period.[5] Each of these runs starts from new correct initial conditions and uses *ex post* values for the exogenous variables.

(b) Nonstochastic simulations over the entire sample period covered by each model; also based on the initial conditions (actual value) at the beginning of that period and on the historical values of the exogenous variables.

(c) Stochastic simulations projecting the models for a period of twenty-five years starting at the end of the sample period. In these experiments, the exogenous variables are generally continued along smooth growth trends based on their compound interest rates of growth during the sample period.

One set of short and one of long nonstochastic simulations (a and b) was required for each model, but for the stochastic simulations (c) as many as fifty computer runs per model were made, so as to gain information on the variability of responses to different configurations of shocks and to avoid excessive reliance on any particular, and possibly idiosyncratic, shock distribution. Completed work covers nonstochastic simulations of type (a) for three models (Wharton, OBE, FMP), those of type (b) for all four models, and the stochastic runs for three (Wharton, OBE, and Brookings).

Regrettably, the results for the different models are not strictly comparable, for at least two reasons. First, the sample periods differ: the Wharton model covers seventy-nine quarters, from Q3 1948 through Q1 1969; the OBE model covers fifty-five quarters from Q2 1953 through Q4 1966; the FMP model covers forty-four quarters from Q1 1956 through Q4 1966; and the Brookings model covers thirty-six quarters from Q1 1957 through Q4 1965. Thus, the Wharton period includes four of the completed contractions or recessions in the postwar economic history of the U.S. (as well as such milder retardations as those of 1951-52, 1962-63, and 1966-67), the OBE period includes three, and the FMP period and Brookings period each include two of these contractions. Such differences can strongly affect the relative performance of the models and, as a task for the future, it would

[5] The business cycle peaks and troughs are dated according to the NBER "reference chronology" (in quarterly terms) and are also referred to as "reference turns."

be very desirable to recalculate the simulations with one common sample period for all included models. Second, models differ in coverage: in particular, what is endogenous in one of them may be exogenous in another. This must be accepted and only some partial remedies are available here depending on the cooperation of the model builders; but this study reduces the problem by concentrating upon a subset of selected variables that are basically common to, and endogenous in, all of the models covered.

The endogenous variables used in the simulations are listed in Table 1, which classifies the series according to their typical timing at business cycle turns, as historically determined. The list includes eight series from the national income accounts, of which five are in constant and three in current dollars; five series relating to employment and unemployment, hours of work, and unit labor costs; four relating to commitments to produce durable goods and invest in equipment and housing; and three relating to interest rates and money. The main sources are the U.S. Department of Commerce, the Bureau of Labor Statistics (BLS), and the Federal Reserve Board (FRB). Most series are used after seasonal adjustment. In addition, three variables unclassified by cyclical timing and not included in Table 1 were also represented in the simulations for all three models: the implicit price deflator for the GNP (P); private wage and salary compensation per man-hour in dollars (W); and net exports in billions of 1958 dollars (NE). Some variables were selected because of their importance for macroeconomic theory in general and business cycle analysis in particular, some in view of their cyclical sensitivity and timing, and some for both reasons. With relatively few exceptions but frequent modifications, they appear in most of the recent econometric models of intermediate or large size.

Although simulation is a powerful tool of economic analysis, its inherent limitations are substantial. Inferences drawn from simulation results about the properties of the economic system are only as good as the model that is used as the analogue of that system. However, evidence from studies based on different models and applications to different periods may to some extent cumulate and reduce this weakness. This argues in favor of comprehensive and diversified coverage of econometric model simulations in business cycle analysis.

2. SIX-QUARTER SIMULATIONS AROUND BUSINESS CYCLE TURNS

The determination of cyclical turning points in these nonstochastic simulations (described under point (a) above) presents considerable difficulties because the data refer to short, unconnected periods and it is sometimes uncertain whether the observed changes in direction are cyclically

TABLE 1

List of Variables and Data Definitions For Simulations of Four Models

Symbol	Variable by Timing Group	Available for Models
	Leading Series	
1. IH	Investment in nonfarm residential structures[a]	Wharton, OBE, FMP, Brookings
2. II	Change in nonfarm business inventories[a]	Wharton, OBE, FMP, Brookings
3. CPR	Corporate profits before taxes and inventory valuation adjustment[b]	Wharton, OBE, FMP, Brookings
4. AWW	Average work week, private employment, hours per week, BLS	Wharton, OBE, FMP, Brookings
5. LH	Total hours per man per annum in nonfarm private domestic sector, BLS	FMP
6. OMD	New orders, durables manufacturers' goods[a]	OBE
7. UMD	Unfilled orders, durable manufacturers' goods end of quarter[a]	Wharton, OBE, Brookings
8. OUME	Unfilled orders, machinery and equipment industries, end of quarter[b]	FMP
9. HS	Private nonfarm housing starts, annual rate, thousands, Census	OBE
10. M	Demand deposits adjusted and currency outside banks[c]	OBE, FMP
	Roughly Coincident Series	
11. GNP	Gross national product[b]	Wharton, OBE, FMP, Brookings
12. GNP58	Gross national product in constant dollars[a]	Wharton, OBE, FMP, Brookings
13. C	Personal consumption expenditures[a]	Wharton, OBE, FMP, Brookings
14. YP	Personal income[b]	Wharton, OBE, FMP, Brookings
15. LE	Total civilian employment, millions of persons, BLS	Wharton, OBE, FMP, Brookings
16. UN	Unemployment rate, per cent (of labor force), BLS	Wharton, OBE, FMP, Brookings

Table 1 (Concluded)

Lagging Series

17. ISE	Investment in nonresidential structures and producers' durable equipment[a]	Wharton, OBE, FMP, Brookings
18. RS	Average yield, 4–6 months prime commercial paper, per cent per annum, FRB	Wharton, OBE, FMP, Brookings
	Government bill rate per cent	Brookings
19. RL	Average yield, corporate bonds, Moody's per cent per annum	Wharton, OBE, FMP, Brookings
	Government bond rate, per cent	Brookings
20. L/CO	Private employee compensation per unit of private GNP in constant dollars, OBE	OBE

[a] Annual rate, billions of 1958 dollars. National income accounts; OBE, Census, seasonally adjusted.
[b] Annual rate (except line 8), billions of current dollars. National income accounts; Census, seasonally adjusted.
[c] Daily average of quarter, billions of current dollars. Currency is exogenous, deposits endogenous.

significant or merely reflect short random movements. This is particularly true when the suspected turns fall close to the beginning or end of the six-quarter period. Consideration of events outside this period——turns in the actual series that occurred shortly before or after——may be helpful, but it too is not always clearly legitimate. Alternative measures were, therefore, computed, one set including and the other excluding comparisons between outside actual and inferred simulated turns.[6] In some cases, doubts remained but were met by deciding in favor of recognizing turns in the simulations if this seemed at all reasonable.

Two models succeeded fairly well, and one (FMP) rather better, in reproducing the turns in the actuals at business cycle peaks and troughs. When the inferred turning points are included, the percentages of the turns matched are 60-67 for Wharton, 66-73 for OBE, and 76-90 for FMP (see Table 2, lines 1-3 for the underlying numbers).[7] When they are excluded, the corresponding percentages are lower, averaging 58, 66, and 75 for the respective models.

The evidence does not indicate that the simulations beginning closer to the reference turn are systematically more successful than those beginning earlier. (The former, it may be noted, cover fewer specific-cycle turns in the actuals than do the latter.) Neither is the expectation that troughs are better reproduced than peaks definitely met, although troughs are often more sharply defined and more closely clustered. This may be due to the constancy of the lag structure used by the models. However, in the simulations that start one or two quarters prior to the reference dates, the percentages of troughs matched do tend to be somewhat higher than the corresponding figures for peaks.

Coincidences with the actual turns account for 21, 39, and 45 per cent of the simulated turns in the six-quarter periods for the Wharton, OBE, and FMP models, respectively. The corresponding figures for leads of the simulated relative to the actual turns are 54, 36, and 19 per cent, while for lags the percentages are 25, 25, and 36. When the series are classified by historical timing groups and the comparisons are made relative to the business cycle

[6]To illustrate such comparisons, if the actual series showed a peak shortly before the beginning of the simulation period and the simulated series continued downward locally, the latter was presumed to have produced a peak.

[7]The higher attainment rate of the FMP model cannot be simply discounted on the presumption that fluctuations are more easily simulated for the period 1957-61; the better performance of the FMP model is retained also if the comparisons for all three models are limited to the turning points of this shorter period. Still, it is possible that the fits are better for 1957-61 and that this explains at least partly the superiority of the FMP model.

TABLE 2

Nonstochastic Six-Quarter Simulations Around Reference Turns,
Selected Statistics Relating to Cyclical Conformity, Timing,
and Amplitudes of Simulated and Actual Series, Three Models

	Wharton Model (1949–61)		OBE Model (1954–61)		FMP Model (1957–61)	
	Actual (1)	Simulated (2)	Actual (3)	Simulated (4)	Actual (5)	Simulated (6)
Frequency of Turning Points (number)						
Simulations starting						
1. 3 Qtrs. before ref. turns	95	64	88	58	50	38
2. 2 Qtrs. before ref. turns	95	61	88	60	50	44
3. 1 Qtr. before ref. turns	95	57	88	64	50	45
Relative Frequency of Leads and Lags (per cent of all turns)[a]						
Leading series:						
4. Leads	46	80	55	70	45	33
5. Coincidences	44	2	36	10	31	30
6. Lags	10	17	9	20	24	37
Roughly coincident series:						
7. Leads	39	88	38	55	32	47
8. Coincidences	48	2	50	21	53	19
9. Lags	13	10	12	24	15	34
Lagging series:						
10. Leads	11	36	14	12	12	32
11. Coincidences	30	40	21	46	53	20
12. Lags	59	23	64	41	35	48
Average Percentage Amplitudes, by Cycle Phase[b]						
13. Expansions	7.8	6.4	7.4	3.5	7.6	3.7
14. Contractions	−7.0	−3.6	−6.6	−3.1	−6.5	−4.8

NOTE: Observations in lines 1–3 include, and those in lines 4–12 exclude, the inferred turning points in simulations, corresponding to the known actual turns that occurred outside the simulation period. See text. For the classification of series by cyclical timing (lines 4–12), see Table 1.

[a]The entries in columns 2, 4, and 6 refer to all simulations regardless of starting date.

[b]The figures in columns 2, 4, and 6 refer to simulations starting two quarters before reference turns (the results for the other simulations are similar). Expansions and contractions are phase movements in the actual and simulated series within the six-quarter periods.

peaks and troughs, leads are found to be much more frequent in the simulations than in the actuals for the Wharton simulations in all groups (Table 2, lines 4-12, columns 1-2). The same statement applies to the OBE model, though less strongly and not for the lagging series, but there is no comparable bias towards early turns in the FMP simulations (lines 4-12, columns 3-6). On the whole, these simulations discriminate but weakly (and much less effectively than the actuals) between the historically leading, coincident, and lagging variables.

The simulated series show rises and falls that tend to be substantially smaller than their counterparts in the actual series within the selected turning-point segments (Table 2, lines 13-14). Of course, nonstochastic simulations must be expected to vary less than the actuals on the average, because they do not include the component of random disturbances that is present in the actuals. However, this factor often seems to explain only a part of the observed underestimation of amplitudes. Good estimation and simulation of systematic, cyclical amplitude components is in any event desirable. The Wharton series approximate relatively well the average size of the actual rises, the FMP series give better results for the declines.

3. SAMPLE-PERIOD SIMULATIONS

In Chart 1, each of the models shows the real GNP (taken to represent the aggregate economic activity) as declining during at least some portion of the first recession period covered. (For Wharton, this means the 1948-49 recession; for OBE, the one in 1953-54; and for FMP and Brookings, the one in 1957-58.) The Wharton and the FMP model also have *GNP58* contracting during the second recession, in 1953-54 and 1960-61, respectively. Neither Wharton nor OBE produces a fall in *GNP58* during either the 1957-58 or the 1960-61 recession. Although the FMP model does produce such declines in these two periods, it would be wrong to conclude that it is therefore better, because the initial conditions for this model, being as of Q1 1956, are much closer to these episodes than the initial conditions for Wharton and OBE. Where the simulated series fail to match the declines in *GNP58,* they at least flatten off, however (e.g., Wharton and OBE in 1957-58, Brookings in 1960-61).

This leads to the important inference that there appears to be a progressive *dampening* of the fluctuations the further away a model's simulation proceeds from its initial conditions period. This type of movement would be characteristic of a hypothetical economy representing a stable macrodynamic

CHART 1

Nonstochastic Sample-Period Simulations of GNP in Constant Dollars, Four Models

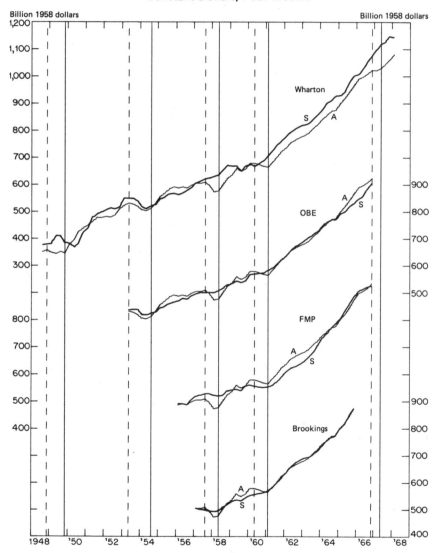

Note: A = actual; S = simulated. Broken vertical lines indicate business cycle peaks; solid lines, troughs. The last pair of such lines, however, refers to a business retardation in 1966-67, which did not develop into another recession.

system insulated from external disturbances.[8] It is the response of such a system to the irregular but persistent outside shocks that is supposed to convert the damped fluctuations into a maintained movement of the type historically observed as the recurrent "business cycles."

Under this hypothesis, therefore, the failure of nonstochastic sample-period simulations to re-create the continuous cyclical developments that did actually occur need not constitute any adverse evidence about the structure of the underlying model. Instead, such results could be due to the suppression of the disturbance terms. It must be noted, however, that the simulations here reviewed use *ex post* values of exogenous variables. Changes in the latter include a large subset of "autonomous" shocks——variations in government expenditures, tax rates, monetary base, reserve requirements, population, exports, etc. Important effects of monetary and fiscal policy changes are thus incorporated. What these simulations suppress, then, is essentially the stochastic components of the endogenous variables. We cannot be certain that it is the disregard of this source of variability that is predominantly responsible for the errors of the nonstochastic sample-period simulations. There are undoubtedly misspecifications in the models, which could be just as important. The autocorrelations of the disturbance terms in some of the original structural equations are high enough to be disturbing. The failures of the simulations to track major cyclical movements can often be traced to the weakness of certain specific relations, e.g., those for inventory investment or the price levels.

Nonstochastic simulations, which refer to the periods to which the models were fit and use the correct *ex post* values of the exogenous variables, do not provide tests of the predictive powers of the models. They do, however, subject the models to rather demanding tests of a different kind, since, in simultaneous estimation, errors are liable to cumulate across a model and, through the effects of lagged dependent variables, errors are also liable to cumulate over time. There is evidence that the calculated values do tend to drift away, though not necessarily continuously, in simulations that cover more than one or two business cycles. For trend-dominated variables such as *GNP, GNP58,* or *C,* the drift appears sometimes as an increasing overestimation, more often as an increasing underestimation of the levels of the series. (In Chart 1, the former is illustrated by the Wharton simulation for

[8] The diminishing oscillations in this model originate in the divergencies from equilibrium that are likely to exist in any initial state of the system; they tend to disappear as the system approaches its equilibrium rate of growth. This hypothesis, completed by the notion that external disturbances or "erratic shocks" do in fact impinge upon the economy continually, gained influence following the important contribution by Ragnar Frisch, "Propagation Problems and Impulse Problems in Dynamic Economics," *Essays in Honor of Gustav Cassel,* London, 1933.

the 1960's and the latter by the OBE and FMP simulations in part of that decade.) Generally, the discrepancies between the levels of the simulated and actual (S and A) series are much greater than those between the corresponding quarterly changes. The reason lies in autocorrelated errors, which cumulate, thus throwing off base the long multiperiod predictions that are here involved.

Common to both short and long nonstochastic simulations is a strong tendency to underestimate the amplitudes of the observed cyclical movements. Contractions in the series, however, are often missed altogether by the simulations rather than merely underestimated. About one-third of the recorded turning points are not matched by the sample-period simulations.

In Table 3 are some measures of the kind that would be helpful to answer the question, how do the models compare with one another in terms of the relative accuracy of their simulations? (See lines 1-5.) However, because of the (already noted) differences in coverage among the models, this question cannot be answered conclusively. The errors of the Wharton simulations are on the average considerably larger than those of either the OBE or the FMP or the Brookings simulations, except for the price level, P, where the differences are small (compare columns 1, 3, 5, and 7). But the Wharton simulations cover a much longer period than the others, including the unsettled and difficult-to-fit developments of the late 1940's and the Korean war.

Dividing the mean absolute errors of relative change (MAERC) by the mean absolute values of actual relative change (MAARC) is a standardizing procedure which probably tends to correct for the differences in the sample periods but does not guarantee an unbiased comparison.[9] The resulting ratios (columns 2, 4, 6, and 8) show smaller differences between the models than do the MAERC figures, but the models would be ranked rather similarly according to the two measures. (Brookings comes out somewhat better than FMP and OBE, and Wharton ranks fourth for most variables; for the price level, however, FMP and Wharton show the lowest ratios and Brookings the highest.)

The second part of Table 3 (lines 6-14) shows that the simulations do discriminate broadly between the groups of leading and lagging indicators but they do not carry this differentiation nearly as far as the actual timing distributions do. The OBE model yields good approximations for both leaders

---

[9] As elsewhere in the analysis of predictive accuracy, the comparisons with changes are on the whole much more meaningful than those with levels. The smaller the ratio (MAERC)/(MAARC), the better it speaks of the model; and a ratio that exceeds unity signifies that the errors are on the average larger than the recorded changes, that is, the model does worse than a type of "naive" extrapolation.

TABLE 3

Nonstochastic Sample-Period Simulations for Four Models, Average
Error Statistics, and Relative Frequency Distributions of
Leads and Lags at Business Cycle Turns

	Wharton Model (Q3 1948–Q1 1968)		OBE Model (Q2 1953–Q4 1966)		FMP Model (Q1 1956–Q4 1966)		Brookings Model (Q1 1957–Q4 1965)	
	(1)	(2)	(3)	(4)	(5)	(6)	(7)	(8)
Selected Variables[a]	MAERC % points	MAERC ÷ MAARC	MAERC % points	MAERC ÷ MAARC	MAERC % points	MAERC ÷ MAARC	MAERC %points	MAERC÷ MAARC
1. GNP	1.17	0.681	0.70	0.459	0.61	0.377	0.57	.363
2. GNP58	1.12	0.852	0.64	0.518	0.65	0.524	0.57	.428
3. P	0.27	0.453	0.24	0.488	0.22	0.429	0.22	.544
4. ISE	3.12	1.036	1.90	0.812	1.79	0.746	1.40	.557
5. UN	17.80	2.502	6.00	0.890	6.26	1.155	5.63	.895
	Relative Frequency of Leads and Lags (per cent of all turns)							
Leadings[b]	Actual	Simulated	Actual	Simulated	Actual	Simulated	Actual	Simulated
6. Leads	62	56	73	74	68	67	56	60
7. Coincidences	32	17	20	15	14	17	38	30
8. Lags	5	26	7	12	18	17	6	10
Roughly Coincident Series[b]								
9. Leads	35	44	38	42	31	30	27	33
10. Coincidences	51	9	50	17	50	30	60	33
11. Lags	14	48	12	42	19	40	13	33
Lagging Series[b]								
12. Leads	8	32	8	11	17	30	18	60
13. Coincidences	42	23	21	28	42	20	45	20
14. Lags	50	46	71	61	42	50	37	20

[a]For meaning of the symbols, see Table 1.

[b]For the classification of series by cyclical timing, see Table 1.

and laggers, the FMP and Brookings models for the leading series only.
Brookings is particularly weak on the timing distribution for the laggers. The
worst results are obtained for the six roughly coincident indicators, where
exact coincidences make up 50-60 per cent of the timing observations for the
actual series but only 9, 17, 30, and 33 per cent of the observations for the
Wharton, OBE, FMP, and Brookings models, respectively.[10] It is for this
category, too, that the simulations have the poorest record on cyclical
conformity: the S series for GNP and other comprehensive aggregates of
income, employment, and consumption show few turning points and
frequently "skip" the peaks and troughs of business cycles.

4. HUNDRED-QUARTER EX ANTE SIMULATIONS

These simulations (see point (c) above) have so far been computed only for
the Wharton, OBE, and Brookings models and their analysis is incomplete.
Each of them covers a period of a hundred quarters, beginning past the space

[10]Note that the large shares of leads and lags tend to approximately balance each
other in this group (Table 3, lines 9-11).

of sample experience (in Q3 1968 for Wharton, in Q1 1966 for OBE and Brookings). The "control solutions" (nonstochastic simulations) produce, over these long future periods, smooth series with uninterrupted growth trends for the comprehensive indicators of over-all economic activity such as GNP, personal income, and employment. The trend-like control series contrast with the nonstochastic sample-period simulations that do show some recurrent, if damped, fluctuations. A probable reason for the contrast lies in the fact that, in these control solutions, the exogenous variables are projected along smooth monotonic upward trends without any fluctuations. The historical series for the same variables, which were used in the nonstochastic sample-period simulations, often show considerable short-term fluctuations. However, this need not be the only or the main reason: another one may be provided by the specification errors of the models.[11]

The lack of fluctuations in the control series for the comprehensive aggregates (GNP, etc.) indicates that none of these models generates cyclical movement endogenously. Evidently the models contain no mechanisms that would cause the simulated aggregates to fluctuate in the absence of shocks in either the exogenous quantities or in the relationships with endogenous variables.

The random shocks used in the stochastic simulations for both models were generated so that the expected value of the variance-covariance matrix of the shocks over the simulation period is equal to the variance-covariance matrix of the observed residuals over the sample period. In another set of experiments, serially correlated shocks were used, their lag correlations for a sufficiently large number of observations being also equal to the corresponding sample values obtained from the residual matrix.[12] For the OBE model, twenty-five simulations use serially uncorrelated random shocks and twenty-five use serially correlated shocks; for the Wharton model, the number is twice as large in each set. Only autocorrelated shocks were used in the fifty simulations for the Brookings model.

---

[11] The control solutions suggest that, at least in this context of long-term projections, all three models are confronted with difficult problems of internal consistency. They include some series that are either made to behave in a more or less arbitrarily predetermined fashion or are permitted to behave in ways that would seem difficult to rationalize. Such questionable simulations (as illustrated particularly by the control series for unemployment and interest rates) are perhaps best viewed as concomitants of the search for a broadly satisfactory control solution for the over-all aggregates. In short, to get a plausible projection for GNP, the simulation of, say, the unemployment rate may have had to be compromised.

[12] The method of generating the shocks is that of Michael D. McCarthy. See his "Some Notes on the Generation of Pseudo Structural Errors for Use in Stochastic Simulation Studies," Appendix to Michael K. Evans, Lawrence R. Klein, and M. Saito, "Short Run Prediction and Long Run Simulation of the Wharton Model" (paper prepared for the Harvard Conference of November 1969), note 1.

The stochastic simulations are strongly trend-dominated for *GNP* in current and constant dollars and several other comprehensive aggregates (*YP, C, LE, P, W, and M*). There are systematic differences between the series with nonautocorrelated shocks (S_u) and those with autocorrelated shocks (S_c). The latter are far smoother than the former and hence tend to have larger average durations and smaller average percentage amplitudes of rises and declines.[13] The Wharton S_u series for *GNP* and *GNP58* show somewhat shorter and smaller declines than the sample-period actuals (*A*), while the S_c series show much fewer declines, all of them short and separated by overly long rises. In the corresponding OBE simulations of either type, declines are altogether rare, short, and small. The same can be said about the Brookings S_c series for *GNP* (in those for *GNP58*, declines are also small and short but more frequent). The simulated series that have weaker trends and stronger fluctuations (relating to investment processes, orders, unemployment, average workweek, and interest rates) tend to have shorter movements than the corresponding *A* series, in either direction. The S_c series often underestimate the length of the recorded movements of *A* less than the S_u series.

These experiments suggest that the use of autocorrelated shocks is helpful in many but by no means all cases and that it works better for the more volatile series than for the comprehensive aggregates with dominant growth trends and subdued fluctuations. The declines in S_c tend to be longer but also smaller than those of S_u. The criterion of duration is presumably more important than that of amplitude.[14] When this is taken into account, the balance of the comparisons favors the S_c over the S_u simulations for most variables in both models, but not without some important counterexamples (notably for *GNP* and *GNP58* in the Wharton model). In general, the cyclical aspects of the simulated series are much weaker than those observed in the

---

[13] A rise (decline) is used to denote any upward (downward) movement in a series, however short or small. In this analysis such changes are distinguished from cyclical movements that must be sufficiently long and pronounced to qualify as "specific cycle" expansions and contractions (as defined by NBER).

[14] The random shock hypothesis here considered asserts, in the formulation by Frisch (*op. cit.*, p. 171), that

> the majority of the economic oscillations ... seem to be explained most plausibly as free oscillations .... . The most important feature of the free oscillations is that the length of the cycles and the tendency towards dampening are determined by the intrinsic structure of the swinging system, while the intensity (the amplitude) of the fluctuations is determined primarily by the exterior impulse.

This suggests that the amplitudes of movements in the stochastic *S* series would depend mainly on the simulator's decision as to the magnitude of the shocks applied. They may be quite different from the amplitudes of the actuals, not because of any failure of the model to reproduce the basic structure of the economy, but because the impulses (shocks) have not been properly scaled.

historical series, in contrast to the long trends and short erratic variations that are often considerably stronger in the S than in the A series.

That the cyclical movements get blurred in the stochastic simulations could be due in large measure to the inadequate handling or scaling of the shocks, in particular to the neglect of disturbances in the exogenous variables. Hence we have also analyzed the relative deviations of shocked from control series, in the expectation that they would be more indicative of the cyclical effects of relatively weak impulses. This expectation was confirmed, but the ratios of the stochastic to the control series are also much more erratic than the shocked series proper, reflecting not only greater sensitivity to the effects of the shocks but presumably a telescoping of "measurement" errors as well. It is particularly the ratios of S_u to the control series that tend to be highly erratic, the ratios of S_c are much smoother and generally appear more plausible.

Ratios of the historical series to their exponential trends were computed to provide measures for the sample-period actuals that correspond to the measure for the simulated ratio series. As shown in Table 4, lines 1 and 2, the trend-adjusted GNP series are better approximated by the S_c than by the S_u ratios, in terms of the durations (and therefore also the frequencies) of rises and declines. Comparisons of amplitudes alone would point to the reverse (lines 3 and 4), but, again giving more weight to the duration than to the amplitude criterion, the results for the ratio series generally favor the S_c over the S_u simulations, and do so rather more strongly than the findings based on the level comparisons. This conclusion also applies to the simulations for $GNP58$ and other variables.

Using the ratio series, cumulated diffusion indexes (CDI) were constructed for three randomly chosen runs of the Wharton model and three of the OBE model. For either model, the selection includes one set of series based on S_u and two based on S_c simulations. For the Brookings model, the CDI indexes were computed for two sets of the S_c series. The indexes are of the "historical" type: after the cyclical turning points have been identified in each of the simulated ratio series in a given set, the percentage of the series undergoing specific cycle expansion is calculated for each quarter, then the deviations of these percentage figures from 50 are cumulated. Each of the CDI shows reasonably well-defined cyclical movements, whose turning-point dates can be used as a reference chronology with which to compare the timing of the simulated series in the given set. The average durations of the specific cycles in the CDI (about 13, 15, and 18 quarters for Brookings, OBE, and Wharton, respectively) are smaller than those of the postwar (1948-68) cycles in trend-adjusted GNP and $GNP58$ (18-20 quarters). This reflects mainly short expansions in the indexes, but the over-all differences for some of the runs are not large.

TABLE 4

Stochastic 100-Quarter Simulations (Ratio Series) for Three Models, Selected Summary Measures of Duration and Amplitude and Relative Frequency Distributions of Leads and Lags at Turns in Cumulated Diffusion Indexes

	Wharton Model			OBE Model			Brookings Model	
	Sample-Period Actuals (A)	Simulations with Nonautocorrelated Shocks (S_u)	Simulations with Autocorrelated Shocks (S_c)	Sample-Period Actuals(A)	Simulations with Nonautocorrelated Shocks(S_u)	Simulations with Autocorrelated Shocks(S_c)	Sample-Period Actuals (A)	Simulations with Autocorrelated Shocks(S_c)
	(1)	(2)	(3)	(4)	(5)	(6)	(7)	(8)
Durations (quarters)[b]								
Quarterly Movements in GNP (Actual and Simulated)[a]								
1. Rises	3.4(2.1)	1.7(0.8)	2.2(1.4)	3.1(3.4)	1.9(1.1)	2.7(1.9)	3.3(1.7)	2.4(1.5)
2. Declines	2.6(1.6)	1.7(0.8)	2.3(1.9)	2.3(1.9)	1.9(1.1)	2.6(1.8)	2.5(1.3)	2.3(1.4)
Amplitude (per cent)[c]								
3. Rises	0.9	0.9(0.1)	0.4(.05)	0.6	0.4(.05)	0.3(.04)	0.8	0.34(0.06)
4. Declines	1.0	0.9(0.0)	0.4(.05)	0.6	0.4(.05)	0.3(.05)	0.9	0.33(0.06)

Relative Frequency of Leads and Lags (per cent of all turns)[e]

Group of Variables[d]	Wharton			OBE			Brookings		
	Leads	Coincidences	Lags	Leads	Coincidences	Lags	Leads	Coincidences	Lags
5. Leading	48	26	26	43	28	29	43	21	36
6. Roughly Coincident	23	43	34	23	47	30	33	44	23
7. Lagging	28	21	51	24	25	51	31	24	45

NOTE: See text for the explanation of simulations with nonautocorrelated and autocorrelated shocks (S_u and S_c), of the form in which they are used here (as ratios to the corresponding control series), and of the timing comparisons underlying the entries in lines 5–7 (observations at reference—CDI—peaks and troughs).

[a] Actual (A): Relative deviation of GNP from its exponential trend. Simulated (S_u and S_c): Relative deviation of shocked from control series for GNP. On the meaning of "rises" and "declines," see note 13. The entries in lines 1–4, cols. 2, 3, 5, and 6 are based on all available simulation runs.

[b] I or S: mean duration per run, with standard deviation in parentheses. I or S: mean duration per run, with mean standard deviation of the durations "within the run" in parentheses.

[c] For A: mean amplitude. For S: mean amplitude per run, with standard deviation of means per run in parentheses (in per cent, at quarterly rate).

[d] Classified according to the timing of the historical series. See Table 1.

[e] Based on comparisons of the turning points in the simulated ratio series with the corresponding reference dates—peaks and troughs in the cumulated diffusion indexes (CDI).

In general, the series resulting from simulations with autocorrelated shocks conform better to the reference indexes (CDI) than the series resulting from simulations with nonautocorrelated shocks, because the former have fewer "extra" turns than the latter. The comprehensive indicators of national product, income, and expenditures, which historically rank high on conformity, also score relatively well according to these comparisons.

There is considerable correspondence between the relative timing of the *ex ante* stochastic simulations and of the historical data for the same variables, as indicated by the average leads and lags of the ratio series at the major turns in the CDI. Indeed, the distributions of the timing observations for the ratio series (Table 4, lines 5-7) appear to be appreciably better than those for the sample-period simulations in identifying the coinciders. However, they are not so sharp in differentiating between the groups of typical leaders and laggers (see Table 3, lines 6-14), particularly because of discrepancies relating to several of the leading series. Also, the total picture is less favorable than the distributions alone would imply, for many turns in the more volatile ratio series (particularly from the S_u runs) cannot be matched with the reference turns and some that can be are difficult to date, so that the timing comparisons are rather uncertain.

5. CONCLUDING REMARKS

To produce any cyclical movements, the models included in this study seem to require perturbations in either the exogenous variables or the relationships with endogenous variables or both. Even the best stochastic simulations here obtained——those with serially correlated shocks to the equations——show only residual cyclical elements, much weaker than those observed in the historical series used in the estimation of the models. This is a disappointing result, assuming that it is reasonable to expect the stochastic simulations to reproduce the recent pattern of the economy's movement at least over several years beyond the sample period. Errors in either the estimates of the disturbances or in the structure of the models could account for this finding.

The absence of shocks or fluctuations in the projected exogenous variables is an unrealistic feature that is likely to be partly responsible for the weakness of the cyclical elements in the stochastic *ex ante* simulations. Further experiments should test whether this weakness can be remedied by imposing more or less sporadic disturbances on the exogenous factors——or, better, to what extent it can be reduced. There are some indications that the role of such exogenous movements may be large, but the evidence is still very fragmentary.[15] Moreover, it is possible that the general picture conveyed by the simulations is seriously distorted by specification errors in the models; certainly, important errors of this sort would tend to obscure the meaning of the evidence that the simulations can provide.[16] Future simulation studies, therefore, should be combined with a comparative analysis of misspecifications in the models covered.

A more limited task that could be readily accomplished with the materials already collected is to examine larger samples of the stochastic simulations. Also, to compare the models with regard to their ability to approximate the main characteristics of major short-term fluctuations of the economy, there is need for more standardized simulations——at least for a suitable common sample period for the different systems. Even in terms of our present program, the coverage of the Brookings and FMP models is still to be completed. Finally, the simulation studies should be extended to other recent models and to revised versions of the included models. The more varied the assortment of the represented systems, the more we are likely to learn from this research.

[15] See the report by Green, Liebenberg, and Hirsch on stochastic simulations with the OBE model in the forthcoming volume of the proceedings of the *1969 NBER Conference on Econometric Models of Cyclical Behavior.*

[16] This point has been repeatedly made in discussions at the 1969 conference. See Bert G. Hickman's introduction to *Econometric Models of Cyclical Behavior, op. cit.*

A Study of Discretionary and Nondiscretionary Monetary and Fiscal Policies in the Context of Stochastic Macroeconometric Models

Yoel Haitovsky
The Hebrew University of Jerusalem

Neil Wallace
University of Minnesota

I. INTRODUCTION

In this paper we study stochastic or random versions of three quarterly representations or models of the U.S. economy: the FRB-MIT, Wharton, and Michigan econometric models.[1] For each model, we examine the results of imposing a set of macroeconomic policy rules——rules comprised of different combinations and magnitudes of monetary and fiscal responses to what is occurring in the economy. The results that flow from each of the policy rules according to each representation of the economy are obtained from sixteen-quarter simulation experiments designed to answer the following question: If the economy is represented by a particular model that is stochastic and if a

---

[1] The FRB-MIT model is described and discussed in F. deLeeuw and E. Gramlich, "The Federal Reserve-MIT Econometric Model," *Federal Reserve Bulletin,* January 1968, and by the same authors in "The Channels of Monetary Policy: A Further Report on the Federal Reserve-M.I.T. Model," *The Journal of Finance.* The Michigan model is described by S. H. Hymans and H. T. Shapiro, *The DHL-III Quarterly Econometric Model of the U.S. Economy,* Research Seminar in Quantitative Economics, University of Michigan, Ann Arbor, 1970. The Wharton model is an outgrowth of an older model described in M. K. Evans and L. R. Klein, *The Wharton Econometric Forecasting Model,* Economic Research Unit, Wharton School of Finance and Commerce, University of Pennsylvania, 1967. The version used here, which has more price equations and an extended financial sector, exists at the Economic Research Unit at Wharton.

particular policy rule is followed, what is the distribution of possible outcomes?

Our work differs from previous work on the policy implications of large econometric models precisely in that we obtain for each model and each policy a distribution of outcomes. With only partial and rare exceptions, previous studies have been conducted as if the models were deterministic; and, presumably, as if they were exact representations of a deterministic economy, this in spite of the fact that those models were estimated under the assumption that there are random elements in the economy.[2] Consistent with the estimation procedures, we view the economy as random, and accept as descriptive of its randomness the estimates of the residual variances turned out by the models. In addition, we take account of uncertainty about the parameter values and accept as descriptive of that uncertainty the estimates of the variance-covariance matrices of the coefficients. Because we take randomness into account, we come to grips with two related macroeconomic policy issues: the choice between discretionary and nondiscretionary policies, and the choice among instruments for a discretionary policy. The instruments question includes both the monetary-fiscal controversy and the interest-rate—monetary-aggregate controversy. Let's first consider the discretion-nondiscretion issue.

More than 20 years ago, Milton Friedman argued that most discussions of macroeconomic policy were being conducted as if the economy were a deterministic system.[3] He showed that if the policy instrument is connected to the target variable by way of random variables, then the policy action affects the stability (as measured by the variance) of the target variable, and seemingly reasonable policies that depend on recent observations, the usual way of defining discretionary policies, may lead to worse outcomes than

[2] There are few exceptions, but there is the pioneering study by I. Adelman and F. Adelman, "The Dynamic Properties of the Klein-Goldberger Model," *Econometrica,* 1959. Recently three related studies on the FRB-MIT, OBE, and Wharton models were undertaken. They are summarized by Zarnowitz, Boschan, and Moore, "Business Cycle Analysis of Econometric Model Simulations," in *Econometric Models of Cyclical Behavior,* Bert G. Hickman, ed., NBER Conference on Research in Income and Wealth, forthcoming. (See also the references therein.) However, the only random element considered there is the randomness of the additive disturbance. Another approach to the investigation of stochastic properties of econometric models was taken by G. C. Chow and R. E. Levitan, "Nature of Business Cycles Implicit in a Linear Economic Model," *Quarterly Journal of Economics,* Vol. LXXXIII, August 1969, pp. 504-517, and more recently by E. P. Howrey, "Dynamic Properties of a Condensed Version of the Wharton Model," in *Econometric Models of Cyclical Behavior, op. cit.*

[3] See M. Friedman, "The Effects of a Full Employment Policy on Economic Stabilization: A Formal Analysis," in his *Essays in Positive Economics,* University of Chicago Press, 1953.

policies that ignore recent observations, the usual way of defining nondiscretionary policies. In general, the more random the connections between the instruments and the targets, the less the instruments should respond to recent observations. Thus, resolution of the dispute between those who favor discretion and those who do not depends on determining the degree of instability that attaches to the effects of policy actions. Those who favor discretion must argue that the gain outweighs the instability that might result. Those who favor nondiscretion must argue that given the way discretionary policy is currently formulated, the instability dominates. Until now, neither side has presented evidence.

While the discretion versus nondiscretion issue is bound up with the degree to which the connections between instruments and targets are random, the second issue, the choice among instruments for a discretionary policy, depends on how that randomness is distributed. For example, in the monetary versus fiscal instruments controversy, one aspect concerns the degree to which fiscal instruments can be made responsive to macroeconomic policy needs. In this paper we disregard that question and proceed as if the personal and corporate income tax rates were instruments of macroeconomic policy; as if the President had the power to vary those rates each calendar quarter. A second aspect of the controversy involves relative potency, with an imaginary fiscalist arguing that monetary policy has almost no effect and an imaginary monetarist arguing that fiscal policy has almost no effect. The relative potency question has received a great deal of attention, but deserves that attention, if at all, only within a stochastic framework. In a deterministic framework, if a $1 billion open market operation gives an undesirably small effect, then try a $10 billion operation; and, similarly, for tax rate changes. In a deterministic framework, it is only important that instruments work in the desired direction; and, moreover, in a linear system, one instrument is sufficient to attain one target. Once we take randomness into account, however, the variance of the target is affected by the movements of the instruments, and we expect that the use of combinations of instruments will do better than the use of any one instrument, even if there is only one target variable.[4] However, this presumption for monetary and fiscal policy has never been tested.

We present evidence on both the discretion versus nondiscretion issue and on the choice of instruments question primarily in terms of (i) average growth rates of real output and the price level, (ii) dispersion of outcomes around

---

[4] Brainard shows that diversification among instruments is analogous to diversification among assets. See "Uncertainty and the Effectiveness of Policy," *American Economic Review*, May 1967.

their respective growth rates (within-path variance that serves as a measure of instability), and (iii) degree of uncertainty about the particular growth rates that will occur (among-path variance). We also compute expected utility for a class of utility functions.

We find that our discretionary policies,[5] indeed, affect the average growth rates of real output and the price level in the expected directions. That is, when restrictive policy actions are taken, as they are in the Michigan model, both growth rates decline; while when expansionary policy actions are taken, as they are in the FRB-MIT model, both growth rates increase. As that suggests, we find high correlations between the growth rates for real output and the price level across different policies. Moreover, we find that for given instruments the stronger the action taken, the greater the effects on growth rates. We find that our fiscal policies have a stronger effect than our monetary policies in the FRB-MIT model, but find the reverse in the Michigan model. This may be accounted for by asymmetry in the effects of policy actions; monetary policy, it is often suggested, is more potent when applied to restrict the economy than when applied to stimulate the economy.[6]

Our discretionary policies failed to reduce the within-path (over time) instability of either real income or the price level. Indeed, we persistently find for real income that such instability increases with the strength and, hence, with the average effect of the discretionary policy applied. As among instruments, we have evidence from the FRB-MIT model that within a given range a given effect on the growth rate of real income can be achieved with less accompanying instability of real income by the use of fiscal policy than by the use of either monetary policy or a combination of the two.

Although policies have significant effects on average growth rates, there is great uncertainty about the particular growth rate that will occur under any policy. Moreover, that uncertainty varies across policies. On this score strong policies generally outperform weak policies which, in turn, outperform the nondiscretionary policies. That is, given the uncertainty about the parameters implied by estimation and about the time paths of noninstrument exogenous variables, there is least uncertainty about the particular growth rates that will occur under our strong discretionary policies and most uncertainty under our nondiscretionary policies.

Those findings, however, both for the discretion versus nondiscretion and for the monetary versus fiscal instruments questions are subject to two basic limitations. First, we examine only a few specific discretionary policy rules.

[5] These results are based only on the FRB-MIT and Michigan models.
[6] We gladly acknowledge Bert Hickman for this remark.

Necessarily, there are other discretionary rules that would do better. The problem is finding them. For any model, there exists an optimal policy which is discretionary and which, almost certainly, would involve using both monetary and fiscal instruments. But, deriving that policy for a large, stochastic, dynamic economic model seems beyond present capabilities. It involves solving a horrendously large dynamic programming problem. Thus, we attempted to postulate only plausible rules. Second, our findings with respect to all the rules, both discretionary and nondiscretionary, are only as good as the models from which we infer them. If the models are seriously in error, then our results give no indication of what would happen if any of our rules were actually implemented.[7] One should recognize, however, that, barring experiments on the economy itself, the questions raised above must be studied within the context of estimated models of the economy.

As for the contrast between outcomes from stochastic and nonstochastic simulations, our results show that outcomes from nonstochastic or deterministic policy simulations can be poor estimates of the distributions of outcomes that result from stochastic simulations of the same policies. We find that nonstochastic simulations may not produce reliable estimates of the mean paths of outcomes. For the FRB-MIT model, we generally reject the hypothesis that the nonstochastic outcome for real GNP in any quarter is the mean of the distribution of the corresponding stochastic outcomes. We also find that nonstochastic simulations generally produce estimates of instability that understate the degree of instability found in the stochastic results. And, more serious, they often rank policies on the basis of expected utility differently than do the stochastic outcomes. Thus, even if our results are not accepted as indicative of the outcomes that would result from the application of the rules we study because of skepticism about the models, our experiments are still important because they show how to derive the implications of these models in a way consistent with the underlying stochastic assumptions.

II. THE NATURE OF THE EXPERIMENTS

For each policy rule and each model, we obtain a sample of sixteen-quarter simulation runs for the period 1969-I through 1972-IV. The sample elements are generated by three kinds of randomness: randomness of coefficients, of

[7]While several comparative studies of the forecasting performance of econometric models were published, the forecast errors were not compared to the standard errors of forecasts for the models and, thus, their specifications were not tested against the forecast errors they produced.

additive disturbances, and of exogenous variables. The randomness is such as to generate distributions of outcomes consistent with the estimated models.

The coefficients are taken as random from run to run, but as fixed from quarter to quarter within each sixteen-quarter run, a view consistent with the specifications assumed by the model builders.[8] The random parameters are generated equation by equation.[9] If the ith estimated equation of a model contains a vector of parameters, b_i, then random values of b_i are generated according to the following matrix equation,

$$b_i = \bar{b}_i + R_i v,$$

where $\bar{b}_i$ is the vector of point estimates of b_i, R_i is a matrix such that $R_i' R_i$ equals the estimated variance-covariance matrix of $\bar{b}_i$, and v is a vector of random variables chosen independently of one another, all from a distribution with mean zero and variance one.[10] It follows, then, that b_i has a distribution with mean $\bar{b}_i$ and a variance-covariance matrix equal to the

---

[8]If the true parameters are, instead, random from period to period, we are understating the degree to which parameters are random and overstating the degree to which residuals are random. Such misassignment of randomness would seem to bias our results in favor of discretionary policies, but such an effect is limited by the nonlinearities of the models we are examining. Disturbances that are additive equation by equation can end up determining solutions multiplicatively, while the converse can be true for parameters. Only in linear systems is there a sharp distinction between the effects of random parameters and the effects of random disturbances.

[9]It was claimed that we should have taken account of possible correlation among disturbances from different equations, which would, of course, imply correlations among parameter estimates from different equations. In the presence of such correlations, both ordinary least squares and two-stage least squares are inefficient procedures. Since the authors of the models did not state explicitly their model assumptions regarding this question, and since they did not choose an estimation procedure to deal with it--e.g., three-stage least squares--we proceeded under the assumption that the authors did not regard possible correlations among disturbances as a problem that warranted action.

[10]The elements of v and all the underlying random variables used are generated independently from a single distribution, a truncated normal distribution. Let x be a normal zero-one random variable. We draw values of x and accept only those for which $|x|$ is less than 2. The accepted x's have mean zero and variance $(.880)^2$, so that $v = (1.137)x$ has mean zero and variance one, the desired distribution.

estimated variance-covariance matrix.[11] This procedure is followed for every estimated equation of every model.

The additive disturbance for each estimated equation is treated as random from run to run and from quarter to quarter within each run. It is chosen independently over time from a distribution with mean zero and variance equal to the estimated residual variance for that equation. The independence assumption is needed if we are to attribute consistency to the estimated variances and covariances that we use.[12]

The third kind of randomness pertains to the noninstrument exogenous variables. The variables in that class differ from model to model, but often include, for example, population, exports, and federal government expenditures. (Since we have chosen to use as fiscal instruments only certain tax rates, all other potential fiscal instruments are treated as uncontrolled.) We assume that all noninstrument exogenous variables are generated by third-order autoregressive schemes of the form:

$$Z_t = a_0 + a_1 Z_{t-1} + a_2 Z_{t-2} + a_3 Z_{t-3} + u_t,$$

where Z_t is the value of a noninstrument exogenous variable in quarter t. We have estimated such equations by ordinary least squares for each of the noninstrument exogenous variables in each of the models.[13] Those equations are treated as are all other estimated equations of the models; the parameters are chosen randomly from run to run, and the disturbance randomly from quarter to quarter. But, here, the residual variance is taken to be one-half the estimated residual variance, the argument being that if one had set out to build a model that explained all noninstrument variables, one could have

---

[11]We do, however, require that each element of b_i have the same sign as the corresponding element of $\overline{b}_i$. If the sign constraint is violated, we choose a new random vector, v. The sign constraint expresses our prior views about the distributions of the true parameters. In no instance did it turn out to be binding.

[12]If the true residuals are serially correlated, we are, in a sense, attributing too much variance to them. But, that may be more than offset by the adjustments that should then be made in the estimated variances. Serial dependence has the effect of reducing degrees of freedom, and the implied adjustment would lead to larger estimated variances.

[13]In a few cases, multicollinearity prevented us from inverting the moment matrix of the right-hand side variables. In those cases, we used a lower order scheme.

done better explaining the noninstrument exogenous variables than we do with the autoregressive schemes. Those schemes can imply very large forecast variances when used, as we use them, to forecast many periods ahead; in any particular sixteen-quarter simulation run, the values in each quarter depend on the corresponding values in all previous simulated quarters. Thus, as we proceed quarter by quarter, the effects of the disturbances drawn in the early quarters can be magnified.

We simulate all policy rules for a given model on the same sample of random variables so that differences among the distributions of outcomes for different policies can be attributed entirely to the policies. The basic random sample is determined from simulations of a nondiscretionary policy. Those simulations are conducted as follows. To each set of random parameters a sixteen-quarter set of random disturbances is associated, both for the structural equations and for the autoregressive schemes. If a solution is obtained for all sixteen quarters on such a sample, then all other policies are run on that sample. If a solution is not obtained in any quarter of the sixteen-quarter run, then that sample is discarded and is not used for any other policy.[14] In either case, we proceed to a new random sample of both parameters and disturbances and start a new sixteen-quarter run.

The procedure for a nonconvergence turned out never to be implemented for the Michigan model. For that model, sixteen-quarter solutions were obtained for all random samples tried. Moreover, no nonconvergences resulted when the other policies were applied to that basic sample. The record was very different for the FRB-MIT and Wharton models. There, as shall be described below, for the nondiscretionary policy the model failed to converge to a solution or converged to a nonsensical solution on many random samples and, when other policies were applied to the FRB-MIT model, it did not converge to a sensible solution on some of the samples in the basic sample.

For any policy rule and model, a particular sixteen-quarter element of the sample of outcomes is obtained as follows. The first policy decision is made at the beginning of the first quarter of 1969 and determines the 1969-I values of the instruments on the basis of actual data up through 1968-IV. That first policy action and a sample of values of parameters and disturbances——both for the "structural equations" and for the autoregressive schemes we supply——determine the 1969-I values of all noninstrument variables. Then, those values together with actual data up through 1968-IV determine the 1969-II values of the instruments. The 1969-II values of the instruments and

[14] All three models are nonlinear and are solved by way of an iterative procedure that may not always converge to a solution, let alone a plausible solution.

a new sample of disturbances, both for the "structural" and autoregressive equations, determine the 1969-II values of all noninstrument variables. The process is continued through the fourth quarter of 1972, with the parameters held fixed through all sixteen quarters.

Note that for any discretionary policy rule, the policy actions taken from 1969-II to 1972-IV may differ from sixteen-quarter run to sixteen-quarter run, because the action taken at any time within a particular simulation run depends on what has happened previously within that run. For example, for any policy rule that allows for discretionary fiscal action, tax rates in 1969-II depend on the 1969-I values of endogenous variables which are functions of random variables. The 1969-I policy actions are an exception, because they depend entirely on events prior to 1969-I which are described by actual data. Actual data are used when and only when we need values of variables for dates prior to 1969-I. In that sense, the simulations are entirely endogenous; they could have been performed at the beginning of 1969-I, as soon as data for 1968-IV became available. Moreover, in a sense, there are no exogenous variables in our experiments. The policy rules to be described below are, in effect, the equations for the instrument variables; the autoregressive schemes are the equations for the noninstrument exogenous variables; and the estimated equations and identities that constitute the models are, of course, the equations for the endogenous variables.

Finally, in addition to generating distributions of outcomes for each policy rule, we also obtain one nonstochastic outcome for each policy. The nonstochastic path is obtained by setting all parameters and disturbances equal to their means, both in the structural equations and in the autoregressive schemes.

III. THE MODELS

The three models chosen for our experiments range in size from Michigan with 24 behavioral equations, to Wharton with 51, to FRB-MIT with 75. Each of them was constructed by a group of economists who continuously modify their models and use them to forecast and to evaluate policies. The models differ in the attention they give to different sectors of the economy. For example, in the FRB-MIT model, the largest block of behavioral equations (17) is devoted to the financial sector; in Wharton 6 equations describe the financial sector; while in Michigan there is only one equation, that describing the relationship between long- and short-term interest rates. The models also differ with respect to the degree of interdependence: the FRB-MIT is the most highly interdependent and also has the richest lag structure; Michigan is almost recursive. Despite this, the FRB-MIT model was estimated by ordinary least squares, while Wharton and Michigan were estimated by two-stage least squares.

All the models respond similarly to the usual instruments of economic policy. Monetary policy works via changes in short-term interest rates, with long-term rates affected by way of a distributed lag. Those rates, in turn, affect aggregate demand——investment in residential housing, business and government fixed investment, and, in the FRB-MIT model, consumption. Tax rate changes affect aggregate demand in two ways. They affect disposable incomes of businesses and firms, and, therefore, their expenditures. In the FRB-MIT model, they also affect rates of return.

All three models use quarterly data. A special attempt was made in the FRB-MIT model to take account of serial correlation in the equation residuals. First-order autocorrelation coefficients were estimated, and the implied partial first differences taken. Most of the equations of the Michigan model were estimated in simple first difference form. A special adjustment for autocorrelation was made in only two equations. In Wharton, no account was taken of serial correlation.

The sample periods used for estimating the models also differ. Wharton's sample period starts as early as the first quarter of 1948 and ends in the last quarter of 1968.[15] The FRB-MIT typically uses the post-Korean War period up to late 1966 or early 1967, but a few important equations were fit to data up through 1968-III. In Michigan all stochastic equations were fit to data for the period 1954-I to 1967-IV.[16]

The number of exogenous variables varies with the size of the model, Michigan having less than 20, Wharton 53, and FRB-MIT 70. However, there are only 14 exogenous variables that required autoregressive schemes in Michigan, 34 in Wharton, and 40 in the FRB-MIT model. The others were dummies, time trends, or strictly legally determined variables such as the maximum rate payable on time deposits which, except for the trends, were maintained at their 1968-IV values.

In addition to the model description normally required for simulation experiments, we required estimates of residual variances and of parameter covariance matrices. Wherever possible, the residual variances were taken from the published or mimeographed versions of the models. For Michigan, the coefficient covariance matrices were supplied to us by the authors. For

[15]We have replaced the total labor force equation with one based only on the post-Korean War period. It was given to us by Professor L. Klein.

[16]However, for two equations, the authors supplied us with coefficient estimates different from those that appear in the published version.

the FRB-MIT model, they were estimated for a project being undertaken under the auspices of the Federal Reserve Bank of Minneapolis, and were made available to us.[17] For Wharton, we computed for each structural equation the inverse of the moment matrix of the right-hand side variables and multiplied that by the residual variance reported in the model description. Admittedly, for all equations estimated by two-stage least squares, such moment matrices are not identical to those that would be obtained from the two-stage procedure. However, no disservice was done to Wharton. Any quadratic form of the inverse of the moment matrix computed from the original series cannot exceed the corresponding quadratic form of the inverse computed from the predictors estimated in the first-stage regressions of two-stage least squares. Thus, if anything, we understate the variance of the coefficients.

IV. THE POLICY INSTRUMENTS

Our experiments involve the use of both monetary and fiscal instruments. The fiscal instruments are the personal and corporate income tax rates, which, however, are used as a single instrument; the same percentage change is always imposed on both tax rates. There are two alternative monetary instruments: the rate on 4- to 6-month prime commercial paper and unborrowed reserves. They are alternative instruments because when one of them is the instrument, the other is necessarily endogenous.[18] Both the commercial paper rate and unborrowed reserves are potential instruments because the Federal Reserve can, if it wishes, peg the rate on commercial paper from quarter to quarter, or can, if it wishes, control unborrowed reserves almost perfectly. (It cannot, of course, do both simultaneously.) The rate on commercial paper was chosen as one of the monetary instruments because it is the only potential monetary instrument common to all three models. All discretionary monetary policies are carried out with that rate as the instrument. Nondiscretionary monetary policy is carried out in two ways: with the interest rate exogenous and constant for all sixteen quarters, and with unborrowed reserves exogenous and growing by one per cent per quarter. The unborrowed reserves experiments can be attempted only in the FRB-MIT and Wharton models.

[17]The procedure is described in a forthcoming paper by J. Kareken, T. Muench, T. Supel, and N. Wallace, "Determining the Optimum Monetary Instrument."

[18]If the models are correctly specified, it is valid to use them to inquire about the effects of using alternative instruments. Large structural models of the economy are constructed in order to allow us to study the effects of changes in structure, and a change in instruments is one kind of change in structure.

Unborrowed reserves was chosen as an instrument because it was the model builders' choice as the monetary instrument and because control of it is generally thought to imply approximate control of the money stock. In the models, as in the economy, complete control of unborrowed reserves does not imply complete control of the money stock. One reason for the lack of control is the ability of banks to borrow from the Federal Reserve. In order to reduce changes in bank borrowings from the Federal Reserve, or, to put it differently, to reduce changes in banks' desired holdings of free reserves, the discount rate is always set one-half of a per cent above the rate on commercial paper in the previous quarter.[19] While that rule should make the connection between unborrowed reserves and the money stock closer than it would otherwise be, our stochastic treatment still allows for a number of slippages. We treat required reserves as a stochastic function of the levels of demand and time deposits because given legal reserve requirements——which we hold fixed throughout our experiments——required reserves depend on the distribution of deposits by class of bank, a stochastic element. And we treat the demand for free reserves stochastically, just as we do all other structural relationships.

Tax rates were chosen as the fiscal instrument because we believe they are closer to being actual instruments of macroeconomic policy than are government expenditures, even though legislation would be required in order to allow tax rates to vary quarter by quarter in accord with a macroeconomic criterion.[20] Even assuming such an institutional change, however, serious questions about controllability were posed because the models do not, in general, contain as variables the tax schedules that would be altered by policy. An exception is the FRB-MIT treatment of corporate taxes, and, to a certain extent, its treatment of personal taxes.

In the FRB-MIT model, corporate tax liabilities are determined by an estimated equation in which the maximum corporate tax rate appears as a variable. The treatment of personal taxes is similar. There exists a variable, defined as the average tax rate under Federal personal income tax, which was

[19]The discount rate has an effect on income and the price level only when unborrowed reserves is exogenous. When the commercial paper rate is exogenous, the discount rate is irrelevant; it affects only free reserves and unborrowed reserves.

[20]Again the question arises: Are the models appropriate for studying the effects of such fiscal policies, given that such policies were not in effect during the sample periods? First of all, as will become clear in the next section, even if the fiscal rules are known, one can predict the course of tax rates only by predicting the course of the economy. But, more important, if these models cannot be used to study the effects of such fiscal policies, those effects cannot be studied at all.

constructed independently of current data on tax revenue and which appears in an estimated equation determining revenue. We treat both tax rates as controllable instruments. They appear in structural equations that we treat as we do all other structural equations; namely, we allow randomness in these relationships too.

In the Wharton and Michigan models, tax rates do not appear as variables. There are estimated equations for tax revenues, which for personal and corporate taxes in both models can be represented schematically as,

$$T = a_0 + a_1 B + u,$$

where T is revenue, B is the assumed tax base, and u is a disturbance. The parameters, a_0 and a_1 are estimated from data for short periods over which tax laws are uniform. We adapt such equations as follows. (i) The coefficient a_1 is replaced by the product of a tax rate, τ, and a coefficient, a^*. (ii) The mean of a^* is set at unity. The variance-covariance matrix of (a_1, a^*) and the variance of u are taken to be the relevant estimated variances and covariances in the linear regression of T on B over the whole data period. (iii) The tax rate, τ' is treated as controllable with an initial value equal to the point estimate of a_1 supplied by the model. For example, the Wharton personal tax equation is

$$TP = -12.8 + (.16 + SLTP)(\text{Base}),$$

where TP is personal tax and nontax payments in current dollars, and $SLTP$ is a "slope adjustment." We rewrite the equation as

$$TP = a_0 + a^*(\tau_p)(\text{Base}) + u.$$

The parameters a_0 and a^*, which vary randomly from run to run, are given by the equation,

$$\begin{bmatrix} a_0 \\ \\ a^* \end{bmatrix} = \begin{bmatrix} -12.8 \\ \\ 1.0 \end{bmatrix} + R \begin{bmatrix} v_1 \\ \\ v_2 \end{bmatrix}$$

where R is such that RR' equals the estimated variance-covariance matrix from a linear regression of TP on the base over the whole data period, and where the v's are random variables, independently chosen from a distribution with mean zero and variance one. The disturbance, u, which varies from quarter to quarter, has mean zero and variance equal to the estimated residual variance from the same regression. The tax rate, τ_p, is assumed controllable, with an initial, 1968-IV value of .16.

A controllable corporate tax rate for the Wharton model and controllable personal and corporate tax rates for the Michigan model are defined in the same way. In each case we use the form of the revenue equation given in the model and use as initial values for the tax rates the point estimates supplied by the model. The initial values of the controllable tax rates for the different models are listed below.

Model	Personal	Corporate
FRB-MIT	.231	.528
Wharton	.16	.46
Michigan	.20	.47

One way to rationalize the differences among models is to say that the models summarize the same tax law in different ways. As a consequence, they apply their resulting "average" rate to different bases. For example, the Wharton personal tax base includes social security contributions of individuals, while the Michigan base does not.

In our experiments, fiscal policy is conducted by making the same percentage changes in the rates for all the models. The implicit assumption is that a given percentage change in all those rates corresponds to a given change in tax laws of the surcharge type. We start, by the way, with the 1968 surcharge fully in effect.

V. THE POLICY RULES

The policy rules we propose to investigate recognize the policy makers' utility tradeoff between growth and inflation and take some account of lags. Our operating criteria are based on the per cent unemployed (un) as a measure of the departure from attainable growth and on the percentage rate of change of the GNP deflator (p) (1958 = 1.0). Thus, for purposes of determining policy, we compute at the beginning of each quarter, t, the following weighted averages:

$$P_t = 100 \sum_{1}^{4} a_i (p_{t-i} - p_{t-i-1})/p_{t-i-1}$$

$$U_t = \sum_{1}^{4} a_i \, un_{t-i}$$

where P_t is the weighted average of the percentage change in the price level, U_t is the weighted average of the unemployment rate, and $a_1 = .4$, $a_2 = .3$, $a_3 = .2$, and $a_4 = .1$.

Action is taken based on the values of P_t and U_t according to the following discrete classes.

P

	$-.5\%$		$.5\%$		1.5%		$+\infty$

		P		
	$-.5\%$	$.5\%$	1.5%	$+\infty$
0	(1,1) No action	(1,2) Moderate tightening	(1,3) Extreme tightening
4%	(2,1) Moderate ease	(2,2) No action	(2,3) Moderate tightening
6%	(3,1) Extreme ease	(3,2) Moderate ease	(3,3) No action
100%			

U is the row variable.

Here, for example, cell (1,1) represents all combinations of P and U such that P, the weighted average of the percentage change in the price level over the past four quarters, is between $-.5$ and $.5$ per cent, and U, the weighted average of the unemployment rate over the past four quarters, is less than 4 per cent. If (P_t, U_t) lies in (1,1), no action is taken. Actions are defined as follows.[21]

No action means keep all instruments unchanged.

Moderate action means move the instrument(s) a moderate amount subject to the following proviso. Unless the situation at t is worse than at $t-1$, action may be taken at t only if action in the same direction was not taken either at $t-1$ or $t-2$.

Extreme action means move the instrument(s) an extreme amount subject to the following proviso. Unless the situation at t is worse than that at $t-1$, action may be taken at t only if action in the same direction was not taken at $t-1$. But this waiting rule is waived if in cell (3,1), $U_t - U_{t-1} > 1$; and if in cell (1,3), $P_t - P_{t-1} > .25$.

---

[21]We also specified actions for $P < -.5$ per cent, but such values were not encountered.

In the provisos, worse means that (P_t, U_t) lies in a worse cell than (P_{t-1}, U_{t-1}), where for this purpose, iso-utility lines run diagonally southwest in the table above, with cell (1,1) having the highest utility. Thus, for example, if (P_t, U_t) lies in cell (3,1) and (P_{t-1}, U_{t-1}) had been in (2,1), then instruments are moved an extreme amount in the direction of ease even if they had been moved in the direction of ease at t-1, because of the extreme action proviso.

Given that scheme, we now define moderate and extreme actions in terms of our instruments: the interest rate for discretionary monetary policy, tax rates for discretionary fiscal policy. The scheme above applies, of course, only when discretionary policies are in effect. Altogether, we examine ten policy rules defined in terms of percentage changes in the instruments in Table 1. In the table, R stands for the rate on four- to six-month commercial paper (R_{cp}), and τ for both the personal and corporate tax rates. The plus (+) is used whenever tightening action is called for, and the minus (−) whenever easing action is called for.

TABLE 1

Policy Actions at Time t

Policy	$\pm (R_t - R_{t-1})/R_{t-1}$		$\pm (\tau_t - \tau_{t-1})/\tau_{t-1}$	
	Moderate	Extreme	Moderate	Extreme
1. Nondiscretionary, R_{cp} exogenous	0	0	0	0
2. Monetary I, R_{cp} exogenous	.1	.2	0	0
3. Fiscal I, R_{cp} exogenous	0	0	.05	.10
4. Joint I, R_{cp} exogenous	.05	.1	.025	.05
5. Monetary II, R_{cp} exogenous	.2	.4	0	0
6. Fiscal II, R_{cp} exogenous	0	0	.1	.2
7. Joint II, R_{cp} exogenous	.1	.2	.05	.1
8. Nondiscretionary, unborrowed reserves exogenous	Endogenous		0	0
9. Fiscal I, unborrowed reserves exogenous	Endogenous		.05	.10
10. Fiscal II, unborrowed reserves exogeneous	Endogenous		.1	.2

For policies 8, 9, and 10, unborrowed reserves grow one per cent per quarter.[22] Thus all three involve nondiscretionary monetary policy, just as do policies 1, 3, and 6, but of a different kind. Note that extreme action is always twice moderate action, that the Roman two (II) policies, hereafter called strong policies, are always twice the Roman one (I) or weak policies, and that

[22] And the discount rate is set one-half of a percent above the value of R_{cp} in the previous quarter.

the joint policies are a simple average of the corresponding monetary and fiscal policies. Wherever possible, all rules are applied to all three models.

Although the rules are necessarily arbitrary, they seem not unlike those that might be applied.[23] They were chosen prior to any experimentation by us on the three models to which we apply them. It would have been desirable to standardize, on the one hand, all the weak policies and, on the other hand, all the strong policies so that within each group all policies have the same effect on some criterion, say, the two-quarter expected change in the unemployment rate. The problem is that it would take a great deal of experimentation to determine such equivalences, nor is it easy to single out a criterion of equivalence.

VI. SUMMARY STATISTICS

1. Growth Rates and Variances Around Constant Growth Rate Paths

We analyze the results mainly in terms of growth rates of real GNP and of the GNP deflator and in terms of variance around the respective constant growth rate paths. We assume that

$$X_{tj} = X^0 e^{\gamma_j t} e^{\mu_{tj}} \tag{1}$$

where X_{tj} stands either for real GNP in quarter t of the jth sixteen-quarter run, y_{tj}, or for the GNP deflator in quarter t of the jth run, p_{tj} (or for the money stock); X^0 is the 1968-IV value of X, the value in the quarter before our runs begin, and is common to all runs; the disturbance, u_{tj}, is assumed to have expected value zero and variance independent of t, $t=1,2,\ldots,16$; and, although we shall not always mention it, all tests for significance depend on the assumption that u is normally distributed. Equation 1 says that X_{tj} grows on the average at a constant rate of growth per quarter, γ_j, starting from its 1968-IV value.

We estimate γ_j and σ_u^2 the variance of u, in a least squares regression. Taking the natural logarithm of each side of (1):

[23]These rules seem reasonable to us and seem to conform to Phillip's recommendation: "A strong proportional element is needed as the main basis of the policy, sufficient integral correction should be added to obtain complete correction of an error within a reasonable time and an element of derivative correction is required to overcome the oscillatory tendencies which may be introduced by the other two elements of the policy." (A. P. Phillips, "Stabilization Policy in a Closed Economy," *Economic Journal*, June 1954.) The proportional element in our rule is the relatively heavy weighting given to the most recent observation. The integral element is the positive weighting of lagged observations, which, in any case, seems desirable for a stochastic model. The derivative element is the set of waiting rules.

$$\log X_{tj} - \log X^0 = \gamma_j t + u_{tj}. \qquad (t = 1, 2, \ldots, 16)$$

Thus, we regress $\log X_{tj} - \log X^0$ on t, constraining the intercept to be zero. For example, for the Michigan model, there are 50 sixteen-quarter runs for each of seven policies, so that there are 7(50) such regressions for prices (X_{tj} = p_{tj}) and 7(50) such regressions for real output ($X_{tj} = y_{tj}$). We, henceforth, denote the individual growth rate estimates by $\gamma \ldots \gamma_y$ for real income, γ_p for prices, and the individual residual variances by $\sigma^2 \ldots \sigma_y^2$ for the estimated variance of u when $X = y$, σ_p^2 when $X = p$.

For each policy, we compute average growth rates

$$\bar{\gamma}_y = (1/N) \sum_j \gamma_y \qquad\qquad (j = 1, 2, \ldots, N)$$

and

$$\bar{\gamma}_p = (1/N) \sum_j \gamma_p \qquad\qquad (j = 1, 2, \ldots, N)$$

where N is the number of sixteen-quarter runs for which we have output ($N = 50$) for the Michigan model; $\bar{\gamma}$ is identical to the regression coefficient of time in a pooled regression of $\log X_{tj} - \log X^0$ on t run on all $16N$ observations; and the standard error of estimate of $\bar{\gamma}$, denoted $\sigma(\bar{\gamma})$ and always presented in parentheses beneath the corresponding $\bar{\gamma}$, is, in effect, estimated in that pooled regression.

In addition to the average growth rates, we focus on two kinds of variance, within-path variance and among-path variance. For each sixteen-quarter run, within-path variance is measured by σ^2, a measure of within-path stability. For each policy, we compute

$$\bar{\sigma}_y^2 = (1/N) \sum_j \sigma_y^2$$

and

$$\bar{\sigma}_p^2 = (1/N) \sum_j \sigma_p^2$$

average within-path variance. We report corresponding standard deviations, $\bar{\sigma}_y$ and $\bar{\sigma}_p$. Note that those are average standard deviations based only on the residual variance within each sixteen-quarter regression.

Since the time path of the economy is, according to the particular model under consideration, characterized by a sixteen-quarter path like one in our sample of N, the $\bar{\gamma}$'s are measures of the growth rates that will be experienced, and the $\bar{\sigma}$'s are measures of the instability that will be experienced. According to the models, those statistics are representative of characteristics of the economy. Finally, note that $\bar{\gamma}$'s and $\bar{\sigma}$'s are also computed for the single nonstochastic path produced for each policy.

The second kind of variance we examine, among-path variance, is in part attributable to our lack of knowledge about the economy, in particular, to our uncertainty about the true parameters. For a given policy, the among-path variance is a function of the distribution of the N individual growth rate estimates. As measures of those distributions, we report for each policy

$$\sigma(\gamma) = [\Sigma(\gamma-\bar{\gamma})^2/(N-1)]^{1/2}$$

for both real income, $\sigma(\gamma_y)$, and prices, $\sigma(\gamma_p)$. In addition, we report the correlation among the γ_y's and γ_p's for each policy, denoted by $\rho(\gamma_y,\gamma_p)$.

For testing purposes, we can summarize the above by an analysis of variance table.[24] In the RMS column, the total-residuals entry is the residual standard deviation from the pooled regression. $\sigma(\bar{\gamma})$ is equal to that divided by $(N\Sigma t^2)^{1/2}$. The among-samples entry in that column is the standard deviation of the distribution of the individual γ's multiplied by the square root of the second moment of the independent variable, time, about its 1968-IV value, which is zero. The within-samples entry in the RMS column is simply the average within-path standard deviation.

We wish to test for the following comparisons: (i) $\bar{\gamma}$'s across policies for stochastic and nonstochastic outcomes, (ii) $\bar{\sigma}$'s across policies for stochastic and nonstochastic outcomes, (iii) $\sigma(\gamma)$'s across policies, and, finally, (iv) individual γ's within each policy. The appropriate test statistics are as follows: (i) If $|\bar{\gamma}-\bar{\gamma}'|/[\sigma^2(\bar{\gamma}) + \sigma^2(\bar{\gamma}')]^{1/2} > t_c$, then we accept $\bar{\gamma} \neq \bar{\gamma}'$, where t_c is the critical value from the t distribution with a chosen significance level and the appropriate degrees of freedom. When $\bar{\gamma}$ and $\bar{\gamma}'$ are stochastic means for different policies, there are $2(16N-1)$ degrees of freedom. (ii) If $\bar{\sigma}/\bar{\sigma}' > (F_c)^{1/2}$ (where $\bar{\sigma} > \bar{\sigma}'$), then we accept the hypothesis $\bar{\sigma} > \bar{\sigma}'$, where F_c is the critical value from the F distribution with a chosen significance level and $15N$ and $15N$ degrees of freedom, and, where for nonstochastic outcomes, $N=1$. (iii) This test is the same as for (ii), except that $\sigma(\gamma)$ replaces $\bar{\sigma}$ and F_c now has $N-1$ and $N-1$ degrees of freedom. (iv) The second entry in the RMS column divided by the third is distributed as the $(F)^{1/2}$ with $N-1$ and $15N$ degrees of freedom, so that if that ratio exceeds the appropriate $(F_c)^{1/2}$, we accept the hypothesis that the individual γ's are not all equal.

[24]The appendix contains a sample table.

Finally, note that all tests for comparisons across policies are only suggestive, because they are based on statistics computed from the same samples of random variables; not from independent samples, the assumption that underlies the tests.

2. Expected Utility

Another related way to summarize outcomes is to compute expected utility for each policy for a class of utility functions. We represent utility by

$$U = (1/16) \sum_{1}^{16} \left[y_t^{1/2} + b \ 10^4 \ (p_t - p_{t-1} / p_{t-1})^2 \right]$$

where in this subsection y is per capita real GNP in 1958 prices, and p is the GNP deflator. The subscript t ranges over the sixteen simulated quarters.

The parameter b, which takes only nonpositive values, determines the tradeoff between per capita real income and percentage price variance around the value of the price level in the previous quarter. At any time and at a given value of y_t, the tradeoff is given by

$$\left. \frac{dy_t}{10^4 d \left[(p_t - p_{t-1} / p_{t-1})^2 \right]} \right|_{dU=0} = -2by_t^{1/2}$$

Thus, for y_t =$3,600, which is approximately the 1968-IV value, and b=−.3, the utility function implies indifference between an addition to per capita real income of one per cent and an addition to the percentage variance of prices of one percentage point. The closer b is to zero, the less concern there is for price variance. We shall compute expected utility for values of b ranging from zero to −.3.

Note that because y appears in the utility function raised to a power less than one, the tradeoff between real income and price variance also depends on y. The larger y is, the more y is willingly given up to reduce price variance. Raising y to the power one-half also imposes risk aversion. At a given value for price variance, fair gambles on y are always rejected. Put differently, raising y to the power one-half makes expected utility inversely dependent on the variance of y. A second-order Taylor expansion of $y^{1/2}$ about the expected value of y implies

$$E(y^{1/2}) = (Ey)^{1/2} \left[1 - (1/8)E \left(\frac{y - Ey}{Ey} \right)^2 \right]$$

Thus, the expected value of $y^{1/2}$ is a decreasing function of the percentage variance of y, but only a mildly decreasing function.[25]

For each policy, we compute expected utility by averaging over the N outcomes of U for that policy. The policies are then ranked. The nonstochastic outcomes are also ranked by U.

VII. RESULTS, THE FRB-MIT MODEL

1. Convergence and the Sample

The basic random sample was generated by applying to random samples, as described in Section II, nondiscretionary policy with tax rates held constant and unborrowed reserves growing one per cent per quarter (policy 8). Out of 83 sixteen-quarter runs attempted, 50 sensible sixteen-quarter solutions were obtained; in 30 cases the model failed to converge during some quarter of the run, and in three of the runs the unemployment rate converged to a negative value which led us to discard those runs. The record of sensible sixteen-quarter solutions that were obtained when the other nine policies were applied to the basic 50 random samples is shown in Table 2.[26]

The result, though, is a common random sample of only 35 on which sensible sixteen-quarter solutions were obtained for all ten policies. All our subsequent analysis and discussion of the FRB-MIT model are based on that sample of 35.

2. Average Stochastic Growth Rates

The average stochastic growth rates, $\bar{\gamma}_y$'s for real GNP and $\bar{\gamma}_p$'s for the GNP deflator, are shown in the first and third columns of Table 3. The $\bar{\gamma}_y$'s range from .05 for policy 1, the policy in which the interest rate and tax rates are held constant, to .84 for policy 6, the strong fiscal policy with the interest rate held constant. That is, they range from a rate slightly above zero to one

[25]For example, the average percentage within-path standard deviation of real output in the FRB-MIT model is as high as 6 per cent. If that represented the percentage standard deviation of per capita income around its expected value, it would imply $E[(y-Ey)/Ey]^2 = (.06)^2$. According to our utility function, there is indifference between, on the one hand, that variance and $Ey = \$360.00$, and, on the other hand, zero variance of y and $Ey = \$359.50$.

[26]A solution is not sensible if variables have economically meaningless values. This criterion resulted in discarding a number of runs for which the unemployment rate was negative.

TABLE 2.

FRB–MIT Model, the Convergence Record by Policy

Policy	Number of Sensible Sixteen-Quarter Solutions Out of Fifty Attempts
1. Nondiscretionary, R_{cp} exogenous	47
2. Monetary I, R_{cp} exogenous	47
3. Fiscal I, R_{cp} exogenous	47
4. Joint I, R_{cp} exogenous	46
5. Monetary II, R_{cp} exogenous	44
6. Fiscal II, R_{cp} exogenous	46
7. Joint II, R_{cp} exogenous	46
9. Fiscal I, reserves exogenous	49
10. Fiscal II, reserves exogenous	45

implying an annual growth rate of 3.75 per cent. Note that each $\bar{\gamma}_y$ for the weak version of each policy is substantially lower than that for the corresponding strong version, and that the fiscal policies (3 and 6) produce higher real growth rates than do the corresponding joint policies, which, in turn, produce higher growth rates than do the corresponding monetary policies. (It turned out that after the initial moderate tightening action in 1969-I, which is exogenous and common to all runs, our policy rules implied easing actions, on the average, throughout the remaining fifteen quarters of the stochastic runs of this model.) In contrast, the $\bar{\gamma}_p$'s vary very little. They range from .11 for policy 8 to .27, only slightly greater than 1 per cent per year, for policy 7. The correlation between the $\bar{\gamma}_y$'s and $\bar{\gamma}_p$'s across policies is .89; on average, higher rates of growth of real output are accompanied by higher rates of growth of the price level, as shown in Figure 1. Although the direction of tradeoff between the average growth rates of real output and prices is what one expects to find, the relative unresponsiveness of prices is somewhat surprising. Given our policy rules, the relative constancy of prices helps account for the easing actions taken in this model.

3. Average Stochastic Within-Path Variance

Policies, of course, are not judged solely by growth rates, but also by the degree of stability around the constant growth rate path. For the 35 paths for each policy, instability is measured by the average within-path standard

TABLE 3

FRB-MIT Model, Rates of Growth and Standard Deviations of Real Income and Price Level

Policy	$\bar{\gamma}_y$		$\bar{\gamma}_p$		$\bar{\sigma}_y$		$\bar{\sigma}_p$		$\sigma(\gamma_y)$	$\sigma(\gamma_p)$	Among Divided by Within		$\rho(\gamma_y\gamma_p)$
	S	NS	S	NS	S	NS	S	NS			y	p	
	(1)	(2)	(3)	(4)	(5)	(6)	(7)	(8)	(9)	(10)	(11)	(12)	(13)
1. Nondiscretionary, R_{cp} exogenous	.05 (.03)	.43 (.07)	.16 (.01)	.18 (.01)	2.31	2.84	0.89	0.39	.75	.27	12.5	11.6	.66
2. Monetary I, R_{cp} exogenous	.25 (0.3)	.74 (.12)	.16 (.01)	.21 (.01)	3.83	4.56	0.89	0.42	.70	.23	7.1	10.0	.57
3. Fiscal I, R_{cp} exogenous	.48 (.03)	.81 (.11)	.20 (.01)	.24 (.01)	4.32	4.27	0.82	0.45	.54	.20	4.8	9.4	.46
4. Joint I, R_{cp} exogenous	.44 (.03)	.78 (.12)	.19 (.01)	.23 (.01)	4.64	4.45	0.89	0.44	.57	.21	4.8	9.0	.47
5. Monetary II, R_{cp} exogenous	.57 (.03)	.96 (.15)	.19 (.01)	.25 (.02)	6.04	5.71	1.34	0.74	.57	.20	3.6	5.6	.34
6. Fiscal II, R_{cp} exogenous	.84 (.03)	1.04 (.13)	.26 (.01)	.29 (.02)	5.65	5.12	1.35	0.93	.33	.14	2.3	4.2	.09
7. Joint II, R_{cp} exogenous	.83 (.03)	1.04 (.14)	.27 (.01)	.28 (.02)	6.56	5.56	2.09	0.93	.45	.16	2.7	2.9	.35
8. Nondiscretionary, reserves exogenous	.12 (.03)	.50 (.11)	.11 (.01)	.15 (.01)	3.56	4.17	0.78	0.40	.62	.20	6.7	10.0	.52
9. Fiscal I, reserves exogenous	.54 (.03)	.77 (.12)	.17 (.01)	.20 (.01)	5.10	4.81	0.89	0.53	.41	.16	3.1	6.8	.20
10. Fiscal II, reserves exogenous	.72 (.03)	.92 (.13)	.21 (.01)	.25 (.02)	5.26	4.96	0.95	0.74	.30	.14	2.2	5.9	.12

NOTE: All rates and standard deviations are expressed in per cent per quarter. S is stochastic and NS is nonstochastic. Standard deviations are in parentheses.

Figure 1. FRB-MIT Model, Average Quarterly Growth Rates,
Price Level vs Real Income

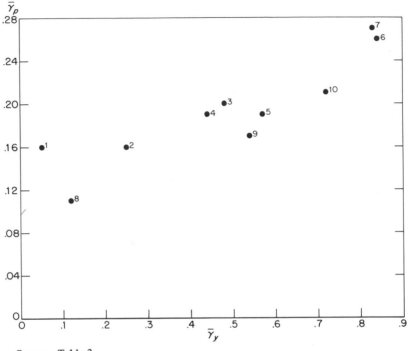

Source: Table 3.

deviations of real output and prices given in columns five and seven of Table
3. For example, for policy 1, the average within-path standard deviation for
real GNP is 2.3 per cent, meaning that the square root of the average squared
deviation of real income for that policy lies 2.3 per cent above or below its
respective constant rate of growth path. If the deviations of log y around each
constant growth rate path are normally distributed, almost one-third of the
real income outcomes for policy 1 deviate by more than 2.3 per cent from
the values determined by those paths.

The $\bar{\sigma}_y$'s are lowest for the nondiscretionary policies, 1 and 8; next lowest
for the four weak policies, 2, 3, 4, and 9; and highest for the four strong
policies, 5, 6, 7, and 10. (At a 10 per cent significance level, any ratio of
those standard deviations in excess of 1.1 is significant.) The pairs $(\bar{\sigma}_y, \bar{\gamma}_y)$
are plotted in Figure 2. There is clearly a positive correlation. Thus, the
relatively high growth rates achieved by the strong discretionary policies (6,

Figure 2. FRB-MIT Model, Real Income, Rates of Growth vs
Within-Path Standard Deviations

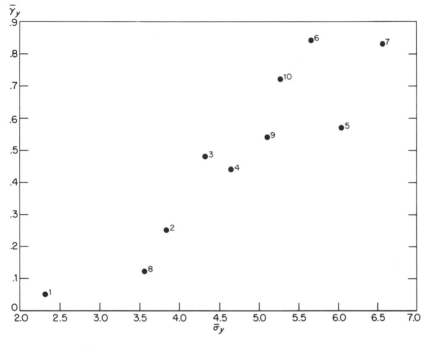

Source: Table 3.

7, and 10) are accompanied by relatively large degrees of instability as we measure it. But care should be taken in interpreting that result. Sixteen quarters may be too short a time interval for measuring instability. Given the lags between changes in the instruments and the effects on real output, each of our runs may constitute only a few "observations," each consisting of an endogenous stimulus to policy, a policy action, and a response. One would like to measure instability over a long sequence of such "observations."

Figure 2 does, however, suggest a pattern among kinds of policies with the interest rate exogenous. The line segment connecting the points for policies 3 and 6 (the fiscal policies) lies above the line segment connecting the points for policies 4 and 7 (the joint policies) which, in turn, lies above a line segment connecting the points for policies 2 and 5 (the monetary policies). If it is assumed that points on those line segments are attainable by different strengths of each respective kind of policy, then those segments suggest that with the interest rate as policy instrument fiscal policies are superior to joint policies, which, in turn, are superior to monetary policies; for any given $\overline{\sigma}_y$ in the range covered by those line segments, the use of fiscal policy gives the highest $\overline{\gamma}_y$, joint policies the next highest, and monetary policies the lowest. Those segments, therefore, are not consistent with the presumption noted in the introduction; namely, that random connections between instruments and targets imply that any expected value can be attained with smaller variance by the use of multiple instruments than by the use of a single instrument. We should note, though, that one way to interpret these results is that fiscal policy works with a shorter lag than monetary policy. Figure 2 also contains a hint that superior combinations of $(\overline{\sigma}_y, \overline{\gamma}_y)$ are attainable with the interest rate constant and various doses of fiscal policy (policies 1, 3, and 6) than with unborrowed reserves growing at 1 per cent per quarter and various doses of fiscal policy (policies 8, 9, and 10).

For prices, the results are less clear-cut, but again the strong policies give rise to the highest $\overline{\sigma}_p$'s. Focusing just on prices, and assuming, of course, that low values for both the growth rate of prices and the variance are preferable to high values, there is a clear-cut preference for each weak policy over its strong counterpart. That being the case, there is no way to rank by kind of policy––monetary, fiscal, and joint––simply on the basis of price performance.

4. Among-Path Variance

For each policy and each variable, among-path variance is a function of the distribution of the 35 individual growth rates. If the true individual growth rates are identical, among-path variance would on average equal within-path variance. If they are not identical, the among variance should exceed the within variance. For each policy, the ratios of the among-path standard deviation to the within-path standard deviation are given in columns 11 and 12 of Table 3. (Ratios that exceed 1.22 are significant at a 10 per cent level of significance.) The hypothesis that the individual growth rates are identical is always rejected for both real output and the price level.

The standard deviation of the distributions of the individual γ's allows us to pose questions like the following: How likely is it that a single path of outcomes for, say, policy 6, is characterized by a real output growth rate smaller than, say, .5 per cent per quarter? The relevant statistic is the difference between the mean growth rate for policy 6, .84, and the posited value, .5, divided by $\sigma(\gamma_y)$ for policy 6, .33. That statistic has the t distribution with 34 degrees of freedom. For the question just posed, its value is just over unity, so the probability for policy 6 of observing a single path with real income growth rate smaller than .5 is about .17. This suggests that even though the mean output growth rates for different policies are estimated quite precisely, for any policy there is substantial uncertainty about the particular path that will occur.

Among-path variance follows a different pattern across policies from that of within-path variance. This may be seen by examining the standard deviations of the distributions of the individual growth rates in columns 9 and 10 of Table 3. Ratios of any $\sigma(\gamma_y)$ to any smaller one, or of any $\sigma(\gamma_p)$ to any smaller one are distributed as the square root of F with 34 and 34 degrees of freedom, the 10 per cent critical value for which is 1.3. There are, therefore, highly significant differences across policies in uncertainty about the growth rates that will prevail.

In Figure 3, we plot $[\sigma(\gamma_y), \sigma(\gamma_p)]$ by policy. The strong fiscal policies do best, while the nondiscretionary policies do very poorly. Indeed, in the result for policy 1, we have a qualified confirmation of what many view as a fundamental proposition; namely, that great uncertainty attaches to a policy of holding the interest rate constant over a substantial period of time. The confirmation is qualified because policy 6——strong fiscal policy with the interest rate held constant——is only insignificantly worse than policy 10——strong fiscal policy with unborrowed reserves growing steadily. Those with very strong a priori attachment to what we have just called a fundamental proposition will take our fairly weak confirmation of it as grounds for rejecting the FRB-MIT model. They might find it hard to believe that policy 8——nondiscretionary policy with unborrowed reserves growing steadily——does almost as poorly by these measures of uncertainty as does policy 1. Such skepticism might be reinforced by the surprising stability of prices remarked upon above.

Finally, note that the individual growth rates for real output and prices for a given policy are positively correlated. (See the last column of Table 3.) That means that when a particular random sample implies a higher than average rate of growth of real income, it is likely to imply a higher than average rate of growth of the price level. That is consistent with the positive correlation of average growth rates across policies. The correlation is strongest for the nondiscretionary policies and weakest for the strong policies, a finding consistent with the general unresponsiveness of prices in this model. Policies tend to affect real output without having much effect on the price level.

5. Stochastic Versus Nonstochastic Outcomes

The average stochastic outcomes and the nonstochastic outcomes for each quarter are shown in Tables 4 (for real output) and 5 (for the price level). The

Figure 3. FRB-MIT Model, Among-Path Standard Deviations,
Price Level vs Real Income

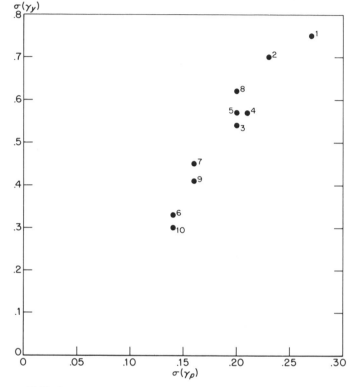

Source: Table 3.

standard deviation of the distribution of stochastic outcomes for each quarter
is presented beneath the corresponding mean. For almost all policies and for
both real income and prices, those standard deviations increase quarter by
quarter from 1969-I on. That was to be expected because those standard
errors are analogous to standard errors of forecast which grow with the
forecast span.

Note that the nonstochastic values for real GNP and for prices are equal to
or exceed the corresponding mean stochastic outcomes. The discrepancy is
small for the price level, fairly large for real output. The consistency of the
discrepancies is explained by the dependence among outcomes across policies
and over time. Dependence across policies arises because the outcomes for

TABLE 4

FRB-MIT Model, Means and Standard Deviations of Real GNP Obtained Each Quarter by Application of the Various Policy Rules

| Year and Quarter | Commercial Paper Rate Exogenous | | | | | | | | | | | | | | | | Unborrowed Reserves Exogenous | | | | | |
| | Non-discretionary | | Monetary 1 | | Fiscal 1 | | Joint 1 | | Monetary 2 | | Fiscal 2 | | Joint 2 | | | Non-discretionary | | Fiscal 1 | | Fiscal 2 | |
	NS	S	NS	S	NS	S	NS	S	NS	S	NS	S	NS	S		NS	S	NS	S	NS	S
1969–I	719	718 (6.8)	719	718 (6.7)	717	716 (6.8)	718	717 (6.7)	718	717 (6.6)	715	715 (6.7)	716	716 (6.7)		718	717 (6.4)	716	716 (6.4)	715	714 (6.3)
1969–II	724	720 (13.2)	722	719 (12.9)	719	716 (13.1)	720	718 (13.0)	719	717 (12.5)	714	713 (12.8)	716	715 (12.7)		720	718 (11.7)	715	714 (11.6)	713	711 (11.4)
1969–III	724	717 (18.4)	720	715 (17.7)	718	712 (18.0)	719	713 (17.9)	716	712 (16.9)	710	707 (17.3)	713	710 (17.2)		717	712 (15.3)	711	708 (15.0)	708	704 (14.5)
1969–IV	722	713 (26.7)	716	709 (25.4)	715	708 (25.5)	716	708 (25.5)	712	706 (24.7)	707	703 (24.2)	709	704 (24.1)		711	706 (21.6)	707	702 (20.8)	704	699 (20.1)
1970–I	718	709 (34.1)	712	705 (32.2)	713	705 (31.9)	712	705 (32.2)	708	701 (30.5)	707	702 (30.1)	706	701 (30.0)		706	700 (27.0)	703	697 (25.7)	702	697 (25.0)
1970–II	717	707 (39.1)	712	702 (36.5)	713	705 (35.0)	712	703 (35.9)	709	699 (34.1)	709	705 (31.1)	708	701 (32.4)		704	697 (30.2)	703	697 (27.5)	704	700 (25.7)
1970–III	707	708 (43.5)	714	703 (40.4)	717	710 (37.1)	715	706 (38.8)	713	701 (37.5)	720	715 (31.9)	716	708 (33.8)		705	697 (33.2)	709	703 (28.8)	714	710 (26.0)
1970–IV	718	710 (49.0)	718	707 (45.4)	725	717 (40.5)	722	712 (42.7)	721	707 (42.2)	733	728 (33.7)	726	719 (36.4)		708	700 (38.5)	718	712 (32.3)	727	724 (28.8)

(continued)

Table 4 (continued)

Year and Quarter	Commercial Paper Rate Exogenous																				Unborrowed Reserves Exogenous						
	Non-discretionary		Monetary 1		Fiscal 1		Joint 1		Monetary 2		Fiscal 2		Joint 2		Non-discretionary		Fiscal 1		Fiscal 2	
	NS	S	NS	S	NS	S	NS	S	NS	S	NS	S	NS	S	NS	S	NS	S	NS	S
1971–I	721	713 (52.4)	727	712 (48.4)	737	726 (42.5)	732	719 (44.7)	734	716 (45.0)	752	744 (34.7)	743	733 (37.5)	714	705 (42.2)	732	724 (34.2)	746	740 (30.3)
1971–II	727	719 (57.8)	741	722 (53.6)	754	739 (47.1)	748	731 (49.0)	753	730 (50.0)	774	765 (37.8)	765	754 (42.4)	726	713 (48.7)	750	740 (39.5)	768	760 (35.1)
1971–III	737	725 (62.3)	759	733 (59.2)	773	752 (51.5)	766	744 (53.2)	777	747 (55.3)	801	785 (39.9)	792	776 (47.7)	741	722 (54.6)	771	758 (45.5)	794	780 (39.2)
1971–IV	748	728 (66.2)	780	743 (65.2)	794	764 (54.5)	788	758 (57.0)	803	766 (59.4)	827	803 (40.4)	820	799 (52.5)	758	729 (58.4)	793	775 (50.6)	818	796 (41.6)
1972–I	762	730 (70.8)	803	754 (71.8)	815	777 (56.5)	810	773 (61.0)	831	787 (63.7)	850	823 (42.6)	847	824 (60.8)	778	738 (62.9)	816	791 (54.2)	838	811 (42.9)
1972–II	780	733 (75.5)	828	765 (78.9)	836	791 (59.1)	833	789 (67.1)	862	810 (67.6)	870	841 (44.8)	873	846 (67.6)	800	748 (66.8)	837	805 (51.8)	856	824 (39.7)
1972–III	798	739 (79.8)	853	778 (83.1)	856	807 (60.2)	856	806 (70.4)	892	838 (71.6)	887	858 (46.0)	896	868 (67.6)	820	762 (71.1)	854	819 (46.9)	868	837 (35.4)
1972–IV	816	745 (84.4)	878	793 (83.4)	874	824 (59.1)	877	823 (69.1)	924	868 (77.4)	903	874 (48.8)	917	895 (92.0)	835	775 (73.1)	867	830 (42.1)	877	847 (32.4)

NOTE: NS is nonstochastic and S is stochastic. Standard deviations are in parentheses.

TABLE 5
FRB-MIT Model, Means and Standard Deviations of Prices Obtained Each Quarter by Application of the Various Policy Rules

Year and Quarter	Commercial Paper Rate Exogenous														Unborrowed Reserves Exogenous					
	Non-discretionary		Monetary 1		Fiscal 1		Joint 1		Monetary 2		Fiscal 2		Joint 2		Non-discretionary		Fiscal 1		Fiscal 2	
	NS	S	NS	S	NS	S	NS	S	NS	S	NS	S	NS	S	NS	S	NS	S	NS	S
1969–I	124	(.3)	124	(.3)	124	(.3)	124	(.3)	124	(.3)	124	(.3)	124	(.3)	124	(.3)	124	(.3)	124	(.3)
1969–II	124	(.5)	124	(.5)	124	(.5)	124	(.5)	124	(.5)	124	(.5)	124	(.5)	124	(.5)	124	(.5)	124	(.5)
1969–III	125	(.7)	125	(.7)	125	(.7)	125	(.7)	125	(.7)	125	(.7)	125	(.7)	125	(.7)	125	(.7)	124	(.7)
1969–IV	125	(.9)	125	(.9)	125	(.9)	125	(.9)	125	(.9)	125	(.9)	125	(.9)	125	(.8)	125	(.8)	125	(.8)
1970–I	125	(1.2)	125	(1.2)	125	(1.1)	125	(1.2)	125	(1.1)	125	(1.1)	125	(1.1)	125	(1.1)	125	(1.1)	125	(1.0)
1970–II	125	(1.5)	125	(1.4)	125	(1.4)	125	(1.4)	125	(1.3)	125	(1.3)	125	(1.3)	125	(1.3)	125	(1.2)	125	(1.2)
1970–III	126	(1.9)	125	(1.8)	125	(1.7)	125	(1.7)	125	(1.7)	125	(1.5)	125	(1.6)	125	(1.6)	125	(1.5)	125	(1.4)
1970–IV	126	(2.3)	125	(2.1)	125	(2.0)	125	(2.1)	125	(2.0)	125	(1.8)	125	(1.8)	125	(1.9)	125	(1.7)	125	(1.6)

(continued)

Table 5 (continued)

Year and Quarter	Commercial Paper Rate Exogenous														Unborrowed Reserves Exogenous					
	Non-discretionary		Monetary 1		Fiscal 1		Joint 1		Monetary 2		Fiscal 2		Joint 2		Non-discretionary		Fiscal 1		Fiscal 2	
	NS	S	NS	S	NS	S	NS	S	NS	S	NS	S	NS	S	NS	S	NS	S	NS	S
1971–I	126	125 (2.8)	125	125 (2.5)	126	125 (2.3)	125	125 (2.4)	125	125 (2.3)	125	125 (2.0)	125	125 (2.0)	125	125 (2.2)	125	125 (1.9)	125	125 (1.8)
1971–II	126	125 (3.2)	125	125 (2.8)	126	125 (2.6)	126	125 (2.7)	125	125 (2.5)	126	125 (2.1)	126	125 (2.2)	125	124 (2.4)	125	125 (2.1)	125	125 (1.9)
1971–III	126	125 (3.6)	126	125 (3.1)	126	126 (2.8)	126	125 (2.9)	126	125 (2.7)	126	126 (2.2)	126	126 (2.2)	125	124 (2.7)	125	125 (2.2)	126	125 (2.0)
1971–IV	126	126 (4.1)	126	125 (3.4)	127	126 (3.0)	126	126 (3.1)	126	125 (3.0)	127	127 (2.3)	127	126 (2.3)	125	125 (3.0)	126	125 (2.3)	127	126 (2.1)
1972–I	126	126 (4.6)	127	126 (3.8)	127	126 (3.3)	127	126 (3.5)	127	126 (3.3)	128	128 (2.6)	128	127 (2.5)	126	125 (3.5)	127	126 (2.7)	128	127 (2.4)
1972–II	126	126 (5.2)	127	126 (4.4)	128	127 (3.8)	128	127 (3.9)	128	127 (4.0)	129	129 (3.0)	129	129 (3.3)	126	125 (4.0)	127	127 (3.0)	128	128 (2.8)
1972–III	127	127 (5.9)	128	127 (5.1)	129	128 (4.4)	128	128 (4.6)	129	128 (4.6)	131	130 (3.4)	131	130 (4.8)	126	126 (4.5)	128	128 (3.5)	129	129 (3.3)
1972–IV	127	127 (6.8)	129	128 (5.8)	130	129 (4.9)	129	129 (5.2)	131	130 (6.4)	132	132 (4.9)	132	134 (9.0)	127	126 (5.0)	129	129 (3.9)	131	130 (3.8)

NOTE: NS is nonstochastic and S is stochastic. Standard deviations are in parentheses.

different policies are generated from a common random sample, while dependence over time arises because of lags in the model. Nevertheless, two related questions can be posed. First, if the mean and standard deviation of the true distribution of outcomes are given by the statistics for the stochastic runs, how likely is it that the nonstochastic outcomes come from that distribution? Quite likely. All nonstochastic outcomes are within one standard deviation of the mean of the distribution of stochastic outcomes. Second, and more important given the widespread use of nonstochastic forecasts and analyses, it may well be asked, How likely is it that the nonstochastic outcome is the mean of the distribution of outcomes? Quite unlikely. The relevant test statistic is the difference between the nonstochastic outcome and the average stochastic outcome divided by the standard deviation of the stochastic *average,* which in each case is the standard deviation (given in parentheses) divided by the square root of 35. Assuming normality, that statistic is distributed as t with 34 degrees of freedom, the critical value for which at a 5 per cent significance level for a two-tailed test is 2.03. For real income, the test statistic exceeds that by a wide margin for most 1972 observations. Thus, for real income, we must either reject the hypothesis that the nonstochastic outcome represents the true mean, or must reject the hypothesis that the sample of 35 stochastic paths for real income is representative of the distribution of possible solution values of the model. One reason for rejecting the first of these is that there is no a priori support for it. Dependent variables are complicated functions of the underlying random variables——the parameters and disturbances. The expected or average value of a function of random variables is in general equal to the function of the expected values (the nonstochastic outcome) only if the function is linear in the random variables. We know in our case that the functions determining real income and the price level are not linear.

Summary data for the comparison of stochastic and nonstochastic outcomes are presented in Table 3. The difference between average values for the stochastic and nonstochastic outcomes is revealed in terms of growth rates in columns 1-4. Columns 5-8 of the table allow us to compare stochastic and nonstochastic within-path standard deviations. Surprisingly, there is no general pattern between the nonstochastic within-path standard deviation for real income and the stochastic for each policy. None of the ratios of the stochastic to the nonstochastic is significantly different from unity. (Such ratios have to exceed 1.33 to be significant at the 10 per cent level.) For prices there is a general pattern. The stochastic within-path standard deviation exceeds the nonstochastic and significantly so except perhaps for policy 10.

Obviously, there is no nonstochastic analogue to the $\sigma(\gamma)$'s so that one cannot deduce from nonstochastic results the substantial differences in uncertainty that accompany the different policies.

6. Utility Rankings

The policies are ranked by expected utility in Table 6 according to the utility function described above. Rankings of both the stochastic and nonstochastic outcomes are given. For the stochastic outcomes, policy 6, which produced the highest average growth rate of real output, holds first place when no weight is given to the price variance term in the utility function. Its standing drops steadily the greater the weight given to that term. Policy 10, strong fiscal policy with unborrowed reserves growing steadily, is the best policy when any of the nonzero weights are given to the price variance term.

The nonstochastic and stochastic rankings differ more the greater the weight given the price variance term. That is not surprising, because the less weight given to the price variance term, the more are policies being judged almost solely on the basis of expected values. As noted in Section VI, while our utility function implies risk aversion with respect to y, it implies only very mild concern for the variance of y.

TABLE 6
FRB-MIT Model, Policies Ranked by Expected Utility

						b					
	0.0		−0.6		−.12		−.18		−.24		−.30	
Ranking	S	NS	S	NS	S	NS	S	NS	S	NS	S	NS
1. (best)	6	6	10	6	10	6	10	6	10	3	10	3
2.	7	7	6	7	9	7	9	7	9	6	9	4
3.	10	5	9	5	3	5	3	10	3	10	3	10
4.	5	10	3	10	6	10	4	3	4	4	4	2
5.	9	3	4	3	4	3	6	5	2	5	2	6
6.	3	4	5	4	2	4	2	4	8	2	8	9
7.	4	2	7	2	5	2	8	2	1	7	1	5
8.	2	9	2	9	8	9	1	9	6	9	6	7
9.	8	8	8	8	1	1	5	1	5	1	5	1
10. (worst)	1	1	1	1	7	8	7	8	7	8	7	8

NOTE: Utility $= U = (1/16) \sum_{1}^{16} \left[y_t^{1/2} + b\,10^4\,(p_t - p_{t-1}/p_{t-1})^2 \right]$

7. The Money Stock

We begin by describing the behavior of the money stock in the runs with unborrowed reserves exogenous and growing at 1 per cent per quarter, the policy 8, 9, and 10 runs. Table 7 contains summary statistics based on the same computation scheme for growth rates as is used throughout for real output and the price level. The money stock, m, is the sum of demand deposits and currency.

The $\bar{\sigma}_m$'s, which measure the average within-path variance of m, reveal a high degree of instability for the stock of money under policies 8, 9, and 10. If log m is normally distributed, almost one-third of the stochastically determined quarterly values of the money stock deviate by more than 2.5 per cent from their respective constant rate of growth paths, even though unborrowed reserves are growing steadily at 1 per cent per quarter. At a base of about \$200 billion, that amounts to a quarterly "miss" in excess of \$5

TABLE 7

FRB-MIT Model, Growth Rates and Standard Deviations of the Money Stock

Policy	$\bar{\gamma}_m$		$\bar{\sigma}_m$		$\sigma(\gamma_m)$	Among Divided by Within	Total Standard Deviation
	S	NS	S	NS			
1. Nondiscretionary, R_{cp} exogenous	.35 (.04)	.61 (.03)	2.37	1.26	.87	14.2	8.60
2. Monetary I, R_{cp} exogenous	1.13 (.03)	1.60 (.15)	4.64	5.64	.48	4.0	6.42
3. Fiscal I, R_{cp} exogenous	.65 (.03)	.90 (.06)	2.88	2.50	.64	8.5	6.67
4. Joint I, R_{cp} exogenous	.91 (.03)	1.21 (.10)	3.93	3.78	.52	5.1	6.25
5. Monetary II, R_{cp} exogenous	2.35 (.06)	2.64 (.25)	9.84	9.79	.90	3.5	12.84
6. Fiscal II, R_{cp} exogenous	.94 (.03)	1.09 (.09)	4.06	3.60	.47	4.5	5.95
7. Joint II, R_{cp} exogenous	1.57 (.04)	1.72 (.15)	6.87	5.94	.51	2.9	8.27
8. Nondiscretionary, reserves exogenous	.55 (.01)	.59 (.06)	2.69	2.18	.21	3.0	3.29
9. Fiscal I, reserves exogenous	.51 (.02)	.61 (.06)	2.55	2.29	.27	4.1	3.56
10. Fiscal II, reserves exogenous	.49 (.02)	.63 (.06)	2.46	2.41	.29	4.5	3.62

NOTE: All rates and standard deviations are expressed in per cents per quarter. S is stochastic and NS is nonstochastic. Standard deviations are in parentheses.

billion about one-third of the time, and that is only the within-path "miss." There is, in addition, significant among-path variance. For example, the probability for policies 8, 9, and 10 of experiencing a growth rate 50 per cent above or below the average for those policies is about .18. The last column of Table 7, which gives the average standard deviation around the pooled growth rate path, combines within- and among-path variance. Given normality, it implies that about one-third of the quarterly observations for policies 9 and 10 lie more than 3.5 per cent from the average constant growth path for those policies.

These results raise questions both about (i) the usefulness of unborrowed reserves as an exogenous monetary instrument in a quarterly model, and about (ii) the validity of the assumption made in these models that unborrowed reserves was an exogenous monetary instrument during the sample period. It is obvious that the Federal Reserve can, if it wishes, control the stock of money much more closely than is suggested by the variances in Table 7. It is no less obvious that the Federal Reserve has never set a value for the average stock of unborrowed reserves for a calendar quarter independent of what was occurring during the quarter. Even if unborrowed reserves is the day-by-day instrument, the Federal Reserve receives information on other financial variables and responds to it almost continuously. That makes the stock of unborrowed reserves over a quarter or even over a month dependent on the values of other variables in that quarter or month. In a quarterly model, the best surrogate for control of the money stock may well be the money stock, in the sense that the use of any other variable understates greatly the degree of control of the quarterly stock of money that can, in fact, be attained. Unfortunately, we did not examine policies with the money stock exogenous.

Despite the erratic behavior of the money stock under policies 8, 9, and 10, there is a sharp contrast between its behavior under those policies and its behavior under policies 1-7. That difference is traceable to the fact that under policies 1-7, the money stock is demand determined, while under policies 8-10 it is largely "supply" determined. For example, the $\bar{\gamma}_m$'s for policies 1, 3, and 6 are directly related to the average growth rates for income under those policies, while under policies 8-10, there is almost no relationship between the average growth rates of the money stock and those of income.

VIII. RESULTS, THE MICHIGAN MODEL

1. The Sample

As noted above, we encountered no convergence difficulties with the Michigan model. Solutions were obtained for nondiscretionary policy 1 for the first 50 sets of random variables we tried, and solutions were obtained from all those sets for the other six policies. (Recall that unborrowed reserves does not appear in the Michigan model, so that we have results only for the seven interest-rate exogenous policies.) Thus, our analysis and discussion of the Michigan model are based on that sample of 50.

2. Average Stochastic Growth Rates

The average stochastic growth rates for real GNP and for the GNP deflator are shown in the first and third columns of Table 8. For policy 1, the average stochastic growth rate for real output is .698 per cent per quarter, while that for the price level is .794 per cent per quarter. Those contrast sharply with what we found for that policy for the FRB-MIT model. There we found that holding the interest rate and tax rates constant for sixteen quarters resulted in an average stochastic growth rate of real output near zero and a growth rate for the price level of .16 per cent per quarter. Thus, for policy 1, the Michigan model predicts an annual real income growth rate 2.6 per cent higher than that for the FRB-MIT model and an annual rate of growth of prices 2.5 per cent higher. Growth rate outcomes for nondiscretionary policy 1 are the only ones comparable across these models, because our policy rules implied very different courses of action in the two models. In FRB-MIT, after the initial tightening common to all models, the course of the economy called for easing actions, on average, throughout the period, while in this model, the opposite occurred. Thus, we find for Michigan that the average growth rates for real output and the price level are lower when discretionary policies are applied.

The pairs $(\bar{\gamma}_y, \bar{\gamma}_p)$ are plotted in Figure 4. Just as in the FRB-MIT model, there is an obvious positive correlation—indeed, a perfect rank correlation—between the growth rates. (The correlation coefficient is .99.) The real output growth rates range from .445 per cent per quarter for policy 5 to .698 per cent for policy 1, while the price level growth rates range from .745 to .794 per cent. Each strong policy is characterized by lower growth rates for real output and prices than its corresponding weak version. Given that tightening actions were taken, that is to be expected. Note, in addition, that the monetary policies produce greater effects than the joint policies, which, in turn, produce greater effects than the fiscal policies. In the FRB-MIT model, the positions of monetary and fiscal policies were exactly the reverse; there fiscal policy had the largest effect and monetary policy the smallest effect. Moreover, while in FRB-MIT each strong policy dominated all weak policies, in Michigan weak monetary policy is more effective in terms of growth rates than both versions of fiscal policy.[27]

[27]This may reveal another inconsistency between the two models, or may, as suggested by Bert Hickman and noted above, arise because of asymmetry in the effects of monetary and fiscal policy.

TABLE 8

Michigan Model, Growth Rates and Standard Deviations of Real Income and Price Level

| Policy | γ_y | | γ_p | | $\bar{\sigma}_y$ | | $\bar{\sigma}_p$ | | $\sigma(\gamma_y)$ | $\sigma(\gamma_p)$ | Among Divided by Within | | $\rho(\gamma_y,\gamma_p)$ |
	S	NS	S	NS	S	NS	S	NS			y	p	
1. Nondiscretionary, R_{cp} exogenous	.698 (.016)	.739 (.033)	.794 (.007)	.765 (.023)	1.67	1.27	.97	.87	.445	.164	10.33	6.53	+.323
2. Monetary I, R_{cp} exogenous	.553 (.015)	.562 (.032)	.768 (.005)	.745 (.024)	1.70	1.23	.94	.94	.400	.139	9.05	5.74	+.166
3. Fiscal I, R_{cp} exogenous	.666 (.016)	.696 (.031)	.789 (.006)	.763 (.023)	1.67	1.21	.95	.89	.427	.157	9.90	6.38	+.282
4. Joint I, R_{cp} exogenous	.616 (.015)	.622 (.035)	.777 (.006)	.750 (.024)	1.72	1.37	.94	.92	.420	.146	9.46	6.02	+.223
5. Monetary II, R_{cp} exogenous	.445 (.015)	.459 (.053)	.745 (.005)	.727 (.025)	2.12	2.04	.95	.95	.382	.122	6.95	4.99	+.054
6. Fiscal II, R_{cp} exogenous	.636 (.015)	.652 (.030)	.785 (.006)	.761 (.023)	1.67	1.15	.94	.90	.410	.150	9.45	6.20	+.242
7. Joint II, R_{cp} exogenous	.530 (.015)	.586 (.034)	.765 (.006)	.748 (.024)	1.74	1.33	.94	.93	.385	.136	8.54	5.57	+.126

NOTE: All rates and standard deviations are expressed in per cents per quarter. S is stochastic and NS is nonstochastic. Standard deviations are in parentheses.

Figure 4. Michigan Model, Average Quarterly Growth Rates,
Price Level vs Real Income

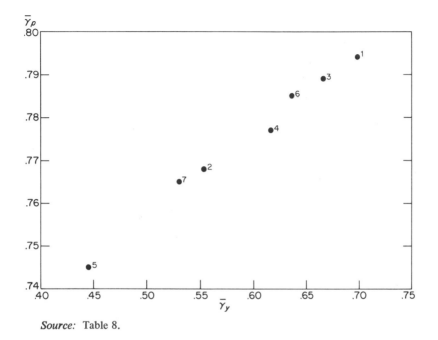

Source: Table 8.

3. Average Stochastic Within-Path Variance

Figure 5 shows that for other than fiscal policy, as discretionary policies are applied, within-path variance of real income increases. That is consistent with the FRB-MIT results, but here the differences are relatively slight. Moreover, policy by policy, within-path variance for real income is lower in the Michigan model than in the FRB-MIT model. In Michigan, the within-path standard deviation of real income ranges from about 1.7 to 2.1 per cent, while in FRB-MIT it ranged from 2.3 to 6.6 per cent. When $\bar{\sigma}_y$'s for strong policies are compared to those for weak policies, significant differences are found only for monetary policy.

The within-path standard deviation of prices varies almost not at all across policies. Its value is, on the average, lower than that found for the FRB-MIT model. Thus, the Michigan model exhibits more within-path stability for both real income and the price level than does the FRB-MIT model.

Figure 5. Michigan Model, Real Income, Rates of Growth vs Within-Path
Standard Deviations

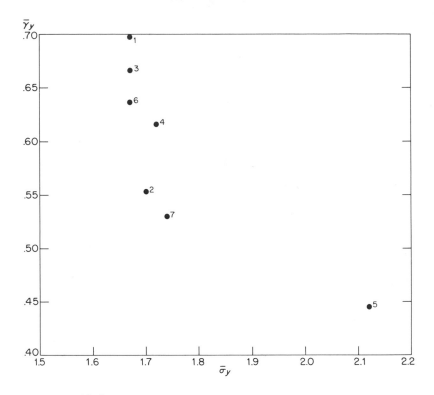

4. Among-Path Variance

On the average, there is also less dispersion among the individual real
income growth rates for the Michigan model than for FRB-MIT. Despite that
there is still great uncertainty about the particular real income growth that
will occur under any policy. For example, the probability under policy 5 of
observing a real income growth rate larger than .698——the value of the
highest average growth rate obtained, that for policy 1——is about one-third.

In Figure 6, we plot $[\sigma(\gamma_y), \sigma(\gamma_p)]$ by policy. Least uncertainty attaches
to policy 5 and most to policy 1. That is consistent with our findings for
FRB-MIT in two respects: (i) nondiscretionary policy with the interest rate

Figure 6. Michigan Model, Among-Path Standard Deviations,
Price Level vs Real Income

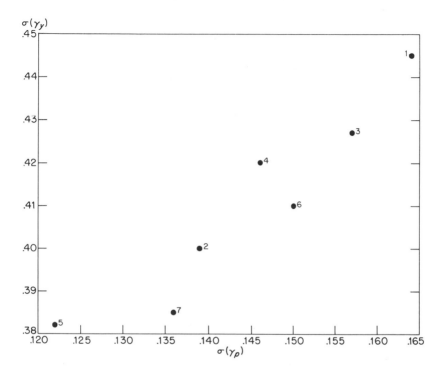

Source: Table 8.

held constant does worst; and (ii) that policy which is most effective in terms
of growth rates does best.

As in the FRB-MIT model, individual growth rates for real income and
prices for a given policy are positively correlated (see the last column of Table
8).

5. Stochastic Versus Nonstochastic Outcomes

Table 9 for real output and Table 10 for the price level show the average
stochastic outcomes (and associated standard deviations) and the nonstochastic outcomes for each quarter. As one expects, the standard deviations

TABLE 9

Michigan Model, Means and Standard Deviations of Real GNP Obtained
Each Quarter by Application of the Various Policy Rules

Year and Quarter	Commercial Paper Rate Exogenous													
	Control		Monetary 1		Fiscal 1		Joint 1		Monetary 2		Fiscal 2		Joint 2	
	NS	S	NS	S	NS	S	NS	S	NS	S	NS	S	NS	S
1969–I	717	718 (6.1)	717	718 (6.1)	717	718 (6.1)	717	718 (6.1)	716	717 (6.2)	717	718 (6.0)	717	718 (6.1)
1969–II	716	717 (9.7)	716	716 (9.7)	716	717 (9.7)	716	716 (9.6)	712	715 (10.2)	716	716 (9.7)	716	716 (9.6)
1969–III	720	719 (13.1)	719	718 (13.0)	720	719 (13.2)	718	719 (13.0)	714	715 (13.8)	720	719 (12.9)	718	718 (12.9)
1969–IV	725	724 (16.7)	722	722 (16.4)	725	723 (16.6)	722	722 (16.4)	716	717 (17.6)	724	723 (16.4)	721	721 (16.3)
1970–I	732	731 (20.6)	727	727 (20.1)	731	730 (20.3)	727	728 (20.1)	718	720 (20.9)	730	729 (20.1)	726	726 (19.9)
1970–II	739	738 (26.5)	733	732 (26.0)	738	737 (26.1)	733	734 (25.8)	723	724 (26.0)	737	736 (25.8)	732	731 (25.7)
1970–III	747	745 (29.5)	739	738 (28.6)	746	744 (28.9)	740	740 (28.5)	727	728 (28.0)	744	742 (28.3)	738	736 (28.0)
1970–IV	756	753 (32.4)	743	744 (30.6)	753	752 (31.5)	747	748 (30.8)	731	733 (29.7)	751	750 (30.6)	745	742 (29.8)

(continued)

Table 9 (continued)

Year and Quarter	Commercial Paper Rate Exogenous												
	Control		Monetary 1		Fiscal 1		Joint 1		Monetary 2		Fiscal 2		Joint 2	
	NS	S	NS	S	NS	S	NS	S	NS	S	NS	S	NS	S
1971–I	764	762 (36.1)	749	750 (33.7)	761	760 (35.0)	754	755 (34.4)	736	739 (32.9)	759	758 (33.8)	751	748 (32.7)
1971–II	772	770 (38.5)	756	757 (35.0)	769	768 (37.0)	761	763 (36.4)	744	746 (33.9)	766	765 (35.6)	758	755 (33.8)
1971–III	780	780 (42.7)	762	765 (38.2)	776	777 (40.9)	768	772 (40.0)	753	754 (37.0)	773	774 (39.2)	765	763 (36.7)
1971–IV	788	788 (45.8)	770	772 (40.3)	784	785 (43.7)	775	780 (42.6)	762	761 (39.1)	780	782 (41.7)	772	770 (38.5)
1972–I	796	795 (48.5)	777	779 (41.8)	791	792 (46.1)	783	787 (44.8)	773	768 (39.8)	786	788 (43.9)	779	776 (39.9)
1972–II	803	803 (49.7)	784	786 (41.2)	798	799 (46.8)	792	794 (45.1)	784	776 (37.9)	793	796 (44.3)	787	783 (39.2)
1972–III	811	811 (53.1)	792	793 (43.6)	805	806 (49.7)	800	801 (47.9)	793	784 (39.9)	800	802 (46.7)	795	790 (41.3)
1972–IV	819	817 (57.1)	799	800 (45.8)	813	812 (52.9)	808	807 (50.8)	803	791 (41.9)	807	808 (49.4)	803	796 (43.2)

NOTE: S is stochastic and NS is nonstochastic. Standard deviations are in parentheses.

TABLE 10

Michigan Model, Means and Standard Deviations of Price Obtained
Each Quarter by Application of the Various Policy Rules

Year and Quarter	Control		Monetary 1		Fiscal 1		Joint 1		Monetary 2		Fiscal 2		Joint 2	
	Commercial Paper Rate Exogenous													
	NS	S	NS	S	NS	S	NS	S	NS	S	NS	S	NS	S
1969–I	126	126 (.4)	126	126 (.4)	126	126 (.4)	126	126 (.4)	126	126 (.4)	126	126 (.4)	126	126 (.4)
1969–II	127	126 (.8)	127	126 (.8)	127	126 (.8)	127	126 (.8)	127	126 (.8)	127	126 (.8)	127	126 (.8)
1969–III	128	128 (1.0)	128	128 (1.0)	128	128 (1.0)	128	128 (1.0)	128	128 (1.0)	128	128 (1.0)	128	128 (1.0)
1969–IV	129	129 (1.2)	129	129 (1.2)	129	129 (1.2)	129	129 (1.2)	129	129 (1.2)	129	129 (1.2)	129	129 (1.2)
1970–I	130	130 (1.3)	130	130 (1.3)	130	130 (1.3)	130	130 (1.3)	130	130 (1.2)	130	130 (1.3)	130	130 (1.3)
1970–II	131	131 (1.4)	131	131 (1.4)	131	131 (1.4)	131	131 (1.4)	131	131 (1.3)	131	131 (1.4)	131	131 (1.4)
1970–III	131	131 (1.5)	131	131 (1.5)	131	131 (1.5)	131	131 (1.5)	131	131 (1.5)	131	131 (1.5)	131	131 (1.5)
1970–IV	132	132 (1.7)	132	132 (1.7)	132	132 (1.7)	132	132 (1.7)	132	132 (1.6)	132	132 (1.7)	132	132 (1.7)

(continued)

Table 10 (continued)

Year and Quarter	Commercial Paper Rate Exogenous												
	Control		Monetary 1		Fiscal 1		Joint 1		Monetary 2		Fiscal 2		Joint 2	
	NS	S	NS	S	NS	S	NS	S	NS	S	NS	S	NS	S
1971–I	133	133 (2.0)	133	133 (1.9)	133	133 (2.0)	133	133 (1.9)	132	133 (1.8)	133	133 (1.9)	133	133 (1.9)
1971–II	134	134 (2.2)	133	134 (2.1)	134	134 (2.2)	133	134 (2.1)	133	133 (1.9)	134	134 (2.1)	133	134 (2.1)
1971–III	134	135 (2.4)	134	134 (2.2)	134	135 (2.4)	134	135 (2.3)	134	134 (2.0)	134	135 (2.3)	134	134 (2.2)
1971–IV	135	136 (2.8)	135	135 (2.5)	135	136 (2.7)	135	135 (2.6)	134	135 (2.2)	135	136 (2.6)	135	135 (2.4)
1972–I	136	137 (3.3)	135	136 (2.7)	136	137 (3.1)	136	136 (2.9)	135	136 (2.3)	136	136 (3.0)	136	136 (2.7)
1972–II	137	138 (4.1)	136	137 (3.1)	137	137 (3.8)	136	137 (3.4)	136	136 (2.6)	137	137 (3.5)	136	137 (3.0)
1972–III	138	139 (4.9)	137	138 (3.5)	137	139 (4.5)	137	138 (3.9)	137	137 (2.8)	137	138 (4.1)	137	138 (3.3)
1972–IV	138	140 (5.3)	138	139 (3.7)	138	140 (4.8)	138	139 (4.2)	137	138 (2.9)	138	139 (4.4)	138	139 (3.5)

NOTE: S is stochastic and NS is nonstochastic. Standard deviations are in parentheses.

increase continuously from 1969-I on. Although differences among the 1972-IV average stochastic outcomes for real GNP seem slight, the ranking is the same as the ranking by average growth rate in Table 8. Note that for prices the average stochastic values for each quarter are almost the same across policies, which is consistent with the near identity of growth rates for prices across policies. In contrast to what was found in FRB-MIT, for this model the hypothesis that the nonstochastic outcomes represent the means of the distributions of outcomes can not be rejected. Here, each nonstochastic outcome could be the mean of the corresponding distribution of outcomes.

The nonstochastic within-path variance estimates for real GNP are significantly lower than the stochastic except for policy 5. For prices, the differences are not significant (see Table 8). Underestimation of within-path instability is what one expects to find in the nonstochastic runs.

6. Utility Rankings

The policies are ranked by expected utility in Table 11. For the stochastic outcomes, the ranking for values of b near zero is the same as the ranking by real output growth rates. Only when the price variance term is given substantial weight, does the ranking change; the nondiscretionary policy, policy 1, falls in the rankings, ending as the fifth best policy for $b-.3$. In contrast, the nonstochastic expected utility ranking is the same for all values

TABLE 11
Michigan Model, Policies Ranked by Expected Utility

							b					
	0.0		−0.6		−.12		−.18		−.24		−.30	
Ranking	S	NS	S	NS	S	NS	S	NS	S	NS	S	NS
1. (best)	1	1	1	1	1	1	1	1	3	1	6	1
2.	3	3	3	3	3	3	3	3	6	3	4	3
3.	6	6	6	6	6	6	6	6	1	6	3	6
4.	4	4	4	4	4	4	4	4	4	4	2	4
5.	2	7	2	7	2	7	2	7	2	7	1	7
6.	7	2	7	2	7	2	7	2	7	2	7	2
7. (worst)	5	5	5	5	5	5	5	5	5	5	5	5

$$U = (1/16) \sum_{1}^{16} \left[y_t^{\frac{1}{2}} + b\,10^4\,(p_t - p_{t-1}/p_{t-1})^2 \right]$$

of b. It is almost the same as the stochastic for values of b near zero. For $b = -.24$ and $-.30$, the discrepancy between the stochastic and nonstochastic ranking can be explained by the fact that the nonstochastic ranking, by definition, takes no account of among-path variance.

IX. RESULTS, THE WHARTON MODEL

We did not carry out our experiments on the Wharton model. The problem centered on the determination of the unemployment rate, un. In the Wharton model,

$$un = 1 - (x + y)/(z - w),$$

where $z - w$ is the civilian labor force——the total labor force, z, minus the number of military personnel, w, and $x+y$ is total employment——the number of private nonfarm employees, x, plus the sum of civilian government employees, farm workers, and the nonagricultural self-employed, y. We tried a number of extrapolation procedures for the exogenous variables, y and w, but for all of them, un took on negative values in a high percentage of the sixteen-quarter runs attempted. We could have constrained the unemployment rate to be positive, but since its value in any quarter helps determine wages, prices, and other variables in that and subsequent quarters, those solutions would depend on the lower bound——necessarily nonzero——chosen by us. Rather than report results dependent on an arbitrarily chosen lower bound for un, we chose not to perform the experiments.

APPENDIX

In this appendix we illustrate the computations required for deriving the summary growth rate and variance statistics. For this purpose we use two sets of results for real income from the FRB-MIT model obtained from the application of nondiscretionary policy with the interest rate exogenous. The natural logarithms of those real income results are plotted in Figure 7.

The constant growth rate paths shown in Figure 7 were computed from least squares regressions as described in part 1 of Section VI. The constant growth rates are .956 and $-.525$ per cent per quarter for runs I and II, respectively. The residual standard deviations around those constant growth rate paths were used as measures of instability. They are .64 for run I and 1.85 for run II. In the text we report the average (pooled) growth rate, $\overline{\gamma}_y$, and the average standard deviation, $\overline{\sigma}_y$. If a sample consisted of these two runs, then $\overline{\gamma}_y = (.956 - .525)/2 = .216$ and $\overline{\sigma}_y = [(.64^2 + 1.85^2)/2]^{1/2} = (1.916)^{1/2}$. We also report the standard deviation of the individual growth rates, which for this sample of two is $\sigma(\gamma_y) = [(.956 - .216)^2 + (-.525 - .216)^2]^{1/2}/2^{1/2} = (.496)^{1/2}$. The analysis of variance table for this sample of two is as follows:

Source of Variation	Degrees of Freedom	Sum of Squares	Root Mean Square (RMS)
Total residuals from pooled regression	$16N-1 = 31$	$\sigma^2(\gamma_y)\sum_1^{16} t^2 + 15N\bar{\sigma}_y^2 = 799.5$	$(799.5)^{1/2} = 28.3$
Among samples	$N-1 = 1$	$\sigma^2(\gamma_y)\sum_1^{16} t^2 = (.496)(1,496)$ $= 742.0$	$(742.0)^{1/2} = 27.2$
Within	$15N = 30$	$15N\bar{\sigma}_y^2 = 30(1.916) = 57.5$	$(1.916)^{1/2} = 1.38$

Figure 7. Two Stochastic Paths of Real Income and Their Respective Constant Growth Rate Regressions

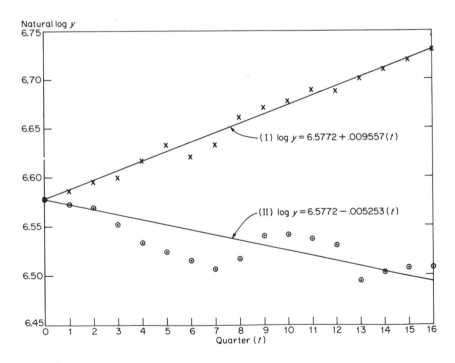

The standard deviation of the average growth rate is the first entry in the RMS column divided by $(N \Sigma t^2)^{\frac{1}{2}}$; for this example, .52. In the text in Tables 3 and 9 under the heading "Among Divided by Within," we report ratios of the second entry in the RMS column to the third. For this sample of two that ratio is 19.7. Aside from the correlation coefficient between income and price level growth rates, that completes the description of all growth rate and variance statistics.

DISCUSSION—AFTERNOON SESSION

Includes comments by F. Thomas Juster, vice president–research of the National Bureau, who was chairman of this session; Bert Hickman, of Stanford University, and Arthur Okun, of The Brookings Institution, who acted as formal panelists, and Otto Eckstein, of Harvard University, who offered some additional remarks. Again, the oral discussion was recorded and edited with the cooperation of the speakers. The exchange of views during the open discussion period was not recorded.

Introductory Remarks by F. Thomas Juster

The only comment I'd like to add to the content of this morning's discussion refers to what many people have viewed, incorrectly, as the National Bureau's simplistic public rule which says that two quarterly declines in a row in real GNP is a recession. The outcome of applying this rule may depend, among others, on whether you look at GNP from the expenditure or the income side. If you do as I do, and look at it from the income side, real GNP did not turn up in the second quarter because the statistical discrepancy turned around the wrong way, and you have *three* quarterly declines in a row. Now, that's a curiosity; it has no substantive content. It does suggest, I think, that it would be important to have somewhat better numbers than the ones we now have, which is a useful thing to bear in mind generally.

The subject matter of this afternoon's session is quite different from the morning's discussion in that we move from talking about the indicators, which one can view as variables that reflect a consensus about where things are going, to relationships which are more specifically behavioral. Our concern is largely with the performance of econometric models—what they can or cannot tell us about the path business activity is taking. It may not be familiar to all of you that the Bureau as an institution has for some time now gone well beyond our traditional interest in tracking business cycle movements with indicators. We have taken the view that what we can appropriately do in the area of econometric models is not what some would have us do and just build one more, yet another, full-scale model—which we think would probably be a mistake on our part; but essentially to focus on evaluation of the record and the structure of the model, which we think is something that has been greatly underdone in terms of the professional work in this area, and we've been doing this now for several years. We view it as

having a considerable amount of potential, and it does bear, I think, on
the broad question before us today, which is: What ought to be the
scope of National Bureau research in this area in future years?

*   *   *

Bert Hickman: I want to start with a few remarks about the Zarnowitz
paper. The parts that I found the most interesting in this paper concern
the econometric model forecasts. Many of the results that Zarnowitz is
reporting here and the results reported earlier by Evans, Haitovsky, and
Treyz were first presented at a conference jointly sponsored by the
Committee on Economic Stability of the Social Science Research Council
and the Conference on Income and Wealth last November [1969] at
Harvard University. Those papers are presently being edited, and I hope
that that volume will be out within six months to nine months from now.
It has a very impressive amount of evidence on these issues. Zarnowitz
has had only a chance to scratch the surface in this presentation today.
I think this is a very useful research activity which is being undertaken.
I might also put in that this reminds me of another conference which
was recently sponsored by the SSRC Committee on Economic Stability,
in April 1967, entitled "Is the Business Cycle Obsolete?" That volume
of papers came out with the usual two-year lag; it's been out two months.
It was edited by Martin Bronfenbrenner. I don't want to keep you in
suspense; we decided the business cycle was not obsolete, particularly
if you move toward a concept of something like a Japanese growth-rate
cycle; so you may find some parallelism between the proceedings from
that earlier conference in 1967 and the proceedings today.

Now, I want to say a few things about the issue of econometric
versus judgmental forecasts. It seems to me that on a priori grounds,
structural econometric models (or structural models in general) have
much more to offer than do other methods of forecasting, in particular,
than do any extrapolative forecasts whether they're naive models of the
very simple type that Zarnowitz used here or more complex autoregressive models. There are several reasons why I think the econometric models are much more meaningful and interesting. In the first
place, it seems to me that, if we are economists, we ought to try to use
economic theory in our forecasting, and a structural econometric model
is a deliberate attempt to use economic theory in creating hypotheses
about behavior. And unless economic theory is a set of empty boxes, we
ought to be able to improve on mechanical methods of forecasting by

using it in some systematic way. Second, if we have a structural econometric model, it does give us entry points for the use of exogenous information, and these entry points are, I think, very important. Of course the real problem with using an econometric model, or any other kind of model, for forecasting is that structural change does occur. But the structural econometric model should give you some entry points to try to make use of exogenous information as it comes up in ex ante forecasting. And of course the primary applications here are things like adjusting tax-rate parameters and tax functions in the models, if you know that a tax change is coming, or making an adjustment in your external estimate of government spending, if you know that's coming; also, making adjustments for things like strikes that are coming up, and so forth. There are various ways of entering that information into an econometric model. I don't know of any systematic way of handling that information unless you do have some sort of structural model; it tells you what functional relationships *ought* to be affected by those extraneous changes.

Third, the large-scale econometric models in particular include a great deal of sectoral detail. Of course there is an argument about whether big models or small models forecast better, and I'm not going to try to get into that. But I do want to say that it seems to me that sectoral detail is very important for its own sake. If people are interested in sectoral detail, they're not interested simply in how well you can forecast total GNP; they want a breakdown of GNP, they want an industrial breakdown; if possible they want a breakdown of prices, and so forth. Also, if you have a large-scale structural model with many endogenous variables, it gives the person evaluating the forecast the possibility of examining the internal structure of that GNP forecast. This gives some better means of judging whether he thinks it's a good or bad forecast because he can examine the individual assumptions of what's happening internally in the model and need not simply accept or reject the aggregate forecast.

Another important reason for preferring structural models, particularly econometric models, is that they can be used directly for policy analysis. That is, they can be used to ask the question, If you don't like the predicted outcome, what can you do to try to achieve a better outcome? In particular, if they have been built with an eye to policy analysis, they will have included structural instruments of policy which can then be used to answer questions about what would happen if you changed tax rates or what would happen if you changed the rediscount rate, and so forth. So they permit, in other words, not only forecasting but also the analysis of the effects of alternative policies. And finally, a structural econometric model allows you to conduct the analysis of dynamic properties of the economic system represented by that model, and this in itself is a very interesting and relevant topic.

So it seems to me that it is very important for us to continue the work, which has become more prevalent recently, of systematically testing econometric models; among other things, testing their forecasting ability—both ex ante and ex post—and doing our best to improve the specification of models and hence their ability to forecast as we go along. It does seem to me that it is important to continue that work in the econometric area as well as in other areas of forecasting because the inherent promise of the econometric models is so very great. From that point of view, I very much welcome that last part of Victor Zarnowitz's paper, where he talks about plans for future research. Most of these future plans—research activities which he hopes will be undertaken at the National Bureau—deal with the analysis of the properties of econometric models, as well as other methods of forecasting. I think this is important work which was sort of opened up in that conference of last November and which I hope will be continued.

I have a few very brief remarks about the Haitovsky and Wallace paper, partly because it is a very meaty paper and hard to read. I did read it, but it will take a long time to digest. I think this paper illustrates what can be done with these models, the very interesting questions that can be asked with them. It reinforces what I have just been saying about econometric models. I think it is a very important methodological paper. It's incomplete right now, and I am sure they are going to be working further with it, but it is a very interesting pilot study. The authors clearly recognize that they have only dealt with certain particular kinds of discretionary policy rules and that their conclusions therefore relate just to those rules and not to all rules. They also recognize that they have used a very simple welfare function which involves a trade-off only between unemployment and prices. Well, there I have some problem because the policy rules deal with unemployment and prices, whereas the welfare function deals with the rates of growth of GNP and prices. Unemployment drops out of the welfare function, which contains just the growth rates of prices and GNP, whereas unemployment is in the decision function as to the policy. I think I know why this is handled this way, or one reason that it might be handled this way, but it is something that perhaps they should have a chance to talk about.

Now, as compared with previous stochastic simulations I think the major difference introduced by the authors is the following: Previous stochastic simulations have by and large dealt with shocks to the disturbance terms in the individual structural equations. In particular, that was true of all the stochastic simulations done for the conference last November. It was also true of the stochastic simulations done on the Brookings model some years ago, and so those simulations of very large-scale models generally just dealt with random disturbance terms. The earlier study by Irma and Frank Adelman also dealt with shocks to the exogenous variables, and in that sense it is similar to this current study. But the current study is the only one I am personally familiar with which has also dealt with shifts in the multiplicative coefficients in the individual functions. So they are letting really everything vary in these experiments: The exogenous variables are also subject to random variation. There is an awful lot of randomness, and that certainly turns up some interesting results. One of the most interesting ones to me was that, given the fact that they have all these kinds of shocks going on, the mean of the stochastic simulations is not close to the nonstochastic simulation, whereas in the earlier experiments, say, with the Brookings model or with the models at the November conference, where only disturbance terms were shocked, it was still generally true that the mean of the stochastic simulations was close to the nonstochastic simulation, despite the nonlinearities in the models. So that apparently what is causing this to diverge in these models now is that shocks are going on also in the coefficients and in the exogenous variables.

Aaron Gordon had raised a point which I had also wanted to mention briefly; namely, that the procedure used in this simulation implies that you can change tax rates from one quarter to the next. And that is OK, I think, but the point really is whether those tax-rate changes will be viewed as permanent or temporary by persons who perceive them. It is the permanent income question, really. You know the response will be at least potentially different if the tax increase is viewed as a temporary one. Now, this may be partly handled in these models to the extent that, for example, they have distributed lags in the consumption functions, so that a change in disposable income has only a partial effect in the current period. In a sense that is a way of getting at the difference between a permanent and a transitory movement in the tax function. But this raises an important question. Do the estimated parameters in the models, which were not estimated under the assumption of such frequent and temporary tax changes, reflect the structure of the models that would obtain if tax changes were as frequent as quarter by quarter?

Another interesting point the authors noted was that there was an asymmetry in policy between the FRB-MIT model and the Michigan model, namely, the fiscal policy was stronger in the FRB-MIT model, which in itself is interesting, since that model was really constructed to try to emphasize the effects of monetary policy, and the reverse was true in the Michigan model. This may well be due to the different structures of the models, but I also wonder if it is possibly due to the asymmetry of monetary policy itself. At least, it used to be argued that monetary policy is much more efficient as a restraining device on economic activity than as a stimulating device; that is, when you had excess capacity and were operating at a high level of unemployment, increasing the money supply might have a smaller effect than if you were trying to restrict the growth rate of activity. Whether that is the case with these models I don't know. It partly involves a question of what the structures of the models are like and whether they differ in respect to possible asymmetries in monetary response. But it is one possible thing that could account for this asymmetry, it seems to me, because, in the policy simulations that Haitovsky and Wallace present, the Michigan model leads to restrictive policies and the other model to expansionary policies. So that is a difference between them in addition to the difference in their structure.

Arthur Okun: The most constructive and most important contribution of the Haitovsky-Wallace paper in my view is its underlining of the problems of uncertainty, the stochastic elements, in judging policy and models, and applying them to the world. We have been aware for a considerable period of time that the effectiveness of policy is not primarily a matter of a bang for a buck. It isn't a question of how much GNP we get by moving the money supply or changing tax rates a given amount. As the authors point out, if the effects are small, then larger shifts in policy are required. If there were no problem of uncertainty about the effects, larger shifts in policy would be justified, and they would not come through as larger shifts in the economy. Similarly, it is clear that uncertainty and lags interact; in making a decision to take an expansionary action now on the basis of the current economic situation, you are implicitly tying yourself to a forecast that the expansionary effects of that policy will still be appropriate during the period in which it is going to be stimulating the economy.

Thus, we have become aware of the importance of questions about how reliable a policy tool is in generating some extra GNP and about how reliable our forecasts are in guiding us to want some extra GNP. But, until now, I believe we have always assumed that the *average* expected impact of an instrument can be derived from multipliers of a model without worrying about the stochastic element. Haitovsky and Wallace come up with a *dramatic* discovery as applied to the FRB-MIT model, that the average effect expected from a policy move when uncertainty is ignored is just a different world from the average result of the stochastic process, which does take randomness and uncertainty into account. This result comes through so clearly that it dominates everything else in the paper. And that result makes it hard to interpret the findings for the stochastic world.

The stochastic world, particularly in the FRB-MIT simulation, is a disaster area. Uncertainty keeps putting a deflationary bias into the results—and it isn't at all clear why the process of generating uncertainty always pulls *down* on real output. The difference between the stochastic and nonstochastic answers is enormous by 1972. Perhaps the random number generator has a built-in dummy variable for Republican occupancy of the White House. Perhaps the Alvin Hansen of the 1930's is generating the residuals and creating a tremendously stagnationist bias in the stochastic version. Starting with the initial boom conditions of the fourth quarter in 1968, the problem becomes that of fighting deflation rather than inflation in no time flat. Although policy seems to be doing reasonable things and is interpreted through a model which has turned out to be reasonable in other exercises, it just can't make this economy go up.

I am not going to be happy until I know what makes that deflationary result come out of the black box, and the authors don't tell me. Moreover, once the economy is in a disastrous situation, the comparisons between the policies merely reveal ones that are a little less disastrous versus ones that are a little bit more disastrous. Nothing is any good. I can't take any satisfaction in the less disastrous results that emerge for some fiscal policy instruments. Some of the conclusions on the monetary instruments need modification. If for some reason a given growth of unborrowed reserves is translated into a smaller growth of the money supply, then a good monetary rule would simply raise the growth target of unborrowed reserves. Before Milton Friedman or some other monetarist tears this test apart, let me go on record saying that I don't think it is a fair test.

It is apparently a property of the FRB-MIT model that a growth rate of the money supply of 4 per cent a year is inadequate to produce healthy growth. Thus, a 4 per cent rule in itself would produce a deflationary bias, although that would apply to the nonstochastic as well as the stochastic version. In his research for the Brookings Papers on Economic Activity, William Poole tried to get the economy on a full employment path by 1973, and estimated the monetary growth requirements with a given fiscal policy. It took a thumping 8 per cent growth rate of M_1 to do the job. Since money GNP had to rise at a rate of even more than 8 per cent, it shouldn't be surprising that it took an 8 per cent growth of M_1, since there is no secular uptrend in velocity in the FRB-MIT model.

Haitovsky and Wallace raise many other interesting issues I could discuss. I do feel, however, that their technique tends to raise too many issues at once in a way that makes it hard to sort out the key factors in operation. For example, if they took a single move of policy and traced out its implications compared with the nondiscretionary model through sixteen quarters, that would give a valuable benchmark of the size and time-shape of the effects. The results of implementing this rather complicated dynamic set of rules for decision-making tell us whether the package works as a package, but does not reveal much about the pieces.

Let me turn to the Zarnowitz paper. I have just a few comments on the earlier part. One, in looking at the CEA [Council of Economic Advisers] comparison table—which I have an historical attachment to—I was particularly struck by the fact that the quantitative errors recorded year by year really don't always match my ex post feeling about the adequacy of the various forecasts. The numbers in the table say that the forecast for 1964 was great while that for 1962 was poor, and my ex post feelings agree; but 1969 was a very good year and 1967 only a little bit better than an average year according to the table. I feel that 1969 was a poor year in terms of the policy implications of the forecast, largely because the 1969 expectation was for slower growth during the first half, and a speedup in the second half, and we got just the reverse. The profile during the year was quite different from what was contemplated at the beginning. Also, the real and price parts of the forecast were off the track, but balanced out. On the other hand, 1967 was a jewel in terms of its policy implications. It really did catch the profile of the year: a flat first half and the danger of an upsurge in the second half. Although the GNP number did not come out exactly on the nose, the accuracy of the profile dominated the slightly larger error in the annual forecast.

I am not suggesting that Zarnowitz can do anything to adjust for such matters, particularly since the data come to him in annual form. But the illustrations suggest, more generally, that a full evaluation of forecasts has to ask other questions: What is the forecast used for? Is it doing the job it is supposed to do? And sometimes the magnitude of the GNP error will not be a good indication.

Like Bert Hickman, I was most interested in the part that Zarnowitz did not get time to summarize, namely: Where do we go from here? I'm concerned about the possibility of answering the question: Do econometric models do well? The sample of econometric models remains small, even with the additional ones that Zarnowitz is planning to include in the future. And they are special in ways other than being econometric. Most of them were developed by very proficient, expert economists, who were able to finance a large investment in a forecasting system. Novices in the field don't get that opportunity. Whether econometric models work better may be a little like the question of whether baseball players from Oklahoma have better batting averages than all baseball players as a group. I don't find the latter question very interesting, and I don't see any use to the answer. Similarly, I have no particular reason to believe that econometric models will be better or worse as a group than equally serious judgmental forecasts. And I would conjecture that forecasting differences *among* econometric models will be as large as the differences between them and judgmental forecasts. I doubt that the forecasts that come off a computer and are very formalized are going to have anything in common. Some of the reasons for my skepticism are illustrated by the wonderful paradox cited in the paper: If perfect foresight on exogenous variables is plugged, ex post, into some of the econometric models, they come out worse than they actually did ex ante without that foresight. I'd throw another possible explanation for the paradox into the hat: the possibility that an econometrician who feels a little more bullish than his model may let that bullishness show up in higher projections of exogenous variables. And when he feels more bearish than his model, he may unconsciously hold down the exogenous variables for the next several quarters rather than make a specific residual adjustment. I wonder how the model builders feel about this paradox. It is a great personal tribute to their ability to make adjustments. But it is capable of an interpretation they wouldn't like: "If this smart fellow wants a toy to play with, it's all right because he's smart enough to correct it anyway." I don't believe that that is the proper interpretation. I think that the model is a tool for developing forecasting techniques, and it is a constructive one, provided it is not used as a substitute for good judgment and provided it is not so structural that it can't absorb barometric and anticipatory data that don't fit into nice causal relationships.

I don't know whether I may be disagreeing with Bert Hickman in that last proviso. I worry about forecasting and analytical objectives getting confused, and thereby compromising the effort to forecast by insisting on structural explanations and nice causal relationships which exclude indexes and surveys. The barometers help forecast, and if we don't take advantage of them, we pay a considerable price in our forecasting ability.

In looking ahead to future research, I would underline the set of questions in Zarnowitz's paper, that ask the why's about the mistakes in the models. The models do provide, as Bert Hickman noted, a unique opportunity to trace the errors and nail them down and determine why mistakes were made. That should help reveal the relationships we're most weak on, what we need to know, whether particular relationships in particular models are outstandingly good (quite apart from whether the model does well as a whole). What kinds of situations seem to lead *all* economists astray? There is a high payoff in focusing on some key surprises; for example, why plant and equipment turned up so strongly at the end of 1968; why the consumer keeps changing his mind; why prices accelerated in 1969. What do these surprises tell us about the world?

It seems to me that there are opportunities to explore the why's of the results on the judgment forecasts in the ASA [American Statistical Association] survey. Could you get a "postmortem" reinterview with some of the people who answer the questionnaires? Give it back to them after a year and say: "Here's what you were predicting. Here's where the economy came out. How do you feel about that forecast? Did it meet your needs? How would you grade yourself? Where do you feel you went wrong? What have you learned from this experience that might help you in the future? Where does the result point to in your own research?"

We do want to be sure that we're not just collecting batting averages of baseball players arranged by state. It's fine to collect averages of left-handed hitters against left-handed and right-handed pitchers; that might suggest whether platooning is a good idea. Similarly, the research should help guide decisions on how to improve forecasting. The work that Zarnowitz has done already has answered several important questions. It demonstrates beyond any shadow of doubt that economists are better forecasters than any naive models, and yet that we have a long way to go before we achieve the predictive accuracy we'd like.

Incidentally, forecasting accuracy interacts with policy issues. Suppose our ability to forecast improved greatly and was translated into economic policy, because the politicians finally accepted our forecasts and advice. In that world, presumably, economic activity would move pretty smoothly over time, and extrapolative methods of forecasting would do very well, just as well as professional economic forecasts. So, in some ultimate sense, the economic forecaster can't win both games of being right and of convincing the politicians to take his advice. In fact, the time the economic forecaster will look best is when the profession is very smart and the politicians are very stubborn. If there were a tremendous gap between what we know policy ought to be doing and what it is doing, then we could confidently predict the major fluctuations. Maybe that would maximize the economic welfare of the profession but it would be sad for the nation.

*   *   *

Otto Eckstein: Let me try to clarify the puzzle about ex ante and ex post forecasting. There are three essential elements in all forecasting of this type: (1) the information that is used; (2) the extrapolation methods based on past relationships; and (3) judgments about policies and other key elements.

The models contain a lot of information, but they don't reflect all available, useful information. If you run a model in the ex post method, you use only that information which happens to be for variables incorporated in the model and throw away all the rest. The use of constant adjustments or add factors is a method to bring other known information, including leading indicators, expectational swings, industry information, and many other things into the forecasting process.

Extrapolation, which every forecaster employs, is essentially a process of taking past relationships, some primitive, some sophisticated, and projecting them into the future. The computers do that much better than the pencil. Models assure consistency and accuracy.

The third element is judgment. The human brain filters information and analyzes it; the informal forecaster has an informal model in his head. The extent of judgment used depends very much on the personality, interest, and ability of the forecaster. Whether models are used or not has little impact on the extent of judgment exercised.

The superiority of ex ante forecasts is explained, I think, essentially in this way. Outside information and judgment help correct for errors that would otherwise occur in the model. You don't really start out on the next quarter (or the current quarter, which usually is forecast) knowing nothing about the error terms. The first error term in large part is observed, and even the second and third error terms are observed in part, and can be corrected.

Let me make another point regarding the reported FRB-MIT model simulations. The FRB-MIT model is a delicate race horse, more sensitive than the Michigan or Wharton models. Its intricate financial structure and the role of the stock market heighten the possibility of unstable model runs. In the hands of an experienced forecaster, the FRB-MIT model would not be allowed to explode. In the hands of amateurs, the model produces results that are not totally serious. The enormous stochastic variation in the reported runs shows nothing about the economy and only a little about the model. It only proves something about the interactions of the model and the men using it on that particular occasion.

INDEX

(The discussions have not been included in the index.)

Abramovitz, Moses, 12, 12*n*, 14

Accelerator principle, 14*n*, 19*n*, 22, 23

Accelerator variables, 14, 14*n*, 22

Adelman, Frank L., 25*n*, 26, 27*n*, 242, 243, 262*n*

Adelman, Irma, 25*n*, 26, 27*n*, 242, 243, 262*n*

Aggregate economic activity
  in business cycle recessions and slowdowns, 90–92, 99, 110–12, 125
  and the conceptions of business cycles, 2–3, 39–40, 125–26
  and the definition of growth cycles, 41, 47
  indicators of
    in 1948–70, 93, 94–97*t*, 98–99
    in 1969–70, 112, 113, 114*t*, 115, 115*t*, 116*t*, 117
  pecuniary and real measures of, 90–92, 117–21
  relation to price-level changes, 118–19
  See also Business cycle indicators; Business cycles; GNP (gross national product)

Andersen, Leonall C., 31*n*, 32*n*

Ando, Albert, 15, 15*n*, 29*n*

Anti-inflationary measures, effects on fluctuations and growth, 10

ASA-NBER (American Statistical Association and National Bureau of Economic Research) Quarterly Survey of Economic Outlook, 185, 185*n*, 228

AT&T trend in production, 130–31*t*, 132, 133*t*

Average workweek, 244, 245*t*

Balance of payments, 6

Banking and financial system reforms, 7

Barger, Harold, 109

Becker, Gary S., 11

Benchmark forecasts. *See* Business cycle indicators; Extrapolative models

Bernstein, Martin, 12, 12*n*

Blyth, C. A., 39*n*

Boschan, Charlotte, 26*n*, 43, 43*n*, 44, 45, 54*n*, 59*n*, 63, 67, 140, 185, 185*n*, 240, 241*n*, 252*n*

Boschan-Bry computer program. *See* Bry-Boschan computer program for cycle dating

Brady, Dorothy S., 15*n*

Brainard, William C., 247*n*

Bronfenbrenner, Martin, 2*n*, 10*n*, 14*n*, 34*n*

Brookings model, 14*n*, 26*n*, 33*n*, 233*n*
  in business cycle analysis of econometric model simulations, 242, 243–44, 245–50*t*, 259
  hundred-quarter *ex ante* simulations with, 253–56, 257*t*, 258
  sample-period simulations with, 249, 250*t*, 251–53, 253*t*

Brumberg, R. E., 15, 15*n*

Bry, Gerhard, 12, 43, 43*n*, 44, 45, 54*n*, 59*n*, 63, 67, 140

Bry-Boschan computer program for
cycle dating, 42–43, 44, 45, 53–
57, 69–70, 70n, 140
Bureau of Labor Statistics, 154n,
166, 244
Burns, Arthur F., 1, 2n, 3n, 7n, 8n,
12n, 13n, 14n, 15n, 16n, 18n,
24n, 39n, 40, 40n, 41n, 42, 42n,
44, 44n, 90n, 91n, 99n, 121,
122n, 123, 126n, 127n, 134,
134n, 135–36, 136n, 137, 139,
147
Business Conditions Digest (BCD),
53, 53n
Business cycle analysis of econometric model simulations
conclusions from, and their interpretation, 25–27, 258–59
exogenous variables in, 243–44,
251, 254–55
hundred-quarter *ex ante* simulations, 253–56, 257t, 258
methods and data, 243–44, 245–
46t
questions addressed to, 241–42
sample-period simulations, 249,
250t, 251–53
six-quarter simulations around
business cycle turns, 244, 247,
248t, 249
See also Business cycles; Econometric models
Business cycle indicators, 16, 50–53
deviation cycles in, 65–67, 72t
leading, in business cycles and
growth cycles, 36, 47n, 82, 82n,
83–84
in 1948–70 and in contractions
since 1920, 93–99, 94–97t,
100–109t
in 1969–70, compared with earlier
episodes, 115, 116t, 117
"roughly coincident," in 1969–70,
114t, 115t

step cycles in, 67–73, 72t
turning points in, 54–55
used in dating U.S. business cycles
by computer methods, 88t
used in dating U.S. growth cycles,
73, 73n
used in forecasting GNP, 200–202
See also indicators of *under* Aggregate economic activity
Business cycles, 8–9, 10
and agriculture, 120n
and "built-in stabilizers," 6–8, 134
causes of, in economic theory,
17–25
changes in, 2–8, 36–37, 39–40,
134–35
chronologies of, handpicked and
programmed, 42–43, 57–65, 82–
83, 138–39
chronology, compared with price
cycle chronology, 145, 146t, 147
"classical" and new, concepts of,
2–5, 39–42
compared with "growth cycles,"
36–37, 44–49, 81, 135
cumulation of knowledge about,
10–16
definition of, 2, 40, 41, 44, 90, 99,
111–12, 121–22, 139
and econometric models, 20, 24–
28, 32, 33, 35, 234–35, 241–44,
247–53
endogenous and exogenous factors
in, 17–18, 21–35, 37, 123–26,
234, 241–42, 258–59
endogenous and exogenous models
of, 17–18, 21–22, 23
foreign, 2, 10, 10n, 40n, 42
Keynesian analysis of, 8, 20, 21–
25
labor force changes and changes
in, 8, 120n
mathematical models of, 20–22
monetary analysis of, 28–34

multiplier-accelerator models of, 20–23

National Bureau studies in, 1–2, 11–16, 18–20, 23–24, 25–26, 41, 137–38, 183–84

and "policy cycles," 10, 34, 34n

research needed, 36–37, 39n, 82–83, 135–36, 166, 227 ff, 258–59

and stabilization policies, 7–10, 31–35, 134–35

and structural changes in the economy, 6–7, 36, 134–35

See also Aggregate economic activity; Business cycle analysis of econometric model simulations; Business cycle indicators

Cagan, Phillip, 11, 12, 31n, 68n

Cairncross, Alec, 50n

Capital appropriations, backlog of, 114t

Carlson, Keith M., 31n, 32n

Chiang, A. C., 236n

Chow, Gregory C., 37n, 262n

Christ, Carl F., 17n, 27n, 184, 239

Civilian labor force, 1948–70, 96–97t

Cloos, George W., 46n, 58n, 59n, 62, 62n, 63

Cold War, 5

Cole, Rosanne, 121n, 184, 239

Compensation per man-hour, 158, 159t, 161, 165t, 166

Composite indexes

amplitudes of, 78n, 79n

of growth cycles and business cycles, 84

and identification of deviation cycles, 65, 72t, 73n

for selected cyclical indicators, 73–79, 75t, 77t

for step cycles, 74n

Computerized cycle dating, 42–43

See also Bry-Boschan computer program for cycle dating

Conard, Joseph W., 11

Conference on the Economic Outlook, 196, 196n

Construction costs in expansion prior to 1969, 124

Consumer buying intentions and attitudes, 188n

Consumer goods and services, diffusion of price changes in, 147, 148t

Consumer Price Index

diffusion of changes in, 147, 148t

forecasts of, 195, 195n

rates of change in, 142t, 145, 146t, 147, 149, 151t

reference chronology for prices based on, 139–44, 144t, 163–64

timing of, 149, 152–53t, 154, 156t, 157–58

See also Price cycle chronology; Prices

Consumption expenditures

and built-in stabilizers, 6–7

in economic forecasts, 193, 209, 210t, 217, 219t, 220t

errors in forecasts of, 193, 219t, 220t

Consumption theory, 11n, 14–15, 15n

Contractions in economic activity

and business cycle recessions, 111–12, 125–26

and increase in monetary growth, 29

irregularities in, 121–23

and low-rate phase of growth cycle, 45, 81

and price changes, 145, 146t

and rates of increase in GNP and industrial production, 68, 86t, 87t

Contractions in economic activity (Cont.)
  selected measures of, 99, 100–10*t*, 111–12
  See also Recessions
Costs of production
  in expansion before 1969–70 recession, 124, 165, 165*n*
  labor costs per unit of output, 14*n*, 72*t*, 158, 159–60*t*, 161, 162*t*, 165, 165*t*, 166
  other unit costs, 158, 160*t*, 161, 162*t*, 165, 165*t*
  relation to cyclical behavior of prices, 13*n*, 14*n*, 19, 23, 118–19, 138, 158–63, 165–66, 165*t*
Council of Economic Advisers (CEA) forecasts, 212, 212*n*, 213*t*, 214, 236
Courchene, Thomas J., 15*n*
Cox, Garfield V., 184, 239
Creamer, Daniel, 12, 12*n*, 137
Cunnyngham, Jon, 196, 239
Cyclical characteristics of the economy, simulations study of. *See* Business cycle analysis of econometric model simulations

Damped fluctuations, 21, 22, 26, 234, 249, 251
Darling, Paul G., 15*n*
deLeeuw, Frank, 27*n*, 29*n*, 32, 32*n*
Demand deposits and currency, 245*t*
Department store sales, 100–107*t*
Depression of the 1930's, 4, 7–8
Diffusion indexes, 16, 19, 73–75, 76*t*, 77–79, 118*n*, 126
  cumulated, for *ex ante* simulations, 256, 257*t*, 258
  of employment on nonagricultural payrolls, 97*t*, 98–99, 108–109*t*
  of price changes, 147, 148*t*, 164
  of production changes, 108–109*t*, 111, 111*n*

Diller, Stanley, 239
Dividend distribution, 6
Duesenberry, James S., 15, 15*n*, 23, 23*n*, 29*n*
Durand, David, 11
Dynamic models of business cycles, 17–18, 21–23
Dynamic properties of models, 17–19, 21–26, 29–30, 36–37, 234, 242, 249, 251, 254

Easterlin, Richard A., 11
Eckstein, Otto, 2, 15*n*, 29*n*
Econometric model forecasts
  accuracy of, compared with judgmental forecasts, 196, 222–23, 224–25*t*, 225, 226*t*, 227*t*
  and benchmark forecasts with leading indicators, 200, 200*n*, 201–202
  ex ante and *ex post*, 197–99, 218, 219–20*t*, 221–22, 232–33
  and extrapolative benchmark forecasts. *See* Extrapolative models
  "fine tuning" of, 197
  and judgmental forecasts of exogenous variables, 27–28, 196, 196*n*, 197–98, 232
  large and small models, 200–201
  monthly, 237–38
  reduced-form, 201–202
  single-equation, 201–202
  and specification errors, 27–28, 232–33, 251, 259, 265*n*
  See also Econometric models; Economic forecasts; GNP forecasts
Econometric models, 24, 28–33
  and accelerator variables, 14, 14*n*
  and business cycle analysis and forecasting, 4, 20, 24–28, 32–33, 36–37
  exogenous variables in, 25–28, 196*n*, 197–98, 232–33, 258–59

monetary and financial sectors in, 28, 28–29*n*

and simulation studies of economic policies, 4, 32–33, 35

See also Business cycle analysis of econometric model simulations; Econometric model forecasts; Economic policy simulations with econometric models

Economic forecasts, 4, 192, 196, 230–31

accuracy of, 50, 50*n*, 186–87, 187–88, 215, 216*t*, 217

agenda for new studies, 227–28

average errors of, 185–86, 203, 204*t*, 205–206

base values, changes and levels of, 203, 204*t*, 205, 209

before and since 1964, 206, 207*t*, 208, 209, 210–11*t*, 212

bias in, 188–89

of business economists, 184–85, 187, 215, 216*t*, 217

CEA forecasts. *See* Council of Economic Advisers (CEA) forecasts

and cyclical characteristics of forecast period, 173

and cyclical turning points, 189–92

and econometric models. *See* Econometric model forecasts

and economic growth, 188–89

and extrapolative benchmark models. *See* Extrapolative models

feedback effects of, 235–37

of FOMC. *See* Federal Open Market Committee (FOMC) minutes

of gross national product (GNP). *See* GNP forecasts

of industrial production. *See* forecasts of *under* Industrial production index (Federal Reserve)

leading indicators model as benchmark, 184–86

of major expenditure components of GNP, 192–94, 209, 210–11*t*, 217–22, 219–20*t*

and national income accounts, 16*n*

NBER studies of, 16, 16*n*, 27–28, 183–85

predictive record of, updated, 202–27

of price level, 195–96

private and governmental, compared, 212, 213*t*, 214–15

private judgmental, 203, 204*t*, 205–06, 207*t*, 208–09, 210–11*t*, 215, 216*t*, 217

recent and current research on, 183–202

sources and uses of, 183–84

in Western Europe, 236

Economic instability

and changes in business cycles, 2–7

and expectations, 7, 40, 40*n*

and stabilization policies, 6–10, 31–35

and the structure and institutions of the economy, 3–4, 6–7, 36, 134–36

Economic policy

and business cycle research, 2–3, 13, 13*n*

correction of errors in, 277*n*

discretionary vs. nondiscretionary, 252–55

and economic forecasts, 235–37

endogenous and exogenous elements in, 32–34, 235

and implications of growth cycle concept, 42

and 1969–70 recession, 37, 93

role in business cycles, 7–10, 30–35, 134–35

short-term vs. longer-term effects, 9, 34

Economic policy (Cont.)

See also Economic policy simulations with econometric models; Fiscal policy; Monetary policy

Economic policy simulations with econometric models

discount rate in, 272, 272n, 276n

expected utility for each policy, 280–81

experimental simulations described, 265–69

growth rates resulting from, summary statistics of, 277–80, 307, 308t, 309

models used for, 269–71

monetary and fiscal instruments used for, 271–74

personal income tax rate as policy instrument, 271ff

policy rules, 274–77, 294, 294t, 306, 306t, 307

results with FRB-MIT model, 281–85, 286t, 287–88, 289–92t, 293–96

results with Michigan model, 296–97, 298t, 299–301, 302–305t, 306–307

results with Wharton model, 307

stochastic vs. nonstochastic outcomes, 35, 265, 287–88, 289–92t, 293, 301, 302–305t, 306

unborrowed reserves, 271ff, 295, 295t, 296

variances

among-path, 285, 286t, 287, 300, 301t

around constant growth rate paths, 277–80

average stochastic within-path, 282–85, 284t, 299, 300t

See also Economic policy; Fiscal policy; Monetary policy

Economic Report of the President,

forecasts in, 200, 212, 212n, 213t, 214

Employment, 114t

cyclical contraction measures, 100–109t, 116t

"full," meaning and measurement of, 98, 124

and man-hours, nonagricultural, 72t, 95t, 96t

nonagricultural, diffusion indexes and related measures, 97t, 98–99, 108–109t

total civilian, in econometric model simulations, 244, 245t

Employment Act of 1946, 7

Epstein, Lillian, 11n

Evans, Michael K., 24n, 27, 185, 239, 254n

Expansions in economic activity

changes in length, 5, 5n

and high-rate phase of growth cycle, 45, 68, 81

irregularities in, 121–23

and price changes, 145, 146t

prior to 1969–70 recession, 91, 122–25

and rate of increase in GNP, 68

and restrictive forces, 91, 124–25

Expectations, 7, 7n

Explosive fluctuations, 18, 18n, 22

Exports, 120n

changes in, as "autonomous" shocks, 23, 251

Extrapolative models

as aid in explaining structure of forecasts, 186

autoregressive projections, 186

as benchmarks of predictive performance, 186–87, 189–90, 197–99, 230

comparison of errors of forecast with errors of judgmental forecasts, 204t, 205–206, 207t,

208–209, 210–11*t*, 212, 214, 215, 216*t*, 217
with errors of econometric model forecasts, 218, 219–20*t*, 221, 222
for consumption and investment, 193, 193*n*, 230–31

Fabricant, Solomon, 1, 3, 4, 4*n*, 11, 38, 47*n*, 48*n*, 47–49, 89, 137
Federal Open Market Committee (FOMC) minutes, 191–92
Federal Reserve Bank of Minneapolis, 271
Federal Reserve Bank of St. Louis, monetarist model, 32, 32*n*, 33*n*, 37*n*
Federal Reserve Board, 244
and money stock, 296
Fels, Rendigs, 46*n*, 62, 62*n*, 63, 174, 190*n*, 239
Ferber, Robert, 15*n*
Fiscal policy
built-in stabilizers, 6–7, 8, 134
discretionary, 7–8, 9–10, 31, 32–33, 35, 125, 263–65
instruments for, 271–74
relative effectiveness of, vs. monetary policy, 9, 32–33, 262–65
rules for, 261, 276, 276*t*, 277
simulation results, 281ff
See also Economic policy; Economic policy simulations with econometric models; Monetary policy
Fisher, Irving, 30
Forecasting. *See* Econometric model forecasts; Economic forecasts
FRB-MIT-PENN (FMP) model, 26*n*, 29*n*, 37*n*, 185, 185*n*
in business cycle analysis of econometric model simulations, 242–44, 245–46*t*, 259, 262*n*
in policy simulations study, 261,

261*n*, 264–65, 268–72, 274, 281–96, 307
vs. Michigan model, 297, 299, 300–301, 306
sample-period simulations with, 199, 249, 250*t*, 251–53, 253*t*
six-quarter simulations around business cycle turns with, 247, 248*t*, 249
Free reserves, 114*t*
Frickey, Edwin, 126*n*
Friedman, Milton, 7*n*, 10*n*, 11, 12, 15, 15*n*, 18*n*, 19*n*, 24*n*, 25, 28, 28*n*, 29*n*, 30*n*, 31*n*, 34, 34*n*, 36*n*, 45*n*, 67, 67*n*, 126, 126*n*, 137, 262, 262*n*
Friedman, Rose D., 15*n*
Frisch, Ragnar, 17*n*, 20, 21, 21*n*, 25, 26, 251*n*
Fromm, Gary, 15*n*, 29*n*, 233*n*

Gilbert, Milton, 10*n*
GNP (gross national product)
actual and potential in 1958 dollars, compared, 96*t*, 97*t*, 98
and aggregate economic activity, 93
alternative measures of deviation from trend, in 1958 dollars, 127, 128–29*t*, 132, 133*t*
in business cycle contractions since 1920, 100–107*t*, 111
in cyclical analysis of econometric model simulations, 244, 245*t*, 249, 250*t*, 251–53, 253*t*, 254–56, 257*t*
data revisions and methods of estimation of, 121*n*
and definitions of business cycles and growth cycles, 46–47
deviation cycles and step cycles, in 1958 dollars, 87*t*
in 1948–70, in current dollars and 1958 dollars, 72*t*, 94*t*

GNP (gross national product) (Cont.)
in 1969–70 recession and earlier
episodes, 113, 114t, 115, 115t,
116t, 117
real, in policy simulations with
econometric models, 265, 277ff,
280–84, 283t, 284t, 286t, 288t,
289–90t, 293–94, 297–301,
298–303t, 308t
related to policy variables, 33n
See also Aggregate economic activity; Business cycle indicators;
Business cycles; GNP forecasts
GNP forecasts
accuracy of, 187, 189
before and since 1964, 206, 207t,
208–209, 210t, 212
by business economists, 184, 215–
17
at cyclical turning points, 189–91
with econometric models, 196–97,
200–201, 218, 219t, 221–23,
224–25t, 225, 226t, 227, 227t,
232
and forecasts of major expenditure components of GNP, 192–
93
governmental and private forecasts
of, compared, 200, 212, 213t,
214–15
and industrial production forecasts, 194–95
with leading indicators, 200–202,
200n, 201n
multiperiod, 215, 216t, 217
and price-level forecasts, 195
private judgmental, 203, 204t,
205–206, 207t, 208–209, 210t
See also Econometric model forecasts
GNP implicit price deflator
alternatives to, 121n, 195n
in cyclical analysis of econometric

model simulations, 244, 252,
255
as index of general price level,
121, 139–40
in 1969–70, 164
in policy simulations with econometric models, 264, 274ff,
277ff, 280–83, 283t, 285, 286t,
287–89, 289t, 291–92t, 293,
294, 297–301, 298t, 299t, 301t,
304–305t, 306
and price cycle chronology, 139,
140
for private sector, 154, 157t
rate of change in, 142t
timing relative to Consumer Price
Index, 154, 157–58, 157t
Wharton and OBE econometric
model forecasts of, 218, 219t,
221–22
See also Price cycle chronology;
Prices
Goldberger, Arthur, 23n, 24, 196
Goldsmith, Raymond W., 11
Goodwin, R. M., 22n
Gordon, Robert Aaron, 13n, 14n,
17n
Gordon, Robert J., 233n
Government expenditures, forecasts
of, 193, 209, 211t, 217
implications of data errors in, 198,
198n
Gramlich, Edward M., 29n
Green, George R., 26n, 27n, 239,
259n
Griliches, Zvi, 33n, 233n
Gross private domestic investment
(GPDI), forecasts of, 193, 209,
210t, 217
Growth cycles, 127, 128–32t
amplitudes of, 79–80, 79n
and business cycles (Burns-
Mitchell definition), 39–42,
44–45, 81, 82–83, 135

chronology of, 73–75, 73n, 74n, 75t, 83–84

  comparison according to deviation cycles and step cycles, 75–79, 76t, 77t

and computerized cycle dating, 42–43

concepts of, alternative, 44–46, 46–49

criteria for selecting indicators for, 49–53

deviation cycles and step cycles in indicators of, 41–42, 53, 65–71, 72t, 73

diffusion of, 80

in Germany, 40n, 42, 49, 78n

"growth recessions" and their social costs, 92, 132, 134, 135

and leading indicators, 82, 83, 84

low-rate and high-rate phases of, 42, 68–69, 83

in 1947–70, 76t, 77t

in 1951–52, 80–81

in 1969–70, 84

objections to concept of, 42

periods covered, 39n, 73n, 84

trend adjustments for identification of, 65–66, 126–34

See also Business cycle indicators; Business cycles; Growth rates

Growth rates

  analysis of, and measurement errors, 69, 69n

  of money stock, resulting from policy simulations, 295, 295t, 296

  of output and employment, and the economy's performance, 98–99

  of real GNP and GNP deflators, resulting from policy simulations, 274ff, 277ff, 281–94, 297–306, 307–308

retardation of, in expansion before the 1969–70 recession, 124

of series from stochastic 100-quarter econometric model simulations, 243, 253

and stabilization policy, 9–10

tradeoff between inflation and growth, 93, 274–75

See also Growth cycles

Grunberg, Emile, 236

Gurley, John G., 7n

Guttenberg, Jack M., 11

Haberler, Gottfried, 12, 17n, 18n, 20n

Haitovsky, Yoel, 1, 4, 27, 37, 185, 235, 239, 261

Hansen, Alvin, 23n

Harkins, C., 121n

Harrod, Roy F., 21n

Heller, Walter W., 127n

Help-wanted advertising, 114t

Hickman, Bert G., 2, 10n, 14n, 24n, 25n, 26, 27, 32 241n, 259n, 262n, 264n, 298n

Hickman, W. Braddock, 11

Hicks, John R., 18n, 24n

Hinshaw, C. Elton, 184, 191n, 239

Hirsch, A. A., 26, 239, 259n

Holland, Daniel M., 12

Holzman, Franklyn D., 34n

Hours per man, 245t

Housing expenditure forecasts. See Residential construction forecasts

Housing starts, 245t

Howrey, E. Philip, 262n

Hultgren, Thor, 12, 12n, 14n, 137

Hymans, Saul H., 261n

Import prices and GNP, 120n

Income

  distribution of, and changes in the price level, 119–20

Income (Cont.)
in monetary analysis of business cycles, 28–29, 126
real, in policy simulations. *See under* GNP
Income tax collection, 6
Industrial capacity (Wharton), 1947–70, 133t
Industrial production index (Federal Reserve)
alternative measures of deviation from trend, 127, 130–131t, 132, 133t
in business cycle contractions since 1920, 100–107t, 111
deviation cycles and step cycles in, 72t, 86t
diffusion of components of, 108–109t, 111, 111n
forecasts of, 171, 178–79
in 1948–70, 94t
in 1969–70 recession and earlier episodes, 113, 114t, 115, 116t, 117
Inflation
diffusion of prices and costs in, 138, 163
and economic policies, 7, 31, 34
and measurement of aggregate economic activity, 118–21
and policy implications of growth cycle concept, 42
and recession, 37, 145
tradeoff with growth, 93, 274–75
Interest rates
and economic policies, 34
in expansion before 1969, 124
and monetary changes during business cycles, 7n, 29
role in policy simulations with econometric models, 271ff
turning-point dates, 72t, 114t
Inventory investment (net change in inventories)

and accelerator variables, 14, 14n, 22
in business cycle analysis of econometric model simulations, 245t
determination of, 14, 22
forecasts of, 193–94, 220t, 221
Investment in capital goods, 72t
and accelerator variables, 14, 14n
autonomous and induced, 22, 23
in business cycle analysis of econometric model simulations, 245t, 246t
decisions and realizations, lagged relationship of, 19, 21
in expansion before 1969–70 recession, 124
expectations and forecasts of plant and equipment expenditures, 194
as main "real" factor in business cycles, 30
and monetary changes during business cycles, 29
and profit variables, 14, 14n, 19, 23, 23n
Wharton and OBE econometric model forecasts of, 220t
See also Gross private domestic investment forecasts; Residential construction forecasts

Jenks, Elizabeth, 11n
Johnson, Harry G., 11n
Jordan, Jerry L., 32n
Juster, F. Thomas, 2, 11, 239

Kahn, C. Harry, 12
Kalchbrenner, John, 32, 33n
Kaldor, Nicholas, 21, 21n
Kalecki, Michal, 19, 19n, 20, 21 21n
Kareken, John, 255n
Kemp, Murray, 220
Kendrick, John W., 11, 14n

Keynes, John Maynard, 8, 11n, 14, 15, 20, 21n
Kindahl, James K., 138, 154n
King, W. I., 11n
Klein, Lawrence R., 13n, 14n, 17n, 22n, 24n, 26, 29, 109, 196, 233, 239, 254n, 261n, 270n
Klein-Goldberger econometric model, 25, 242
Knauth, O. W., 11, 11n
Knowles, J. W., 127n
Koopmans, Tjalling, C., 13n
Korean War, 5, 145
Kravis, Irving B., 11, 137, 138
Kuh, Edwin, 14n, 23n, 29n
Kurihara, Kenneth K., 15
Kuznets, Simon, 11, 11n, 14n, 15, 15n, 126n

Labor costs per unit of output. See Costs of production
Latané, Henry A., 7n
Leads and lags. See Timing measures
Lempert, Leonard M., 41
Levitan, R. E., 246n
Liebenberg, Maurice, 26n, 239, 259
Lipsey, Robert E., 11, 137, 138
Liu, Ta-Chung, 221n
Long, Clarence D., 11
Lovell, Michael C., 15n
Lundberg, Erik, 6n, 10n, 40n, 46n

Macaulay, Frederick R., 11, 11n
McCarthy, Michael D., 238n
McGraw-Hill Survey of Investment Intentions, 194
Mack, Ruth P., 12, 12n, 14n, 37n, 49n, 92, 92n
Maddison, Angus, 10n
Man-hours in nonagricultural industries, 72t, 95t, 100–107t, 114t, 116t
Manufacturing and trade inventories, 72t

Manufacturing and trade sales, 95t, 100–107t, 114–15t, 116t
Meiselman, David, 28n
Metzler, Lloyd, 22, 22n, 31n
Meyer, John R., 2
Michigan model
  forecasts of percentage changes in real GNP, 180, 180n
  in study of policy simulations, 245, 245n, 248–49, 252, 253–55, 257–58, 280–81, 282t, 283–85, 286–89t, 290–91
  See also under FRB-MIT-PENN model
Mills, Frederick C., 111, 137
Mincer, Jacob, 11, 120n, 168, 223
Minsky, Hyman P., 28n
Mintz, Ilse, 1, 3, 12n, 36, 37, 38, 39, 40, 52n, 78n, 92n, 109, 110, 113n, 126, 132, 133t
Mitchell, Wesley C., 1, 2n, 3n, 11n, 12, 12n, 16n, 18, 19n, 23, 30, 30n, 40, 41n, 42, 42n, 44, 44n, 68n, 90n, 99n, 121, 122n, 123, 126n, 134, 134n, 137, 139, 147, 163, 166
Models of business cycles. See Business cycles
Modigliani, Franco, 15, 15n, 29n, 172n, 220n
Monetary policy
  and goals of combating inflation and unemployment, 9, 34
  instruments for, 262–63, 263n, 271–72
  relative effectiveness of, vs. fiscal policy, 9, 32–33, 262–65
  role in the economy, 33–34, 33n, 235
  rules for, 245, 260, 260t, 261
  short-term vs. longer-term effects, 9, 34
  simulation results, 281ff

Monetary policy (Cont.)
See also Economic policy; Economic policy simulations with econometric models; Fiscal policy
Money stock
autonomous changes in, 29
changes in composition of, 30–31
changes in, and economic fluctuations, 28, 30
effects on money income and spending, 28–29, 32, 32n, 33n
fluctuations in, and economic instability, 31
in policy simulations with FRB-MIT model, 279, 279t, 280
Moore, Geoffrey H., 1, 12, 12n, 14n, 16n, 19n, 26n, 36, 37n, 38, 46n, 50n, 52n, 57n, 59n, 61n, 62, 62n, 63, 65n, 89n, 92n, 109, 112n, 137, 184, 185, 196, 212, 212n, 239, 241n, 262n
Muench, T., 271n
Musgrave, John C., 53n

"Naive" models, 186, 199, 205–12, 204t, 207t, 210–11t, 214–22, 216t, 219–20t
See also Extrapolative models
National Bureau of Economic Research
business cycle research of. *See under* Business cycles
econometric model simulations, studies of, 25–27, 241n, 262n
economic forecasting, studies of, 16, 16n, 27–28, 183–85
price behavior, studies of, 137–38
reference cycle chronology and national income accounting, 11, 11n, 13, 37, 42–43, 50–52, 55–65, 75n, 82, 99, 110–11, 111n, 135, 138–39

National income accounting, 11, 11n, 16n, 24
Nerlove, Marc, 14, 24n
New orders, durable goods, 245t
Nourse, Edwin G., 127n

OBE (Office of Business Economics) model, 26n, 185, 185n
accuracy of forecasts with, relative to judgmental forecasts, 223, 225, 226–27t, 227
in business cycle analysis of econometric model simulations, 242–44, 245–46t
ex ante and *ex post* forecasts with, 197, 197n, 198, 218–22, 219–20t
hundred-quarter *ex ante* simulations with, 253–56, 257t, 258
sample-period simulations with, 198–99, 249, 250t, 251–53, 253t
six-quarter simulations around business cycle turns, 247, 248t, 249
OBE-SEC investment anticipations, 188n, 194
Okun, Arthur M., 2, 184n, 188n, 239
Output
actual and potential, 46–47, 98, 124, 127, 127n
per man-hour, 158, 159t, 161, 165t, 166
See also GNP (gross national product)

Pecuniary vs. real or deflated indicators, 48–49, 90–92, 113, 117, 118–21, 119n
Personal income, 72t, 94t, 102–107t, 114t, 116t, 245t
Phelps, Edmund S., 34n
Phillips, A. P., 277n
Phillips curve, 34

Policy instruments. *See* Economic policy simulations with econometric models; Fiscal policy; Monetary policy

Price cycle chronology
and business cycle chronology, 138–39, 145–46t, 147
computerized and judgmental identification of turning points, 140
construction of, 139–43
measurement and smoothing of rates of change in indexes for, 141, 143, 143n
reference dates of, 143, 144t
seasonal adjustments used for, 140–41

Prices
behavior in inflation, 138
changes in comprehensive indexes during business cycles, 142t, 145, 146t
of commodities other than food (CPI), 149, 150t, 151t, 156t
of consumer finished goods (WPI), 152t, 155t, 156t
of consumer goods and services (CPI), 147, 148t
of crude materials (WPI), 152t, 154, 155t, 158, 164
decomposition into cost and profit components, 161–62, 162t
diffusion of changes in, 147, 148t
of food, 147, 149, 150t, 151t, 152t, 156t, 158, 164
of industrial commodities (WPI), 148t, 149, 152t, 154, 164
of industrial materials (spot market), 147, 148t, 152t, 154, 164
of intermediate materials (WPI), 152t, 155t, 158
leads and lags in, 149–58, 150t, 152t, 157t

of manufactured goods (WPI), 147, 148t, 149
manufacturers' selling, diffusion index, 148t
of producers' finished goods (WPI), 152t, 154, 155t
and production costs and profits, 158, 159t, 160t, 161, 162t, 163, 165, 165t, 166
of purchased materials, diffusion index, 148t
recent developments in, 117–18, 163–66, 165t
retailers' selling, diffusion index, 148t
of services (CPI), 149, 150t, 151t, 158, 164
transaction index, 154n
See also Consumer Price Index; GNP implicit price deflator; Wholesale Price Index

Producers' durable goods, forecasts of, 193, 193n

Profits, 72t, 245t
cyclical changes in, 14n, 19, 158–63, 160t, 162t, 165t
in expansion before the 1969–70 recession, 124, 165–66, 165t
in inflation, margins of, 138, 163
and investment, 14, 14n, 19, 23, 23n
per unit of output, 158, 160t, 161, 162t, 163, 165, 165t

Random elements in econometric models, 262, 262n, 263, 265–69, 266n
See also Shocks, exogenous

Rasche, Robert H., 240

Recession of 1969–70
and antecedent developments, 122–25

Recession of 1969–70 (Cont.)
  and anti-inflationary policy, 92–93
  and changes in business cycles, 134–37
  compared with developments in 1926–27, 1960–61, and 1966–67, 115, 116*t*, 117
  and conception of business cycles, 125–26
  and criteria for identification of recessions, 89–92
  indications of 1969 reference peak, 113, 114–15*t*
  and measures of deviation from trend, alternative, 127–34, 128–31*t*, 133*t*
  pecuniary and real activity indicators in, 118–21
  and revised definitions of recession, 48, 126–27
  viewed as low-rate phase of growth cycle, 83, 84
Recessions
  and amplitudes of decline in economic activity, 110, 110*n*
  changes in duration and intensity of, 5–7, 39–40
  and changing distribution of income and wealth, 119–20
  compared with low-rate phases of growth cycles, 45, 83
  definitions of, 3, 48, 90–93, 99*n*, 126–27, 134–36
  historical characteristics of, 99–112, 100–109*t*
  of 1918–19 and 1926–27, 110–11
  See also Contractions in economic activity
Rees, Albert, 11
Reference cycles. *See* Business cycles
Reference dates (chronologies). *See* Business cycles; Price cycle chronology

Research Seminar in Quantitative Economics, 196, 196*n*
Residential construction forecasts, 193, 193*n*, 209, 211*n*
Retail sales, 72*t*, 100–107*t*, 115*t*, 116*t*, 117

Saito, M., 26*n*, 238*n*
Samuelson, Paul A., 2, 4, 20, 20*n*, 21*n*, 22
Sauerlander, Owen H., 172*n*
Saulnier, Raymond J., 12
Schumpeter, Joseph A., 21, 21*n*
Schwartz, Anna Jacobson, 7*n*, 10*n*, 11, 12, 15, 28*n*, 29*n*, 30*n*, 36*n*, 45*n*, 67, 67*n*, 82*n*
Seltzer, Lawrence H., 11
Shapiro, Harold T., 224, 245*n*
Shaw, Edward S., 7*n*
Shay, Robert P., 11
Shiskin, Julius, 12, 16*n*, 50*n*, 52*n*, 53*n*, 57*n*, 59*n*, 63, 65, 65*n*, 109, 184
Shocks, exogenous
  autocorrelated and nonautocorrelated, 26–27, 27*n*, 254–56, 254*t*, 257*t*, 558
  autonomous, 21, 27, 251, 251*n*
  and changes in business cycles, 5–6, 8
  deviations of shocked from control series, 256
  in downturns and recovery, 23, 23*n*
  in econometric model simulations, 25–27, 234, 254–56, 257*t*, 258
  Frisch hypothesis, 25, 251
  interaction with endogenous factors, 17–18, 17*n*, 21, 23, 33
  in mathematical models of business cycles, 21
  monetary and other, 29–31, 32*n*
  random "type I" and "type II," 25
  wars as cause of, 5–6, 17

Sills, David L., 136*n*
Slutsky, Eugen, 26
Speculative booms, causes of, 23
Spencer curve, 54, 54*n*, 55
Stabilization policies. *See* Economic policy; Fiscal policy; Monetary policy
Stanback, Thomas M., Jr., 12*n*, 14
Stein, Herbert, 2
Stekler, Herman O., 168, 224
Stigler, George J., 11, 137, 138, 154*n*
Stochastic simulations. *See* Business cycle analysis of econometric model simulations; Economic policy simulations with econometric models
Stock market, 23, 124
Su, Josephine, 25*n*, 241*n*
Su, Vincent, 239
Subcycles, 37*n*, 49, 92
Suits, Daniel, 14*n*, 29*n*, 184, 196, 240
Supel, T., 271*n*

Theil, Henri, 184, 188, 240
Timing measures
    of composite and diffusion indexes at business cycle turns, 57–65, 58*t*, 64*t*
    at growth cycle turns, 74–75, 75*t*
    of rates of change of various price indexes at CPI turns, 149, 150*t*, 152–53*t*, 154, 157*t*, 157–58
    of sample period simulations for four econometric models at business cycle turns, 252–53, 253*t*
    of six-quarter simulations for three models at business cycle turns, 247, 248*t*, 249
    of stochastic 100-quarter simulations for three models at turns in cumulated diffusion indexes, 256, 257*t*, 258

Tinbergen, Jan, 14, 20, 21*n*, 23, 23*n*, 24, 24*n*, 242*n*
Tintner, Gerhard, 126*n*
Transfer payments, 6
Treasury bill rate, 72*t*, 114*t*
Treyz, George I., 27, 169, 223
Trueblood, Norman, 51*n*, 58*n*, 59*n*, 61*n*, 62, 62*n*, 63
Turning points
    computerized selection
        in business cycle indicators, 54–55
        See also Bry-Boschan computer program for cycle dating
    in deviation cycles and step cycles for selected indicators, 71, 72*t*, 73
    in reference cycles, identification by diffusion and composite indexes, 55–57, 56*t*
    in six-quarter econometric model simulations, 244, 247, 248*t*, 249
    See also Business cycles; Growth cycles; Price cycle chronology

Unemployment rate, 66*n*, 72*t*, 100–107*t*, 114*t*, 116*t*, 245*t*, 281
    and definition of recession, 127, 127*n*
    and economic policies, 6, 7, 34
    in expansion before 1969–70 recession, 124
    in 1948–70, 97*t*
    Wharton and OBE econometric model forecasts of, 218, 220*t*, 221–22
Unfilled jobs, 66*n*, 72*t*
Unfilled orders, of manufacturers, 114*t*, 245*t*
U.S. Department of Commerce, 244

Vietnam War, 5
Vining, Rutledge, 13

Wages and salaries, 72t, 114t
Wages, real, in inflation, 138
Wage-price spirals, 23
Wallace, Neil, 1, 4, 37, 235, 261, 271n
Wallich, Henry C., 2
Wars, as cause of shocks to economy, 5–6, 17
Wartime cycles, 6, 6n
Weather cycle, 17
Wharton estimate of industrial capacity, 130–31t, 132
Wharton model, 24n, 26n, 185, 185n
    accuracy of forecasts of, relative to judgmental forecasts, 223, 224–25t, 225, 227
    in business cycle analysis of econometric model simulations, 242–44, 245–46t
    ex ante and ex post forecasts with, 197, 197n, 198, 218–22, 219–20t
    hundred-quarter ex ante simulations with, 253–56, 257t, 258
    sample-period simulations with, 198, 198n, 199, 249, 250, 251–53, 253t
    six-quarter simulations around business cycle turns with, 247, 248t, 249

    in study of policy simulations, 261, 261n, 269–71, 273, 307
Wholesale Price Index, 72t, 115t
    diffusion of changes in, 147, 148t
    forecasts of, 195, 195n
    leads and lags in rates of change of major components of, 149, 152–53t, 154
    leads and lags relative to CPI, 149, 152–53t, 154, 156t
    rates of change in comprehensive price indexes and, 142t
    rates of change, by stage of process, 155t
    recent developments, 164
    See also Price cycle chronology; Prices
Wholesale sales, 114t
Wicksell, Knut, 26
Wolman, Leo, 11

Yields, average, on commercial paper and bonds, 114t, 246t
Young, Allan H., 53n, 121n

Zarnowitz, Victor, 1, 14, 14n, 16n, 25n, 26, 26n, 27n, 28n, 46n, 61n, 62, 62n, 183, 184, 185, 189n, 199n, 202n, 239, 240, 241, 262n